The Reign of Terror in America
Visions of Violence from Anti-Jacobinism to Antislavery

In the 1790s, American conservatives were profoundly shaken when their French "sister republic" collapsed into violent factionalism and civil war. Fearful that civic bloodshed and chaos might overwhelm their own new republic, northern Federalists and their Congregationalist allies reacted with a war of words directed at the French Revolution and at the Americans who supported it.

The Reign of Terror in America traces the paths by which American fears of the French Revolution's violence gave rise, over the course of two generations, to antislavery, antiwar, and public-education movements in the United States. The first history of the American response to the Reign of Terror, this book shows how the violence in France permeated political thought in the United States. Ultimately, the bloodshed in France inspired northeastern conservatives to oppose the violence of slaveholding, provided material for their attacks on Southern slavery, and helped to spark the Civil War.

Rachel Hope Cleves is assistant professor of American history at Northern Illinois University.

The Reign of Terror in America

Visions of Violence from Anti-Jacobinism to Antislavery

RACHEL HOPE CLEVES

CAMBRIDGE
UNIVERSITY PRESS

CAMBRIDGE UNIVERSITY PRESS
Cambridge, New York, Melbourne, Madrid, Cape Town,
Singapore, São Paulo, Delhi, Mexico City

Cambridge University Press
The Edinburgh Building, Cambridge CB2 8RU, UK

Published in the United States of America by Cambridge University Press, New York

www.cambridge.org
Information on this title: www.cambridge.org/9781107403987

First published 2009
First paperback edition 2012

A catalogue record for this publication is available from the British Library

Library of Congress Cataloging in Publication data
Cleves, Rachel Hope, 1975–
The reign of terror in America : visions of violence from anti-Jacobinism to antislavery /
Rachel Hope Cleves.
p. cm.
Includes index.
ISBN 978-0-521-88435-8 (hardback)
1. United States – History – 1783–1865. 2. United States – Social conditions – To 1865.
3. Violence – United States – History – 19th century. 4. Nonviolence – United States –
History – 19th century. 5. Antislavery movements – United States – History.
6. United States – History – Civil War, 1861–1865 – Causes. 7. France – History –
Reign of Terror, 1793–1794. 8. France – History – Revolution, 1789–1799 –
Influence – United States. I. Title.
E301.C585 2009
973.3–dc22   2008045087

ISBN 978-0-521-88435-8 Hardback
ISBN 978-1-107-40398-7 Paperback

For Galen Gibson, Nacuñán Sáez,
Gayle Dubowski, Catalina Garcia, Julianna Gehant, Ryanne Mace,
and Daniel Parmenter, victims of violence.

Contents

List of Illustrations

Preface

Two hundred years ago, in the small town of Medford, Massachusetts, the Reverend David Osgood, a corpulent older man of middling height and homely appearance, ascended the pulpit and delivered a sermon on the subject of self-government. He began with Proverbs 16:32, "He that is slow to anger, is better than the mighty; and he that ruleth his spirit, than he that taketh a city." The minister had his sermon committed to memory from repeated delivery. Perhaps he spoke with no particular urgency at the beginning, but as he expounded, Osgood's speech grew quick and excited, coming "down upon his audience with the overwhelming force of a torrent." His "heavy brow" creased and his "authoritative eye" gazed searchingly upon his congregants.

In impassioned tones, Osgood warned the assembly that "unrestrained anger" made "men as void of understanding – as fierce and dangerous, as the wild beasts of the forest." People too often took pleasure in reading the battle stories that filled newspapers and history books. But Osgood deplored the glorification of war; "humanity weeps at those scenes of blood and ruin." Wars and fighting came from ungoverned passions. When men learned to practice self-government, Osgood promised, "then would wars cease in the world; there would be no acts of violence and oppression, and no complaining in our streets." Self-government held the key to a redeemed world, where civil government would cease to be necessary, swords would be beaten into ploughshares, and each person would sit under his own fig tree and vine.[1]

---

[1] "Sermon XIII: Self-Government," David Osgood, *Sermons* (Boston, Mass., 1824), 233–249. For physical descriptions of Osgood and his preaching style, see William Buell Sprague, *Annals of the American Pulpit, or, Commemorative Notices of Distinguished American Clergymen of Various Denominations: From the Early Settlement of the Country to the Close of the Year Eighteen Hundred and Fifty-Five with Historical Introductions* (New York, 1857), 2:72–84.

Historians have long looked to the early national era to understand how the American belief in self-government developed. The early republic is depicted as a battleground between Democratic-Republicans like Thomas Jefferson, who believed that men could and should govern themselves, and Federalists like John Adams, who wanted to preserve government in the hands of a "natural aristocracy."[2] In this binary, David Osgood falls unquestionably on the side of Adams. Osgood earned a national reputation by publishing a 1794 sermon attacking the French Revolution and the American democrats who Osgood believed wished to imitate its example.[3] In the following decades, Osgood embraced the Federalist Party, publishing eleven political sermons attacking Jacobinism and democracy, defending religious orthodoxy, pillorying the Jefferson and Madison administrations, and protesting the War of 1812.[4] An aloof man who vividly personified the privileges of his caste by eschewing any familiarity with his parishioners, Osgood was a leader among that set of men, purportedly narrow-minded and certainly elitist, who fought viciously to prevent the expansion of popular politics.

Osgood feared deeply that the United States suffered a threat from "the wild fury of popular sedition and insurrection." Ironically, it was this conservative terror of popular political power that drove Osgood to insist upon the need for self-government. Taking off his spectacles and gazing with significance upon his congregants, Osgood insisted that the danger of insurrection should "convince us of the necessity, importance, and excellence of self-government above any other rule or power!"[5] To Osgood, self-government

---

[2] The most recent synthesis of this historical interpretation is Sean Wilentz, *The Rise of American Democracy: Jefferson to Lincoln* (New York, 2005), 40–140.

[3] David Osgood, *The Wonderful Works of God Are to Be Remembered: A Sermon, Delivered on the Day of Annual Thanksgiving, November 20, 1794* (Boston, 1794). The sermon sold through multiple editions and was even exported to Europe, where British conservatives read it; see William Playfair, *The History of Jacobinism, Its Crimes, Cruelties and Perfidies . . . With an Appendix, by Peter Porcupine, Containing a History of the American Jacobins, Commonly Denominated Democrats* (Philadelphia, Pa., 1796), 179–81.

[4] For example, David Osgood, *A Discourse, Delivered February 19, 1795: The Day Set Apart by the President for a General Thanksgiving through the United States* (Boston, Mass., 1795); David Osgood, *Some Facts Evincive of the Atheistical, Anarchical, and in Other Respects, Immoral Principles of the French Republicans Stated in a Sermon Delivered on the 9th of May, 1798, the Day Recommended by the President of the United States for Solemn Humiliation, Fasting, and Prayer* (Boston, Mass., 1798); David Osgood, *The Devil Let Loose, or the Wo Occasioned to the Inhabitants of the Earth by His Wrathful Appearance among Them Illustrated in a Discourse Delivered on the Day of the National Fast, April 25, 1799* (Boston, Mass., 1799); David Osgood, *A Discourse Delivered before the Lieutenant-Governor, the Council, and the Two Houses Composing the Legislature of the Commonwealth of Massachusetts, May 31, 1809, Being the Day of General Election* (Boston, Mass., 1809); David Osgood, *A Solemn Protest against the Late Declaration of War in a Discourse Delivered on the Next Lord's Day after the Tidings of It Were Received*, 2nd ed. (Exeter, N.H., 1812). Osgood also published many nonpolitical texts, such as ordination and funeral sermons.

[5] "Sermon XIII: Self-Government"; Osgood, *Sermons*, 249. For the description of Osgood removing his glasses, see Sprague, *Annals of the American Pulpit*, 2:80.

connoted an emotional style that subordinated the violent passions to reason and equipped citizens to be orderly political subjects. This definition of self-government as obedience to authority does not conform to contemporary understandings of self-government as independence from authority.[6] Historians' present admiration for the virtue of resistance has left little sympathy for the story of antidemocratic conservatives like David Osgood. Yet Osgood's account of self-government penetrates through the fog of the past, demanding attention. Although I cannot place myself within the walls of his church, his voice reaches out to me. His tears for the "scenes of blood" wreaked by "acts of violence" compel my interest as a historian dedicated to approaching history as a moral enterprise and as an individual who has suffered from acts of violence.[7]

Two times in the past seventeen years I have had the misfortune to experience massacres committed by savage men and the good fortune to survive. The first incident took place in December 1992 at Simon's Rock College of Bard, where I was enrolled, when one of my classmates went on a shooting rampage, killing a student and a professor and wounding four others on campus. I knew everyone involved. The shooter and I used to get in screaming fights at the seminar table; the murdered student, Galen Gibson, was a friend, and the murdered professor, Nacuñán Sáez, was my professor that semester. I published an article about this shooting a couple of years ago, to explore the ethical dilemma in writing about violence, and then I thought that I had buried the topic, so to speak.[8] But gun violence unfortunately will continue to plague the United States as long as there are hundreds of millions of guns in circulation. And in February 2008 a student at Northern Illinois University, where I am a professor, went on a shooting rampage in the building next to my office, killing five students and wounding seventeen more. I had taught one of the injured students, and many of my colleagues and students had close connections with other victims of the shooting. The shooting at NIU viscerally restored my sense that human violence is not an exceptional phenomenon, tragic yet inexplicable, but a predictable behavior, which we must work to suppress.

Although I feel no kinship with the religious or political conservatism of David Osgood, I sympathize with his perspective that human beings are dangerously violent. In the eighteenth-century United States, the dominant religious outlook taught that all human beings were prone to sin and that homicide represented only an extreme manifestation of the violent proclivities shared by all people. But during the nineteenth century, the murderer

---

[6] The moral failing of obedience as a virtue is most eloquently explored in Hannah Arendt, *Eichmann in Jerusalem: A Report on the Banality of Evil* (New York, 1977; repr., 1994).

[7] Steven Mintz explores the function of history as a "moral enterprise" in his introduction to Steven Mintz and John Stauffer, eds., *The Problem of Evil: Slavery, Freedom, and the Ambiguities of American Reform* (Amherst, Mass., 2007).

[8] Rachel Hope Cleves, "On Writing the History of Violence," *Journal of the Early Republic* 24 (Winter 2004).

became reconfigured as a "moral monster" utterly unlike normal people.[9] Today, American culture identifies human violence as a deviation from the norm. Nonviolence is assumed; bloodshed is the aberration that must be explained. The fact that I do not share this assumption has led me to approach the history of violence from an alternative starting point, which posits not an initial premurderous moment but the continuous ever-present potential for violence, subject to both limiting and expanding historical tendencies. This book seeks to understand the pressures that the exigencies of a new republican political culture placed on violence in the early national era.

Searching for the cultural dynamics of violence in the early republic led me to David Osgood, and the vast conservative political and religious literature in which his sermon is embedded. During the late eighteenth and early nineteenth centuries, Federalists and their allies among the Calvinist ministry waged a fierce reaction against the violence of the French Revolution and what they perceived to be the potential for violence within American political culture. This reaction, although antidemocratic, inspired and fueled criticism of violent institutions within the United States, including southern slavery most significantly. Put off by the elitism of men like David Osgood, historians have been reluctant to study the origins or consequences of their sentiments against violence. But perhaps we can extend more sympathy to a young girl who sat in the pews each week, listening to Osgood. Born in Medford in 1802, she attended Osgood's church and acquired an education by borrowing books from his personal library. Her beloved older brother, the Reverend Convers Francis, idolized Osgood. As an adult, she became a leading abolitionist, opponent to capital punishment, critic of animal cruelty, and advocate for women's rights and Indians' rights. Lydia Maria Child devoted her life to causes that transcended her childhood pastor's vision of a well-ordered society, but her commitment to reform in many ways signified a logical extension of Osgood's sermons against "acts of violence." How American political culture moved from David Osgood to Lydia Maria Child is the subject of this book.

[9] Karen Halttunen, *Murder Most Foul: The Killer and the American Gothic Imagination* (Cambridge, Mass., 1998).

Acknowledgments

What a pleasure to acknowledge the goodness of other people rather than to dwell ceaselessly on their depravity. Like all books, and most especially books that begin as dissertations, *The Reign of Terror in America* owes an enormous debt of gratitude to the kindness of teachers, friends, colleagues, librarians, family members, and even strangers at conferences, who aided its author from inception to completion.

Thank you first to Paula Fass, who seemed to know what my book was about long before I did but never let me in on the secret. There were numerous times that I wished she would just come out and tell me what it was I was trying to say, but like a true mentor, Paula enabled me to discover the argument for myself.

Additional thanks to all the other fabulous teachers on whose criticism and encouragement I have long depended, including Tom Laqueur, who asked the questions that got me started, and David Henkin, who asked the questions that forced me to move beyond the starting point. Thank you to two professors of early American history, Herbert Sloan and James Kettner, whose open doors encouraged me to enter this field. My gratitude extends to all the members of the Berkeley History Department who made Dwinelle an exciting intellectual home, although feeling so at home could have had disastrous consequences for ever finishing the dissertation that led to this book.

I feel especially lucky that my home at Dwinelle was crowded with *siblings*, to fight with at the seminar table and to turn to for support. I am grateful to all the members of my cohort, most especially my fellow dissertators Susan Haskell, Caroline Hinkle, and Ellen Berg. Biggest thanks to the friend who incited me to enlarge my family beyond the confines of the university, and to enlarge myself along the way – Amanda Littauer shepherded the birth of more than my book. My gratitude to Heather McCarty for the same.

The dissertation benefited from institutional as well as personal support. I appreciate the generous funding of the Center for Children and the Working Family; the University of California, Berkeley, Graduate Division and Department of History; and the Harry Frank Guggenheim Foundation. After completing the dissertation, I received support from the Gilder Lehrman Institute of American History, as well as the Graduate Division of Northern Illinois University, for additional research.

More than money, the transformation from dissertation to book depended on the insightful feedback of numerous scholars in the field who gave generously of their most precious commodity, time. Thank you to John L. Brooke, Matthew Mason, and Padraig Riley, who each offered detailed feedback on the manuscript. Chapter 6 benefited especially from extensive workshopping, both at the Omohundro Institute of Early American History and Culture, where it received critical attention from Ronald Hoffman, Sally Mason, Fredrika Teute, Patrick Erben, Alexander Haskell, and others, as well as at a brown-bag seminar organized by the History Department at Northern Illinois University, where I benefited greatly from the feedback of Taylor Atkins, Sean Farrell, Susan Fry, Beatrix Hoffman, James Schmidt, and many more. Since arriving at NIU, I have received amazing intellectual and personal encouragement from my colleagues, whom I am honored to call friends. Many thanks to all the faculty and student members of the Atlantic history reading group at NIU, whose discussions helped redefine the book. Sean Farrell deserves particular thanks for on occasion rereading successive drafts of the same five pages. Beatrix Hoffman, most of all, helped to make NIU my home, from the pint-sized Huskies gear she sent the kids before we decamped California, to the many glasses of wine she has poured me since we arrived. Thanks are also due to my editor, Eric Crahan, for taking a chance on the dissertation and offering friendly encouragement along the way.

My sincere appreciation to the librarians at NIU, UC Berkeley, and the New York Public Library. Additional thanks to Kate Pinkam and Susan Chase, archivist and librarian at the Governor's Academy, in Byfield, Massachusetts. And deep thanks to everyone who ever participated in the digitization of early American history sources. I began the dissertation during the age of micro-opaques. Having lived through the digital revolution, I may have to embrace the paradigm of whig history after all!

Most of all, I wish to thank my wonderful family: Jonathan Sinnreich, who has probably read more drafts of the book than anyone else; Aram Sinnreich, who took time out from his own dissertation to read mine; Masha Zager, who taught me how to write; Emily Pines, who showed me what it means to love your work; Daniel Sinnreich, who stayed up too late watching bad movies with me; Kim Graves, who offered nutritious support; and the *gantze mishpoche* – readers, writers, thinkers, every one. Lastly, thank you to Elias and Maya, for bringing me joy, and to Tim, my love, for everything.

INTRODUCTION

Revolutionary Violence in the Atlantic World

> We live, my Friends, in an age of revolution and disorganization.
> – Simeon Doggett, *An Oration, Delivered at Taunton,*
> *on the 4th of July, 1799*

In the fall of 1792, reports of revolutionary bloodshed in France electrified the American atmosphere. News of the September Massacres rolled like black storm clouds across the Atlantic, bristling North American shores with potential energy and polarizing the body politic.[1] Newspaper reportage swiftly condemned "the hellish faction of Robertspierre, Marat, [and] Chabot," blaming the leaders of the Jacobin political club in Paris for purportedly designing the mass slaughter of prisoners and priests.[2] Rumors that the Jacobins planned more violence held readers' attention into the next year; subscribers to the Charleston *City Gazette and Daily Advertiser* read anxiously in January 1793 that "the sanguinary faction" of Robespierre and Danton was "planning another bleeding," and that Marat "wished to see 260,000 heads fall at his feet."[3] Accounts of the events in France preceded

[1] "Intelligence from France," *Diary or Loudon's Register*, Nov. 1, 1792; "Monday, September 3," *Dunlap's American Daily Advertiser*, Nov. 1, 1792; "Arrived at Philadelphia," *Baltimore Evening Post*, Nov. 2, 1792; "Massacre at Paris. Extract of a Letter from Paris, Dated September 3," *Essex Journal*, Nov. 21, 1792; "Extract of a Letter from a Gentleman Belonging to This Town," *Salem (Mass.) Gazette*, Nov. 13, 1792; "France. Paris, Sept. 7," *Columbian Centinel*, Nov. 14, 1792; "Extract of a Letter from Paris, Sept. 17," *New-Hampshire Gazette, and General Advertiser*, Nov. 14, 1792; "By Capt. Rich, Arrived at Boston in 36 Days from Bristol," *United States Chronicle*, Nov. 15, 1792; "Extract of a Letter from Paris, September 17," *The Mirrour*, Dec. 3, 1792; "Paris, Sunday Morning. From the French Gazette," *Virginia Chronicle and Norfolk and Portsmouth General Advertiser*, Dec. 8, 1792.

[2] "Foreign Intelligence. Paris, September 17," *The Mail; or, Claypoole's Daily Advertiser*, Nov. 14, 1792. The Jacobins were named after the former convent in which they met.

[3] "France. National Convention, Tuesday October 30," *City Gazette (Charleston, S.C.) and Daily Advertiser*, Jan. 24, 1793. Early national sources frequently misspelled the names of Robespierre, Dumouriez, and other French revolutionaries; the variation Robertspierre appeared in multiple sources.

local affairs in the news columns as editors provided eager readers with details of the increasing bloodshed of the incipient Reign of Terror.[4] During the summer of 1793, the Jacobin faction seized control of the French National Convention and began to purge perceived state enemies. Over the following year at least thirty thousand French citizens were executed by the guillotine or died in prisons; the vast majority of those were commoners. Meanwhile, the French Republican army fought wars against Britain, Austria, and Prussia, and combated a civil war in the Vendée, which took more than one hundred thousand lives (many by massacre).[5] Throughout these events, the violence of the French Revolution, in all its bloody iterations – massacres, guillotines, foreign wars, civil wars, cannibalism, mass drownings, patricides, and infanticides – kept American readers transfixed.

For seven decades, from the rise to power of the radical Jacobin club in 1792 until the fall of the southern Confederacy in 1865, French Revolutionary discourse pervaded American newspapers, religious literature, political orations, broadsides, private letters, fiction, poetry, pedagogy, drama, and periodicals. Readers were bombarded by countless narratives of violent Jacobinism, a catchall term that Americans used incorrectly to capture every stage of the revolution in France – from the Reign of Terror through the Directory, even to the Napoleonic era.[6] Americans also extended the term *Jacobinism* geographically, to describe violent political radicals in Ireland, Continental Europe, the Caribbean, and the United States. The literature describing the violence of what R. R. Palmer has famously described as "the age of democratic revolution" is best understood as anti-Jacobin, because descriptions of bloodshed were almost always used to demonstrate the revolutions' failures.[7] (Although for a brief window in 1793 some American Francophiles used depictions of French violence to argue that revolution was divine punishment for the Bourbon monarchs' crimes.) Why did Americans

---

[4] Judah Adelson, "The Vermont Press and the French Revolution, 1789–1799" (Ph.D., New York University, 1961); Beatrice F. Hyslop, "American Press Reports of the French Revolution, 1789–1794," *New-York Historical Society Quarterly* 42 (Oct. 1958); Davis R. Dewey, "The News of the French Revolution in America," *New England Magazine* 7 (Sept. 1889).

[5] William Doyle, *The Oxford History of the French Revolution* (Oxford, 1989), 258–9. Although the seventeen thousand lives taken by the guillotine may seem low by modern standards, it represented "almost twice as many lives as the United States lost in all the battles of the War of Independence and the War of 1812 combined." David Brion Davis, *Revolutions: Reflections on American Equality and Foreign Liberations* (Cambridge, Mass., 1990), 31.

[6] Searches in digital databases for terms such as *Jacobin*, *Robespierre*, and *Bastille* produce hundreds of thousands of hits (many of which, of course, overlap). When sources such as nonpublished sermons or orations, foreign prints, private letters, and live performances are taken into consideration, it is probably fair to say that people in the United States were exposed to millions of anti-Jacobin narratives between 1792 and 1865. See the appendix.

[7] R. R. Palmer, *The Age of the Democratic Revolution: A Political History of Europe and America, 1760–1800*, 2 vols. (Princeton, N.J., 1959).

write and read so much about the violence of Jacobinism, and what effects did that discourse produce? Pro-French radicalism is broadly understood to have made an important contribution to democratic ideas during the early national era. What ideological consequences resulted from concerns about French Revolutionary violence?

Although the question of Americans' reactions to the violence of the French Revolution may seem antiquarian in light of U.S. global dominance today, the structure of geopolitics in the late eighteenth and early nineteenth centuries gave events in France a transforming significance for American political culture.[8] Americans' fascination with the French Revolution reflected their immersion in the late-eighteenth-century Atlantic World. Early national citizens viewed themselves as participants in a transnational community, drawn together by sinews of trade, migration, and information. Americans saw the Atlantic Ocean not as a barrier that cut them off from Europe but as a concourse that connected them to the Old World. In the late eighteenth century, the United States' population still hugged the continent's eastern shore; as of 1790, less than 5 percent of the nation's nonnative population lived west of the Appalachian Mountains. The great cities were port cities, and their busiest streets were by the docks. Ships arrived and departed daily, traveling across the ocean, traveling between American ports, traveling to and from the Caribbean Sea. When American readers sought out the news from France, they were seeking news of their own world. The streets of Paris led directly to the streets outside their doors.[9]

Those streets, the narrow walkways of the growing cities and villages of the early republic, were unquiet in the fall of 1792. The creation of a new national government in 1789, far from securing consensus among the nation's citizens, had opened a new era of political conflict. The impulse and resistance to democratic politics that had caused conflicts during the 1780s prompted renewed battles following the ratification of the Constitution.[10]

---

[8] Matthew Rainbow Hale, "'Many Who Wandered in Darkness': The Contest over American National Identity, 1795–1798," *Early American Studies* 1 (2003). Lloyd S. Kramer, "The French Revolution and the Creation of American Political Culture," in *The Global Ramifications of the French Revolution*, ed. Joseph Klaits and Michael H. Haltzel (Washington, D.C., 1994).

[9] For theoretical and historiographical treatments of the Atlantic World, see Alison Games, "Atlantic History: Definitions, Challenges, and Opportunities," *American Historical Review* 111 (June 2006); Bernard Bailyn, *Atlantic History: Concept and Contours* (Cambridge, 2005); David Armitage, "Three Concepts of Atlantic History," in *The British Atlantic World, 1500–1800*, ed. David Armitage and Michael J. Braddick (New York, 2002); Nicholas Canny, "Writing Atlantic History; or, Reconfiguring the History of Colonial British America," *Journal of American History* 86 (1999); Aaron Fogleman, "The Atlantic World, 1492–1860s: Definition, Theory, and Boundaries," in *Soundings in Atlantic History*, ed. Bernard Bailyn (Cambridge, forthcoming).

[10] Alfred F. Young, *Liberty Tree: Ordinary People and the American Revolution* (New York, 2006); Woody Holton, "An 'Excess of Democracy' – or a Shortage?" *Journal of the Early*

The 1790s have famously been described as an age of passion: a time when paranoia and emotionalism fractured American politics.[11] The American streets routinely boiled over with political conflict during the early 1790s, heightened by the connections between domestic affairs and international politics. Democratic American supporters of the French Revolution demonstrated their continuing commitment to politics out of doors by gathering in the streets to celebrate French accomplishments and to protest the federal administration. Federalist opponents of the French Revolution sought to enforce a model of republicanism that limited political participation to voting and speech, by attacking the Democratic-Republicans rhetorically, legally, and with arms.

In the United States, news of the French Revolution encountered a passionately interested, and passionately divided, audience. Deeply embedded in the Atlantic World, Americans viewed the French Revolution from its beginning as a local as well as an international event. As W. M. Verhoeven has argued, "the many revolutions that produced the national ideologies, identities, and ideas of state of present-day America and Europe" were shaped by a "trialogue (between France and Britain and America)."[12] If anything, Verhoeven is understating how multivectored the revolutionary spirit of the late eighteenth century was. The revolutionary Atlantic included far more places than Britain, France, and the United States. To Americans, the French Revolution involved not only the political activities of men and women in Paris, London, and Philadelphia but also the legislative wranglings, visionary theories, and brutal warfare of men and women in Ireland, Geneva, Saint Domingue, Guadeloupe, and beyond. Radicalism and repression in Ireland, and slave rebellions and suppression in the Caribbean, furthermore drove thousands of revolutionary and counterrevolutionary migrants to the

---

Republic 25 (Fall 2005); Woody Holton, "Did Democracy Cause the Recession That Led to the Constitution?" *Journal of American History* 92 (2005); Paul Douglas Newman, *Fries Rebellion: The Enduring Struggle for the American Revolution* (Philadelphia, Pa., 2004); Leonard L. Richards, *Shays's Rebellion: The American Revolution's Final Battle* (Philadelphia, 2002); Terry Bouton, "A Road Closed: Rural Insurgency in Post-Independence Pennsylvania," *Journal of American History* 87 (2000).

[11] For classic statements of this argument, see John R. Howe, "Republican Thought and the Political Violence of the 1790s," *American Quarterly* 19 (Summer 1967); Marshall Smelser, "The Jacobin Phrenzy: The Menace of Monarchy, Plutocracy, and Anglophilia, 1789–1798," *Review of Politics* 21 (1959); Marshall Smelser, "The Federalist Period as an Age of Passion," *American Quarterly* 10 (1958); Marshall Smelser, "The Jacobin Phrenzy: Federalism and the Menace of Liberty, Equality, and Fraternity," *Review of Politics* 13 (Oct. 1951).

[12] W. M. Verhoeven, ed., *Revolutionary Histories: Transatlantic Cultural Nationalism, 1775–1815*, Romanticism in Perspective (New York, 2002), 3. See also Andrew W. Robertson, "'Look on This Picture...And on This!' Nationalism, Localism, and Partisan Images of Otherness in the United States, 1787–1820," *American Historical Review* 106 (Oct. 2001).

United States.[13] Early national audiences treated the French Revolution as an event of profound local significance.

When news of the September Massacres crossed the Atlantic, American conservatives immediately questioned what implications the violence had for the United States. In Massachusetts, Abigail Adams received newspaper accounts of the violence in early December, soon after the roads had been cleared from a bad snowstorm. In Adams's next letter to her husband, Vice President John Adams, she expressed the hope that Republicans in the House of Representatives would "not follow the French example and Lop of Heads." Perhaps she had in mind the reported September 3 assault on the Princess de Lamballe, Marie Antoinette's close friend, whom a Parisian mob had reportedly gang-raped and mutilated, by cutting off her breasts, before they impaled her decapitated head on a pike and paraded it in front of the queen's window. When John Adams received his wife's letter in early January, he wrote back from the capital, agreeing that "Danton Robertspiere, Marat &c. are Furies," and warning, in humor cut with fear, "We have our Robertspierres and Marats."[14] By "our Robertspieres and Marats," Adams probably had in mind his most powerful political enemies in the executive and legislative branches of the national government: Thomas Jefferson, the secretary of state, and James Madison, leader of the emerging opposition party in the House of Representatives. Both Virginia Republicans continued to praise the French Revolution throughout the 1790s, despite its purported violence. Adams may also have been referring to the democratic opposition within his own state, some of whom openly identified with the French Revolutionaries.

James Sullivan, a Republican political leader in Massachusetts, assumed the French nom de plume "Citoyen de Novion" in a pamphlet defending France from the charge of excessive bloodshed. Sullivan explained that "excess is the carrying the means beyond what is necessary to obtain the end" and exculpated France by asking, "But have we yet obtained our end?"

[13] Susan Branson and Leslie Patrick, "*Étrangers dans un pays étrange*: Saint-Domingan Refugees of Color in Philadelphia," in *The Impact of the Haitian Revolution in the Atlantic World*, ed. David Patrick Geggus (Columbia, S.C., 2001); R. Darrell Meadows, "Engineering Exile: Social Networks and the French Atlantic Community, 1789–1809," *French Historical Studies* 23 (Winter 2000); David A. Wilson, *United Irishmen, United States: Immigrant Radicals in the Early Republic* (Ithaca, N.Y., 1998); Gary Nash, "Reverberations of Haiti in the American North: Black Saint Dominguans in Philadelphia," *Pennsylvania History* 65 (1998); Michael Durey, *Transatlantic Radicals and the Early American Republic* (Lawrence, Kan., 1997); Richard J. Twomey, "Jacobins and Jeffersonians: Anglo-American Radicalism in the United States, 1790–1820" (Ph.D., Northern Illinois University, 1974).

[14] Letter from Abigail Adams to John Adams, Nov. 26, 1792; Letter from Abigail Adams to John Adams, Dec. 4, 1792; Letter from John Adams to Abigail Adams, Jan. 14, 1793 (electronic edition). *Adams Family Papers: An Electronic Archive*, Massachusetts Historical Society, http://www.masshist.org/digitaladams/.

By identifying himself as Citoyen de Novion, Sullivan both located himself at the center of the Revolution (Novion-Porcien is a French district north of Paris) and slyly winked at his true American identity (his name suggests "citizen of the new place"). By asking his American audience "But have we yet obtained our end?" Sullivan described the French Revolution as a transnational event, occurring simultaneously in France and the United States, and he identified himself as a member of the radical party pushing for more democracy despite the costs. American Republicans' willingness to identify themselves with French Revolutionaries, even after the Reign of Terror devoured its own leaders, fueled Adams's and other conservatives' fears of American Robespierres. Both anti-Jacobins and Francophiles shared an understanding of the French Revolution as a transatlantic event that directly involved the United States.[15]

The transatlantic sensibility of the 1790s made the French Revolution a turning point in American political culture, with profound effects on national attitudes toward democracy, violence, slavery, and war. Yet regional factors strongly shaped the national reaction to the French Revolution. The American response followed a sectional and political logic, which pitted anti-French northeastern political and religious conservatives against a pro-French cross-sectional coalition of democrats and religious dissenters, led by southern elites. Historical Francophobia in New England, stemming from Puritanism's fervent anti-Catholicism and from the region's long involvement in Britain's imperial wars against New France, fueled northeastern antipathies toward Jacobinism.[16] In addition, northeastern conservative elites faced contemporary political and religious challenges from local democratic opponents, which sensitized them to the threat of disorder abroad and at home. When American democrats linked their cause to France, it prompted northeastern conservatives' historical fears of French violence and their contemporary concerns about democratic political challenges to fuse into a hideous chimera that haunted them for decades.[17]

In the southern states, where Anglophobia was more pronounced than Francophobia as a result of planters' indebtedness to British merchants, as

---

[15] James Sullivan, *The Altar of Baal Thrown Down; or, The French Nation Defended, against the Pulpit Slander of David Osgood, A. M. Pastor of the Church in Medford: A Sermon* (Stockbridge, Mass., 1795), 23.

[16] Francis D. Cogliano, *No King, No Popery: Anti-Catholicism in Revolutionary New England*, Contributions in American History (Westport, Conn., 1995), 23–35; Linda Colley, *Britons: Forging the Nation, 1707–1837* (New Haven, Conn., 1992); Nathan O. Hatch, "The Origins of Civil Millennialism in America: New England Clergymen, War with France, and the Revolution," *William and Mary Quarterly* 31 (July 1974); Kerry Arnold Trask, "In the Pursuit of Shadows: A Study of Collective Hope and Despair in Provincial Massachusetts during the Era of the Seven Years War, 1748 to 1764" (1971).

[17] Paul Douglas Newman, "The Federalists' Cold War: The Fries Rebellion, National Security, and the State, 1787–1800," *Pennsylvania History* 67 (2000).

well as to British efforts to foment slave rebellion, elites welcomed the French Revolution. In addition, the local elites continued to sustain a powerful deference from the lower classes during the 1790s that made democratic politics a less significant challenge to their local power. Consequently, democratic southern elites continued to support the French Revolution throughout the 1790s. In South Carolina, where backcountry democrats posed a strong challenge to coastal elites, Charleston Federalists turned against the French Revolution in the early 1790s. But not until the turn of the century did anxieties about slave rebellions in the Caribbean and at home finally turn most southern whites against Jacobinism.[18]

Religious beliefs also played an important role in dividing opponents from supporters of the French Revolution. Many Americans interpreted news of French Revolutionary violence in a religious framework. During its first years, enthusiastic Protestant ministers had greeted the French Revolution as a providential event that brought retribution on the bloodstained Catholic Bourbon monarchy. Prophetic ministers, such as Joseph Eckley of Boston, believed that France's struggle represented the breaking of the "sixth vial" and the beginning of the "reign of virtue."[19] However, the dechristianization measures of the Jacobin era, accompanied by its seemingly anarchic violence, problematized that prophetic vision. The radical revolutionaries who ascended to power in France in late 1792 complemented their use of terror with an assault on religion. More than two hundred priests were killed in the September Massacres, and during 1793 radical French Revolutionaries sought to institute a cult of reason to take the place of Christianity. In 1793, a law passed condemning all suspected priests to death, and in the years following thousands more were executed or fled the nation.

Orthodox ministers in the United States, especially Congregationalist and Presbyterian ministers in New England who shared a conservative political orientation based in a fear of human depravity, responded to accounts of Jacobin violence and dechristianization with horror and began to preach against the Revolution in the fall of 1792. The Reverend Samuel Williams, a Congregationalist minister in Rutland, Vermont, who later became a newspaper editor, preached an election sermon in October 1792, arguing that humans were fallen creatures who needed the restraints of a strong government in order to avoid violence and savagery. When religion degenerated,

---

[18] Elizabeth Fox-Genovese and Eugene D. Genovese, *The Mind of the Master Class: History and Faith in the Southern Slaveholders' Worldview* (New York, 2005), chap 1, Simon Newman, "American Political Culture and the French and Haitian Revolutions," in *The Impact of the Haitian Revolution in the Atlantic World*, ed. David Patrick Geggus (Columbia, S.C., 2001), Rachel N. Klein, *Unification of a Slave State: The Rise of the Planter Class in the South Carolina Backcountry, 1760–1808* (Chapel Hill, N.C., 1990), chap. 7.

[19] Joseph Eckley, *A Sermon, Preached at the Request of the Ancient and Honourable Artillery Company, June 4, 1792 Being the Anniversary of Their Election of Officers* (Boston, Mass., 1792), 16–20.

Williams warned, "it produces a fierce and savage spirit, which aims to please God by the abuses, cruelties, and murders it entails on men." That Williams had seen evidence of such degeneration in France is evident from his rueful reflection that corrupt men too often sought revolution "through war and slaughter; a fearful combination of evils and miseries, and the collected curses of mobs, and murders." By fall 1792, the word *mob* was becoming shorthand for Jacobin violence. Religious conservatives like Samuel Williams avidly consumed accounts of violence in France because it conformed to their Calvinistic worldview and illustrated the necessity of religion. Williams treated the French Revolution as a reason to uphold religious orthodoxy in the United States.[20] Certain northeastern dissenting ministers, on the other hand, viewed the disestablishment of the Catholic Church in France as a victory for religious freedom that portended the crumbling of religious tyranny at home.

Whether from a religious or a political worldview, Americans of the early 1790s reacted to the French Revolution in terms that revealed their identification with the conflict. The *Oxford English Dictionary* dates the first transference of the word *Jacobin* – its use to describe a person who shared traits with the Jacobins in France, yet was not actually a member of the Jacobin Club – to a letter written by Edmund Burke in Britain in 1793. But the transference of the word *Jacobin* to articulate the violent threat posed by domestic insurgents began at least the year before in the United States.[21] At a fall 1792 political gathering in New York City, "a large Company mixed of Federalists and Antis, Whigs and Tories, Clintonians and Jaysites" entered into a heated discussion about the recent turn in French affairs. Initially, all who attended the New York meeting "condemned and execrated" the violence, until one "Jaysite" declared, "We had Jacobins in this Country who were pursuing objects as pernicious by means as unwarrantable as those of France."[22] The conversation quickly dissolved into furious disagreement. The September Massacres had polarized American political culture. In the years following, Federalists described the French Revolution as an immediate domestic danger imperiling the American republic, while Republicans repudiated Federalist criticism of French democracy as a betrayal of the American Revolution.

Most historians have assumed that anti-Jacobinism was a British argot, which conservatives in the United States cynically adopted to disguise their

[20] Samuel Williams, *The Love of Our Country Represented and Urged: In a Discourse Delivered October 21, 1792, at Rutland, in the State of Vermont* (Rutland, Vt., 1792), 3, 9, 20.

[21] *Oxford English Dictionary*, 2nd ed., s.v. "Jacobin." There are likely earlier examples to be found in Britain as well.

[22] Letter from John Adams to Abigail Adams, Dec. 7, 1792 (electronic edition). *Adams Family Papers: An Electronic Archive*, Massachusetts Historical Society, http://www.masshist.org/digitaladams/.

domestic agenda for a brief window during the late 1790s.[23] Even the most recent scholarship has accepted the dictum of Vernon Parrington, who argued that American anti-Jacobinism "was little more than an echo of the old-world debate."[24] Yet only by taking seriously the domestic significance and domestic authorship of American anti-Jacobin propaganda can we begin to understand the impact that French Revolutionary violence had on the United States. The Atlantic context gave anti-Jacobinism powerful local significance. For seven decades, graphic images of Jacobin cannibalism, corpse mutilation, and decapitation pervaded American literature. Even in the face of the unparalleled bloodshed at Antietam and Gettysburg, Americans called on the memory of the French Revolution to understand their suffering.[25] These pervasive and persistent images of bloodshed deeply affected American beliefs about the legitimacy of violence within American politics and society.

The onslaught of bloody French Revolutionary narratives following the September Massacres heightened awareness of the dangers that violence posed to the new American republic. Americans who avidly produced and consumed anti-Jacobin literature developed a suspicion of bloodshed during the 1790s, which led them to attack institutions of violence within American society. The French Revolution became an example of how uncontrolled bloodshed could propel a republic into anarchy. Anti-Jacobinism problematized violent actions by private citizens, and ultimately violent actions by the state, as dangerous to social order. Counterrevolutionary ideology served as a critical lens that focused American awareness of violence and inspired a new opposition to the bloodshed caused by slavery, war, and ignorance. This book rediscovers the vital role that the fear of democratic violence played in the genesis of abolitionism, the antiwar movement, and support for public education.

Anti-Jacobinism was both a stimulus and a conduit for the humanitarian sensibility that revolutionized transatlantic attitudes toward pain and suffering in the late eighteenth and early nineteenth centuries. Norbert Elias's

---

[23] Seth Cotlar, "The Federalists' Transatlantic Cultural Offensive of 1798 and the Moderation of American Democratic Discourse," in *Beyond the Founders: New Approaches to the Political History of the Early American Republic*, ed. David Waldstreicher, Andrew W. Robertson, and Jeffrey L. Pasley (Chapel Hill, N.C., 2004); Michael Lienesch, "The Illusion of the Illuminati: The Counterconspiratorial Origins of Post-Revolutionary Conservatism," in *Revolutionary Histories: Transatlantic Cultural Nationalism, 1775–1815*, ed. W. M. Verhoeven, Romanticism in Perspective (New York, 2002).

[24] Vernon Louis Parrington, *Main Currents in American Thought: An Interpretation of American Literature from the Beginning to 1920* (New York, 1939), 324.

[25] Frank P. Blair, "The Jacobins of Missouri and Maryland," *Congressional Globe*, House of Representatives, 38th Cong., 1st Sess., appendix, 46–7; Republican Party, *McClellan and the People!* (1864) *American Broadsides and Ephemera*, Series I, no. 11780. See also James M. McPherson, *Abraham Lincoln and the Second American Revolution* (New York, 1991), 7.

wonderfully funny and vastly influential treatise *The Civilizing Process* (1939) argues that beginning in the Middle Ages and proceeding over many centuries, everyday violence in Europe lessened as a consequence of a changing political structure that produced a new emotional style of self-control.[26] Such a vast narrative of social progress has inevitably stimulated a wide range of dissent, both by historians critical of the statistical evidence for declining violence and by historians suspicious of a grand theory that fails to take into account the "complexity of emotional life" as constructed in specific communities and places.[27] Yet Elias's argument for declining rates of personal violence does seem to hold true for Western Europe and North America from the seventeenth through the early nineteenth centuries.[28] Moreover, the circumscription of everyday violence coincided with a new ethical awareness of the need to remediate human suffering. The cultural nexus of restraining violence and correcting suffering that manifested most dramatically in the early nineteenth century is often described as humanitarianism.

Historians have identified many different origins and principles of nineteenth-century humanitarianism, and abolitionism in particular. Scholars of Quakerism have located the origin of humanitarianism in the Quaker reformation of the 1750s.[29] Another important literature within Anglo-American historiography traces the emergence of a humanitarian sensibility to the Scottish school of common sense, which taught an increased empathy for other people's suffering and provided a rationale for criticizing physical violence and cruelty.[30] Other historians have emphasized the Universalist origins of humanitarianism; the rejection of the Calvinist doctrine of innate depravity seems to have logically led people to experience greater

---

[26] Norbert Elias, *The Civilizing Process: Sociogenetic and Psychogenetic Investigations*, rev. ed., trans. Edmund Jephcott (Malden, Mass., 2000), 369–374.

[27] Randolph Roth, *American Homicide* (Cambridge, Mass., forthcoming); Barbara H. Rosenwein, "Worrying about Emotions in History," *American Historical Review* 107 (June 2002).

[28] For recent treatments that support Elias, see Martin J. Weiner, *Men of Blood: Violence, Manliness, and Criminal Justice in Victorian England* (New York, 2004), 10–12; Eric Monkkonen, "Homicide: Explaining America's Exceptionalism," *American Historical Review* 111 (Feb. 2006); Pieter Spierenburg, "Democracy Came Too Early: A Tentative Explanation for the Problem of American Homicide," *American Historical Review* 111 (Feb. 2006).

[29] Sydney V. James, *A People among Peoples: Quaker Benevolence in Eighteenth-Century America* (Cambridge, Mass., 1963); Jack D. Marietta, *The Reformation of American Quakerism, 1748–1783* (Philadelphia, Pa., 1984).

[30] Philip Gould, *Barbaric Traffic: Commerce and Antislavery in the Eighteenth-Century Atlantic World* (Cambridge, 2003); Andrew Burstein, *Sentimental Democracy: The Evolution of America's Romantic Self-Image* (New York, 1999); Karen Halttunen, "Humanitarianism and the Pornography of Pain in Anglo-American Culture," *American Historical Review* 100 (Apr. 1995); G. J. Barker-Benfield, *The Culture of Sensibility: Sex and Society in Eighteenth-Century Britain* (Chicago, Ill., 1992); Norman Fiering, "Irresistible Compassion: An Aspect of Eighteenth-Century Sympathy and Humanitarianism," *Journal of the History of Ideas* 37 (1976).

empathy for their fellow beings.[31] Calvinism was hard soil, incapable of giving life to soft sympathy; in fact, the Calvinist use of terror to promote conversion served as the negative source that religious liberals were reacting against when they generated the age of reform.[32] But an alternative genesis story credits humanitarianism to the Calvinist New Divinity theology formulated by the followers of Jonathan Edwards. Particular credit is given to the doctrine of disinterested benevolence promoted by the Reverend Samuel Hopkins, an early leader of New England antislavery.[33] Breaking from religious origin stories, another school of thought argues that humanitarianism emerged out of a capitalist sensibility, as the consequence of new cognitive understandings of cause and effect.[34] Most recently, a thesis has emerged that Britain's need to regain moral capital during and following its war against the American colonies turned antislavery sentiment into action in Great Britain.[35] Each of these arguments draws attention to an important constituting element of humanitarianism. As Elizabeth Clark aptly argued, "The rise of a sympathetic or affective mode of moral reasoning is an overdetermined phenomenon."[36]

Yet Quakerism, sensibility, Universalism, Edwardsean Calvinism, capitalism, and American independence did not generate as many overt criticisms of bloodshed between 1790 and 1865 as did opposition to the French Revolution. To look for negative descriptions of human violence in

[31] Dan McKanan, *Identifying the Image of God: Radical Christians and Nonviolent Power in the Antebellum United States* (New York, 2002); Twomey, "Jacobins and Jeffersonians"; John L. Thomas, "Romantic Reform in America, 1815–1865," *American Quarterly* 17 (1965); Vernon Louis Parrington, *Main Currents in American Thought: An Interpretation of American Literature from the Beginning to 1920* (New York, 1948), 339–41.

[32] Ava Chamberlain, "The Theology of Cruelty: A New Look at the Rise of Arminianism in Eighteenth-Century New England," *Harvard Theological Review* 85 (1992).

[33] Peter Hinks, "Timothy Dwight, Congregationalism, and Early Anti-Slavery," in *The Problem of Evil: Slavery, Freedom, and the Ambiguities of American Reform*, ed. Steven Mintz and John Stauffer (Amherst, Mass., 2007); Kenneth P. Minkema and Harry S. Stout, "The Edwardsean Tradition and the Antislavery Debate, 1740–1865," *Journal of American History* 92 (2005); Joseph Conforti, "Samuel Hopkins and the New Divinity: Theology, Ethics, and Social Reform in Eighteenth-Century New England," *William and Mary Quarterly* 34 (1977).

[34] Thomas Haskell, "Capitalism and the Origins of the Humanitarian Sensibility (Two Parts)," *American Historical Review* 90 (1985). An alternative highly contested thesis argues that antislavery was the result of capitalist economic motives; Barbara L. Solow and Stanley L. Engerman, eds., *British Capitalism and Caribbean Slavery: The Legacy of Eric Williams* (New York, 1987).

[35] Christopher Leslie Brown, *Moral Capital: Foundations of British Abolitionism* (Chapel Hill, N.C., 2006). My argument, like Brown's, credits the political pressures of the age of revolution for the rise of American abolitionism. However, whereas Brown sees the rise of British abolitionism as essentially self-serving, I recognize an ethical continuity linking the concerns about political revolution to growing antislavery.

[36] Elizabeth B. Clark, "The Sacred Rights of the Weak: Pain, Sympathy, and the Culture of Individual Rights in Antebellum America," *Journal of American History* 82 (1995): 46.

late-eighteenth- and early-nineteenth-century sources is to discover anti-Jacobinism. The novels of Henry Mackenzie and the philosophical treatises of Adam Smith instructed readers in how to become men of sensibility by experiencing an aversion to witnessing or causing pain. But anti-Jacobinism described human heads decapitated and impaled on spikes, bodies flayed of skin to make boot leather, hearts torn out and bitten when still beating, and pregnant women's corpses repeatedly raped – images designed to physically sicken people at the thought of French violence. Anti-Jacobin writings are the most explicitly violent writings of the late eighteenth and nineteenth century. Their role in the development of antiviolent humanitarianism within the United States must be taken into account.

The aspiration of American anti-Jacobin authors to make their readers sick, and my earlier claims that anti-Jacobinism bombarded and assaulted the United States, however, indicates the need to complicate this whig narrative about ethical change. While anti-Jacobinism could be used to problematize violence, its graphic language served at the same time as a weapon that enacted violence. Raymond Williams notes in his definition of violence in the book *Keywords* that it "can include the reporting of violent physical events" but also indicates "the dramatic portrayal of such events."[37] In other words, graphic descriptions of violence themselves constitute a form of violence with the implicit power to wound.[38] The authors of American anti-Jacobinism used discourse as a weapon to assault their political and religious enemies. Until 1798, conservatives dominated the use of anti-Jacobin discourse and used it very effectively to club their opponents (again, note how natural it is to envisage using words as weapons). Yet the language proved so seductive that in 1798 Jeffersonian Republicans began to use it themselves, describing the Alien and Sedition Acts under which they suffered as a Federalist "reign of terror." In the nineteenth century, anti-Jacobinism expanded as a discourse and was employed frequently on opposing sides of violent political debates.

The fact that anti-Jacobinism served as a weapon for early national partisans is an important reason historians have been reluctant to take it seriously. Historians, many of whom admire the democratic Jeffersonian vision as well as the liberating ideology of the French Revolution, have long argued that early national opposition to the French Revolution was never really about its violence. Instead, opposition to the French Revolution has been attributed to deeper concerns about social order, religious orthodoxy, and property.

---

[37] Raymond Williams, *Keywords: A Vocabulary of Culture and Society* (London, 1976), 278.

[38] Two recent histories that take into consideration how language itself constitutes a form of violence include Jill Lepore, *The Name of War: King Philip's War and the Origins of American Identity* (New York, 1998); and Christopher Tomlins, "Law's Wilderness: The Discourse of English Colonizing, the Violence of Intrusion, and the Failures of American History," in *New World Orders: Violence, Sanction, and Authority in the Colonial Americas*, ed. John Smolenski and Thomas J. Humphrey (Philadelphia, Pa., 2005).

American complaints about the Revolution's bloodiness are read as rhetorical cover for elite agendas. Historians argue that elites used frightened accounts of French violence merely as a persuasive language to consolidate their social position; they never meant what they said. This position was advanced most influentially in a 1965 article by Gary Nash, who argued that the New England ministry rejected the French Revolution only after the end of the Reign of Terror in 1795, and not because of violence in France but because of the threat posed by deism at home.[39] Marshall Smelser also contributed to the formulation of this historiographical consensus by arguing that Federalist opposition to Jacobinism was attributable not to events occurring in France but rather to the Federalists' "social paranoia" and "aristocratic" hostility to equality.[40] Almost every historian who has since published any treatment of the American reaction to the French Revolution cites both Nash and Smelser.[41]

Historians who have dismissed American concerns about the violence of the Revolution have based their arguments on a very important truth: accounts of violence make exceptionally persuasive rhetoric. Accounts of Jacobin atrocities were incredibly persuasive in disaffecting Americans from the French Revolution and in discrediting democratic radicalism at home. When words serve so transparently as political weapons, historians are sometimes reluctant to consider them meaningful. However, the power of violent words as an instrument of battle is what drives this study. If violent words make powerful rhetoric, we must ask what consequences they entail. One obvious consequence of American anti-Jacobinism was to sanction an antidemocratic political offensive during the early 1790s. But that was not the language's only outcome. The expansion of anti-Jacobinism into a weapon against conservatives during the late 1790s demonstrates that its

---

[39] Gary Nash, "The American Clergy and the French Revolution," *William and Mary Quarterly* 22 (July 1965). See also Ruth H. Bloch, *Visionary Republic: Millennial Themes in American Thought 1756–1800* (New York, 1985), 207; Ann B. Lever, "Vox Populi, Vox Dei: New England and the French Revolution, 1787–1801" (Ph.D., University of North Carolina, 1971). A much older historiography takes the role of violence more seriously; John Bach McMaster, *A History of the People of the United States, from the Revolution to the Civil War*, vol. 2 (New York, 1883), chap. 8; Charles Downer Hazen, *Contemporary American Opinion of the French Revolution* (Baltimore, 1897); Howard Mumford Jones, *America and French Culture, 1750–1848* (Chapel Hill, N.C., 1927).

[40] Smelser, "Jacobin Phrenzy"; Smelser, "Federalist Period." John Howe makes the related argument that republican paranoia sparked the Federalists' reaction against the French Revolution; Howe, "Republican Thought." The new cultural history of the early republic has been no more sympathetic to fears of violence than have earlier interpretations; see Andrew Burstein's argument that the Federalists transformed sensibility into a negative force: "now passion was merely exposing the destructive sentiments of terror and panic instead of feeding sympathy and generosity," in Burstein, *Sentimental Democracy*, 182.

[41] Jonathan D. Sassi, *A Republic of Righteousness: The Public Christianity of the Post-Revolutionary New England Clergy* (Oxford, 2001); Davis, *Revolutions*; Henry Farnham May, *The Enlightenment in America* (New York, 1976).

discursive power extended beyond the initial political debate in which it was framed. A second, less obvious consequence of American anti-Jacobinism was to empower nineteenth-century abolitionists in their crusade against the cruelty of the slave system.[42] *The Reign of Terror in America* argues that the violence of anti-Jacobin language evolved into a powerful abolitionist weapon during the 1800s. Anti-Jacobinism both raised awareness that violence against enslaved people was a threat to American social and political order and served as a weapon that antislavery leaders used to attack the slave system.

Historians of the early American republic have also been skeptical of the significance of anti-Jacobinism because of the language's sensationalist power to titillate. While many American readers read and wrote about the French Revolution for political or religious reasons, the broad popularity of anti-Jacobin literature in the United States suggests that it also served to entertain. Accounts of the violence in France could be dramatic and bloody. The *Federal Gazette* printed a story in October 1792 about a massacre in Bordeaux, during which savage villagers danced around their victims, singing the "Ça Ira," before they cut the victims with sabers, pikes, bayonets, and daggers. After the victims died, one was "torn piecemeal by some of these cannibals"; another was decapitated and his head impaled on a pike while his body was thrown onto a dunghill to rot.[43] Some readers of this news item must have attended to every word, rereading to be clear who had lost his head and who had been torn to pieces. Other readers, no doubt, skimmed quickly – fascinated by the news, yet not wishing to know too much. But even readers whose eyes merely alighted on the words *France, massacre, cannibal,* and *pike* without settling in to determine whose body had suffered which injury could feel the attraction of the violent words. A headline like "Massacre at Bourdeaux" attracted the bloodthirsty and the squeamish; both temperaments could experience the stimulating attraction of reading about violence.

If violent writing is written and read for sensation, can its ethical posturing against violence be credited? As Karen Halttunen has shown, violent language gained the power to sensationalize precisely because of the expanding belief that human beings should be nonviolent.[44] Sensationalism and the formation of an ethical nonviolent sensibility are not at odds with

---

[42] This claim runs contrary to the arguments of Winthrop Jordan, David Brion Davis, Elizabeth Fox-Genovese, and Eugene Genovese that the violence of the French Revolution had a stifling impact on American antislavery; David Brion Davis, *Inhuman Bondage: The Rise and Fall of Slavery in the New World* (New York, 2006), chap. 8; Fox-Genovese and Genovese, *Mind of the Master Class*; David Brion Davis, *The Problem of Slavery in the Age of Revolution, 1770–1823* (Ithaca, N.Y., 1975); Winthrop Jordan, *White over Black: American Attitudes toward the Negro, 1550–1812* (Chapel Hill, N.C., 1968).

[43] "Paris. Aug. 9. Massacre at Bourdeaux," *Federal Gazette, and Philadelphia Evening Post,* Oct. 4, 1792.

[44] Halttunen, "Humanitarianism and the Pornography of Pain."

each other; they are mutually defining processes. The spectacle of violence presents a contradiction: it both repels and attracts. These bipolar qualities are mutually constituting. Violent imagery commands attention by upsetting us, and it upsets us by commanding attention. The dialectic of attraction and repulsion endows violent imagery with great power. We are absorbed into a feedback loop when we read, listen to, or view accounts of violence. Disturbed, entranced, disturbed, entranced – violence keeps our attention in play, ricocheting back and forth.[45] *Reign of Terror* follows the path of a violent discourse that reverberated powerfully throughout the early years of the American republic.

As is true for any widespread and long-lived discourse, American anti-Jacobinism had many uses and meanings. It could express the political concerns of committed patriots, and it could be used cynically by political partisans to discredit their local rivals for power; it could communicate a deeply held religious belief in human depravity, and it could be a tool for establishment ministers to retain their monopoly on tax monies; it could reflect an emerging ethical concern with bloodshed, and it could feed people's sensationalistic taste for bloody literature. *Reign of Terror* explores each of these uses and meanings within the vast public discourse against the violence of the French Revolution authored between 1789 and 1865. Because this study is primarily concerned with the development and consequences of a public discourse, it makes use primarily of published sources. The book draws heavily on published sermons, political orations, newspaper and periodical writings, pamphlets, memoirs, and political debates. The book also draws on letters written by prominent individuals, which often served a quasi-public function during the early national era.[46] The concern here is how narratives of the French Revolution penetrated and transformed the American public sphere.

John L. Brooke has recently defined Jürgen Habermas's concept of the public sphere as "a specific space in civil society for discourse, communication, and association, mediating between the state and the people in their private capacities." Habermas's initial formulation of the public sphere emphasized rational deliberation as the sphere's media, provoking criticisms from historians who argued that public communication is often nonrational, defined by emotional persuasion and vast power imbalances. Brooke seeks to remedy this contradiction by offering a "revised model of the public sphere" during the early American republic that acknowledges how "formal 'rational deliberation is intermingled in the public sphere with a much

---

[45] Karen Halttunen has brilliantly explored the dialectical reactions aroused by violent discourse in Halttunen, "Humanitarianism and the Pornography of Pain"; Halttunen, *Murder Most Foul: The Killer and the American Gothic Imagination* (Cambridge, Mass., 1998), 82.

[46] For a wonderful exploration of how private writings served very public purposes, see Joanne B. Freeman, *Affairs of Honor: National Politics in the New Republic* (New Haven, Conn., 2001).

more pervasive, informal cultural persuasion.'"[47] Narratives of Jacobin violence entered the public sphere as a discourse of cultural persuasion, used to secure political consent, and played a key role in constituting the relationship between a pacified civil society and the state. Anti-Jacobin discourse suffused the public sphere in the first half of the nineteenth century, transforming the ethics of personal violence, and refashioning American citizenship from the revolutionary model of personal virtue and resistance to tyranny to the nineteenth-century model of self-control and abidance by law. Much work remains to be done on the integration of anti-Jacobin discourse into the private sphere, yet this study will focus on the very public questions of how opposition to the French Revolution entered into debates about democracy, war, education, and slavery, thereby refashioning the relationships among the state, the civil society, and the citizen.

Quite fortuitously, this book arrives at a time when British interest in anti-Jacobinism has also been on the rise. Recent works insist on the significant influence that anti-Jacobin writings had on transforming British political culture during the 1790s and 1800s.[48] Anti-Jacobin discourse also pervaded British newspapers, periodicals, political pamphlets and treatises, sermons,

---

[47] John L. Brooke, "Consent, Civil Society, and the Public Sphere in the Age of Revolution and the Early American Republic," in *Beyond the Founders: New Approaches to the Political History of the Early American Republic*, ed. Jeffrey L. Pasley, Andrew W. Robertson, and David Waldstreicher (Chapel Hill, N.C., 2004), 207, 228.

[48] Kevin Gilmartin, *Writing against Revolution: Literary Conservatism in Britain, 1790–1832*, ed. Marilyn Butler and James Chandler, Cambridge Studies in Romanticism (New York, 2007); Ian Haywood, *Bloody Romanticism: Spectacular Violence and the Politics of Representation, 1776–1832*, ed. Anne K. Kellor and Clifford Siskin, Palgrave Studies in the Enlightenment, Romanticism, and Cultures of Print (New York, 2006); M. O. Grenby, "'A Conservative Woman Doing Radical Things': Sarah Trimmer and 'the Guardian of Education,'" in *Culturing the Child, 1690–1914: Essays in Memory of Mitzi Myers*, ed. Donelle Ruwe (Lanham, Md., 2005); Emily Lorraine De Montluzin, "The *Anti-Jacobin Review* after John Gifford: Contributions by Identified Authors, 1807–1821," *Library* 6 (Sept. 2005); Kevin Gilmartin, "'Study to Be Quiet': Hannah More and the Invention of Conservative Culture in Britain," *English Literary History* 70 (2003); Jennifer Mori, "Languages of Loyalism: Patriotism, Nationhood, and the State in the 1790s," *English Historical Review* 118 (Feb. 2003); M. O. Grenby, "Politicizing the Nursery: British Children's Literature and the French Revolution," *The Lion and the Unicorn* 27 (2003); Kevin Gilmartin, "In the Theater of Counterrevolution: Loyalist Association and Conservative Opinion in the 1790s," *Journal of British Studies* 41 (July 2002); M. O. Grenby, *The Anti-Jacobin Novel: British Conservatism and the French Revolution*, ed. Marilyn Butler and James Chandler, Cambridge Studies in Romanticism (Cambridge, 2001). Significant studies of British anti-Jacobinism published before 2000 include Mark Philp, "Vulgar Conservatism, 1792–3," *English Historical Review* 110 (Feb. 1995); John Dinwiddy, "Interpretations of Anti-Jacobinism," in *The French Revolution and British Popular Politics*, ed. Mark Philp (New York, 1991); David Bindman, ed., *The Shadow of the Guillotine: Britain and the French Revolution* (London, 1989); H. T. Dickinson, "Popular Conservatism and Militant Loyalism, 1789–1815," in *Britain and the French Revolution, 1789–1815*, ed. H. T. Dickinson (London, 1989).

ballads, broadsheets, caricatures, addresses, resolutions, and petitions. Even recipes were enlisted in the British anti-Jacobin offensive.[49] The list of British genres to be co-opted by anti-Jacobinism strongly resembles the American list. In fact, British anti-Jacobin authors were frequently republished in the United States and enjoyed great popularity here. Yet the 1790s and early 1800s were by no means a friendly interlude in the Anglo-American diplomatic relationship, and American anti-Jacobins often positioned the United States in opposition to Great Britain.

In addition, the Haitian Revolution also serves as a context for understanding American anti-Jacobinism. From 1791 onward, the United States was suffused in accounts of the slave revolt in Saint Domingue and in the other islands of the Caribbean.[50] In addition, thousands of white, mixed-race, and black refugees from the French Caribbean flooded American cities, including Philadelphia, Baltimore, and Charleston, throughout the decade.[51] Although it has often been assumed that the Haitian Revolution was universally despised in the United States, the truth is much more complicated. At numerous moments, the most rabid opponents to French Revolutionary violence expressed a surprising sympathy for the black Jacobins in the former French colony. Meanwhile the most passionate Francophiles, such as Thomas Jefferson and other southern Republican leaders, did all in their power to defeat the Haitian Revolution. The unpredictable relationships among American anti-Jacobinism, British anti-Jacobinism, and Caribbean revolution reveal the complexity of the history related in this book.

Reign of Terror is divided into six chapters that trace the American reaction to the violence of the French Revolution from its origins to its ultimate role in the abolitionist movement, continuing through the Civil War. Chapter 1 sets the stage by investigating northeastern political and religious ideas about violence, social order, and civil society in the era leading up to the French Revolution. It finds precedents for the anti-Jacobin reaction in historical Francophobia, concerns about human depravity, and beliefs about New World violence. Chapter 2 describes the American reaction to the violence of the French Revolution between 1789 and the early 1800s, exploring in depth the construction of anti-Jacobin rhetorical tropes that persisted into the nineteenth century. The chapter argues that anti-Jacobins embraced a new style of bloody writing to persuade readers to reject the French Revolution. Chapter 3 describes the connection between anti-Jacobinism and antislavery sentiment in the 1790s. It explains why American anti-Jacobins criticized the

---

[49] Susan Pederson, "Hannah More Meets Simple Simon: Tracts, Chapbooks, and Popular Culture in Late Eighteenth-Century England," *Journal of British Studies* 25 (1986).

[50] Matt Clavin, "Race, Rebellion and the Gothic: Inventing the Haitian Revolution," *Early American Studies* 5 (Spring 2007).

[51] Meadows, "Engineering Exile"; Branson and Patrick, "Saint-Domingan Refugees of Color in Philadelphia"; Nash, "Black Saint Dominguans in Philadelphia."

violence of slavery, and how those criticisms shaped abolitionist sentiment in the United States. Chapter 4 examines the transformation of anti-Jacobin discourse in the crucible of the War of 1812. From the passionate anti-Jacobin denunciations of this most unpopular war in American history emerged the first nonsectarian peace movement in U.S. history. Chapter 5 argues that American anti-Jacobins were the strongest supporters of common schooling in the United States during the 1790s and early 1800s, because they viewed education as a necessary corrective to the problem of violence. Popular pedagogy incorporated anti-Jacobin discourse, strongly influencing the rising generation born during the 1790s and early 1800s. Chapter 6 completes the book's narrative arc, arguing that children who were born in the anti-Jacobin milieu of the 1790–1815 era went on to become leaders of the abolitionist movement in the United States. The chapter employs both prosopography and textual analysis to reveal the connections between anti-Jacobinism and abolitionism, and provides a new answer to long-standing questions about the Federalist origins of antislavery. Finally, the conclusion examines whether the anti-Jacobin critique of bloodshed succeeded in limiting social violence, and suggests that anti-Jacobin discourse helped pave the path to the totalizing violence of the Civil War.

Reign of Terror is structured to form a narrative arc, leading from concerns about the French Revolution to the emergence of a new understanding of the problem of violence during the antebellum era. I am holding out the promise of nonviolence as the reason to pursue the violent language that fills the following chapters. Nonviolence is the ending that will redeem both my subjects' and my own relentless and repetitive descriptions of spilling blood, mutilated bodies, and tortured suffering. But is nonviolence the only ending? A shadow hangs over this book – the negative power of violent language to seduce and to wound. It too should end the introduction, not as a promised reward to drive the reader forward, but as a warning to consider.

In J. M. Coetzee's novel *Elizabeth Costello* (2003), the eponymous heroine, an old and increasingly feeble author, considers a novel that she has read about torture – a novel written with the conscientious intention to open its readers' eyes "to human depravity in another of its manifest forms," and to prevent that evil's recurrence. Reading the book, however, makes Costello feel touched by evil in a way that she concludes is not good for her or any reader. Reading the book, "she felt, she could have sworn, the brush of Satan's hot leathery wings. Was she deluded? *I do not want to read this*, she said to herself; yet she had gone on reading, excited despite herself. *The devil is leading me on*: what kind of excuse is that?"[52] Perhaps those hot, leathery wings also brushed many of the authors and readers captured in this book; perhaps they brush me and you, too. The seduction of violence

---

[52] J. M. Coetzee, *Elizabeth Costello* (New York, 2003), 176–8.

poses a constant challenge to the book's origins in my commitment against violence.

Last, the historical arc of *Reign of Terror* casts a shadow. While anti-Jacobinism inspired a reaction against violence that became a powerful ingredient of nineteenth-century humanitarianism, it also contained a seductive element that fueled and justified the violence of the Civil War. Anti-Jacobin fantasies helped enable the destruction of 620,000 lives, which may be judged as a worthwhile price for eliminating slavery but must nonetheless be viewed as a tragedy of massive proportions. By demonizing French Revolutionary disorder, anti-Jacobins contributed to the emergence of humanitarian movements against bloodshed during the nineteenth century. But at the same time, their rhetorical extremism contained a moral rationale for total war. This historical shadow has darkened the world in the century and a half since. We await the time when the ameliorative properties of concerns about the problem of violence overshadow the destructive potential of those concerns.

I

Violence and Social Order in the Early American Republic

> Man, unrestrained by law and religion, is a mere beast of prey.
> – Timothy Dwight, *A Discourse on Some Events of the Last Century Delivered in the Brick Church in New Haven, on Wednesday, January 7, 1801*

New England Calvinist ministers of the late eighteenth century bear the historical reputation of having bored their audiences with arcane doctrinal disputes. Seated in pews ordered by wealth and status, orthodox New Englanders endured Sunday sermons said to be "dry as a remainder biscuit after voyage."[1] Colorless men in black robes preached from elevated pulpits about the subtleties of divine sovereignty and human inability. Did Adam's sin impute sinfulness on his posterity? Did that imputation follow from Adam's status as man's legal representative? Was all humanity truly guilty of sin because Adam lost the supernatural ability to love God in proper proportion? Was imputation best understood as a reflection of God's moral law? Or should the doctrine of imputation be abandoned altogether, and depravity be interpreted as a consequence of humanity's consent to Adam's sin? (Calvinists refused to even consider the possibility that man was morally neutral or good.)[2] Starting with a biblical passage, continuing through exegesis of its grammar and context, then on to proofs of the doctrine leading – hopefully – to rational conviction, a sermon could last for two stifling hours. Between the emotional high points of the First Great Awakening and the Finneyite revivals seems to lie the declivity of the early national era, when unhappy congregants could be forgiven for worrying more about eternal boredom than eternal damnation. Some historians have

---

[1] Vernon Louis Parrington, *Main Currents in American Thought: An Interpretation of American Literature from the Beginning to 1920* (New York, 1939), 2:317.
[2] E. Brooks Holifield, *Theology in America: Christian Thought from the Age of the Puritans to the Civil War* (New Haven, Conn., 2003).

observed the vitality of early national Calvinism, drawing attention to its social engagement. Leaders of the faith promoted humanitarian endeavors, including education, antislavery, and temperance.[3] Yet the reappraisal of early national Calvinism should not rest solely on the basis of its ends. The means of the clergy's publicly oriented faith also deserves a second look, for sermons on the subject of man's sinfulness held more interest than might be imagined.[4]

The Reverend Elijah Parish of Byfield, Massachusetts, chose man's sinfulness as the subject for his tenth anniversary sermon in 1797. Born in Connecticut in 1762, a descendant of Myles Standish, the short yet commanding minister preached New Divinity Calvinism from his ordination in 1785 through his death in 1825. Parish had the reputation among religious and political liberals of the era as the typification of the archaic Puritan – a man whose desiccating breath made the currents of faith run dry. And yet he preached to crowded meetings and preserved a remarkable degree of unity within his congregation.[5] When Parish preached on the subject of man's depravity, his congregation listened. At his tenth anniversary sermon, Parish spoke for perhaps half an hour, without diversion, about the terrible brutalities committed by men who had not been redeemed by the saving power of the Gospel. In tones "animated, emphatic, [and] glowing" he focused on the practice of human sacrifice: "the altars of Moloch, in the land of Canaan were stained with human blood. In Gaul they inclosed a man in a kind of wicker work, and burnt him in Honor of the Gods. The banks of the Nile drank the blood of human victims." The list continued across continents and centuries, a dystopian anthropological survey. Along the Danube, parents drowned their children, and children ate their parents. The Romans sacrificed their children. Carthaginians burned their children alive. Africans exposed their children to be eaten by wild beasts. South Sea islanders piled human skulls. In Peru men pulled the flesh off the living and ate it before their eyes. The Tartars sucked the blood of wounded persons. Indians and Africans burned their wives. The natives of Jago, Hispaniola,

---

[3] Jonathan D. Sassi, *A Republic of Righteousness: The Public Christianity of the Post-Revolutionary New England Clergy* (Oxford, 2001); John R. Fitzmier, *New England's Moral Legislator: Timothy Dwight, 1752–1817* (Bloomington, Ind., 1998); Mark Valeri, *Law and Providence in Joseph Bellamy's New England: The Origins of the New Divinity in Revolutionary America* (New York, 1994); David William Kling, *A Field of Divine Wonders: The New Divinity and Village Revivals in Northwestern Connecticut, 1792–1822* (University Park, Pa., 1993); James D. Essig, *The Bonds of Wickedness: American Evangelicals against Slavery, 1770–1808* (Philadelphia, Pa., 1982); Lois Wendland Banner, "Protestant Crusade; Religious Missions, Benevolence and Reform in the United States, 1790–1840" (Ph.D., Columbia University, Columbia University, 1973).

[4] Kling, *Field of Divine Wonders*, chap. 4.

[5] Elijah Parish, *Sermons, Practical and Doctrinal with a Biographical Sketch of the Author* (Boston, Mass., 1826). Matthew Mason, "'Infuriate Ravings': The Rev. Elijah Parish and Federalist Antislavery" (unpublished paper, 2006).

FIGURE 1. Elijah Parish, 1762–1825, from *The Story of Byfield* by John Lewis Ewell. Elijah Parish typified the intersections between Congregationalist ethics and Federalist politics. During his long career, Parish defended the doctrine of innate depravity and attacked the violence of the French Revolution, slavery, and the War of 1812. He also supported education, donating his personal papers to the local academy in his parish of Byfield, Massachusetts. *Collection of the New-York Historical Society.*

and Brazil were cannibals. The Mingrelians buried their children alive. The inhabitants of Britain were so guilty of human sacrifice that the Romans forbade their religion. When Parish spoke on the subject of human depravity, his sermons were not dry; he spoke with a violence that seized his listeners' attention. During his long ministry, the small congregation at Byfield experienced two dramatic revivals. In the words of Moses P. Parish, the minister's only son to survive infancy, "He was fired himself, and never failed to fire his audience."[6]

Parish's vision of men's violence drew on millennia of religious and philosophical teachings about human depravity, as well as on more immediate traditions within American Christianity. Since the Great Awakening, North American Calvinists had employed the doctrine of depravity to terrify their congregants, as a means to catalyze spiritual rebirth and community revival. Far from boring listeners, sermons like Parish's – or Jonathan Edwards's classic frightener "Sinners in the Hands of an Angry God" (1741) – proved

[6] Elijah Parish, *The Excellence of the Gospel Visible in the Wretchedness of Paganism. A Discourse Delivered December 20, 1797, Being the Tenth Anniversary of His Ordination* (Newburyport, Mass., 1798). 9–15; Parish, *Sermons,* ix.

remarkably effective at producing conversions. The Presbyterian minister Gilbert Tennent, a very successful revivalist during the First Great Awakening, belittled ministers who "did not have the Courage, or Honesty, to thrust the Nail of Terror into sleeping souls."[7] According to revivalists, the doctrine of depravity did not alienate congregants; it was key to their conversion.[8] Listening to the exhortations of their Calvinist ministers, New England congregations felt terror at the prospect of human violence, and at their own culpability for bloodshed.[9] Elijah Parish's bloody catalog continued into the present age, ending in the very space that he and his congregants occupied. Perhaps, he concluded, "the spot on which we are has been an altar – perhaps here stood the bloody sacrificer – here lay the agonizing victim – here the dust was crimsoned with human gore."[10] Depravity made human violence a constant threat, its proximity an ever-present reminder of the human need for salvation. Short of salvation, which came only through the grace of God, the threat of violence required the control of human law and social order.

The doctrine of depravity played a central role in Elijah Parish's Christian vision throughout his life. From the first sermons that he preached in 1785 through his final sermons in 1825, Parish relentlessly returned again and again to the vision of depraved human violence. His first sermon following ordination painted a picture of human tyrants who "swam to their imperial seats thro seas of blood."[11] Twenty years after his ordination, when religious liberals had seized control of Harvard and the belief in human goodness was expanding throughout New England religious culture, Parish was still preaching sermons that used hideous examples of violence to justify the Gospel.[12] Even in 1825, long after his doctrinal opponents had gained control of New England Christianity, Parish wrote a letter to his son advising that it was better to attend a mediocre minister than a genius who had abandoned the principle of original sin.[13] Along the way, Parish's conviction in the violent dangers of human depravity inspired him to become one of the nation's most relentless critics of the French Revolution, as well as an opponent of war and a fierce critic of the enslavement of African

---

[7] Gilbert Tennent, *The Danger of an Unconverted Ministry: Considered in a Sermon on Mark VI, 34* (Boston, Mass., 1742).

[8] Holifield, *Theology in America*, 98.

[9] Kling, *Field of Divine Wonders*, 131.

[10] Parish, *Excellence of the Gospel*, 15.

[11] Elijah Parish, "No. 22," 1785, Elijah Parish Papers, Governor's Academy, Byfield Massachusetts (EPP).

[12] Elijah Parish, *A Sermon, Preached before the Massachusetts Missionary Society: At Their Annual Meeting, in Boston, May 26, 1807* (Northampton, Mass., 1807).

[13] William Buell Sprague, *Annals of the American Pulpit, or, Commemorative Notices of Distinguished American Clergymen of Various Denominations: From the Early Settlement of the Country to the Close of the Year Eighteen Hundred and Fifty-Five with Historical Introductions* (New York, 1857), 1:271.

Americans. In the pages that follow, this chapter will describe how the doctrine of human depravity blended with intense anxiety about British New World violence and with communitarian political traditions to create a base of beliefs about violence and social order that, when heated by the French Revolution, reacted explosively.

The story of Elijah Parish, interwoven throughout this book, embodies how deeply rooted religious and political beliefs engendered the American reaction to the violence of Jacobinism in France and at home. Passionately committed to the craft of writing, Parish published multiple editions of more than ten sermons and five books during his lifetime, and he saved thousands of his unpublished sermons as well as many of his poems, correspondence, and ephemera. These unpublished papers bring to light the consistency of Parish's earliest recorded convictions with his later "partisan" publications. The tight cursive hand, tattooed in sepia ink across the darkened pages, reveals a man perpetually focused on death, terror, and depravity. In an oration delivered at his Dartmouth College commencement in 1785, Parish observed that the "history of the world [was] little more than the history of rapine, murder and devastation."[14] Poems in his hand memorialize the deaths of young friends. "O, Sin, thou monster! How dost thou destroy / And blast the hope of every rising joy / How has thou poison'd every thing below / And made this world a scene of death of woe," begins a typical poetic production.[15] Letters he saved express his nearly deranging grief at the death of his brother.[16] Most of all, his sermons unremittingly impressed his congregants with the bloody evidence of human depravity. And, lest Parish be mistaken as unusual, the great popularity of his morbid publications illustrates the attraction that his violent writing held to the age.

The Great Christian Doctrine of Original Sin Defended

The northeastern political and religious leaders who reacted most fearfully to the threat of French violence in the early 1790s were predisposed by a deeply rooted belief in human depravity. Saint Augustine, the bishop of Hippo, fixed depravity as a core Christian belief in his fifth-century criticism of the Pelagian heresy. Although often challenged, depravity remained central to the Western European Christian tradition for the next thousand years. The Puritans situated the concept of original sin at the core of their religious worldview. It was included in the Westminster Confession of 1646, which New England Calvinists adopted as a standard of belief. In colonial North America, ministers often quoted to their congregations from the

---

[14] Elijah Parish, MSS Oration Commencement, Dartmouth College, 16 Aug. 1785, EPP.
[15] Elijah Parish, "Some Reflections Ocasioned [*sic*] by the Death of Mr. William Brewster of Hampton," EPP.
[16] Elijah Parish to Elijah Parish Sr., 1794, EPP.

prophet Jeremiah (17:9): "The heart of man is deceitful above all things and desperately wicked." This teaching was central to the jeremiad sermons that American religious historians once described as the defining feature of New England Puritanism. The portrayal of humanity as utterly corrupt and depraved pulsed vigorously throughout the seventeenth century and into the eighteenth century.[17]

Calvinist professions of human sinfulness were invigorated during the eighteenth century by the challenge from Enlightenment progressives who argued for man's inherent virtue. In the Anglo-American Christian tradition, a set of British theologians known as the Latitudinarian Divines made the most forceful Enlightenment challenge to the doctrine of depravity. Rejecting English Calvinist doctrine, the Latitudinarians argued that "human nature was instinctively sympathetic and that their passions naturally inclined them to virtuous actions."[18] The Latitudinarians drew on the rationalist spirit of the era, basing their conclusions about human nature on the new science of sensational psychology (promulgated by John Locke). A school of moral sense philosophy centered on the premise of man's inherently sympathetic nature took shape in Britain during the eighteenth century, greatly influencing European and American political theories. The Third Earl of Shaftesbury, Anthony Ashley Cooper (1671–1713), is credited as one of the founders of this school, but its true efflorescence took place during the Scottish Enlightenment in the mid-eighteenth century. Francis Hutcheson (1694–1747), professor of moral philosophy at Glasgow, argued in his *Inquiry into the Original of Our Ideas of Beauty and Virtue*, that God had framed human nature to feel benevolence and to act for the good of others. Hutcheson's writings were highly influential in North America; moral sense philosophy also reached a broad audience through its popularization in British periodicals such as the *Spectator* and the *Guardian*, which had many American readers.[19]

The popularity of new beliefs in human benevolence did not silence traditional Calvinists in the northeastern colonies. Instead, the new ideas prompted vociferous resistance from eighteenth-century ministers who were eager to prove how rationality and the doctrine of depravity could be blended harmoniously. Beginning in 1750, a violent paper war erupted within New England over the question of human nature. Jonathan Edwards supplied the authoritative orthodox opinion in *The Great Christian Doctrine of Original Sin Defended* (1758). Of course, the debate continued. Challenges to

[17] Arthur O. Lovejoy, *Reflections on Human Nature* (Baltimore, 1961).
[18] G. J. Barker-Benfield, *The Culture of Sensibility: Sex and Society in Eighteenth-Century Britain* (Chicago, 1992), 67.
[19] Norman Fiering, "Irresistible Compassion: An Aspect of Eighteenth-Century Sympathy and Humanitarianism," *Journal of the History of Ideas* 37 (1976); Barker-Benfield, *Culture of Sensibility*, 105–19.

the doctrine of depravity grew louder during the revolutionary era, as the triumph of republican politics seemed to bolster religious arguments for human ability and virtue. The publication of Charles Chauncy's antidepravity tract, *Five Dissertations on the Fall and Its Consequences*, in 1785 – almost twenty years after it was first written – perpetuated the debate among New England divines after the Revolution.[20] Once again, Calvinist ministers, mostly Congregationalists and Presbyterians, vigorously defended the doctrine of original sin against its detractors. In addition to Old Calvinists such as Jedidiah Morse and David Tappan, who claimed doctrinal conformity with their ancestors, a rising generation of New Divinity theologians incorporated insights from the Scottish Enlightenment into their revitalized defense of depravity.

Ministers of the New Divinity school, also known as consistent Calvinists, were the students and intellectual inheritors of the great revivalist Jonathan Edwards. In their search to systematize and popularize their mentor's theology, New Divinity ministers delved deeply into the writings of the moral sense school. Joseph Bellamy, one of the earliest promoters of the New Divinity, immersed himself for many years in the writings of Shaftesbury, Hutcheson, and David Hume. Although he rejected their vision of human benevolence, he attempted to prove that Calvinism had rational integrity and obeyed moral law. He used sensationalist psychology to justify the correctness of the doctrine of depravity, finding evidence for man's depravity in his often-brutal behavior.[21] Samuel Hopkins, another New Divinity leader, co-opted the term *disinterested benevolence* from a contributor to the liberal journal the *Spectator*, to frame a logic of human virtue that was rooted in the acknowledgment of depravity.[22] Timothy Dwight, a grandson of Jonathan Edwards and the president of Yale College from 1795 through 1817, believed in "the harmonious coexistence of science and religion," and insisted that human imperfection had to be acknowledged and compensated for to advance the progress of civilization. In 1788, Dwight wrote a poem entitled *The Triumph of Infidelity*, which responded to Chauncy's attack on original sin, by using Augustan satire to reveal the fallen world as plunged in war and bloodshed. Dwight drew a clear connection in *Triumph*, and in later works, between the "descent into the material level of existence and the tendency toward brutality and violence."[23]

---

[20] H. Shelton Smith, *Changing Conceptions of Original Sin* (New York, 1955).

[21] Valeri, *Law and Providence*, 42–94.

[22] Joseph Conforti, "Samuel Hopkins and the New Divinity: Theology, Ethics, and Social Reform in Eighteenth-Century New England," *William and Mary Quarterly* 34 (1977); Fiering, "Irresistible Compassion," 203.

[23] Colin Wells, *The Devil and Doctor Dwight: Satire and Theology in the Early American Republic* (Chapel Hill, 2002), 111, 149. Timothy Fitzmier argues convincingly that Timothy Dwight was neither a New Divinity man nor an Old Calvinist but rather a purveyor of his own, influential school of "Godly Federalism"; Fitzmier, *New England's Moral Legislator*, chap. 3.

Man's violence often served as the primary evidence for the terrible doctrine of human depravity. "Among innumerable things which shew this [depravity]," wrote the Reverend Jonathan Edwards in his 1758 treatise, "I shall now only observe this, viz. the degree in which mankind have from age to age been hurtful one to another."[24] Bloodshed signified the ultimate and most terrifying manifestation of depravity; it was where greed, passions, and lusts eventually terminated. In eighteenth-century parlance, the words *passions* and *lusts* carried violent implications very different from today's sexual connotations.[25] In a sermon rallying New Englanders to fight in New France, the Reverend Ebenezer Pemberton argued that unrestrained "passions" were "like a devouring lion" that "would soon cover the face of nature with cruelty and violence if not kept in chains."[26] David Osgood, of Medford, Massachusetts, instructed militia members in attendance at a 1788 sermon that while human "lusts remain, the earth will be more or less *filled with violence*."[27] Like passions and lusts, the word *violence* itself had multiple shades of meaning.[28] During the early national era *violence* could simply connote great force, or it could evoke the more familiar contemporary meaning of shedding blood. Yet both senses were positioned along a continuum, so that the first meaning invariably called the second to mind. For example, a July 1798 article in *Philadelphia Monthly Magazine* commented, "Of political things, how many are violently thrown out of their old places – how few are solidly fixed in new ones! What violence, rage, and bloodshed!"[29] Passions, lusts, and force bled quickly into violence. This human violence, this shedding of blood, pulsed hot and thick beneath the surface of sermons about human inability, supplying the color to a religious movement that has appeared pallid to later generations.

---

[24] Jonathan Edwards, *Original Sin*, ed. Clyde A. Holbrook, The Works of Jonathan Edwards (New Haven, Conn., 1970), 3:168.

[25] This definition of the passions enabled "sexual and violent acts [to] bleed into each other" during the eighteenth century more than they are acknowledged to do today; Sharon Block, *Rape and Sexual Power in Early America* (Chapel Hill, 2006), 17.

[26] Quoted in Kerry Arnold Trask, "In the Pursuit of Shadows: A Study of Collective Hope and Despair in Provincial Massachusetts during the Era of the Seven Years War, 1748 to 1764," (Ph.D., University of Minnesota, 1971), 56.

[27] David Osgood, *A Sermon, Preached at the Request of the Ancient and Honourable Artillery Company, in Boston, June 2, 1788 Being the Anniversary of Their Election of Officers* (Boston, Mass., 1788), 15. See also Nathaniel Thayer's warning that "'the casting of fire-brands, arrows and death' is the natural product of excessive passions." Nathaniel Thayer, *A Sermon, Delivered before the Ancient and Honorable Artillery Company, in Boston, June 4, 1798 Being the Anniversary of Their Election of Officers* (Boston, Mass., 1798), 7. And John Andrews's reference to "those lusts and passions, which uncontroued, degrade our nature, and produce wars and fightings." John Andrews, *A Sermon, Delivered February 19, 1795: Being a Day of Public Thanksgiving, throughout the United States of America* (Newburyport, Mass., 1795), 7.

[28] Raymond Williams, *Keywords: A Vocabulary of Culture and Society* (London, 1976), 278–9.

[29] "Brief Summary of Foreign Intelligence," *Philadelphia Monthly Magazine* (July, 1798).

American Violence

Northeastern religious conservatives in the early republic did not have to look far for examples of the human violence they feared. In the sixteenth century, Europe's colonization of the New World acquired a reputation for horrific bloodshed. Within the British Empire, North America and the West Indies developed a reputation as the violent periphery of a well-ordered society. Two sets of social relations in the New World constituted this reputation: interactions between settlers and natives, and interactions between masters and slaves.[30] To rationalize their actions as legitimate, British settlers frequently projected the violence of their social relations onto their victims and their foreign enemies.[31] British literature chiefly targeted Catholics (and French Catholics in particular) as the guilty party in New World violence, yet the projection of violence onto religious and racial others never succeeded in completely relieving Britons from anxieties about their own actions.

Catholic atrocity literature first emerged in England following Queen Mary's persecution of domestic Protestants in the 1550s. The most important example of this genre is John Foxe's *Actes and Monuments* (1563), known familiarly as the *Book of Martyrs*, which contained graphic woodcuts depicting the Catholic torture and execution of Protestants martyrs. The publication of Bartolomé de Las Casas's *Brevísima Relación* (1552–3), which was translated into English in 1656, sealed the British association between Catholic violence and the New World. Las Casas described in horrifying detail the atrocities that Spanish conquerors perpetrated on New World natives; his books, like the *Book of Martyrs*, were illustrated with woodcuts depicting the tortures described in the text. Images of infants being impaled or jumping from the wombs of mothers being burned alive, and images of adults being dismembered, flayed, stretched on the rack, boiled in hot oil, and immolated by bonfire, seared an impression upon readers – or nonreaders – of the extents to which human savagery could reach.

Raised on the "black legend" of Spanish cruelty in the New World, sixteenth-century English theorists of colonization, such as Richard Hakluyt, initially aspired to avoid the violence that had marked earlier European interactions with American natives. The patrons of British settlement both in New England and in the Chesapeake dreamed of creating colonies that coexisted harmoniously with the regions' indigenous peoples. However, reality on the ground soon destroyed those initial pacific fantasies. The expansionist greed of British settlers, and the understandable resistance of Native Americans to dislocation, swiftly resulted in exterminatory conflicts both north and south. British settlers were forced to reconstruct their expectations for

---

[30] Eliga Gould, "Zones of Law, Zones of Violence: The Legal Geography of the British Atlantic, circa 1772," *William and Mary Quarterly* 60 (2003).

[31] Jill Lepore, *The Name of War: King Philip's War and the Origins of American Identity* (New York, 1998).

New World colonization and to recast "intercultural violence as a natural component of a hierarchical, yet intimate relationship" between settlers and natives.[32]

During the late seventeenth century, when Britain and France entered into their century of struggles over empire, Foxe's *Book of Martyrs* grew increasingly popular in Britain and in North America. On both sides of the Atlantic, the book was sold in cheap editions and could be found in many ordinary households. Linda Colley has made the influential argument that British identity developed in the context of the empire's wars against France, which were envisaged as religious battles between martyred Protestantism and violent Catholicism. Spectacular images of French bloodshed pervaded Anglo-American literature throughout the eighteenth century. Meanwhile, anti-French and anti-Catholic sentiment thrived in the British colonies of North America, especially in the northeastern colonies closest to New France.[33]

New England attracted some of the "most uncompromising anti-Catholics" who came to North America. During yearly Pope's Day (Guy Fawkes) celebrations in Boston, dating back to 1623, crowds spurred on by tales of Catholic violence burned effigies of the pope and brawled in the streets – using violence to reunite the Anglo community in a shared sense of social order.[34] Long before the French Revolution, North Americans had a history of violently projecting concerns about domestic disorder onto imagined French enemies. New Englanders enlisted time and again for service in Britain's imperial struggles against New France. One-quarter of New England men enlisted for wars against New France in the mid-eighteenth century.[35] Their defeats abroad (of which there were many) and sufferings at home from assaults by French-allied Native Americans inspired an American genre of anti-French literature. Captivity narratives, sermons, political writings, and newspaper accounts all contributed to the development of an American trope of French violence that conflated natives and Catholics into a horrifying enemy.

During King George's War, when North American colonials seized the French fortress of Louisbourg in Cape Breton, a New York minister rallied his parishioners to the fight by fulminating against the *"inhuman barbarities"* and "methods of *torture* and *violence*" committed by the French.[36] During the French and Indian War, which started in the backcountry of

---

[32] Melanie Perreault, "'To Fear and to Love Us': Intercultural Violence in the English Atlantic," *Journal of World History* 17 (2006).

[33] Linda Colley, *Britons: Forging the Nation, 1707–1837* (New Haven, Conn., 1992), 25–8.

[34] Francis D. Cogliano, *No King, No Popery: Anti-Catholicism in Revolutionary New England*, Contributions in American History (Westport, Conn., 1995), 23–35; Colley, *Britons*; Philippe Rosenberg, "The Moral Order of Violence: The Meanings of Cruelty in Early Modern England, 1648–1685" (Ph.D., Duke University, 1999).

[35] Trask, "Pursuit of Shadows," 8, 244–6. See also Cogliano, *No King, No Popery*.

[36] Nathan O. Hatch, "The Origins of Civil Millennialism in America: New England Clergymen, War with France, and the Revolution," *William and Mary Quarterly* 31 (July 1974): 418.

Pennsylvania and enlisted thousands of colonials alongside British troops, American printers published vast amounts of anti-French propaganda. Works such as *A Specimen of the Unrelenting Cruelty of Papists in France* (1756) offered a typical depiction of France as a site of Catholic violence, by describing the circumstances of the murders of numerous French Protestants.[37] The French strategy of using Native American allies as proxies in their wars against the British settlers fostered propaganda about French violence in America.[38] The Reverend Samuel Woodward of Massachusetts preached a sermon in 1760 that labeled the French in America as "little less blood-thirsty and cruel than the barbarous natives." Woodward used imagery of infanticide, as had Foxe and Las Casas, to demonstrate the utter depravity of French-allied Indians: they "make the inhuman butchery of innocent babes the awful Spectacle of their fond Parents; and the Distresses of the Parents, the affecting entertainment of their loving Children."[39] When war parties of French-allied Indians attacked colonial villages, the French received a large share of the blame. Accounts of French atrocities blended with the American genre of captivity narratives, which routinely described the tortures that Native American captors practiced on their victims. In eighteenth-century captivity narratives, the French were often depicted as complicit in ritual torture. A 1758 captivity narrative titled *French and Indian Cruelty* sold in multiple American and British editions from the 1760s through the end of the century.[40] Colonial North Americans avidly consumed a locally produced and locally referenced French-atrocity literature that played a significant role in creating American identity.

However, this French atrocity literature never completely exculpated Britons from responsibility for New World violence. The expansion of African slavery in North America at the end of the seventeenth century reinscribed the British colonies' reputation for violence. The institution of racial slavery depended on the frequent and public use of physical violence. Terror functioned as the primary means of compelling resistant slaves to work and submit. The physical punishment of slaves was encoded into law

---

[37] *A Specimen of the Unrelenting Cruelty of Papists in France, and the Unshaken Faith & Patience of the Protestants of That Kingdom: Now Entering upon the Seventieth Year of Their Persecutions* (London; repr., Boston, J. Draper, 1756).

[38] Valeri, *Law and Providence.*

[39] Samuel Woodward, *A Sermon Preached October 9, 1760: Being a Day of Public Thanksgiving on Occasion of the Reduction of Montreal and the Entire Conquest of Canada by the Troops of His Britanic Majesty, under the Command of General Amherst* (Boston, Mass., 1760), 13–14, 26.

[40] Peter Williamson, *French and Indian Cruelty Exemplified in the Life and Various Vicissitudes of Fortune of Peter Williamson*... (Glasgow, 1758); Gordon Sayre, ed., *American Captivity Narratives: Selected Narratives with Introduction*, New Riverside Editions (New York, 2000), 177–8.

in the Chesapeake during the 1660s; white violence against slaves may have been legitimized, but it could not be denied. Antislavery advocates as early as the seventeenth century used allusions to the institution's violence to repudiate it.[41] In perhaps the most spectacular incident of antislavery activism during the eighteenth century, the hunchbacked Quaker dwarf, Benjamin Lay, thrust a sword into a "Bible" containing a bladder filled with red pokeberry juice and pretended to spray blood on an audience of slave owners at a Quaker meeting in Burlington, New Jersey, in 1738.[42] Quaker critiques of the institution's violence persisted, in the writings of Anthony Benezet, for example, up through the revolutionary era.[43]

By the beginning of the revolutionary era, "both metropolitan and colonial writers accepted an image of Britain's Atlantic periphery as a region 'beyond the line,' a zone of conflicting laws where Britons were free to engage in forms of violence that were unacceptable" in England, Scotland, or Wales.[44] The American Revolution reinforced North America's reputation for violence by fostering civil war, slave rebellion, and Indian and settler massacres throughout the nation.[45] David Ramsay (1749–1815), a Pennsylvania-born physician, member of the Continental Congress, and historian of the American Revolution, complained that in his adopted state of South Carolina, where the forces of civil war, slave rebellion, and Indian massacre were fully unleashed, "Rapine, outrage and murder, became so common, as to interrupt the free intercourse between one place and another. That security and protection, which individuals expect by entering into civil society, ceased almost entirely." Using an image common to atrocity literature, Ramsay called attention to how "the blood of husbands and fathers

---

[41] Philippe Rosenberg, "Thomas Tryon and the Seventeenth-Century Dimensions of Antislavery," *William and Mary Quarterly* 61 (2004).

[42] Mary Stoughton Locke, *Anti-Slavery in America, from the Introduction of African Slaves to the Prohibition of the Slave Trade, 1619–1808* (Gloucester, Mass., 1965).

[43] Anthony Benezet, *Observations on the Inslaving, Importing and Purchasing of Negroes with Some Advice Thereon Extracted Form [sic] the Yearly Meeting Epistle of London for the Present Year Also Some Remarks on the Absolute Necessity of Self-Denial, Renouncing the World, and True Charity for All Such as Sincerely Desire to Be Our Blessed Saviour's Disciples* (Germantown, Pa., 1760); Anthony Benezet, *Serious Reflections Affectionately Recommended to the Well-Disposed of Every Religious Denomination Particularly Those Who Mourn and Lament on Account of the Calamities Which Attend Us; and the Insensibility That So Generally Prevails* (Philadelphia, Pa., 1778); David Crosby, "Anthony Benezet's Transformation of Anti-Slavery Rhetoric," *Slavery and Abolition* 23 (Dec. 2002); Sydney V. James, *A People among Peoples: Quaker Benevolence in Eighteenth-Century America* (Cambridge, Mass., 1963).

[44] Gould, "Zones of Law."

[45] Sylvia Frey, *Water from the Rock: Black Resistance in a Revolutionary Age* (Princeton, N.J., 1991); Colin Calloway, *American Revolution in Indian Country: Crisis and Diversity in Indian Communities* (New York, 1995); Wayne E. Lee, *Crowds and Soldiers in Revolutionary North Carolina: The Culture of Violence in Riot and War* (Gainesville, Fla., 2001).

[was] inhumanly shed in the presence of their wives and children."[46] The depiction of children exposed to violence against their parents signified for Ramsay the illegitimacy of the violence unleashed in his state.

Yet even the legitimate battlefield violence waged between soldiers in the Continental army and soldiers in the British army exacerbated American anxieties about social violence. During the Revolution's early years, many patriots agonized over the need to create a professional army because they worried that the experience of systematic warfare would brutalize American citizens. State militia members could preserve the fiction that they were ordinary citizens called to defend their home regions. But regular soldiers who joined the army for bounty money and spent a year or more traveling the nation engaged in the business of killing risked becoming "de-moralized" and brutalized.[47] Although the struggle for independence fed Americans' fantasies that their new nation would be an asylum from oppression, the actual experience of warfare exacerbated long-standing concerns about New World violence. At the close of the Revolution, as political and religious leaders sought to guide the new nation to peace, the specter of American violence posed a serious challenge to constructing a civil society.

Civil Society

Like beliefs about human depravity, revolutionary-era concerns about civil society were deeply rooted in a lengthy intellectual tradition that sought knowledge of how to contain human violence. The ancient Greeks identified civil society as the politically organized commonwealths that protected people from the chaos of barbarism. Medieval Christians located the church at the center of civil society, because they feared that man's fallen nature rooted the political sphere "in murder and disorder" and could only foster a peace "founded on violence and fear." During the Renaissance, a secular theory of civil society reemerged, which prized the coercion of the state as the best means to guard humanity against the "continual fear and danger of violent death." For many Protestants, religion retreated to the private sphere. Consistent in each of these very different structures of belief was the understanding that bloodshed signified the opposite to civil society. Whether civil society was vested in the commonwealth, the church, or in a powerful monarch, its defining characteristic was peaceable human relations. Anarchy, by definition, equaled violence.[48]

---

[46] David Ramsay, *The History of the Revolution of South-Carolina, from a British Province to an Independent State* (Trenton, N.J., 1785), 2: 271.

[47] Charles Royster, *A Revolutionary People at War: The Continental Army and American Character, 1775–1783* (Chapel Hill, N.C., 1979). This fear troubled certain southern leaders as well; see Aedanus Burke, quoted in Pauline Maier, "Popular Uprisings and Civil Authority in Eighteenth-Century America," *William and Mary Quarterly* 27 (1970): 18.

[48] John Ehrenberg, *Civil Society: The Critical History of an Idea* (New York, 1999).

During the eighteenth century, the Enlightenment progressives who had called the depravity of human nature into question again reconceived civil society. The new belief in human perfectibility led to calls for new systems of government that transferred power from monarchs to subjects. Human benevolence supported arguments for popular sovereignty, which minimized or eliminated the need for mediating institutions such as the church or the aristocracy to uphold civil society. Benevolist thinkers such as the Third Earl of Shaftesbury argued that civil society blossomed from humanity's innate moral sentiments rather than from the state's coercive power (which therefore should be lessened). Instead of identifying civil society with coercive force, Enlightenment liberals defined it as a sphere of individual action, based on consent and separated from church or government. In this Enlightenment conception, institutional oppression was poised opposite to civil society. However, an alternative Enlightenment tradition, rooted in ongoing skepticism about human nature, identified a continuing need for intermediate political and religious institutions to preserve social stability. Operating from historical knowledge of the civil discord unleashed by the religious pluralism of the seventeenth century, political philosophers like David Hume argued the need to draw on human experience and establish a civil society that balanced between authority and liberty.[49]

These competing visions of civil society as radically consensual versus institutionally mediated played out in the United States during the revolutionary era. During the early years of the new republic, the Federalists increasingly voiced a conservative Burkean conception of the need for religious and political institutions to mediate individual participation in the public sphere, whereas the Republicans, like their French revolutionary models, promoted a more immediate vision of individual participation in the civil society (albeit limited by race and gender).[50] Liberal Jeffersonians embraced immediate participation because they believed that man's innate moral sense made violence only a minor challenge to social order; bloodshed appeared to them merely a temporary human failing – an unfortunate interruption rather than an eternal condition – that could be transcended. This explains why Thomas Jefferson could cheerily proclaim that "the tree of liberty must occasionally be watered by the blood of tyrants

[49] Richard Boyd, "Reappraising the Scottish Moralists and Civil Society," *Polity* 33 (Fall 2000); Richard Boyd, "'The Unsteady and Precarious Contribution of Individuals': Edmund Burke's Defense of Civil Society," *Review of Politics* 61 (Summer 1999); Ehrenberg, *Civil Society;* Marvin B. Becker, *The Emergence of Civil Society in the Eighteenth Century: A Privileged Moment in the History of England, Scotland, and France* (Bloomington, Ind., 1994).

[50] John L. Brooke, "Consent, Civil Society, and the Public Sphere in the Age of Revolution and the Early American Republic," in *Beyond the Founders: New Approaches to the Political History of the Early American Republic*, ed. Jeffrey L. Pasley, Andrew W. Robertson, and David Waldstreicher (Chapel Hill, N.C., 2004), 219.

and patriots."[51] Freed from the fear of depravity, Jefferson did not worry that a little bloodletting would unleash men's passions and subsume the country in chaos.

However, the violence of the revolutionary era terrified political and religious traditionalists, who believed that man's innate depravity, if not strictly controlled by civil society, would lead to anarchic bloodshed and transform the new nation into a den of slaughter. In *Essay on the Influence of Religion in Civil Society*, the Presbyterian minister Thomas Reese argued that "the evils for which [civil society] was designed as a remedy are injustice, violence, rapine, mutual slaughter, and bloodshed." According to Reese, humanity required religious institutions' moderating influence to create a civil society that avoided this catalogue of horrors.[52] The Reverend John Daniel Gros, a German-born Calvinist minister and professor at Columbia College who authored one of the first moral philosophy textbooks in the United States, prioritized the role of law in establishing a civil society that was free of bloodshed. A fear of danger signified the point of origin for civil society. Therefore, Gros theorized, "We hold, that the public good of civil society essentially consists in the enjoyment of *civil liberty*, of *internal and external security*." Government by the rule of law created the necessary conditions for citizens to enjoy civil liberty and physical security. Gros's Calvinist-inflected notions of civil society helped establish the architecture of Federalist political theory.[53]

In Massachusetts, political and religious conservatives argued until the 1830s that the state should control civil society in order to protect the common good.[54] John Adams, the primary author of Massachusetts's 1780 constitution that created an "established" civil society, grounded his political theory in a deeply negative view of human nature. Adams was the son of a fervent Congregationalist deacon. Although in maturity he departed from the Calvinist faith of his childhood, Adams retained a suspicious outlook on humanity throughout his life. Adams rejected the doctrine of depravity per se, but he believed that human appetites were limitless and that man's self-control was weak. He distrusted political theories based on human perfectibility, a point that he explained at great length in a series of letters to

---

[51] Thomas Jefferson to William Stephens Smith, Nov. 13, 1787; Thomas Jefferson, *The Papers of Thomas Jefferson*, ed. Charles T. Cullen, John Catanzariti, and Julian P. Boyd (Princeton, N.J., 1950), 12: 356.

[52] Thomas Reese, *An Essay on the Influence of Religion in Civil Society* (Charleston, S.C., 1788), 5.

[53] John Daniel Gros, *Natural Principles of Rectitude, for the Conduct of Man in All States and Situations of Life: Demonstrated and Explained in a Systematic Treatise on Moral Philosophy* ... (New York, 1795), 353; Wilson Smith, *Professors and Public Ethics: Studies of Northern Moral Philosophers before the Civil War* (Ithaca, N.Y., 1956), 81–94.

[54] Johann N. Neem, "The Elusive Common Good: Religion and Civil Society in Massachusetts, 1780–1833," *Journal of the Early Republic* 24 (Fall 2004).

Benjamin Rush written between 1806 and 1807. While he supported the "amelioration of the condition of Man in this world," Adams denied that every man could become "eternal, almighty and allwise." Political theories that promised to abolish government or religion would leave man to "beat and bruise and murder one another."[55] Adams's distrust in human nature underlay his early, and some have alleged monarchical, attack on the French Revolution, *Discourses on Davila* (1790).

In *Davila*, Adams provided commentary on an Italian historian's accounts of the sixteenth-century French Wars of Religion, to suggest that the violence of those wars would be repeated in the contemporary French Revolution. Adams argued that the French belief in human perfectibility would drive the French Revolution toward disaster. "The perfectibility of man is only human and terrestrial," Adams stated in *Davila*, "the balance of a well ordered government will alone be able to prevent [France] from degenerating into dangerous ambition, irregular rivalries, destructive factions, wasting seditions and bloody civil wars." Adams famously proposed the principle of balance as the only means for popular governments to survive the depravity of men. According to Adams, an improperly balanced government, such as the French constitution of 1790 created, would devolve into horrific bloodshed. In the final chapter of *Davila*, Adams depicted this danger in terrifying terms: the unbalanced government in France threatened to cause slaughters like the St. Bartholomew's Day massacre during the Wars of Religion, in which Catholic mobs murdered tens of thousands of Protestants.[56]

Another son of New England Puritanism, Nathaniel Chipman, a federal judge for the Vermont district, similarly brought his native religious background to bear on his understanding of social order. Nathaniel's brother and biographer, Daniel Chipman, described Nathaniel's childhood as marked "by the staid habits of the Puritans." His parents used fear and affection, the familiar Calvinist childrearing dialectic, to shape his character. As an adult, Chipman became a patriot, serving in the Continental army during the Revolution, and a political conservative, who allied with Alexander Hamilton.[57] In 1793, Chipman published his *Sketches of the Principles of Government*, in which he framed a political theory based, like John Adams's, on a view of human nature driven by antisocial passions. In the *Sketches*, Chipman argued that man in his savage state was not virtuous but violently depraved; for evidence, he called attention to the Native Americans, whom

55 John Adams to Benjamin Rush, Sept. 19, 1806, *Old Family Letters: Copied from the Originals for Alexander Biddle*, 2 vols., series A (Philadelphia, Pa., 1892), 111–12.

56 John Adams, *Discourses on Davila: A Series of Papers, on Political History. Written in the Year 1790, and Then Published in the Gazette of the United States* (Boston, Mass., 1805), 91.

57 Daniel Chipman, *The Life of Hon. Nathaniel Chipman, Ll.D, Formerly Member of the United States Senate, and Chief Justice of the State of Vermont: With Selections from His Miscellaneous Papers* (Boston, Mass., 1846).

he accused of "butchering . . . old men, women, and children" and "torturing and burning prisoners, in cold blood," for pastime. The savage state was ruled by such a "violent state of the passions," Chipman wrote, that people turned to monarchy, itself an "institution of violence," for relief. Like Adams, he believed that popular government was preferable to monarchy or aristocracy, but only if power were carefully divided in order to control men's corruption.[58] The principle of balance articulated by so many conservative political authors of the early republic connoted the violent danger of depravity.

The American concept of balance was strongly influenced by Alexander Pope's theory of counterpoise, which assumed that men were always guided by their depraved passions.[59] It also owed credit to the political theories of Thomas Hobbes, Bernard Mandeville, and Niccolò Machiavelli. John Adams cited Machiavelli in his 1787 political treatise *A Defence of the Constitutions of the Governments of the United States of America*, quoting the Florentine political philosopher's claim that "all men are bad by nature; [and] that they will not fail to show that natural depravity of heart whenever they have a fair opportunity."[60] Federalist political theory in the early 1790s developed in a transatlantic context, blending American political traditions with insights from Italian, English, French, Scottish, and German philosophers and politics. Like their democratic counterparts, American and European conservatives during the age of revolution exchanged political ideas in a lively multivocal and multidirectional conversation. For example, not only was Adams's *Defence* republished in Britain and in France, but also the luminary of British conservatism, Edmund Burke, turned (like Nathaniel Chipman) to the supposedly brutal practices of Native American societies to illustrate the potential dangers that human depravity posed to the French Revolution.[61] American Federalist political theory must be situated within an Atlantic context in order to form a proper understanding of the depth and significance of its beliefs.

Yet the new American conservatism of the 1790s differed vitally from European conservatism in the strategies it propounded to compensate for the threat of depravity. Edmund Burke supported monarchy, the established church, and other pre-Enlightenment institutions as the means to control man's potential for anarchy. American Federalists and Calvinists of

[58] Nathaniel Chipman, *Sketches of the Principles of Government* (Rutland, Vt., 1793), 24, 101.

[59] Lovejoy, *Reflections on Human Nature.*

[60] Cited in John E. Paynter, "The Rhetorical Design of John Adams's 'Defence of the Constitutions of . . . America,'" *Review of Politics* 58 (Summer 1996): 552.

[61] C. Bradley Thompson, "John Adams and the Coming of the French Revolution," *Journal of the Early Republic* 16 (1996); Joyce Oldham Appleby, "The Jefferson–Adams Rupture and the First French Translation of John Adams's 'Defence,'" *American Historical Review* 73 (1968); Edmund Burke, *Reflections on the Revolution in France*, ed. J. C. D. Clark (Stanford, Calif., 2001), 226.

the postrevolutionary age never wavered from an essential commitment to republican governance (although the Jeffersonians alleged otherwise). These ministers and politicians, who had fervently supported the War of Independence, were subscribers to "the Moderate Enlightenment." They retained a fear of human depravity that "Revolutionary Enlightenment" men such as Thomas Jefferson had discarded, but they sought republican solutions to their anxiety. The republican solution to the problem of human depravity employed two strategies, one governmental and the other cultural. Federalists and Calvinists desired a form of government that acquired legitimacy from the people, yet was protected from the people's dangerous passions.[62] They believed in the necessity of hierarchy to subdue popular excess, but they valued a hierarchy of merit rather than of birth, which they described as "natural aristocracy." Conservative political and religious leaders wished to entrust the republican government with adequate power to control the people, but more than anything, they tried to craft a future in which the people would control themselves.

In 1792, James Madison celebrated the emerging democratic opposition party as those people "believing in the doctrine that mankind are capable of governing themselves." His opponents, the Federalists who then controlled the national government, had "debauched themselves into a persuasion that mankind are incapable of governing themselves."[63] Although Madison's characterization is unfair to many of the Federalists, who fought avidly for the privilege of self-government during the Revolution, he was correct that early national conservatives did not trust men to govern themselves without mediating institutions. The Federalists and their Calvinist ministerial allies believed that men should be governed by a strong state of their own choosing and a strong church that they voluntarily attended. The democratic vision that so entranced Madison appeared to his opponents to be laden with the danger of bloodshed. Only by controlling men's destructive passions could the new government guarantee citizens their rights and liberties. Under pressure from political and cultural challenges by the democratic opposition, Federalist and Calvinist leaders developed a political theory, which recognized the dangers that man's violence posed to civil society and devised republican political strategies to compensate.

Liberty with Order

In the early years of the American republic, northeastern Congregationalist and Presbyterian ministers formed an alliance with Federalist politicians

---

[62] Henry Farnham May, *The Enlightenment in America* (New York, 1976), 252–3. See also Russell Kirk, *Edmund Burke: A Genius Reconsidered*, rev. ed. (Wilmington, Del., 1997).

[63] Quoted in Richard Buel Jr., *Securing the Revolution: Ideology in American Politics, 1789–1815* (Ithaca, N.Y., 1972), 25–6.

based on their shared suspicion of man's natural capacities. Many critics have argued that self-interest primarily motivated the alliance, as Calvinist and Federalist elites joined forces to resist their shrinking influence in an increasingly democratic society.[64] Conservatives certainly resisted populist challenges to their moral and political authority, but their vision for the future was not solely self-interested or backward looking. The alliance originated in a strongly aligned ideological orientation, which aspired to create innovative solutions to perceived social problems in the postrevolutionary era. The Calvinist clergy of New England did not, as a body, prostitute their faith to temporal ends; their faith inspired a "social vision" that they sought to fulfill by supporting conservative politics.[65] Very rarely did American Calvinist ministers support the Republican opposition. So exceptional was Thomas Allen, a Calvinist–Jeffersonian pastor, that the Federalist *Hampshire-Gazette* asked, "Did anybody ever hear of such a creature?"[66] Calvinist suspicions of human nature and conservative political understandings of civil society meshed naturally, to create a shared ideological commitment to tamping down popular politics and promoting a pacified social order.

Federalists and their Calvinist religious allies advocated creating a strong national government that would secure the public good against the violent threat of individual interests. They also led a rhetorical initiative to strengthen American attitudes against violent disorder; this cultural solution originated in a new political theory of positive social order that adapted classical republicanism, covenant theory, Hebrew Bible prophecy, and New England civic traditions to the postrevolutionary era. The cultural and political strategies were mutually reinforcing. For example, in sermons, orations, essays, and poems, conservatives depicted the establishment of the Federal government as a triumph of peaceful order over bloody chaos. At the same time, conservatives used the new government to buttress their power against the threat of opposing viewpoints – most famously through the disastrous Sedition Act of 1798, which punished criticism of the national government. The Sedition Act and other Federalist repressions of democratic politics have been richly documented, but Federalist cultural initiatives are less well known.[67] James Banner has bemoaned the failure of historians to treat

---

[64] Gordon S. Wood, *The Radicalism of the American Revolution* (New York, 1993), 229–31; Stephen E. Berk, *Calvinism versus Democracy: Timothy Dwight and the Origins of American Evangelical Orthodoxy* (Hamden, Conn., 1974).

[65] Kling, *Field of Divine Wonders*, 54–7.

[66] Richard D. Birdsall, "The Reverend Thomas Allen: Jeffersonian Calvinist," *New England Quarterly* 30 (June 1957): 147.

[67] Seth Cotlar, "The Federalists' Transatlantic Cultural Offensive of 1798 and the Moderation of American Democratic Discourse," in *Beyond the Founders: New Approaches to the Political History of the Early American Republic*, ed. David Waldstreicher, Andrew W. Robertson, and Jeffrey L. Pasley (Chapel Hill, N.C., 2004); Joanne B. Freeman, "Explaining

Federalism as a vital ideology, like its Jeffersonian counterpart. "That political Federalism might have been a conduit of particular ideological strains and traditions in the United States," Banner writes, "seems rarely, if ever, to be considered."[68] Examining Federalist cultural strategies to excise violence from the social order can help address that historiographical silence.

Federalist and Calvinist leaders of the early republic did not profess merely a nostalgic longing for the past. Rather, these leaders articulated a new ideology that, while antidemocratic, contained ameliorative potentials and influenced the American future. The key to uncovering this new ideology lies in taking seriously ministerial and political fears of violence. The most important ideological strain to be produced by the Federalist–Calvinist alliance, the cultural development with the most lasting impact for the nineteenth-century society, was the disavowal of personal physical violence as politically destabilizing and immoral. The early national period witnessed an outpouring of language condemning bloodshed, which drew on a rich base of beliefs, adopted new forms, and strongly influenced American political culture. In their battle to restrain democracy, Federalists and Calvinists created a new rhetoric of opposition to violence that was not, in itself, elitist.

America's democratic vanguard also articulated a claim to the virtue of nonviolence; in order to survive, "a political culture must maintain a

the Unexplainable: The Cultural Context of the Sedition Act," in *The Democratic Experiment: New Directions in American Political History*, ed. Meg Jacobs, William J. Novak, and Julian E. Zelizer (Princeton, N.J., 2003); Albrecht Koschnik, "The Democratic Societies of Philadelphia and the Limits of the American Public Sphere, circa 1793–1795," *William and Mary Quarterly* 58 (July 2001); Jeffrey L. Pasley, *"The Tyranny of Printers": Newspaper Politics in the Early American Republic* (Charlottesville, Va., 2001); Buel, *Securing the Revolution*; James Morton Smith, *Freedom's Fetters: The Alien and Sedition Laws and American Civil Liberties*, Cornell Studies in Civil Liberty (Ithaca, N.Y., 1956); Eugene Perry Link, *Democratic-Republican Societies, 1790–1800* (New York, 1942).

68 James M. Banner, "The Federalists – Still in Need of Reconsideration," in *Federalists Reconsidered*, ed. Barbara B. Oberg and Doron S. Ben-Atar (Charlottesville, Va., 1998), 248. Works that do take Federalist ideology seriously include Albrecht Koschnik, "Young Federalists, Masculinity, and Partisanship during the War of 1812," in *Beyond the Founders: New Approaches to the Political History of the Early American Republic*, ed. Jeffrey L. Pasley, Andrew W. Robertson, and David Waldstreicher (Chapel Hill, N.C., 2004); Marshall Foletta, *Coming to Terms with Democracy: Federalist Intellectuals and the Shaping of an American Culture* (Charlottesville, Va., 2001); Paul Douglas Newman, "The Federalists' Cold War: The Fries Rebellion, National Security, and the State, 1787–1800," *Pennsylvania History* 67 (2000); William C. Dowling, *Literary Federalism in the Age of Jefferson: Joseph Dennie and the Port Folio, 1801–1812* (Columbia, S.C., 1999); Oberg and Ben-Atar, eds., *Federalists Reconsidered*; James M. Banner, *To the Hartford Convention: The Federalists and the Origins of Party Politics in Massachusetts, 1789–1815* (New York, 1970); Linda K. Kerber, *Federalists in Dissent: Imagery and Ideology in Jeffersonian America* (Ithaca, N.Y., 1970); David Hackett Fischer, *The Revolution of American Conservatism: The Federalist Party in the Era of Jeffersonian Democracy* (New York, 1965).

dominant thesis of non-violence."[69] But the style of Federalist nonviolence differed markedly from its democratic counterpart. The democratic claim to nonviolence rested on the limitations it placed on government oppression of civil liberties. Ultimately, democrats viewed government itself as a form of violence against individual liberties, necessary at some minimal level, but violence nonetheless. Within the democratic viewpoint, a government deserved the adjective *humane* when it abjured power.[70] The Federalist–Calvinist claim, on the other hand, placed faith in strong government as a force capable of civilizing humanity. The political leaders, legal theorists, and newspaper editors who founded the Federalist Party created a republican political theory that defined the state as a remedy for human chaos. It preached that obedience to social order would inculcate personal nonviolence and lead Americans down the path to peace. Through obedience to law and reverence for magistrates "the minds of men lose the ferocity and the degradation of the savage, and rise to the standard of refined, human and rational beings," argued Theodore Dwight, a Federalist political operator and brother to the New Divinity minister Timothy Dwight.[71]

The Federalist–Calvinist ideological campaign against violence commenced with efforts to establish a new federal government in the mid-1780s. American conservatives used Shays's Rebellion as the first exhibit to demonstrate that the decentralized government outlined by the Articles of Confederation was inadequate to restrain the people's destructive passions. In 1786, western Massachusetts farmers, led in part by Daniel Shays, staged a regulation/revolt against the state government, using mob actions and symbolic acts of violence, which culminated in a large-scale attack on the federal arsenal at Springfield. Defenders killed four men before the attackers retreated; had the attackers succeeded, they planned to march on Boston. Concurrent episodes of popular resistance took place in other American states. Democratic theorists argued that the people had a legitimate right to use street politics to correct political and economic injustices. The Revolution had secured sovereignty in the American people, who possessed the authority to correct the state when it monopolized power.[72] The tactics used

---

[69] Marvin E. Wolfgang, "A Preface to Violence," *Annals of the American Academy of Political and Social Science* 364 (March 1966): 3.

[70] The Federalist newspaper the *Columbian Centinel* satirized this point of view acutely in a facetious letter to the editor signed "Mentor," Jan. 21, 1795.

[71] Theodore Dwight, *An Oration, Delivered at New Haven on the 7th of July, A.D. 1801, before the Society of the Cincinnati, for the State of Connecticut, Assembled to Celebrate the Anniversary of American Independence* (Hartford, Conn., 1801), 17.

[72] Woody Holton, "An 'Excess of Democracy' – or a Shortage?" *Journal of the Early Republic* 25 (Fall 2005); Woody Holton, "Did Democracy Cause the Recession That Led to the Constitution?" *Journal of American History* 92 (2005); Woody Holton, "'From the Labours of Others': The War Bonds Controversy and the Origins of the Constitution in New England," *William and Mary Quarterly* 61 (2004); Leonard L. Richards, *Shays's Rebellion:*

by tax resisters in the mid-1780s mirrored the tactics used during the Revolution and therefore were of proven legitimacy. But that continuity only exacerbated the conservatives' fears, because many regarded the American Revolution as an episode of necessary but horrific violence that had created a terrible breach in civil society. Conservatives accepted the legitimacy of the rebellion to overthrow British tyranny, but they hardly viewed its violence as salutary. After the revolutionaries seized power, conservative patriots viewed rioting with increasing suspicion.[73] The emerging conservative faction of the 1780s treated Shays's Rebellion as evidence that a lack of government power, not its excess, proved the true threat to American liberty. As a Calvinist minister would later remark, "It has been thought by many, and still is by some, that government is the only foe to liberty.... But experience is correcting this error."[74] Among conservatives, the revolutionary axiom that political power should be kept in heavy chains was weakening.[75]

In "The Anarchiad," a long poem published serially between fall 1786 and fall 1787, the authors David Humphreys, Lemuel Hopkins, John Trumbull, and Joel Barlow – known collectively as the Hartford, or Connecticut, Wits – used Shays's Rebellion to reappraise the relationship between the people and the state.[76] This satiric poem was modeled after Alexander Pope's "The Dunciad" (a style very popular among Federalist authors of the early national era).[77] "The Anarchiad" depicted Shays's Rebellion as a struggle between the spirits of order and chaos in America. Shays and his fellow farmers were represented as devotees of Anarch, the spirit of revolt. The poem recounted Anarch's effort to topple Hesper, the spirit of American social order, and destroy the people's liberties. Anarch's strongest weapon was

The American Revolution's Final Battle (Philadelphia, Pa., 2002); Terry Bouton, "A Road Closed: Rural Insurgency in Post-Independence Pennsylvania," *Journal of American History* 87 (2000); Robert H. Churchill, "Popular Nullification, Fries' Rebellion, and the Waning of Radical Republicanism, 1798–1801," *Pennsylvania History* 67 (Winter 2000).

73 Barbara C. Smith, "Food Rioters and the American Revolution," *William and Mary Quarterly* 51 (1994); Paul A. Gilje, *The Road to Mobocracy: Popular Disorder in New York City, 1763–1834* (Chapel Hill, N.C., 1987); Maier, "Popular Uprisings."

74 Joseph McKeen, *A Sermon Preached before the Honorable the Council, and the Honorable the Senate, and House of Representatives of the Commonwealth of Massachusetts, May 28, 1800: Being the Day of General Election* (Boston, Mass., 1800), 10.

75 Gordon S. Wood, *The Creation of the American Republic, 1776–1787* (New York, 1993), 409–13.

76 The first three authors became prominent supporters of Federalism in the following decade, but Joel Barlow joined the democratic opposition, which his former coauthors felt was a grave betrayal; Leon Howard, *The Connecticut Wits* (Chicago, 1943). See, for example, Lemuel Hopkins's skewering of Joel Barlow in the anniversary poem published in the rabidly Federalist *Connecticut Courant* in 1799; Richard Alsop, Lemuel Hopkins, and Theodore Dwight, *The Political Green-House, for the Year 1798 Addressed to the Readers of the Connecticut Courant, January 1st, 1799* (Hartford, Conn., 1799).

77 Kerber, *Federalists in Dissent*; Howard, *The Connecticut Wits*; Wells, *The Devil and Doctor Dwight*.

human depravity. He advised his lieutenant, Wronghead (Shays), that "the human soul / Sinks, by strong instinct, far beneath her goal." Through appeal to men's selfishness they could destroy the republic. "Not so, Columbia, shall thy sons be known / To prize the public weal above their own," Anarch taunted. Instead, Wronghead would lead Americans to "forswear the public debt, the public course." He would rally his depraved followers to violent disorder, until "the desperate riot runs, / And maddening mobs assume their rusty guns." By this strategy, the new republic would eventually join her ancient predecessors in ruin, by "fire, and sword, and blood." In Number 10 of the series, published on the eve of the Constitutional Convention, Hesper addressed the politicians gathered at Philadelphia, begging them to forge a stronger republican government to defeat anarchy's threatened "sanguine flood."[78] The Connecticut Wits sought to establish a new cultural model that discredited popular politics as unacceptably violent and dangerous.

The contention of "The Anarchiad" that the United States might imminently succumb to violent disorder drew on widespread knowledge of classical history among eighteenth-century elites. From classical history, early American readers learned that ancient republics had foundered when the citizens substituted their private interests for the public good, splitting nations into contending factions, inviting the rise of demagogues, and leading to eventual civil war. Civil wars were far more dangerous than other wars because they disunited the people, causing extremes of violence and leading to eventual anarchy. Conservative religious and political advocates for the new frame of government written in 1787 argued that the Constitution, by establishing a strong national government, would stifle factionalism and protect the nation from the risk of a brutal civil war.[79] Conservatives described the Constitution as the young nation's reprieve from the immediate and bloody threat of societal disintegration. Of course, this claim served the political purpose of bolstering Federalists in the contentious debate over ratification.[80] But it was deeply grounded in religious sentiment, political theory, and classical history.

In the decades following ratification, ministers and orators offering benedictions on election day or speeches on the Fourth of July would praise the Constitution as the antidote to the poison of men's violent passions. The establishment of a strong national government had rescued American citizens from the precipice of depravity. In this political narrative, the Articles of Confederation functioned to remind audiences of the danger that

---

[78] David Humphreys, *The Anarchiad: A New England Poem, 1786–1787*, ed. Luther G. Riggs (Gainesville, Fla., 1967), 32, 19–20, 57–61.

[79] Wood, *Creation of the American Republic*; Bernard Bailyn, *The Ideological Origins of the American Revolution* (Cambridge, Mass., 1992); John R. Howe, "Republican Thought and the Political Violence of the 1790s," *American Quarterly* 19 (Summer 1967).

[80] David Waldstreicher, *In the Midst of Perpetual Fetes: The Making of American Nationalism, 1776–1820* (Chapel Hill, N.C., 1997).

the young nation once faced. After mourning the recent bloody destruction of republican Poland, the Reverend Andrew Lee reminded the audience at his 1795 election sermon of how close America had once come to a similar fate: "These states, now so happy and respectable, had well nigh afforded another instance of a gallant people ruined thru the deficiency of their national government." Under the weak government created by the Articles of Confederation, the virtue of the American people had degraded from its revolutionary heights. Americans had begun reverting to violent barbarism.[81]

While democratically minded supporters of the Constitution, such as James Madison, believed their new government answered the problems of 1780s, to the advocates of order it represented only a beginning. With a strong government in place, the nation's religious and political leaders could start the process of taming citizens' lusts, thus fashioning the nation into a peaceful asylum. Federalists promoted the new national government as a positive force that would ameliorate the human condition – a challenge to the democratic political theory of the negative role of government. Democrats argued that men's rights were natural or innate, and that a just government should exercise the minimum restraint necessary to ensure man's safety. In the oft-cited words of Thomas Paine, government "even in its best state is but a necessary evil."[82] Federalists responded that rights were not innate but constructed by the social order. The natural freedom of depraved man was nothing but butchery. Only by securing the social order could man gain his rights. Government, early republican conservatives argued, was intended by God to lead man to happiness. The new federal government would create a benevolent social order that led each man to live at peace.

Nathaniel Chipman, the Vermont Federalist, principled his conservative political philosophy upon the "social nature of man." Like many New England ministers of the 1790s, Chipman's belief in human depravity led him to reject Jean-Jacques Rousseau's argument that man was happiest in his savage state.[83] He also patriotically rejected other European philosophers in an effort to construct a new American political theory. He disparaged

---

[81] Andrew Lee, *The Origin and Ends of Civil Government with Reflections on the Distinguished Happiness of the United States: A Sermon Preached Before . . . Samuel Huntington, . . . Governor, And . . . General Assembly of the State of Connecticut at Hartford, on the Day of the Anniversary Election, May 14, 1795* (Hartford, Conn., 1795), 19. Timothy Dwight made a similar argument about the Confederation government: "The influence of a weak and fluctuating government on the morals and happiness of mankind is, to say the least, not less malignant than that of an established despotism." Timothy Dwight, *Travels in New England and New York*, ed. Barbara Miller Solomon (Cambridge, Mass., 1969), 4:263. See also Ezra Weld, *A Discourse, Delivered April 25, 1799 Being the Day of Fasting and Prayer throughout the United States of America* (Boston, Mass., 1799), 12.

[82] Thomas Paine, *Common Sense*, ed. Isaac Kramnick (New York, 1986), 65.

[83] Martha Louise Counts, "The Political Views of the Eighteenth Century New England Clergy as Expressed in Their Election Sermons" (Ph.D., Columbia University, 1956), 205.

John Locke and Cesare Beccaria, both of whom recognized that man was designed for civil government yet still asserted that man had given up some natural rights to enter that state. Chipman did not believe that "the laws of nature" gave man any liberty that he could not "enjoy under civil laws and government."[84] Federalist legal scholarship drew on the English common law tradition as well as Puritan sources to support the claim that liberty was socially constructed. James Kent, a Federalist professor of law from an Anglican background, eloquently supported and explained Chipman's theories to his students in a 1795 lecture at Columbia College:

Man was fitted and intended by the great Author of his being, for society and civil government. It is to speak correctly the law of his nature, and by obedience to this law, he is so far from sacrificing any of his rights, that he preserves them all, brings them into security and exercise, and by this means is enabled to display the various and exalted powers of the human mind. . . . Our civil and social rights are our true natural rights; we can have no other; and in free governments like our own, formed upon the plan of an harmonious coincidence with these rights, we make no renunciations but enjoy in full protection, all the liberty which was intended or granted by the laws of our social nature.[85]

Didactic arguments for the social nature of liberty extended beyond legal texts; they were embraced by the foremost educator of the early republic, the red-haired, prominently chinned Noah Webster. Webster, a Calvinist and a Federalist who instructed generations of American schoolchildren through his spellers, dictionaries, and textbooks, fully shared Chipman's and Kent's understanding of liberty. In a Fourth of July oration delivered in New Haven, Connecticut, Webster attempted to reconcile the American principles of freedom, independence, and equality with the social state. He discarded the abstract reasoning of social contract theory. "It is needless to discuss questions of natural right as distinct from a social state," Webster argued, "for all rights are social. . . . Civil liberty, therefore, instead of being derived from *natural freedom* and *independence*, is the creature of society and government."[86] Like Chipman, Webster was an ardent nationalist who sought to craft a new American political culture that strictly limited personal

---

[84] Chipman, *Sketches*, 13–15.

[85] James Kent, *Dissertations: Being the Preliminary Part of a Course of Law Lectures* (New York, 1795), 6–7. For a recent insightful account of James Kent, see Bryan Waterman, *Republic of Intellect: The Friendly Club of New York City and the Making of American Literature* (Baltimore, Md., 2007), 145–53. See also Benjamin Whitman's more pithy remark: "Our rights and liberties are nothing more, than a privilege secured to us by law." Benjamin Whitman, *An Oration, Pronounced at Hanover, Massachusetts, on the Anniversary of American Independence, July 4, 1803 at the Request of the Officers of the Second Regiment, First Brigade, Fifth Division of the Militia of Massachusett* (Boston, Mass., 1803), 16.

[86] Noah Webster, *An Oration Pronounced before the Citizens of New Haven on the Anniversary of the Declaration of Independence, July, 1802* (New Haven, Conn., 1802).

violence by American citizens.[87] The educator's attitudes toward violence and social order later led him – like Chipman, Kent, and the Connecticut Wits – to oppose the French Revolution.

Although Webster, Chipman, and Kent claimed to reject the precepts of European political thought, they drew heavily on American Puritan theories of governance, especially on the notion of the federal covenant, which they adapted to the republican era. Puritan ministers had theorized that God entered into two covenants with the people of New England. The first covenant, or the covenant of grace, promised salvation to the faithful. The second federal covenant or covenant of state defined the community's collective relationship to God and obligated even the unredeemed to obey the laws of state. The covenant of state imposed order on the chaos that would otherwise result from human sinfulness.[88] Puritan divines conceived of liberty as a positive freedom – the freedom to obey God – not as the absence of civil restraint. The notion of a corporate moral order associated with a positive conception of liberty is an obvious analogue to the early republican theory of "social rights."[89] Yet the latter concept was not equivalent to its predecessor; conservatives of the 1790s placed a lesser emphasis on obedience to the law as a religious duty and a greater emphasis on obedience as a civil duty. The creation of a republican government that invested sovereignty in the people necessitated a greater recognition of the people's political authority than had existed among the Puritans. Chipman and Kent encouraged Americans to obey the government because it had been freely chosen and legitimated by themselves, not because it had been instituted by God.[90]

Calvinist ministers joined politicians in adapting Puritan political theory to the new republican state. The Reverend Samuel Williams, a neighbor of Nathaniel Chipman, formulated a strikingly similar theory of positive social order in his 1792 election sermon before the legislature of Vermont. He began with the premise of man's social nature. Man did not have to give up any natural rights when he entered society; society gave security to rights.

---

[87] Jill Lepore, *A Is for American: Letters and Other Characters in the Newly United States* (New York, 2002); Jonathan Messerli, "The Columbian Complex: The Impulse to National Consolidation," *History of Education Quarterly* 7 (Winter 1967).

[88] Dale S. Kuehne, *Massachusetts Congregationalist Political Thought, 1760–1790: The Design of Heaven* (Columbia, Mo., 1996), 41.

[89] Linda Kerber draws a similar connection between Puritan conceptions of liberty and Federalist ideas about freedom; Kerber, *Federalists in Dissent*, 178–9.

[90] Perry Miller, *The New England Mind: From Colony to Province* (Cambridge, Mass., 1953), 25; Perry Miller, "From the Covenant to the Revival," in *Religion in American Life*, ed. James Ward Smith and A. Leland Jamison, Princeton Studies in American Civilization 5 (Princeton, N.J., 1961), 1. For a recent review of the scholarship concerning covenant theory, see Christopher Grasso, *A Speaking Aristocracy: Transforming Public Discourse in Eighteenth-Century Connecticut* (Chapel Hill, N.C., 1999), chap. 1; Kuehne, *Massachusetts Congregationalist Political Thought*.

Williams held out to his audience a visionary promise, that man could find terrestrial perfection in "a state of society." Religion, education, laws, and government could promote human benevolence; under their guiding influence man could cease his violence and extend his affections to all humanity. The excellent government of the United States, designed to "preserve the natural rights and equality of man," would encourage human progress and initiate a golden age. For Williams, Chipman, and Kent, the achievement of perfect human rights within a benevolent social order would bring an end to violence and bloodshed.[91]

This religious-political theory of positive social order gained wide circulation in the early republican period. It received its strongest endorsement in 1795, when Calvinist ministers used the national Thanksgiving proclaimed by President Washington to loudly demonstrate their support for the Federalist government. A single phrase from the President's proclamation, which offered thanks for the Constitution's achievement of "liberty with order," served as a rallying cry in many of the sermons delivered that day.[92] Washington's proclamation began with a nod toward the "calamities" then afflicting other nations. America's greatest blessing was its freedom from the terrible domestic and international bloodshed gripping the nations of Europe. The proclamation followed by listing those factors responsible for preserving America from bloodshed. Foremost among them was the Constitution's gift of "liberty with order." On February 19, the national Thanksgiving, American ministers followed course, opening with remarks against bloodshed and war, then praising the "liberty with order" that had made the United States into an asylum from European suffering.

In his 1795 Thanksgiving sermon, the Reverend David Tappan, an Old Calvinist and the Hollis Professor of Divinity at Harvard, bemoaned the recent terror gripping France and praised the federal government for its freedom from bloodshed. He attributed the preservation of peace in the United States to a correct balance between liberty and order, which was predicated

---

[91] Samuel Williams, *The Love of Our Country Represented and Urged: In a Discourse Delivered October 21, 1792, at Rutland, in the State of Vermont* (Rutland, Vt., 1792), 3, 17.

[92] This phrase had no prior currency within American political discourse. The most explicit early linking of *liberty* and *order* occurred within a 1674 election sermon published in Massachusetts, which explained the operations of "Christian liberty": "Liberty and Order are inseparable, in the conversation of a Christian: it is the Liberty of *Order*, our Liberty is laid out, and limited by *Order*; those therefore that do plead for Liberty, unto the subversion of *Order*, are Libertines, and dangerous Enemies unto Liberty." Samuel Torrey, *An Exhortation Unto Reformation, Amplified, by a Discourse Concerning the Parts and Progress of That Work, According to the Word of God. Delivered in a Sermon Preached in the Audience of the General Assembly of the Massachusetts Colony, at Boston in New-England, May 27, 1674* (Cambridge, Mass., 1674), 26. After making its appearance in 1795, the phrase remained in circulation among Calvinists and Federalists; see, for example, Nathanael Emmons, *A Discourse, Delivered May 9, 1798. Being the Day of Fasting and Prayer throughout the United States* (Newburyport, Mass., 1798).

upon knowledge of human depravity. The "romantic liberty" professed by the French revolutionaries clashed with "the present frame and condition of man." God had granted man a freedom that was restricted by natural law; law constituted freedom's "perfection and security" by keeping "its possessors, both from injuring and oppressing each other." Freedom, according to Tappan and other conservatives, was a form of restraint. Without limits, men would destroy their liberty through the excess of violent passions. "The design of civil government," Tappan explained, was to promote "the observance of these natural laws, and thereby complete the secure and happy enjoyment of liberty." Unrestrained liberty, as the democrats in France had revealed, led to horrific bloodshed and human misery.[93] The minister's close political ally, Theodore Dwight, described this terrifying form of liberty in a 1798 oration as a "tempestuous sea . . . whose waves are waves of blood, whose storms are the conflicting passions of man – whose inhabitants are ferocious monsters, roaming their sanguinary round for prey – and whose shores are white with the bones of murdered millions."[94]

At its extreme, the conservative understanding of "liberty with order" hinged on a nearly unconditional obedience to civil and religious authorities. Calls for total Christian subordination sounded loudest during the final years of the 1790s, when Federalists attempted to censor opposition opinion through the passage of the Alien and Sedition Acts. The Reverend Jedidiah Morse – an Old Calvinist minister whose intense fears of depraved democracy led him to warn that an international band of Illuminati were conspiring to overthrow world religion and social order – denied that there was ever any justification for "disobedience" to the government.[95] Many of Morse's secular and religious allies agreed, laying the defense for obedience in Christian theology (especially the New Testament teachings of Paul and

[93] David Tappan, *Christian Thankfulness Explained and Enforced: A Sermon, Delivered at Charlestown, in the Afternoon of February 19, 1795. The Day of General Thanksgiving through the United States* (Boston, Mass., 1795), 22. For other examples of other Thanksgiving sermons that describe the relationship between liberty and order, see Samuel Kendal, *A Sermon Delivered on the Day of National Thanksgiving, February 19, 1795* (Boston, Mass., 1795), 17–18, 26; Ezra Sampson, *A Discourse Delivered February 19, 1795: Being the Day of National Thanksgiving* (Boston, Mass., 1795), 11–12; Abiel Holmes, *A Sermon, on the Freedom and Happiness of America: Preached at Cambridge, February 19, 1795, the Day Appointed by the President of the United States for a National Thanksgiving* (Boston, Mass., 1795), 13.

[94] Theodore Dwight, *An Oration, Spoken at Hartford, in the State of Connecticut, on the Anniversary of American Independence, July 4th, 1798* (Hartford, Conn., 1798), 17.

[95] Jedidiah Morse, *A Sermon, Preached at Charlestown, November 29, 1798, on the Anniversary Thanksgiving in Massachusetts. With an Appendix, Designed to Illustrate Some Parts of the Discourse; Exhibiting Proofs of the Early Existence, Progress, and Deleterious Effects of French Intrigue and Influence in the United States* (Boston, Mass., 1798), 14. The Rev. Ezra Weld used Morse's argument to justify his own endorsement of obedience; Weld, *Discourse . . . 1799.*

Peter), as well as in political theory.[96] The call for obedience extended to a defense of social inequality; it instructed the lower classes to defer to their betters. Without obedience to the social order, conservatives argued, men would become slaves to force. John Daniel Gros argued that "to be obedient to...government is the highest liberty."[97] Robert Treat Paine, a Federalist propagandist, put this argument to song in 1802, in the lyric "Order is Freedom – Man, obey!"[98]

Yet even this ultraist vision of positive liberty did not begin and end, as had the Puritans', with the freedom to obey. Federalist–Calvinist ideology incorporated the republican understanding of liberty as freedom from governmental oppression. "Liberty with order" meant a social order that established freedom for the individual by means of representational government. Many of the national Thanksgiving sermons celebrated the federal constitution for securing the greatest possible freedom to American citizens. The Reverend Joseph Dana, after explaining that "liberty can be no where established without order," praised the United States for its exercise of "very little disagreeable restraint." Federalists and Calvinists envisaged America as a land of individuals living in harmony, no one impinging on another's freedom. They were not advocating for a collectivist paradise that subordinated individuals to the whole. Although the people were obliged to exercise self-control and obedience to the social order, their promised reward was each man's freedom to sit peaceably under his own "fig-tree and vine," a common biblical reference from Isaiah.[99]

---

[96] Nathanael Emmons, *A Discourse, Delivered on the National Fast, April 25, 1799* (Wrentham, Mass., 1799); John Smalley, *On the Evils of a Weak Government: A Sermon, Preached on the General Election at Hartford, in Connecticut, May 8, 1800* (Hartford, Conn., 1800).

[97] Smith, *Professors and Public Ethics*, 89.

[98] Robert Treat Paine, *The Works in Verse and Prose, of the Late Robert Treat Paine, Jun., Esq* (Boston, Mass., 1812), 252–3. See also Noah Webster's pithy remark that "subordination, therefore, is the very essence of civil liberty"; Webster, *Oration...1802*, 16. More examples are "Equality No. V," in Fisher Ames, *Works of Fisher Ames: With a Selection from His Speeches and Correspondence*, ed. John Thornton Kirkland and Seth Ames (Boston, Mass., 1854), 2:221. And the *Boston Repertory*, Dec. 18, 1804, excerpted in Ronald P. Formisano, *The Transformation of Political Culture: Massachusetts Parties, 1790s–1840s* (New York, 1983), 9.

[99] Joseph Dana, *A Sermon, Delivered February 19, 1795: Being a Day of General Thanksgiving, throughout the United States of America* (Newburyport, Mass., 1795), 9–10. Other Thanksgiving sermons that praised the United States for its minimal restraints on freedom are Jedidiah Morse, *The Present Situation of Other Nations of the World, Contrasted with Our Own: A Sermon, Delivered at Charlestown, in the Commonwealth of Massachusetts, February 19, 1795; Being the Day Recommended by George Washington, President of the United States of America, for Publick Thanksgiving and Prayer* (Boston, Mass., 1795), 33, Hezekiah Packard, *The Plea of Patriotism: A Sermon, Preached in Chelmsford, on the Day of General Thanksgiving, February 19, 1795* (Boston, Mass., 1795), 12; Henry Ware, *The Continuance of Peace and Increasing Prosperity a Source of Consolation and Just Cause of Gratitude to the Inhabitants of the United States: A Sermon, Delivered February 19, 1795; Being a Day Set Apart by the President, for Thanksgiving and Prayer through the United States* (Boston, Mass., 1795), 8, 26.

Nearly a quarter of the published sermons delivered for the national Thanksgiving of 1795 used quotations from Isaiah to illustrate their arguments.[100] Early national ministers quoted from Isaiah – historically a favorite Puritan text – to argue that peace and bloodshed were attributable to a nation's corporate moral responsibility. Isaiah had warned the people of Judah that God would punish or reward the nation as a whole. Puritan covenant theory was based on this collective political vision (also voiced by other Hebrew Bible prophets). Early national ministers used Isaiah to draw a connection between the biblical covenant and the post-revolutionary theory of positive social order. If Americans gave willing obedience and gratitude to the new national government, ministers argued, the nation would be transformed into a paradise, and men would beat their "swords into ploughshares" (Isaiah 2:9). If they revolted against the government, they would be punished with "garments rolled in blood" (Isaiah 9:5). Ministers used the evocative violent imagery of Isaiah to connect individual disorder to the threat of bloody social chaos.

The new Federalist–Calvinist political theory represented violence as a continuum, rooted in the depravity of man, which led from the personal to the political. The Reverend John Andrews, a Congregationalist minister from Newburyport, Massachusetts, drew this innovative political lesson in his 1795 Thanksgiving sermon, arguing that "private persons have frequently cherished inveterate hatred. Parties and factions have often appeared. Kingdoms, States, and Empires have risen in arms against each other." His parishioners' personal safety depended on the strength of the national government, and the national government depended on individuals renouncing violence. Andrews spoke gravely and at length about the miseries of war and the blessings of peace. He described for congregants the personal tragedies that arose from war, picturing the distraught wives, parents, siblings, children, and friends of the fallen soldiers. In a vivid passage, he attempted to paint a picture of the "mangled limbs" that strewed the battlefield, turning at last to the prophet Isaiah's vision of "garments rolled in blood" (9:5). Andrews proselytized his congregants each to live in friendship with his neighbors. Only by peacefully supporting the social order would they earn their freedom, for "if we hope still to be favored with civil and religious liberty, let us cherish and inculcate a cheerful obedience to the constituted authorities of our country."[101]

---

[100] For example, Thomas Fessenden, *A Sermon, Preached in Walpole, on Thursday, February 19, 1795: The Day Appointed by the President of the United States for a Publick Thanksgiving* (Walpole, N.H., 1795); Ashbel Green, *A Sermon, Delivered in the Second Presbyterian Church in the City of Philadelphia: On the 19th of February, 1795. Being the Day of General Thanksgiving Throughout the United States* (Philadelphia, Pa., 1795); John M. Mason, *Mercy Remembered in Wrath: A Sermon, the Substance of Which Was Preached on the 19th of February, 1795, Observed Throughout the United States as a Day of Thanksgiving and Prayer* (New York, 1795).

[101] Andrews, *Sermon*. Samuel Stanhope Smith drew a similar continuum between personal and political violence in his Thanksgiving sermon; Samuel Stanhope Smith, *The Divine*

While Federalist politicians and their Calvinist allies encouraged Americans to eschew violence in support of the social order, they were not pacifists. They approved of the use of state power against internal and external enemies in order to maintain social order. Conservative politicians and ministers both argued that the reality of human depravity made the use of force for military and civil defense inescapable. They aimed to set in motion a political and cultural process that limited human violence, but the perfection of human society represented only an idealized goal, not a practical possibility. The very impossibility of perfect human goodness is what made strong government so necessary. Temporal social order had to supply restraints where self-control failed. When American society seemed threatened by domestic turmoil or foreign aggression during the early national period, Federalists and Calvinists rallied to the cause of military defense. In many cases, the conservative party continued to espouse its preference for nonviolent solutions. The 1795 Thanksgiving sermons praised the Washington administration for forcefully suppressing the Whiskey Rebellion, yet reasserting order without bloodshed.

In yearly sermons preached during the early national period before the Ancient and Honorable Artillery Company – a Boston militia company – ministers argued that human depravity led inevitably to violence, and they praised militia members for their defensive readiness.[102] They refused to condemn defensive war. Their vision of social order did not altogether renounce force; instead it sought to concentrate force within the hands of an

---

Goodness to the United States of America: A Discourse, on the Subjects of National Gratitude, Delivered in the Third Presbyterian Church in Philadelphia, on Thursday the 19th of February, 1795, Recommended by the President of the United States, to Be Observed Throughout the Union as a Day of General Thanksgiving and Prayer (Philadelphia, Pa., 1795), 28. For other Thanksgiving sermons that stressed the importance of personal nonviolence, see Levi Frisbie, *A Sermon Delivered February 19, 1795: The Day of Public Thanksgiving through the United States. Recommended by the President* (Newburyport, Mass., 1795), 15–17; John Bracken, *The Duty of Giving Thanks for National Blessings: A Sermon, Preached in the Parish Church of Bruton, Williamsburg; on Thursday February 19th, 1795. Being the Day Appointed to Be Kept as a General Thanksgiving to Almighty God Throughout the United States of America* (Richmond, Va., 1795), 21–23, Kendal, *Sermon... 1795*, 25–27.

[102] Osgood, *Sermon...June 2, 1788*; Thomas Barnard, *A Sermon, Preached at the Request of the Antient and Honourable Artillery Company, in Boston, June 1, 1789 Being the Anniversary of Their Election of Officers* (Boston, Mass., 1789); William Bentley, *A Sermon, Preached before the Ancient and Honourable Artillery Company, in Boston, June 6, 1796 Being the Anniversary of Their Election of Officers* (Boston, Mass., 1796). Daniel Adams, in an oration before a different company of militia officers in Fitchburg, Massachusetts, pronounced a very similar note; the militia was necessary because man was "more cruel than savage beasts, he falls on his own species, destroys with violence, and riots in his prey." Daniel Adams, *An Oration, Pronounced at Fitchburg, Oct. 12th, 1801, by the Appointment and at a Meeting of the Militia Officers of the Fourth Regiment* (Leominster, Mass., 1802), 4.

accountable and responsible government. In the new republic, where power was widely dispersed, advocates of order attempted to limit the people's violence and to restrict the use of force to government-sanctioned bodies. According to the Reverend Peter Thacher, who preached the company's 1793 election sermon:

The design of good government is to form a focus to which all the diverging rays of power in a community may be collected, and which may enable a people to bring the force of the whole to one point. This accumulated power protects every individual in his rights; it guards the weak from the violence of the strong, and the few from the oppression of the many.[103]

More sermons to the Ancient and Honorable Military Company were published during the early republican period than before or afterward during its three hundred and fifty year history, reflecting the significance that Americans placed on the question of the proper role of violence within the new social order. The militia's ministerial advisers were firm in their defense of physical force as "publick spirited and humane" when it was employed against murderers or threatening armies.[104] They would not join "the honest Quaker," as Peter Thacher denoted that faith, in condemning all wars as unjust. These Calvinists did not celebrate the light of Christ in every man – they feared the devil in man's heart. Yet even in their sermons to a proud militia company, the ministers emphasized that defensive force was only justifiable where all other measures had failed. They took advantage of these public occasions, as they did every other, to encourage their audiences to participate in a civilizing process to restrain the violence of man.

Despite humanity's "wicked passions," the Reverend John Thornton Kirkland held out the hope that Christianity contained the "rational prospect of the gradual restraint and ultimate termination of the violence of man." This goal he set before the Boston militia company. He praised their national fidelity but held them to the standards of a sacred future, when the world would be blessed by "universal and perpetual peace." Already, he cheered, Christianity was bringing great progress to the depraved world – "the abolition of polytheism and human sacrifices, of domestic slavery, the exposure of infants, and other shocking vices." During the Dark Ages, the spread of Christianity had helped to restrain barbarian ferociousness through a

---

[103] Peter Thacher, *A Sermon Preached before the Ancient and Honorable Artillery Company, June 3, 1793: Being the Day of Their Annual Election of Officers* (Boston, Mass., 1793), 19.

[104] William Emerson, *Piety and Arms: A Sermon, Preached at the Request of the Ancient and Honourable Artillery Company in Boston, June 3, 1799, the Anniversary of Their Election of Officers* (Boston, Mass., 1799), 14.

more humane code of chivalry. In the new era, America would spread the benevolent light of liberty to Europe and beyond.[105]

Some orators before the Boston militia described education as the great force that would civilize man and restrain violence.[106] Others saw the civilizing process as a historical progression that accompanied the strengthening of national governments.[107] Some believed that man's violence would be restrained by the progress of religious science.[108] Others focused on the need for personal self-control, directing their audiences to be "slow to anger."[109] All joined in promoting a new ideological opposition to individual violence. During the revolutionary period, political and religious leaders had called on Americans to support the infant republic by behaving with great virtue. In the years following the ratification of the Constitution, this dream disintegrated. Advocates of order became convinced that human depravity made virtue untenable as the basis of social order.[110] Virtue could not secure American liberty from the onslaught of the destructive passions. Classical history and contemporary experience revealed the danger that American society would unravel under the pressure of men's selfish ambitions. The nation's leaders needed to strengthen the social order before an uncivilizing process cast America from its golden age dreams into dark red anarchy.

"No Amelioration of Society can be Wrought by Violence"

The vision of American peacefulness expounded by the Federalist–Calvinist alliance did not accurately reflect the era's political realities; rather, it served the ideological purpose of forging consent. The ratification of the Constitution had caused contentious debate within the nation. Likewise, the new government swiftly divided between strongly opposing factions. An ideological orientation that problematized social violence worked alongside economic, social, and personal attitudes to fracture supporters of the Constitution into opposing parties. In the presidential cabinet, in the national legislature, in newspapers, and from the pulpit, American leaders fought battles over key issues of governance such as the funding of the national debt, the proper course of foreign policy, and the appropriate role of popular opinion within a republic. The techniques of opposition employed first by anti-Federalist opponents to the Constitution, and later by

---

[105] John Thornton Kirkland, *A Sermon, Preached before the Ancient and Honorable Artillery Company, in Boston, June 1, 1795 Being the Anniversary of Their Election of Officers* (Boston, Mass., 1795), 8, 21.

[106] Osgood, *Sermon...June 2, 1788.*

[107] Barnard, *Sermon...June 1, 1789,* 27.

[108] Joseph Eckley, *A Sermon, Preached at the Request of the Ancient and Honourable Artillery Company, June 4, 1792 Being the Anniversary of Their Election of Officers* (Boston, Mass., 1792), 13.

[109] Thayer, *A Sermon... 1798.*

[110] Noah Webster criticizes the cult of virtue in Webster, *Oration... 1802,* 13.

Democratic–Republican opponents to the Federalist Party, included symbolic violence and actual violence. Dissenters published vituperative newspaper attacks on political and religious leaders, burned their opponents in effigy, rioted, and, in several instances, attacked tax collectors representing the national government and destroyed their property. Fistfights in Congress, political brawls in the streets, mobs, and mayhem played integral roles in the politics in the early republic. Truly radical democrats defended, long after 1789, the use of political violence to reform a free republic that had grown corrupt (although not necessarily oppressive).[111] One function of Federalist–Calvinist rhetoric against violence was to weaken the legitimacy of these opposition techniques in order to consolidate their own hold on power.[112]

To delegitimize political violence, conservatives had to rewrite recent history, to obscure the parallel between revolutionary and postrevolutionary strategies. Some early republican speakers and writers were content to differentiate the two eras of opposition according to the legitimacy of the government itself. American patriots such as John Adams and Thomas Jefferson had worked hard during the Revolution to prove in the courts, in the newspapers, and in such documents as the Declaration of Independence, that England had lost her legitimate right to govern America. The federal government of the 1790s, on the other hand, was elected by the citizens and followed a constitution that the citizens had ratified. However, the distinction of legitimacy left slippery ground for the Federalists to stand on. The opposition could and did accompany acts of political violence with rhetoric that attacked the government's legitimacy. If the Republicans alleged that the Federalists were in the pay of Britain, they could justify the use of riot.

Working backward, many conservatives attempted to paint disorderly violence out of the revolutionary picture. Battles, German mercenaries, and prison ships retained their privileged positions on the mantles of American memory, polished to luster by frequent handling. But riots, lynchings, and mob attacks on suspected Tories retreated to the shadows. Federalist and Calvinist orators recast American revolutionaries as well-reasoned men, committed to the social order even when government itself had failed. According to the Reverend Thomas Fessenden of New Hampshire, whose son, the anti-Jacobin poet Thomas Green Fessenden, was a student of Nathaniel Chipman's, "In all the scenes of confusion and distress which suspended or annihilated our governments, and the regular administration

[111] William Pitt Smith and John Harrisson, *Observations on Conventions: Made in a Tammanial Debate. Published at the Request of the Society* (New York, 1793); Churchill, "Popular Nullification."

[112] Joanne Freeman also emphasizes the explosive quality of early national politics and argues that honor served as a remedy to control the danger; Joanne B. Freeman, *Affairs of Honor: National Politics in the New Republic* (New Haven, Conn., 2001).

of justice, and not withstanding the opposition of some who did not join with the majority, it is remarkable that there were so few acts of violence committed, not even a life lost where arms were not taken up."[113] Federalist–Calvinist orators not only denied that Americans had murdered one another during the Revolution – a claim with some credibility when contrasted to the incredible civil violence then characterizing Republican France, but hardly credible on its own – but also went so far as to deny the role that urban mobs played in the Revolution. During the Revolution, yearly orations had celebrated the date of the Boston Massacre – the Boston riot against the Townshend Acts, in which the rabble-rouser Crispus Attucks was martyred. Attucks's death was counted by some as the very first of the war. But in 1798, Thomas Sparhawk, a Massachusetts Federalist, told a very different story:

It was not a restless, ambitious, *revolutionizing* spirit, which actuated the Colonies in making resistance. It was not the rabble of large cities . . . nor the indigent, unthinking mass of beings, who compose the body of a despotic empire, who have no will but that of their leader – mere machinery, operating in any direction according to the force applied: No – it was the enlightened, the peaceable, the unambitious citizens of the Colonies, always bred in the habits of order, discipline, and submission to government.[114]

Some orators who were initially willing to own up to the violence of the American Revolution changed their perspectives as conservative fears of violence magnified during the 1790s. In a Fourth of July oration in 1794, William Emerson had bemoaned the horrific bloodshed of the war. He made explicit references to lives lost in battle, but his rhetoric was more expansive than that. Emerson regretted the "sanguinary scenes" enacted across the continent; his description acknowledged the generally bloody nature of the conflict. Later, in an Independence Day oration delivered in 1802, Emerson revised this account, drawing sharp distinctions between the American revolutionaries and the radical democrats who had destroyed France and were seemingly threatening the United States. In his 1802 speech, Emerson argued that the uprightness of the revolutionary cause had enabled Americans to resist "those ferocious passions, which commonly desolate society in times of commotion." Never had Americans embraced the "romantick"

[113] Fessenden, *A Sermon . . . 1795*. 7. See also Charles H. Atherton, *An Oration, Pronounced in the First Parish at Amherst, N.H. On the Anniversary of American Independence, July 4, 1798* (Amherst, N.H., 1798); John Lowell, *An Oration, Pronounced July 4, 1799, at the Request of the Inhabitants of the Town of Boston in Commemoration of the Anniversary of American Independence* (Boston, Mass., 1799); Dana, *A Sermon . . . 1795*, 15; Green, *A Sermon . . . 1795*, 26.

[114] Thomas S. Sparhawk, *An Oration, Delivered at Buckston, in the County of Hancock before Capt. Curtis's, and Capt. Hancock's Companies of Militia, and a Number of Other Citizens, July 4th, A.D. 1798. Being the Twenty-Second Anniversary of American Independence* (Boston, Mass., 1798), 8.

liberty that threatened social order. Americans "neither fought nor wished the freedom of an irrational, but that of a rational being; not the freedom of savages, not the freedom of anchorites, but that of civilized and social man."[115] Some historians have argued that these disavowals of the radicalism of the American Revolution were tantamount to a disavowal of the Revolution itself.[116]

To demonstrate that rhetoric against disorderly violence served a political purpose, however, does not necessarily lessen its power. Ideologies function precisely because people do use them to interpret the world. The fear of violence and the projection of a fantasy of American peacefulness were grounded in religious and political beliefs. The friends of order meant what they said, and their words had consequences. The new ideology opposing violence oriented Federalist–Calvinist attitudes not only toward the practice of politics but also toward their society in general. Social institutions that encouraged violence came to be seen as threatening to the civilizing process on which the new republic depended for stability. Opposition to violence placed conservatives in the position of supporting projects that would ameliorate the condition of humanity. Humanitarian reforms became integral to the political agenda of strengthening the social order.

Recognizing the connection between conservative religious and political fears and movements to reform human violence revises the accepted history of humanitarianism. Most American historians have argued that a new positive view of man associated with the Enlightenment inspired the dawn of American humanitarianism. If we look kindly on our fellow human beings, it is natural to desire their gentle treatment. Antislavery, antiwar, opposition to capital and corporal punishment, and opposition to dueling are all credited to newly enlightened religious and political beliefs that placed humanity in a positive light.[117] Some historians who do trace humanitarianism

---

[115] William Emerson, *A Discourse, Delivered in Harvard, July 4, 1794, at the Request of the Military Officers in That Place, Who, with the Militia under Their Command, Were Then Assembled to Commemorate the Anniversary of the American Independence* (Boston, Mass., 1794), 8; William Emerson, *An Oration Pronounced July 5, 1802, at the Request of the Inhabitants of the Town of Boston in Commemoration of the Anniversary of American Independence* (Boston, Mass., 1802), 7, 14. An exception to this effort to cleanse the Revolution of bloodshed can be found in an 1803 oration by Benjamin Whitman, which acknowledged the "popular fury" of the era but celebrated the return to reason in the years following; Whitman, *Oration... 1803*.

[116] Simon Newman, "The World Turned Upside Down: Revolutionary Politics, Fries' and Gabriel's Rebellions, and the Fears of the Federalists," *Pennsylvania History* 67 (2000).

[117] Merle Eugene Curti, *The American Peace Crusade* (Durham, N.C., 1929); Frank Thistlethwaite, *The Anglo-American Connection in the Early Nineteenth Century*, Studies in American Civilization (New York, 1959); Fiering, "Irresistible Compassion"; Myra C. Glenn, *Campaigns against Corporal Punishment: Prisoners, Sailors, Women and Children in Antebellum America* (Albany, N.Y., 1984); David Brion Davis, *From Homicide to Slavery: Studies in American Culture* (New York, 1986); Elizabeth B. Clark, "The Sacred Rights

to more conservative forbearers have debated whether reform movements emerged from self-serving desires to control the lower classes or from altruism inspired by the new republican "optimism" that Federalists and Calvinists shared with their more democratic allies.[118] This debate is reductively characterized as the question of "humanitarianism or control."[119] But these are not necessarily alternatives. An optimistic view of human progress and perfectibility need not be the only source, short of class or status interests, for reform. Early national Federalists and Calvinists were motivated by a deeply negative view of human nature to create reform movements that would ameliorate human violence and control threats to the social order.[120] They were neither optimists nor hypocrites; rather, from their fearful negativism sprang humane efforts to reform society.

Even in the 1790s, the friends of order were self-aware about the humanitarian potentials of their new political theory. They battled the popular assumption that human betterment would come from democratic politics

of the Weak: Pain, Sympathy, and the Culture of Individual Rights in Antebellum America," *Journal of American History* 82 (1995); Karen Halttunen, "Humanitarianism and the Pornography of Pain in Anglo-American Culture," *American Historical Review* 100 (Apr. 1995); Dan McKanan, *Identifying the Image of God: Radical Christians and Nonviolent Power in the Antebellum United States* (New York, 2002).

[118] The question of the relative importance of self-serving versus humane motivations in nineteenth century reform has long been a subject of intense dispute. Progressive historians believed that early national reform was an elite strategy to control the lower classes. During the 1950s and 1960s, a cohort of historians argued that reform movements stemmed from threats to elite status; see John R. Bodo, *The Protestant Clergy and Public Issues, 1812–1848* (Princeton, N.J., 1954); Clifford Stephen Griffin, *Their Brothers' Keepers: Moral Stewardship in the United States, 1800–1865* (New Brunswick, N.J., 1960); W. David Lewis, "The Reformer as Conservative: Protestant Counter-Subversion in the Early Republic," in *The Development of an American Culture*, ed. Stanley Coben and Lorman Ratner (Englewood Cliffs, N.J., 1970). During the 1970s historians described the ways in which reform prepared Americans for capitalist society, Paul Johnson, *A Shopkeeper's Millennium: Society and Revivals in Rochester, New York, 1815–1837* (New York, 1978); Mary P. Ryan, *Cradle of the Middle Class: The Family in Oneida County, New York, 1790–1865* (New York, 1981). David Rothman broke the social control thesis from economic determinism; David Rothman, *The Discovery of the Asylum: Social Order and Disorder in the New Republic* (Boston, Mass., 1971). Lois Banner persuasively challenged the social control school, arguing that evangelical reformers were optimistic republicans in Lois W. Banner, "Religious Benevolence as Social Control: A Critique of an Interpretation," *Journal of American History* 50 (1973); Banner, "Protestant Crusade." Another proponent of the "optimist" interpretation is John L. Thomas, "Romantic Reform in America, 1815–1865," *American Quarterly* 17 (1965). Lawrence Kohl has challenged the very meaning of the term *social control*. Lawrence Kohl, "The Concept of Social Control and the History of Jacksonian America," *Journal of the Early Republic* 15 (Spring 1985).

[119] Martin J. Wiener, *Humanitarianism or Control? A Symposium on Aspects of Nineteenth-Century Social Reform in Britain and America*, vol. 67, Rice University Studies (Houston, Tex., 1981); Thomas Bender, ed., *The Anti-Slavery Debate* (Berkeley, Calif., 1992).

[120] A history that recognizes the connection between the doctrine of depravity and antebellum reform, although without reference to the role of violence, is Leo P. Hirrel, *Children of Wrath: New School Calvinism and Antebellum Reform* (Lexington, Ky., 1998).

and staked a claim to their own powers to improve people's lives and lessen suffering. "I am sensible that modern infidelity pretends to great benevolence and public utility," David Tappan advised a Boston religious society, "but recent facts have proved that no spirit is more bigoted and fanatical, more imposing and sanguinary."[121] The spirit of democracy was bloody, and as such it could not produce positive reforms for the people. "No amelioration of society can be wrought by violence," Noah Webster concurred.[122] Radical politics carried the threat of uncivilizing society and leading the people back along the path toward barbarism.[123] Religious and political traditionalists of the late eighteenth century did not believe that Anglo-American society had left barbarism permanently behind; society could uncivilize swiftly.[124]

Conservatives argued that promise for the future lay in a combination of old traditions and new possibilities. Federalist politicians and Calvinist ministers believed that the influences of Christianity and social order, in the context of the new republican politics with its promise of liberty, held the key to alleviating man's suffering. This recipe gave rise to the network of early-nineteenth-century reform organizations that became known collectively as the Benevolent Empire. Founded by ministers like Timothy Dwight and Jedidiah Morse, alongside their secular allies in the Federalist Party, these groups embraced a self-defined "prudent reform" agenda.[125] Historians have been willing to take Dwight and Morse on their word that the Benevolent Empire represented a conservative approach to early national social problems. Predisposed by the political and religious conservatism of these men, historians haven't sought for radicalism in their actions. However, the cultural agenda of American conservatives in the 1790s was anything but tempered. Inclined by religious doctrine, local history, and political theory to be strongly averse to social violence, Federalists and Calvinists reacted passionately to the sudden threat of Jacobinism that emerged in the fall of 1792. The French Revolution sealed the lid on the pressure cooker, raising fears of violence to a mad boil. The ingredients in the pot melded into a radical anti-Jacobin ideology that violently transformed American political culture.

[121] David Tappan, *A Discourse, Delivered to the Religious Society in Brattle-Street, Boston, and to the Christian Congregation in Charlestown, on April 5, 1798. Being the Day of the Annual Fast in the Commonwealth of Massachusetts*, 2nd ed. (Boston, Mass., 1798), 26.

[122] Noah Webster, *An Oration Pronounced before the Citizens of New-Haven on the Anniversary of the Independence of the United States, July 4th 1798; and Published at Their Request* (New Haven, Conn., 1798), 13.

[123] Samuel Miller, *A Sermon, Delivered May 9, 1798 Recommended, by the President of the United States, to Be Observed as a Day of General Humiliation, Fasting, and Prayer* (New York, 1798), 20.

[124] Philip Gould, *Barbaric Traffic: Commerce and Antislavery in the Eighteenth-Century Atlantic World* (Cambridge, Mass., 2003), 20.

[125] For use of the term *prudent reform*, see Atherton, *Oration . . . 1798*, 20.

A Scene of Confusion and Blood

The American Reaction against the French Revolution

Democracy is always so horribly bloody.
  – John Adams, to Benjamin Rush, March 26, 1806, *Old Family Letters: Copied from the Originals for Alexander Biddle*

No writer has ever yet displayed all the terrors of democracy in our language.
  – John Adams, quoted in Edmund Quincy, *Life of Josiah Quincy of Massachusetts*

At the July 4, 1788, Grand Federal Procession celebrating the ratification of the Constitution, triumphant Federalists led two three-thousand-pound bullocks through the streets of Philadelphia beneath a banner that promised "the death of anarchy and confusion [will] feed the poor and hungry." The butchers put their blades to the beasts' thick bristled necks and cut deeply through the layers of skin, tendon, and muscle. Blood spilled forth, symbolically washing away the "anarchy and confusion" of the revolutionary era. The creation of a new order required more than a few sheets of parchment outlining a new frame of government: the Federalists had to forge consensus. The slaughter of "anarchy" and "confusion" signaled the enthusiastic parade crowd to shout huzzah for the triumph of order and liberty. The people's participation in the rites of celebration gave meaning and force to the Constitution.[1] However, the procession did not eliminate dissent. On the day of the Grand Federal Procession, an anti-Federalist riot

[1] Francis Hopkinson, *Account of the Grand Federal Procession, Philadelphia, July 4, 1788. To Which Are Added, Mr. Wilson's Oration, and a Letter on the Subject of the Procession* (Philadelphia, Pa., 1788), 10; John Bach McMaster, *A History of the People of the United States, from the Revolution to the Civil War* (New York, 1883), 2:89–94; Simon Peter Newman, *Parades and the Politics of the Street: Festive Culture in the Early American Republic* (Philadelphia, Pa., 1997), 122–7; Len Travers, *Celebrating the Fourth: Independence Day and the Rites of Nationalism in the Early Republic* (Amherst, Mass., 1997), 70–83.

broke out in Providence, Rhode Island.[2] When the new government met, divisions soon emerged among the Federalists. James Madison and Alexander Hamilton, allies in the struggle to achieve ratification, famously divided over questions of public finance and regional power. Fights over the distribution of local power divided Federalists within the states. Although the term *Federalist* remained in use during the national government's early years, the coalition that pushed through the Constitution had collapsed. The most important continuity bridging the late 1780s to the early 1790s was political instability.[3]

When news of the violent turn of events in France reached the United States in fall 1792, the crisis acted like a stabilizing agent in the mix, striating the political culture into clearly divided and identifiable camps. Edmund Quincy, the radical abolitionist son of Josiah Quincy, a Federalist political leader from Massachusetts, described the dramatic effect that the French Revolution had on American political culture during the early 1790s:

The contagion of the French Revolution, then at its fieriest height, made the fermentation of popular thought and feeling yet more active and intense. That stupendous phenomenon, which some minds regarded as another Star in the East, – the harbinger of peace and good-will on earth, – and others, as a baleful comet that 'from its horrid hair shook pestilence and war,' shed its influences for good or evil upon the New World as the well as Old. It inspired terror or joy, according as the eyes which watched its progress looked for its issues of life or of death in faith or in fear. The differing elements of the human character subjected to this fierce effervescence soon crystallized into the parties of the Federalists and the Democrats, or, as they at first styled themselves, the Republicans. These were natural parties, having their origin in the constitution of human nature.[4]

The French Revolution split early national political culture into rival partisan clusters determined by their members' orientation to the "constitution of human nature." Few Americans admired the destruction of lives in the Reign of Terror, but some saw in the Revolution only death in fear, while others saw life in faith. Those who believed that human depravity made violence an ever-present threat to civil society reacted fearfully to the danger of Jacobinism in France and at home, and coalesced into the new Federalist Party. Those who shared a more optimistic view of human nature saw the French Revolution – even during its most violent era – as holding the promise

---

[2] Irwin H. Polishook, "An Independence Day Celebration in Rhode Island, 1788," *Huntington Library Quarterly* 30 (1966).

[3] Joanne B. Freeman, *Affairs of Honor: National Politics in the New Republic* (New Haven, Conn., 2001); Stanley M. Elkins and Eric L. McKitrick, *The Age of Federalism* (New York, 1993); James Roger Sharp, *American Politics in the Early Republic: The New Nation in Crisis* (New Haven, Conn., 1993); John C. Miller, *The Federalist Era 1789–1801*, ed. Henry Steele Commager and Richard B. Morris, The New American Nation Series (New York, 1960).

[4] Edmund Quincy, *Life of Josiah Quincy of Massachusetts* (Boston, 1867), 40–1.

for a future of rational humane governance and supported the Democratic-Republican Party.

These political labels encompassed not only a few political elites operating at the national and state levels but also an entire political culture of newspaper writers, religious leaders, lawyers, common voters, free blacks, women, and even youth. American political culture during the 1790s had a populist spirit that reached deeply into the society.[5] This populism is captured in the alternative set of labels used by each party to slander their opponents; to the Republicans, the Federalists were *aristocrats*, and to the Federalists, the Republicans were *Jacobins*. Following 1792, political and religious conservatives viewed Jacobinism as the most pressing threat to political and social order that Americans faced. Anti-Jacobins understood the French Revolution less as a political event than as a social dynamic. American opponents to the French Revolution described it as an "uncivilizing" process, which returned men to savagery and doomed nations to unrestrained bloodshed. Orthodox clergy and Federalist political leaders believed that social order constituted civil liberties by taming man's innate depravity and brutality. They feared that French democracy, by teaching disobedience and overturning hierarchy, would dissolve the social order and introduce anarchy. These fears were reinforced by the French revolutionary assault on Christianity during the Reign of Terror. Only Christianity, American conservatives believed, could save man from his depraved nature, and thereby soften his violent passions. Together with French violence, the rise of religious infidelity persuaded American anti-Jacobins that the world was hurtling toward the millennium, when all humanity would be engulfed in a vortex of bloodshed.

Jeffersonian Republicans and their clerical allies, on the other hand, continued long after the fall of 1792 to believe that the French Revolution was the "harbinger of peace and good-will on earth." When word of the French Republican Army's victories against the Prussians at Jemappes and Valmy reached the United States in January 1793, Republicans organized celebrations across the United States. On January 24, 1793, a roasted ox labeled "Aristocracy" rolled into Boston pulled by a carriage and decorated with French tricolor ribbons. A troop of butchers wearing whites marched alongside, then carved the beast on the "Altar of Democracy." Enthusiasts for the French Revolution devoured the meat to the tune of "Ça Ira." The ox's horns were gilded and hung atop a liberty pole.[6] Federalists believed that they had destroyed the bullocks of anarchy and confusion at the Grand Federal Procession in 1788. But the French Revolution seemingly resurrected

---

[5] Jeffrey L. Pasley, Andrew W. Robertson, and David Waldstreicher, *Beyond the Founders: New Approaches to the Political History of the Early American Republic* (Chapel Hill, N.C., 2004).

[6] "Peace Offering." *Massachusetts Mercury*, Jan. 26, 1793; McMaster, *History of the People*, 96; Newman, *Parades and the Politics*, 125.

the bullock of anarchy in the guise of democracy, compelling terrified conservatives to find new means to quell disorder and forge consent.

The joyful American celebrations of French victories held throughout the late winter and spring of 1793 planted terrified visions of anarchy in the fertile minds of northeastern Federalists and Calvinists. "France is madder than Bedlam," wrote the Massachusetts congressman Fisher Ames to a political colleague, in October 1792. By the spring of 1793, he worried that America would soon become so as well.[7] The Federalist comptroller of the Treasury, Oliver Wolcott Jr., wrote in October 1792 that there existed widespread "apprehension that zeal for liberty may be carried too far, as has been deplorably the case in France."[8] Ames, Wolcott, and their like-minded compatriots reacted to this supposed danger by launching a rhetorical attack on French democracy, focusing in graphic detail on the flowing blood, corpse-strewn fields, and maimed bodies of its victims. Visions of bloodshed did not disguise Federalist concerns about social order; they inspired those concerns. A traditional belief in human depravity, as well as historical anti-Catholicism and anti-Gallicism, drove conservatives' fears. References to bloodshed were persuasive because they drew on a deep well of belief. Yet anti-Jacobinism differed from historic anti-French sentiment by transferring accusations of bloodthirstiness from external to internal enemies. The French Revolution's ideological appeal refashioned Americans into Jacobins who seemingly threatened to destabilize civil society and sink the new United States into chaos.

Bloody Robespierre Commands Our Detestation

At first, Americans offered almost universal support for the French Revolution, perceiving it as a positive reflection of their own political progress. "Liberty will have another feather in her cap," read an item that appeared in at least three newspapers in early September 1789. "The seraphic contagion came to the United States from England across the Atlantic. Now the flame will be communicated to France."[9] Elijah Parish, for example, praised the French Revolution in his 1789 Thanksgiving sermon by emphasizing its

---

[7] Fisher Ames to Thomas Dwight, Oct. 4, 1792; Fisher Ames, *Works of Fisher Ames: With a Selection from His Speeches and Correspondence*, ed. John Thornton Kirkland and Seth Ames (Boston, Mass., 1854), 121.

[8] George Gibbs and Oliver Wolcott, *Memoirs of the Administrations of Washington and John Adams, Edited from the Papers of Oliver Wolcott, Secretary of the Treasury* (New York, 1846), 80.

[9] Beatrice F. Hyslop, "American Press Reports of the French Revolution, 1789–1794," *The New-York Historical Society Quarterly* 42 (Oct. 1958), 11. Another typical expression of this sentiment is Amos Stoddard's remark made at an oration for George Washington's birthday in 1793, "The spark of liberty, enkindled on the American altar, has crossed the wide Atlantick, and now blazes in the palaces of despots"; see *Massachusetts Magazine*, Mar. 1793.

promise to remediate the violence of the Old World. After giving thanks for the Constitution's reestablishment of civil peace in the United States – "we no longer hear the alarming sounds of Death & destruction in our coasts – that the sword sleeps quietly in its scabbard – that the instruments of death & cruelty have become useless" – Parish directed his congregants to give thanks that the Revolution was replacing Catholic despotism in France with reason.[10] Anti-Catholic sentiments as well as concerns about human violence recurred frequently in early positive appraisals of the French Revolution, signaling the continuing influence of these long-standing Anglo-American attitudes in the new United States.

Although early reportage of the French Revolution often contained references to mob violence, Americans initially regarded these incidents as aberrations, not the purposeful design of any particular political party. In fact, before 1792 Robespierre and the Jacobins received approving notices from American newspapers. At least eight newspapers published a speech by Maximilien Robespierre praising freedom of the press in fall 1789.[11] The *Gazette of the United States*, the quasi-official organ of the Federalist administration, published an article praising the Jacobin club in late November 1790.[12] John Adams and John Quincy Adams published early critiques of the Revolution in 1790 and 1791, which led to their vilification by Thomas Jefferson and James Madison.[13] But general opinion about the Revolution remained positive until news of the September Massacres in the fall of 1792. By then, France's rapid and violent changes in government, and its wars with its neighbors, led domestic coverage in American newspapers.[14] Some of the news came from British presses, but Americans also received information from U.S. citizens living in France, from local ship captains who visited European and Caribbean ports, from French and Caribbean refugees who were streaming into the United States, and from French publications shipped across the ocean.[15]

[10] Elijah Parish, "Psalm 136.2," Thanksgiving 1789, EPP.

[11] *Daily Advertiser*, Nov. 20, 1789; *Pennsylvania Mercury*, Dec. 3, 1789; *Independent Gazeteer*, Dec. 7, 1789; *The Freeman's Journal; or, the North American Intelligencer*, Dec. 9, 1789; *The Herald of Freedom, and the Federal Advertiser*, Dec. 15, 1789; *Essex Journal*, Dec. 16, 1789; *Massachusetts Spy*, Dec. 17, 1789; *Salem Mercury*, Dec. 22, 1789.

[12] "Club des Jacobins. Paris, August 18th," *Gazette of the United States*, Nov. 6, 1790.

[13] John Adams, *Discourses on Davila. A Series of Papers, on Political History. Written in the Year 1790, and Then Published in the Gazette of the United States* (Boston, Mass., 1805); Worthington Chauncey Ford, ed., *Writings of Johns Quincy Adams*, 3 vols. (New York, 1913), 1:61–110.

[14] Hyslop, "American Press Reports"; see introduction.

[15] "American Intelligence," *New Hampshire Spy*, Jan. 28, 1792; "Extract of a Letter from a Sea-Faring Man, to the under-Written, Dated Albreda, River of Gambia, June 20, 1792," *Connecticut Gazette*, Jan. 10, 1793; "Extract of a Letter," *Independent Gazetteer*, May 11, 1793; "France," *Herald of the United States*, Sept. 7, 1793; "Extract of a Letter from Londonderry, Dated September 24, 1793," *Baltimore Daily Intelligencer*, Jan. 28, 1794; R. Darrell Meadows, "Engineering Exile: Social Networks and the French Atlantic Community, 1789–1809," *French Historical Studies* 23 (Winter 2000); Catherine Hébert,

These wide-ranging sources persuaded American conservatives that the violence of French Jacobinism was a threat not only to stability in France but also to social order throughout the Atlantic World. From Great Britain, Americans received news of developing radical movements in London, Birmingham, Sheffield, and elsewhere, which were led by self-proclaimed Jacobins. Newspaper articles drew a connection between the threats of violence on both sides of the channel. "The spirit of violence is now so strong against the king in Paris," reported the *Gazette of the United States* in September 1792, that it seemed "to threaten a civil war." Meanwhile, the article proceeded to claim that English Jacobins were threatening to use violence in London.[16] Declarations by the United Irishmen of support for the French cause also appeared in American newspapers during the summer of 1792.[17] Reprints from the British press conveyed the fears of the British government that France was encouraging Ireland to rebel.[18] Meanwhile, mariners and West Indian refugees were spreading accounts of the slave rebellion in Saint Domingue throughout the United States. Critics of the French Revolution frequently attributed the violence in the Caribbean to Jacobin instigators in Paris. An English translation of a French text argued that the slave rebellion was "*committed in the names of philosophy and liberty*," and accused Robespierre of condemning white Saint Dominguans to death.[19] French revolutionary violence and the violence of slave rebellion appeared to flow together in a common river of blood. An extract of a letter from the Colonial Assembly of Saint Domingue to their deputies in Paris, which was printed in a Philadelphia newspaper in June 1792, complained that "cruelties and horrors are constantly committed, the bellies of women with children are ripped open, and they force the husbands (before they cut their throats) to eat the wretched embryo." The letter ruefully noted that no help could be expected from the mother country, which had closed her ears to the planters' plight.[20]

On November 19, 1792, the French National Convention passed a decree that declared republican revolution a universal right and promised to help the common people of foreign nations to gain their liberty.[21] American

"French Publications in Philadelphia in the Age of the French Revolution: A Bibliographical Essay," *Pennsylvania History* 58 (1991).

[16] "London, July 22," *Gazette of the United States*, Sept. 28, 1792.

[17] "The Belfast Second Society of United Irishmen," *Columbian Centinel*, Aug. 4, 1792.

[18] "That in Consequence," *United States Chronicle*, Feb. 21, 1793; "London. December 15," *Connecticut Courant*, Mar. 4, 1793.

[19] *A Particular Account of the Insurrection of the Negroes of St. Domingo, Begun in August, 1791: Translated from the French* (London, 1792), 3, 8, 14.

[20] "Extract of a Letter from the Colonial Assembly of St. Domingo," *The Mail; or Claypoole's Daily Advertiser*, June 4, 1792.

[21] For American and British knowledge and reactions to the decree, see "From a London Paper of January 8th," *Federal Gazette, and Philadelphia Evening Post*, Feb. 23, 1793; "Foreign Affairs. London, January 9," *National Gazette*, Mar. 2, 1793. For the decree itself, see William Doyle, *The Oxford History of the French Revolution* (Oxford, 1989), 199.

conservatives saw the decree as more than an idle threat. Within the United States, political and religious progressives were bringing the French menace home to each section of the new nation. Following the January 1793 celebrations of French battlefield victories, thousands of American democrats filled the streets of towns from Charleston northward to celebrate the arrival of the French ambassador, Citizen Genet, on his mission to drum up military support for France's wars against Europe's monarchies. While Republican partisans called for America to fulfill its revolutionary-era treaty obligation to France and join the wars, anti-Jacobin opponents, led by Secretary of the Treasury Alexander Hamilton, worked assiduously to persuade the president to keep the nation out of conflict. When Washington proclaimed American neutrality in April 1793, political dissension escalated. Unruly public gatherings heaped execrations on the federal government, and Republican newspapers published vituperative attacks on Federalist leaders. Crowds gathered outside the presidential mansion in Philadelphia to protest the decision. Citizen Genet disregarded Washington's proclamation and enlisted ordinary citizens to serve as privateers and to fight against Spanish control of the Mississippi.[22]

Democratic political challengers appeared most ominous when they symbolically appropriated the technologies and methods of the Jacobins, such as the democratic political club and the guillotine. In 1793, multiple local Democratic Societies formed, which issued proclamations supporting the French Revolution and criticizing the "aristocratic" tendencies within the American government. Although these Democratic Societies were not organized by French agents, as conservatives feared, they did encourage support for the Revolution in France and for the spread of its democratic ideals within the United States. Lists of toasts and founding principles published by the Democratic Societies cheered the French Revolution with great enthusiasm.[23] Moreover, many British and Irish Jacobins who fled persecution by the Pitt ministry and British loyalists joined the Democratic Societies upon reaching asylum in America.[24] Having read a radical

[22] Paul Douglas Newman, "The Federalists' Cold War: The Fries Rebellion, National Security, and the State, 1787–1800," *Pennsylvania History* 67 (2000); David Waldstreicher, *In the Midst of Perpetual Fetes: The Making of American Nationalism, 1776–1820* (Chapel Hill, N.C., 1997), Harry Ammon, *The Genet Mission* (New York, 1973).

[23] Philip Sheldon Foner, *The Democratic-Republican Societies, 1790–1800: A Documentary Sourcebook of Constitutions, Declarations, Addresses, Resolutions, and Toasts* (Westport, Conn., 1976); Eugene Perry Link, *Democratic-Republican Societies, 1790–1800* (New York, 1942); Albrecht Koschnik, "The Democratic Societies of Philadelphia and the Limits of the American Public Sphere, Circa 1793–1795," *William and Mary Quarterly* 58 (July 2001).

[24] Richard J. Twomey, "Jacobins and Jeffersonians: Anglo-American Radicalism in the United States, 1790–1820" (Ph.D., Northern Illinois University, 1974), Michael Durey, *Transatlantic Radicals and the Early American Republic* (Lawrence, Kan., 1997), chap. 6; David A. Wilson, *United Irishmen, United States: Immigrant Radicals in the Early Republic* (Ithaca, N.Y., 1998).

pamphlet by the Scottish exile James Callender, John Adams complained that "very soon he will be a Member of the Democratical society.... This country is to be the Asylum of all the discontented, turbulent, profligate and Desperate from all Parts of Europe."[25] The Democratic Societies blended transnational Jacobin enthusiasm, democratic ideology, and dissent against the Federalists into a powerful brew that terrified anti-Jacobins. The rising opposition to the federal administration among supporters of French democracy, coupled with the populist and disorderly nature of the opposition, persuaded American anti-Jacobins that the United States was in imminent danger of Jacobin dissolution and that soon its cities' streets, like those of Paris, might run with blood.

Radical Republicans' praise for Jacobin violence worsened these fears. At civic feasts to welcome Genet, democrats reenacted the king's beheading.[26] In Philadelphia, Republicans set up a model guillotine and demonstrated its operation several times a day.[27] Opposition leaders delivered increasingly vituperative attacks on Federalist party leaders at gatherings organized by Democratic Societies and in Republican newspapers. In South Carolina, enthusiastic Republicans demanded that the Jacobins guillotine all the "moderate men" in France.[28] The Republican *Philadelphia Gazette* included a letter from the planner of a May 1794 civic festival held in celebration of the French Revolution, who argued that it was "in vain the cry is raised of [the French] being atheists, enthusiasts, incendiaries, murderers; of their desiring to overthrow all order and good government – the objects of the revolution still remain the same." Neither the values nor the means of the French Revolution could be criticized according to the letter writer. Rather, the speeches made at the festival praised the Terror, quoted approvingly from Robespierre, and toasted to regicide in Great Britain as well as to democracy in the United States.[29] By uniting the French, the American, and the British democratic cause, supporters of the French Revolution seemed to confirm their opponents' belief that violent Jacobinism was a transatlantic threat.

Two episodes of domestic disorder in the United States during the 1790s gave anti-Jacobins especial cause for concern. In the summer of 1794,

---

[25] Letter from John Adams to Abigail Adams, Nov. 26, 1794 (electronic edition), *Adams Family Papers: An Electronic Archive*, MHS http://www.masshist.org/digitaladams/.

[26] Charles Downer Hazen, *Contemporary American Opinion of the French Revolution* (Baltimore, Md., 1897), 185.

[27] Susan Branson, *These Fiery, Frenchified Dames: Women and Political Culture in Early National Philadelphia*, Early American Studies (Philadelphia, Pa., 2001), 67.

[28] Rachel N. Klein, *Unification of a Slave State: The Rise of the Planter Class in the South Carolina Backcountry, 1760–1808* (Chapel Hill, N.C., 1990), 207.

[29] "Civic Festival," *Philadelphia Gazette*, May 3, 1794. Andrew Brown, the democratic publisher of the *Philadelphia Gazette*, was a Scottish emigrant and radical democrat, further proof to conservatives that Jacobinism was a transatlantic threat.

FIGURE 2. "The Times: A Political Portrait. Triumph Government: perish all its enemies" (1795). This political cartoon, published the year after the Whiskey Rebellion,
shows President George Washington marching a troop of federal volunteers to meet
a French "cannibal" invasion. The invading cannibals wear the bonnet rouge, carry
heads on pikes, and threaten to behead their captives. Meanwhile, Thomas Jefferson
clings to Washington's chariot, shouting in a French accent to "stop de wheels of de
gouvernement." The democratic editor Benjamin Franklin Bache lies under the feet
of the troops, while in the foreground a dog urinates on his newspaper, the *Aurora.*
Collection of the New-York Historical Society.

farmers in western Pennsylvania, encouraged by their local Democratic
Societies, used violent tactics such as arson and tarring and feathering to
protest the federal government's whiskey tax. In July, five hundred local
men engaged in a gun battle with troops who were protecting the home
of the federal excise agent. The rebels' leader, David Bradford, reputedly
threatened to establish a committee for public safety and start building
guillotines.[30] The anti-Federalist leader William Petrikin argued in a public

---

[30] "Lewiston, (*Mifflin County*) July 5th, 1794," *Kline's Carlisle Weekly Gazette,* July 9, 1794;
William Hogeland, *The Whiskey Rebellion: George Washington, Alexander Hamilton, and
the Frontier Rebels Who Challenged America's Newfound Sovereignty* (New York City,
2006), 173. Anti-Jacobins were aware of the insurgents' threats to build a guillotine; see
David Osgood, *A Discourse, Delivered February 19, 1795: The Day Set Apart by the President for a General Thanksgiving through the United States* (Boston, Mass., 1795), 23. Also
see threats to use the guillotine made by the Democratic Society of Kentucky in spring 1794
and the Federalist reaction to that threat; "Pittsburgh, April 22," *General Advertiser,* May 6,
1794; Christopher Gore, *Manlius: With Notes and References* (Boston, Mass., 1794), 30.

meeting that "it was time there should be a Revolution." The French ambassador to the United States, Jean Antoine Joseph Fauchet, publicly applauded the rebellion.[31] While the whiskey rebels had legitimate grievances and were using traditional tactics of disorder to seek redress, the violence of their protest even caused a split within the democratic faction.[32] Three years later, resistance against a national tax to pay for America's Quasi-War against France convinced Federalists that the threat of transatlantic Jacobinism remained strong. Some of the 1799 Fries resisters wore French liberty caps, or cockades, and openly voiced their sense of commonality with the transatlantic cause.[33] Two insurgents threatened to go house to house and "cut the heads off" stamp collectors.[34]

Republican opposition to the 1795 Jay Treaty between the United States and Britain also alarmed Federalists. During protests, Francophiles burned Fisher Ames in effigy and beheaded and exploded effigies of John Jay.[35] Benjamin Bache's ultrademocratic journal the *Aurora* published a list of toasts made at a Republican militia gathering in 1795, which included "The guillotine: May it maintain its empire till all crowned heads are laid in the dust" immediately before "Mr. Jay's treaty with Great Britain; May it never be ratified by our government."[36] Readers surely got the message that American Jacobins continued to embrace violence as a legitimate tool to secure democracy. In response to the disorder, John Adams agonized that American radicals "adopted the very stile and language of the French Jacobines."[37] A humorous extract in the conservative *Massachusetts Mercury* lampooning the Republican opposition to the Jay Treaty asserted that a gathering of democrats in New Hampshire had resolved "that all the Antijacobin members of Congress, take the guillotine and perform a pilgrimage to the tomb

---

[31] Newman, "The Federalists' Cold War," 74.

[32] Saul Cornell, *The Other Founders: Anti-Federalism and the Dissenting Tradition in America, 1788–1828* (Chapel Hill, N.C., 1999), 209, 201. See also Richard H. Kohn, *Eagle and Sword: The Federalists and the Creation of the Military Establishment in America, 1783–1802* (New York, 1975), chap. 8; Steven R. Boyd, *The Whiskey Rebellion: Past and Present Perspectives* (Westport, Conn., 1985); Elkins and McKitrick, *Age of Federalism*, 461–85.

[33] Simon Newman, "The World Turned Upside Down: Revolutionary Politics, Fries' and Gabriel's Rebellions, and the Fears of the Federalists," *Pennsylvania History* 67 (2000).

[34] Robert H. Churchill, "Popular Nullification, Fries' Rebellion, and the Waning of Radical Republicanism, 1798–1801," *Pennsylvania History* 67 (Winter 2000), 118.

[35] McMaster, *History of the People*, 2:210–19; John R. Howe, "Republican Thought and the Political Violence of the 1790s," *American Quarterly* 19 (Summer 1967); Todd Estes, "Shaping the Politics of Public Opinion: Federalists and the Jay Treaty Debate," *Journal of the Early Republic* 20 (Autumn 2000). See also Richard Buel Jr., *Securing the Revolution: Ideology in American Politics, 1789–1815* (Ithaca, N.Y., 1972); Richard Hofstadter, *The Idea of a Party System: The Rise of Legitimate Opposition in the United States, 1780–1840* (Berkeley, Calif., 1969); Elkins and McKitrick, *Age of Federalism*.

[36] "New Jersey. Schallenburg, July 6," *Aurora General Advertiser*, July 20, 1795.

[37] Letter from Abigail Adams to John Adams, Jan. 4, 1795 (electronic edition), *Adams Family Papers: An Electronic Archive*, MHS, http://www.masshist.org/digitaladams/.

of Robespierre, and then be transported to Cayenne."[38] However, it was less funny when democrats bombarded Alexander Hamilton, a prominent public supporter of the Jay Treaty, with stones at a public meeting in New York City in July 1795.

"There is a description of men in this country," Alexander Hamilton wrote, who believe "that the most natural and happy state of Society is a state of continual revolution and change – that the welfare of a nation is in exact ratio to the rapidity of the political vicissitudes, which it under-goes – to the frequency and the violence of the tempests with which it is agitated."[39] These American Jacobins, Hamilton and his allies warned, desired to reduce America to the same bloody anarchy that had terrorized France. Opponents of the French Revolution voiced again and again in their sermons, orations, and publications the dread that Jacobin violence would soon consume the United States. John Adams's fear of the "terrorism" on the streets of Philadelphia during the spring of 1793, which he expressed in an 1813 letter to Thomas Jefferson, is well known.[40] But this feeling was not confined to the self-justifying hindsight of an old man.

Elijah Parish's unpublished sermons reveal the growing fears of one ortho-dox northeasterner during the early 1790s. Although in 1789 Parish had celebrated the beginning of the French Revolution, he became concerned during fall 1792 that violence in France posed a local danger. In a December 1792 sermon, he warned of the destabilizing effects of "parties and cabals" in the United States at a time when "upon the theatre of nations you see armies wallowing in their own blood – the crimson tide flows around & swelling rivers run blushing ... to the sea."[41] A deeply religious man, Parish tried to confine his preaching in 1793 to the sacred world rather than the profane. "We shall avoid the war of words & opinions & only address a few passages of scripture," he promised in March of that year.[42] He preached a subtly disguised and sympathetic funeral sermon for Louis XVI in April, yet even as he recoiled from French violence he resisted condemning the aims of the French Revolution and continued to revile Great Britain.[43] By the spring of 1794, Parish could no longer disguise his disapprobation for the Revolution. "We have seen a great kingdom of old possessed with a political enthusiasm rushing into unheard of cruelties & their soil deluged in blood," Parish cried out in his April Fast Day sermon. Most alarmingly, that spirit threatened to extend to the United States, agitating Parish's perpetual fears

---

[38] "Political Irony," *Massachusetts Mercury*, Aug. 18, 1795.

[39] Alexander Hamilton, *The Papers of Alexander Hamilton*, ed. Harold Coffin Syrett (New York, 1961), 14:502–3.

[40] Adams is quoted by David Brion Davis in *Revolutions*, 65; as well as in many other sources.

[41] Elijah Parish, "Micah 2.10," Dec. 1792, EPP.

[42] Elijah Parish, "John 3.," Mar. 1793, EPP.

[43] Elijah Parish, "Jer 30.9," June 1793; Elijah Parish, "Gen 25.27," July 1793, EPP; Elijah Parish, "Psalm 100.4," Thanksgiving (November) 1793.

of war and death. Parish expressed those fears in the violent language that later became the hallmark of his literary style. "We now see the clouds of war Hanging over our heads," he warned. "A shower of blood seems just ready to crimson our fields. The angel of destruction seems preparing to give the signal; then again will our husbands, our sons, our brothers & our lovers bleed on the field of battle, their corpses will float [and] feed the wild beasts."[44] At this early moment in his career, long before his entry into partisan politics, Parish viewed the events in France through a lens of depravity and violence, which prompted him to write violently in reaction.

By the end of 1794, conservative religious and political leaders had turned almost entirely against the French Revolution.[45] In February 1795, President Washington proclaimed a day of national thanksgiving, during which he suggested that Americans rejoice for the preservation of "liberty with order" within the United States.[46] In many of the thirty-odd Thanksgiving sermons that were published, ministers criticized the violence in France. In his unpublished February 1795 Thanksgiving sermon, Elijah Parish shifted gears from his previous forceful but brief attacks on the French Revolution to a full-scale onslaught. For twelve manuscript pages (in a sermon of twenty pages total), Parish crafted a detailed assault on the violence of the French Revolution and the danger it posed to the United States.

Parish conjured for his congregants all the central tropes of Jacobin violence – overflowing blood, streets filled with dead bodies, bestial murderers, mass drownings, the guillotine, infidelity, and fields of war. His narrative of violence began with the storming of the Tuileries and the September Massacres, when "Tigers in human form forsook not their bloody career, till wearied with the work of death, till 6 or 7000 persons lay mangled under their feet." Parish then focused his attention on the violence of the civil war in the Vendée, where a French soldier reported, "We marched over heaps of the slain," and 1,400 were thrown into the river. He ended with the scene of war, where "fields & rivers [are] crimsoned with human blood." Attacking warfare in the same terms he had used since his commencement oration at Dartmouth, Parish stated, "He that is a friend to war is an enemy to the human race." He then shifted the sermon's attention to giving thanks that President Washington had saved the United States from entering the war in Europe (where "the fields are covered with the bodies of the slain") or from dissolving into civil war. Parish minced no words attacking the

---

44 Elijah Parish, "Ezra 8.23," Fast (April) 1794, EPP.
45 Many of the clerical supporters of the French Revolution represented sects that aligned themselves with Jefferson's Democratic-Republicans. Clerical support for the French Revolution was also more popular among ministers from the southern and middle states rather than New England; Ruth H. Bloch, *Visionary Republic: Millennial Themes in American Thought 1756–1800* (New York, 1985), 156.
46 George Washington, *By the President of the United States of America, a Proclamation* (Philadelphia, Pa., 1795).

democratic opponents to the federal administration who had encouraged the "late insurrection" in Pennsylvania, "these Heroes of the cup violently assault our Constitution." Drawing a direct line from the violence of French Jacobins to the violence of American democrats ("those sons of violence"), Parish warned his congregants against all threats to civil order. Finally, he closed with a vision of the United States as a respite from militarism and as an asylum to the poor. "While despotism, & wars & poverty bear down the mass of the people in other nations; how happy are we to welcome the weeping fugitives to a land of Liberty, peace, plenty."[47] Most of the images in Elijah Parish's 1795 sermon would recur in published sermons during his later years as a partisan standard-bearer, enraging critics who accused him of prostituting the pulpit.

Proclaiming political opinions from the pulpit aroused controversy, and many of the printed 1795 sermons included acknowledgments that their delivery had aroused objections. This sensitivity, as well as the fear of offending Republican members of their congregations, explains why many ministers were reluctant to criticize the Revolution before 1795.[48] Each minister who eventually joined the anti-Jacobin ranks negotiated his own path to public opposition. Some joined the opposition when they learned of the execution of Louis XVI; others were not persuaded until after the beheading of Robespierre, when detailed accounts of the Reign of Terror flooded the United States. Still others held out hope for the Revolution until far later in the decade, when they read accounts of a supposed French conspiracy to overthrow all religion and government. Almost all the opponents who looked back on their change in opinion and tried to explain what had happened agreed that violence had been the leading factor.[49] Benjamin Russell, an influential Federalist newspaper editor, explained his reasoning to his readers:

---

[47] Elijah Parish, "Psal. 92.1," Thanksgiving (February) 1795, EPP.

[48] See Jonathan Freeman, *A Sermon Delivered at New-Windsor and Bethlehem, August 30. 1798. Being the Day Appointed by the General Assembly of the Presbyterian Church, in the United States of America: To Be Observed as a Day of Solemn Humiliation, Fasting and Prayer, in All the Churches under Their Care* (New Windsor, N.Y., 1799); William Linn, *A Discourse on National Sins Delivered May 9, 1798; Being the Day Recommended by the President of the United States to Be Observed as a Day of General Fast* (New York, 1798).

[49] For more personal accounts of how the violent disorder influenced their reactions to the French Revolution, see Thomas Tudor Tucker's July 4, 1795, oration, excerpted in *The Rural Magazine; or Vermont Repository*, Feb. 1796; Thomas McKean to John Adams, quoted in Hazen, *Contemporary American Opinion*, 265; Freeman, *Sermon...1798*, 28; William Linn, *A Discourse on National Sins*, 27; Samuel Parker, *A Sermon Preached before His Honor the Lieutenant-Governor... And House of Representatives of the Commonwealth of Massachusetts, May 29, 1793, Being the Day of General Election* (Boston, Mass., 1793); John Prince, *A Discourse, Delivered at Salem, on the Day of the National Fast, May 9, 1798: Appointed by President Adams, on Account of the Difficulties Subsisting between the United States and France* (Salem, Mass., 1798).

Until the '*reign of terror*' commenced in France, I marked, that the Centinel was foremost in vindicating the liberties of Frenchmen; But if it had applauded the shameful executions of thousands of men, women and children – the destruction of the arts and sciences – in short, had it advocated the catalogue of 'murders, treasons, sacrileges and crimes,' which distinguished that four years reign of terror, it ought to have gone down to posterity loaded with execrations![50]

For Benjamin Russell and many other anti-Jacobins, the violent turn in French politics following the September Massacres caused a sharp break in their support. They did not necessarily deny that the initial goals of the Revolution had been praiseworthy. But for American conservatives who believed that violence negated civil society, the terror extinguished their faith.

Although most of the authors of public discourse in the 1790s were men, there is evidence that women turned against the French Revolution for the same reasons that men did. Nelly Parke Custis, a step-granddaughter of George Washington, informed a correspondent that "in reaction to the Terror in France" she had "become 'perfectly Federal' and denounced the French as '*democratic murderers*'."[51] Elizabeth Drinker, the Philadelphia Quaker doyenne, eagerly participated in the capital city's political culture during the 1790s. She adhered to a conservative interpretation of civil society and was horrified by French Revolutionary violence – which she worried would engender political violence within the United States.[52] Other conservative women published poems and songs condemning Jacobin violence and supporting the Federalist cause.[53]

In a July 4, 1795, oration, George Richards, a Federalist orator in New Hampshire, recapitulated the initial welcome that Americans had given to the Revolution: "It was a spark from the altar flame of liberty on this side of the Atlantic, which alight on the pinnacle of despotism in France, and reduced the immense fabric to ashes, in the twinkling of an eye." He even acknowledged some of the positive accomplishments of the Revolution's early years. However, the violence led to a swift reversal in his opinions: "the tragical excesses of independent mobs, the vile automatons of anarchy, arrest our praise. The iron rein of self created clubs, controlling law, calls forth abhorrence. The horrid despotism of the bloody Robespierre commands our detestation."[54] Spoken in the plural first person, Richards's address was

[50] *Columbian Centinel*, Feb. 28, 1795.

[51] Rosemarie Zagarri, "Women and Party Conflict in the Early American Republic," Pasley, Robertson, and Waldstreicher, eds., *Beyond the Founders*, 111.

[52] Susan Branson, "Elizabeth Drinker: Quaker Values and Federalist Support in the 1790s," *Pennsylvania History* 68 (2001).

[53] Branson, *Fiery Frenchified Dames*, 80–1.

[54] George Richards, *An Oration on the Independence of the United States of Federate America: Pronounced at Portsmouth, New-Hampshire, July 4, 1795* (Portsmouth, N.H., 1795), 30.

intended to draw in his audience, and to construct a conversion experience for anyone in the audience who still sympathized with the Revolution.

Public confessions of conversion to anti-Jacobinism had an expressly pedagogical purpose. Americans had long avidly purchased religious conversion narratives, in which authors described their new birth in Christ. These narratives served as models for readers seeking redemption; conversion narratives created a framework of emotional experiences for a reader to travel through en route to salvation. The anti-Jacobin conversion narratives instructed audiences in the emotional and intellectual steps that would lead them to turn against the French Revolution; their descriptions of violence helped produce the emotional and intellectual impetus for this reaction. A New Hampshire printer even titled one pamphlet "A noble confession and sincere conversion of a Jacobin to a Federal." In the confession, the author began by stating his sins: "I frankly acknowledge myself to have been a warm friend to the French Revolution. I considered their cause to be that of *liberty*, in opposition to *tyranny*, notwithstanding the torrents of innocent blood which they had wantonly shed." Next he described all the mistakes of judgment that his false belief had led to (such as justifying French seizures of American shipping). He even acknowledged entertaining fantasies of treason: "I wanted nothing more than two or three desperate fellows to lead the way, and I was ripe for a revolt. I should have been heartily glad that a powerful French army, and navy, had appeared upon our coasts." But finally, the friendship of a good Federalist led him to read the Jay Treaty more carefully and discover his terrible error. Now he knew that "France is *really that Antichrist*, who opposeth, and exalteth himself above all this is called God." He had been converted quite literally from worshipping Satan to a proper devotion to the one true God. The author concluded by listing his reformed beliefs: "I believe" repeated twenty-two times to cover all the dogmas of political Federalism.[55]

When news of mobs and massacres first reached the United States, many friends of order described the violence as a dark "veil" or cloud spreading over the cause of liberty.[56] Years later, these commentators questioned whether it had been their initial view of the revolution that was obscured.

---

[55] *An Address from a Minister in Virginia, to His People in a Special Meeting on Week Day, March, 1798. Occasioned by Their Opposition to the Measures Adopted by the Federal Government: With an Appendix Containing a Noble Confession and Sincere Conversion of a Jacobin to Federalism* (Hanover, N.H., 1799), 17–23.

[56] For examples, see David Tappan, *A Sermon, Delivered to the First Congregation in Cambridge, and the Religious Society in Charlestown, April 11, 1793; on the Occasion of the Annual Fast in the Commonwealth of Massachusetts* (Boston, Mass., 1793), 28; Enos Hitchcock, *An Oration, in Commemoration of the Independence of the United States of America: Delivered in the Baptist Meeting-House in Providence, July 4th, 1793* (Providence, R.I., 1793), 13; Parker, *A Sermon . . . 1793*, 29; David Osgood, *The Wonderful Works of God Are to Be Remembered: A Sermon, Delivered on the Day of Annual Thanksgiving, November 20, 1794* (Boston, Mass., 1794), 23; Elijah Waterman, *An Oration Delivered before the Society of Cincinnati, Hartford, July 4, 1794* (Hartford, Conn., 1794), 10.

Looking back, it seemed that the veil over French affairs lifted only when information regarding its violence reached American ears.[57] Anti-Jacobins described their discovery of French revolutionary violence as an awakening that startled them from political daydreams and forcefully reminded them of the dangers of democracy.

A Scene of Confusion and Blood

During the 1790s, Federalists and their orthodox allies repeatedly used anti-Jacobin rhetoric to stifle political and religious challenges to their authority. Jeffersonian Republicans groused that the attacks issued from "British hirelings and British presses" who wanted to destroy the reputation of the democratic movement.[58] They were correct to identify the transatlantic context of American anti-Jacobinism. Yet while American anti-Jacobins read and borrowed from British texts, their language signified more than foreign falsehoods designed to discredit American democrats. Conservatives drew from deeply rooted political and religious beliefs to launch their assault on the violence of domestic Jacobinism. To assess the meaning and impact of American anti-Jacobinism, this testimony against bloodshed must be carefully examined.

Following in the wake of many years of domestic support for the French Revolution, American conservatives began their attack on Jacobinism by redefining the French Revolution as a cataclysm of lawless violence rather than as a battle for the rights of man. Federalist–Calvinist political theory emphasized the Anglo tradition of law and order as the basis of men's political rights. The French Revolution, anti-Jacobins argued, had abandoned the processes of law. Its revolutionaries "made a mockery" of justice and the rules of evidence by massacring prisoners and condemning thousands to death at the guillotine.[59] The Reverend Elijah Waterman, a student of Jonathan Edwards Jr., berated French Jacobins for being "mad to fury, seeking for some miserable victim which may be sacrificed to their rage, by an atheistical tribunal, who give judgment without mercy, and inflict death without justice."[60] The revolutionary state was executing citizens without

---

[57] Jedidiah Morse, *A Sermon, Preached at Charlestown, November 29, 1798, on the Anniversary Thanksgiving in Massachusetts. With an Appendix, Designed to Illustrate Some Parts of the Discourse; Exhibiting Proofs of the Early Existence, Progress, and Deleterious Effects of French Intrigue and Influence in the United States* (Boston, Mass., 1798); Freeman, *Sermon . . . 1798*; Robert Treat Paine, *The Works in Verse and Prose, of the Late Robert Treat Paine, Jun., Esq* (Boston, Mass., 1812), 301; Linn, *Discourse*; Timothy Dwight, *Travels in New England and New York*, ed. Barbara Miller Solomon (Cambridge, Mass., 1969), 4:271.

[58] Consider Sterry, *An Address to the Republican Citizens: Delivered at Norwich (Con.) on the 4th July 1806 . . .* (Norwich, Conn., 1806).

[59] *The Massachusetts Magazine; or Monthly Museum*, Jan. 1794.

[60] Waterman, *An Oration . . . 1794*, 13. And Samuel Kendal, *A Sermon Delivered on the Day of National Thanksgiving, February 19, 1795* (Boston, Mass., 1795), 12.

due process or religious sanction. In the absence of law and faith, no bulwarks protected French citizens and secured their "peaceable enjoyment of equal liberty."[61] Without restraint, liberty became licentious; as each man obeyed only his own rude passions, society dissolved and anarchic bloodshed reigned.

A local study of political party formation in Berkshire County, Massachusetts, suggests that ideological orientation to law and order, rather than economic or social differences, divided the populace into anti-Jacobin and Jacobin factions. Those who were most frightened by the disorder of the American Revolution were catalyzed by the violence of the French Revolution to become committed Federalists, whereas Republicans saw disorder as a reasonable price for popular representation.[62] Henry Van Schaack, a prominent Berkshire County Federalist, had a strong aversion to extralegal violence following attacks on him as a suspected loyalist during the American Revolution; he quickly became an opponent to the French Revolution and tried to persuade others in the county that French assaults on law and order would culminate in anarchy.[63] Van Schaack and other conservatives argued that respect for law and order was necessary to establish meaningful equality among a nation's citizens; French equality was only another name for bloodshed.

Theodore Dwight praised the laws of Connecticut that secured education, religion, and order, guaranteeing true equality among the people: "hence equality, not that furious, bloody and demoralizing spirit, which has desolated so large a portion of Europe, but the only equality of which mankind are susceptible in a civilized state, is here enjoyed in its fullest extent."[64] American friends of order sought to establish sole claim to republican freedom and rights. "It may be doubted whether there are many Frenchmen in France, who have a true American idea of the Rights of Man," Joseph Clark, a Federalist lawyer, told the audience attending his July 4, 1794, oration in Rochester, New Hampshire. The French National Convention had acted so irregularly and capriciously that France was not progressing toward freedom but "plunging into the gulph of Anarchy."[65]

---

[61] John Thornton Kirkland, *A Sermon, Delivered on the 9th of May, 1798. Being the Day of a National Fast, Recommended by the President of the United States* (Boston, Mass., 1798).

[62] Thomas Lawrence Davis, "Aristocrats and Jacobins in County Towns: Party Formation in Berkshire County, Massachusetts, 1775–1816" (Ph.D., Boston University, 1977).

[63] Henry Cruger Van Schaack, *Memoirs of the Life of Henry Van Schaack Embracing Selections from His Correspondence During the American Revolution* (Chicago, Ill., 1892), 188.

[64] Theodore Dwight, *An Oration, Delivered at New Haven on the 7th of July, A.D. 1801, before the Society of the Cincinnati, for the State of Connecticut, Assembled to Celebrate the Anniversary of American Independence* (Hartford, Conn., 1801), 11.

[65] Joseph Clark, *An Oration Delivered at Rochester; on the Fourth of July, Seventeen Hundred Ninety Four* (Dover, N.H., 1794), 8.

Anti-Jacobins labored to persuade their audiences that the violence in France was not incidental to the Revolution – a regrettable excess soon to be reined in – but rather its very essence. They distinguished the estimable cause of American liberty from its degenerate lawless French counterpart. True liberty consisted in man's freedom to live a virtuous life, not in freedom from governance. French democracy overthrew all order and allowed the violent passions to seize control. Abigail Adams, learning about the exhibition of a guillotine in London, wrote to her husband: "I see by the N. York papers that the guilotine has been advertized to be seen there. I think it should be as 'advertized in England,' 'Here is to be seen the guilotine of the French, and the Wild Beasts.'"[66] American anti-Jacobins both feared the spread of French violence within the United States and perversely wished to exhibit that violence at home to undermine American affection for the Revolution. However, turning Americans against the Revolution required more than simply demonstrating its bloody qualities.

When confronted with evidence of the September Massacres and the Reign of Terror, many Republicans maintained their support for the French Revolution by denying, apologizing, explaining, or even applauding the violence. Secretary of State Thomas Jefferson, leader of the pro-French party, sought both to deny and apologize for French Revolutionary violence. During the summer of 1792, Jefferson began receiving letters from Gouverneur Morris, the American minister plenipotentiary to France, and William Short, an American diplomat in the Hague, containing allegations that the Jacobins were planning to violently subvert the constitutional government. "We may witness some Outrages of the most flagitious kind," Morris wrote Jefferson in June. "My Heart bleeds when I reflect that the finest Opportunity which ever presented itself for establishing the Rights of Mankind throughout the civilized World is perhaps lost and forever."[67] By August and September, Morris's and Short's letters to Jefferson offered details of massacres, of the gruesome killing of Madame de Lamballe, and of the flight of the Marquis de Lafayette (once a close friend of Jefferson's).[68] Short called the Jacobins "monsters"; soon Morris even stopped referring to the Jacobins by name, calling them simply "the violent party."[69] In January 1793, Jefferson fired back a salvo at his correspondents, rejecting their criticisms of the Jacobins. The Revolution, Jefferson wrote, had saved France from despotism, and

---

[66] Letter from Abigail Adams to John Adams, Apr. 11, 1794 (electronic edition), *Adams Family Papers: An Electronic Archive*, MHS, http://www.masshist.org/digitaladams/.

[67] Gouverneur Morris to Thomas Jefferson, June 17, 1792; Thomas Jefferson, *The Papers of Thomas Jefferson*, ed. Charles T. Cullen, John Catanzariti, and Julian P. Boyd (Princeton, N.J., 1950), 24:94.

[68] See, for example, William Short to Thomas Jefferson, July 31, Aug. 15, Aug. 24, Sept. 18, 1792; Gouverneur Morris to Thomas Jefferson Aug. 16, Sept. 10; Jefferson, *Papers*.

[69] Gouverneur Morris to Thomas Jefferson, Dec. 21, 1792, Jefferson, *Papers*, 24:792.

its violence was entirely justifiable. In fact, a holocaust of the human race would be justifiable if in the cause of freedom:

> In the struggle which was necessary, many guilty persons fell without the forms of trial, and with them some innocent. These I deplore as much as any body, and shall deplore some of them to the day of my death. But I deplore them as I should have done had they fallen in battle. It was necessary to use the arm of the people, a machine not quite so blind as balls and bombs, but blind to a certain degree. A few of their cordial friends met at their hands the fate of enemies.... The liberty of the whole earth was depending on the issue of the contest, and was ever such a prize won with so little innocent blood? My own affections have been deeply wounded by some of the martyrs to this cause, but rather than it should have failed, I would have seen half the earth desolated. Were there but an Adam and an Eve left in every country, and left free, it would be better than as it now is.[70]

That same month, in a letter to his son-in-law Thomas Mann Randolph, Jefferson refused to acknowledge the firsthand accounts of violence that he received: "our news from France continues to be good, and to promise a continuance," he wrote.[71] Jefferson simply did not share the Federalists' fear of the violent disruption of French civil society. At the very height of the Reign of Terror, in May 1794, Jefferson scoffed to another correspondent: "Let Rawhead and bloody bones come."[72] Ultimately forced to acknowledge the bloodshed, he never retreated from defending the revolutionary cause.

Other Francophiles took a more regretful tone about the violence of the Revolution, yet sought to apologize by placing the bloodshed in context. A Republican newspaper argued in 1792 that "the dreadful massacre of the 2d of September cannot be thought of without horror; but can by no means injure the cause of the French in the minds of those who reflect."[73] Moderate Republicans acknowledged that French bloodshed had tragic dimensions, but they sought to minimize its significance by comparing the missteps to the great import of the cause or by blaming the bloodshed on the nation's tyrannical past and its struggles against a counterrevolutionary conspiracy of kings. Authors acknowledged the seriousness of the anarchy that afflicted France, but they encouraged their audiences to maintain enthusiasm for the

---

[70] Thomas Jefferson to William Short, Jan. 3, 1793, Jefferson, *Papers*, 25:14. Jefferson's reply to Gouverneur Morris, who was his political enemy, is briefer; it defends the violence committed by the Jacobins as righteous.

[71] Gouverneur Morris to Thomas Jefferson, June 17, 1792; William Short to Thomas Jefferson, Oct. 6, 1792; William Short to Thomas Jefferson, Aug. 15, 1792; Thomas Jefferson to William Short, Jan. 3., 1793; Thomas Jefferson to Thomas Mann Randolph, Jan. 7, 1793; Jefferson, *Papers*, 24: 94, 271, 298; 25:14, 30.

[72] Thomas Jefferson to Tench Coxe, May 1, 1794, Jefferson, *Papers*, 28: 76.

[73] "Baltimore," *Baltimore Evening Post*, Nov. 6, 1792.

rights of man.[74] Others defended the sacred justice of the bloodshed. The Reverend William Linn of the Reformed Dutch Church, confessed in 1794 that "the news of blood and carnage [from France] shock the feelings of our nature." Linn did not approve of the bloodshed, but he justified the violence as God's punishment of the French monarchy for its sins – and for the St. Bartholomew's Day massacre in particular.[75] Such a providential understanding directly conflicted with the anti-Jacobins' belief that French violence destroyed all meaning.

Far more horrifying, some American Republicans reveled in the bloodshed. Take, for example, the boast James Westcott made at a Fourth of July oration in 1794 that France had "immolated a tyrant at the altar of Liberty, and they will not hesitate at making her fumes to smoke with the sacrilegious blood of those wretched miscreants who violate her mandate and wage war against her votaries."[76] Although the majority of French partisans sought to apologize for the Revolution's errors, some American supporters believed that the terror was a just means to accomplish a glorious end. In 1794, Benjamin Franklin Bache – a Republican organizer, editor of the

---

74 For typical apologies for the Terror, see Samuel Miller, *A Sermon, Preached in New-York, July 4th, 1793: Being the Anniversary of the Independence of America, at the Request of the Tammany Society, or Columbian Order* (New York, 1793), 32–33; Joseph Lathrop, *The Happiness of a Free Government, and the Means of Preserving It: Illustrated in a Sermon, Delivered in West-Springfield, on July 4th, 1794, in Commemoration of American Independence* (Springfield, Mass., 1794), 15; John Phillips, *An Oration, Pronounced July 4th, 1794: At the Request of the Inhabitants of the Town of Boston, in Commemoration of the Anniversary of American Independence* (Boston, Mass., 1794), 17; George Tillinghast, *An Oration, Commemorative of the Nineteenth Anniversary of American Independence: Delivered at the Baptist Meeting-House in Providence, on the Fourth Day of July, A.D. 1794* (Providence, R.I., 1794), 16; Samuel Deane, *A Sermon, Preached before His Honour Samuel Adams, Esq. Lieutenant Governor; the Honourable the Council, Senate, and House of Representatives of the Commonwealth of Massachusetts, May 28th, 1794: Being the Day of General Election* (Boston, Mass., 1794), 20; Henry Channing, *The Consideration of Divine Goodness an Argument for Religious Gratitude and Obedience: A Sermon, Delivered at New-London, November 27, 1794. Being the Day Appointed by Authority, for Public Thanksgiving in the State of Connecticut* (New London, Conn., 1794), 14; Joseph Lyman, *The Administrations of Providence Full of Goodness and Mercy: A Sermon, Delivered at Hatfield, November 7th. A.D. 1793. Being the Day of Public Thanksgiving* (Northampton, Mass., 1794), 16; William Jones, *An Oration, Pronounced at Concord, the Fourth of July, 1794: Being the Anniversary of the American Independence* (Concord, Mass., 1794), 19.

75 William Linn, *Discourses on the Signs of the Times* (New York, 1794), 84. Later in the decade Linn, who was a friend of Alexander Hamilton, recanted. See also Samuel Stillman, *Thoughts on the French Revolution: A Sermon, Delivered November 20, 1794, Being the Day of Annual Thanksgiving* (Boston, Mass., 1795).

76 James D. Westcott, *An Oration, Commemorative of the Declaration of American Independence: Delivered before the Ciceronian Society, on the Fourth of July, M, Dcc, Xciv; and Published at Their Request* (Philadelphia, Pa., 1794), 13; Morgan J. Rhees, *An Oration Delivered at Greenville, Head-Quarters of the Western Army, North West of the Ohio, July 4, 1795* (Philadelphia, Pa., 1795).

democratic newspaper the *Aurora*, and unqualified enthusiast of the Revolution – published a translation of a speech made by Maximilien Robespierre that defended terror as a tactic of revolution. Robespierre argued that the spring of a popular government during a revolution should be "virtue combined with terror: virtue, without which terror is destructive; terror, without which virtue is impotent," then he pithily summarized his argument in the maxim: "Terror is only justice prompt, severe and inflexible."[77] Bache's evident approbation of Robespierre's argument, signified by his desire to publicize and disseminate the speech, must have helped to persuade anti-Jacobins of the violent intentions of American democrats.[78] Benjamin Russell, who reported Robespierre's speech in his Federalist newspaper the *Columbian Centinel*, felt frightened enough to publish rumors that American Republicans had been overheard saying such things as, "It is time we had a guillotine erected," or "I wish to see the National Razor in a state of permanent operation."[79]

Anti-Jacobins sought to persuade their audiences to reject these defenses of the violence of the Revolution by decoupling the association between American freedom and French freedom. In his spring 1793 Fast Day sermon, the Congregationalist minister Joseph McKeen challenged the members of his Massachusetts church who favored the Revolution to rethink their support. The Revolution was not a spectacle of freedom, he thundered, but a "scene of confusion and blood." McKeen's formulation echoed the English Bible scholar Matthew Henry's well-known commentary on Isaiah 34:2–7, verses in which the Hebrew prophet describes in graphic detail God's punishment of nations who are his enemies.[80] Far from a prosperous garden of liberty, France was the site of God's wrath and destruction. "Let us not envy the state of the French, nor wish such liberty as theirs," McKeen exhorted.[81] Without social order, the only right the French could secure was the freedom to slaughter one another indiscriminately; the freedom promised by the Jacobins was the freedom of wild beasts.

---

[77] Maximilien Robespierre, *Report upon the Principles of Political Morality: Which Are to Form the Basis of the Administration of the Interior Concerns of the Republic. Made in the Name of the Committee of Public Safety, the 18th Pluviose, Second Year of the Republic (February 6th, 1794)* (Philadelphia, Pa., 1794).

[78] See also "For the diary," *The Diary, or Loudon's Register*, Apr. 3, 1794, which prints a letter defending the French Revolution immediately before a copy of Robespierre's "Report" promising violent suppression of all domestic enemies.

[79] *Columbian Centinel*, July and Aug. 1794; Mar. 1795.

[80] Matthew Henry describes these verses as a "scene of blood and confusion."

[81] Joseph McKeen, *A Sermon, Preached on the Public Fast in the Commonwealth of Massachusetts, April 11, 1793* (Salem, Mass., 1793). For evidence of the French spirit within McKeen's congregation, see William Buell Sprague, *Annals of the American Pulpit, or, Commemorative Notices of Distinguished American Clergymen of Various Denominations: From the Early Settlement of the Country to the Close of the Year Eighteen Hundred and Fifty-Five with Historical Introductions* (New York, 1857), 2:216–21.

In his first published anti-Jacobin sermon, Elijah Parish pictured France as a monster who degraded the language of freedom. "What a contrast" American "civil and religious freedom" posed to "the Hag of France, named Liberty and Equality," Parish preached. "She tyrannizes over the souls and bodies of men, punishes without form of a trial, persecutes religion, tramples on all law; she gorges four million of her own children and cries 'Give, Give;' she tears out the vitals of her enemy, and with malice more restrained spreads moral death among her friends." Parish argued, like his fellow conservatives, that the Jacobins' attack on law had led to terrible bloodshed. His faithful congregants learned to envisage French liberties and rights as a terrifying ghoul, not a comely sister.[82]

Alexander Hamilton described the distinction between French democracy and American liberty in a May 1793 letter written for publication. After decrying the joyful welcome that Citizen Genet had received in Philadelphia, Hamilton implored Americans to resist being "actuated by the *same spirit* which has for some time past fatally misguided the measures of those who conduct the affairs of France and sullied a cause once glorious and that might have been triumphant." The spirit of French democracy was violent and anarchic; it lacked the "same humanity, the same decorum, the same gravity, the same order, the same dignity, the same solemnity" as American liberty. There could be no confusion between true liberty and French revolutionary principles. "I own, I do not like the comparison," Hamilton wrote. "When I contemplate the systematic massacres of the 2d. & 3rd of September – When I observe that a Marat and a Robertspierre [*sic*], the notorious prompters of those bloody scenes – sit triumphantly in the Convention... When I perceive passion tumult and violence usurping those seats, where reason and cool deliberation ought to preside... I regret whatever has a tendency to confound them."[83] Hamilton saw nothing incidental about the violence of the September Massacres; they were systematic efforts to destroy civil society. Americans who drew direct connections between their own revolution and its Jacobin successor exposed the nation to grave danger.

The prominent role that heroes of the American Revolution, including the Marquis de Lafayette and Thomas Paine, played in the early stages of the French Revolution, contributed to the sense of overlap between the events. Lafayette's leadership in French revolutionary politics from 1787 until 1792 and Paine's service in the National Convention in 1792, seemed to show that American ideas had been transported to Europe by the heroes of 1776 and were now inspiring millions to demand their freedom. America was fulfilling its visionary role as a city on a hill. But anti-Jacobins responded that French heroes of the American struggle for independence were being betrayed by the new Revolution. By spring 1793, many American heroes,

[82] Elijah Parish, *An Oration Delivered at Byfield July 4, 1799* (Newburyport, Mass., 1799), 6.
[83] Hamilton, *Papers*, 14: 475–6.

including Lafayette and Paine, had been imprisoned or exiled from France. King Louis XVI, once celebrated for his generous support of the War of Independence, was executed by guillotine. When Federalists and Calvinists mourned the loss of the king, Republican partisans accused them of being monarchists.

While anti-Jacobins sought to sever the connection between American freedom and French freedom, and between the American Revolution and the French Revolution, they highlighted the similarities between French democrats and American democrats. American souls "were sickened" at the debasement of liberty in the French Revolution, argued the Federalist lawyer Elisha Lee at his July 4, 1793, oration in Lenox, Massachusetts. He continued: "the flame of Liberty, which in America was mild and benign, in France has become a Volcano of fire." However, if the meaning of liberty in the two nations differed sharply, the violent proclivities of each nation's democrats were all too similar. Lee beseeched his audience to disregard the slanders upon the federal administration made by democratic political opponents hungry for power. Their patriotic words and allusions to French liberty, he advised, concealed "a poignard" with which they intended to "stab" America "to her heart."[84] American democrats, like their French idols, were votaries of violence.

Violence both differentiated the revolutions and threatened to unite them. Every grateful remark contrasting American freedom and French freedom suggested the danger that blood would wash away the differences. Far from a rhetorical flourish to consolidate American views against the Revolution, violence was central to the anti-Jacobin assault. In January 1793, the Federalist organ the *Gazette of the United States* used violent imagery to draw a sharp distinction for its readers between the two revolutions:

In America no barbarities were perpetrated – no men's heads were struck upon poles – no ladies bodies mangled, were carried thro' the streets in triumph – their prisoners guarded and ironed, were not massacred in cold blood. The Americans did not, at discretion, harass, murder, or plunder the clergy – not roast their generals unjustly alive. – They set limit to their vices, at which their pursuits rested. And whatever blood was shed, flowed gallantly in the field. The American Revolution, it ought to be repeated, was not accomplished as the French has been, by massacres, assassinations, or proscriptions: battles, severe and honorable, were fought, and the chance of war left to decide.[85]

[84] Elisha Lee, *An Oration Delivered at Lenox, the 4th July, 1793, the Anniversary of American Independence* (Stockbridge, Mass., 1793), 7, 12–15.

[85] *Gazette of the United States*, Jan. 16, 1793. See also Joseph Dana, *A Sermon, Delivered February 19, 1795: Being a Day of General Thanksgiving, Throughout the United States of America* (Newburyport, Mass., 1795), 15; Thomas Fessenden, *A Sermon, Preached in Walpole, on Thursday, February 19, 1795: The Day Appointed by the President of the United States for a Publick Thanksgiving* (Walpole, N.H., 1795), 7; Ashbel Green, *A Sermon, Delivered in the Second Presbyterian Church in the City of Philadelphia: On the 19th of*

As the current of reaction grew stronger, American anti-Jacobins denounced French violence in increasingly graphic terms. Imagery of bloodshed appeared in almost every antirevolutionary text written in the late eighteenth and early nineteenth centuries; the words *blood, bloody, bloodthirsty,* and *bloodshed* recurred incessantly. The imagery drew on a long history of English rhetoric that used blood as a symbol for illegitimate force or cruelty.[86] Anti-Jacobin authors frequently pictured blood as flowing uncontrollably, suggesting that the violence it symbolized, once unleashed, could not be contained. Violence would engulf any political system that released its destructive capabilities. Numerous ministers and orators described France as flooded by "torrents of blood."[87] Others referred to "brooks of human blood" or "rivers of blood."[88] The events in France were described as "scenes of blood" or "bloody scenes."[89] For variety, anti-Jacobins frequently referred to the revolution as "sanguinary."[90] Another phrase repeated in numerous sources that condemn the Terror is "garments rolled in blood" (Isaiah 9:5); this image is used to describe the horrors of war and calls to mind a battlefield so imbrued in blood that its victims are literally wallowing in gore.[91]

American anti-Jacobins frequently pictured France, like the battlefield in Isaiah, as a landscape of death. In this symbolic system, violence dominated all other possible understandings of the Revolution; the imagery of holocaust

February, 1795. Being the Day of General Thanksgiving Throughout the United States (Philadelphia, Pa., 1795), 26; John Lowell, *An Oration, Pronounced July 4, 1799, at the Request of the Inhabitants of the Town of Boston in Commemoration of the Anniversary of American Independence* (Boston, Mass., 1799), 20.

[86] Philippe Rosenberg, "The Moral Order of Violence: The Meanings of Cruelty in Early Modern England, 1648–1685" (Ph.D., Duke University, 1999), chap. 3.

[87] Freeman, *Sermon . . . 1798*; Kendal, *A Sermon . . . 1795*, 11; Linn, *Discourse*; David Tappan, *Christian Thankfulness Explained and Enforced: A Sermon, Delivered at Charlestown, in the Afternoon of February 19, 1795. The Day of General Thanksgiving through the United States* (Boston, Mass., 1795), 27.

[88] Timothy Dwight, *The Duty of Americans at the Present Crisis: Illustrated in a Discourse, Preached on the Fourth of July, 1798* (New Haven, Conn., 1798); David Osgood, *The Devil Let Loose, or the Wo Occasioned to the Inhabitants of the Earth by His Wrathful Appearance among Them Illustrated in a Discourse Delivered on the Day of the National Fast, April 25, 1799* (Boston, Mass., 1799).

[89] "State of French Politicks," *Impartial Herald*, Jan. 13, 1795; "Letter of General Dumourier," *Columbian Centinel*, May 15, 1793; "New-York," *Commercial Advertiser*, Oct. 9, 1797.

[90] *An Impartial History of the Late Revolution in France, from Its Commencement to the Death of the Queen, and the Execution of the Deputies of the Gironde Party* (Philadelphia, Pa., 1794), 1:79.

[91] See, among many examples, Thomas Cushing Thacher, *A Sermon. Preached at Lynn, November 20th, 1794: Being the Day Appointed for the Annual Thanksgiving* (Boston, Mass., 1794); Ezra Sampson, *A Discourse Delivered February 19, 1795: Being the Day of National Thanksgiving* (Boston, Mass., 1795); John Andrews, *A Sermon, Delivered February 19, 1795: Being a Day of Public Thanksgiving, Throughout the United States of America* (Newburyport, Mass., 1795), 9.

denied any power to the Revolution's promise of a utopian future. In his July 4, 1793, oration, John Quincy Adams blamed France for transforming Europe into a "corpse-covered field"; the French had "poured the torrent of destruction over the fair harvests of European fertility; which have unbound the pinions of desolation, and sent her forth to scatter pestilence and death among the nations."[92] Nothing could grow from this wasted countryside. As successive French governments entangled the nation in a series of wars that extended until the close of the Napoleonic era, the imagery of a land blighted by death recurred frequently. In 1799, a Federalist artillery captain, Amos Stoddard, described France as "*a forest of bayonets;*" her countryside, "instead of flowers and the blossoms of vegetation, is covered with the bones of immolated citizens."[93]

France's fatal blight threatened to overspread its neighbors, and to poison even the faraway bounty of the United States. The Revolution's violence had spread pestilence over all of Europe; France's destructive ambitions knew no boundaries. A series of millennialist texts published at the end of the 1790s, when hostilities between the United States and France erupted into a Quasi-War, identified France with Assyria, the terrifying empire of destruction in Isaiah. Jedidiah Morse, as well as David Osgood, Abiel Holmes, and David Tappan, who were France's fiercest clerical opponents during the early 1790s, all compared France with Assyria in their 1798 Fast Day sermons.[94]

[92] John Quincy Adams, *An Oration, Pronounced July 4th, 1793: At the Request of the Inhabitants of the Town of Boston, in Commemoration of the Anniversary of American Independence* (Boston, Mass., 1793), 19–20.

[93] Amos Stoddard, *An Oration, Delivered before the Citizens of Portland, and the Supreme Judicial Court of the Commonwealth of Massachusetts, on the Fourth Day of July, 1799 Being the Anniversary of American Independence* (Portland, Me., 1799). See also Dwight, *Travels*, 4:268; John M. Mason, *Mercy Remembered in Wrath: A Sermon, the Substance of Which Was Preached on the 19th of February, 1795, Observed throughout the United States as a Day of Thanksgiving and Prayer* (New York, 1795), 15; Samuel Miller, *A Sermon, Delivered May 9, 1798 Recommended, by the President of the United States, to Be Observed as a Day of General Humiliation, Fasting, and Prayer* (New York, 1798), 26. The "Ode for Independence, 1793," published in *Massachusetts Magazine*, July 1794, described revolutionary France as "Death's vast empire."

[94] Abiel Holmes, *A Sermon Preached at Brattle-Street Church, in Boston, and at Cambridge, April 25, 1799, the Day Appointed by the President of the United States for a National Fast* (Boston, Mass., 1799); Jedidiah Morse, *A Sermon, Delivered at the New North Church in Boston, in the Morning, and in the Afternoon at Charlestown, May 9th, 1798, Being the Day Recommended by John Adams, President of the United States of America, for Solemn Humiliation, Fasting and Prayer* (Boston, Mass., 1798); David Osgood, *Some Facts Evincive of the Atheistical, Anarchical, and in Other Respects, Immoral Principles of the French Republicans Stated in a Sermon Delivered on the 9th of May, 1798, the Day Recommended by the President of the United States for Solemn Humiliation, Fasting, and Prayer* (Boston, Mass., 1798); David Tappan, *A Discourse, Delivered to the Religious Society in Brattle-Street, Boston, and to the Christian Congregation in Charlestown, on April 5, 1798. Being the Day of the Annual Fast in the Commonwealth of Massachusetts*, 2nd ed. (Boston, Mass., 1798). Also, Ezra Weld, *A Discourse, Delivered April 25, 1799 Being the Day of Fasting and Prayer Throughout the United States of America* (Boston, Mass., 1799).

Elijah Parish reiterated this theme in an unpublished November 1798 sermon (probably preached at Thanksgiving), as many orthodox ministers likely did.[95] Revolutionary France, like ancient Assyria, is described in the sermons as both "the rod" of God's anger – a nation whose bloody appetite for destruction God unleashes upon his enemies – and alternatively as the site of God's anger, a nation terribly punished for its wanton bloodshed. As Assyria, France signified a land of totalizing violence.

Critics also characterized France as a bloody and grotesque monster. Robert Treat Paine's popular song from 1798, "Adams and Liberty," described France as a beast whose "huge limbs bathe recumbent in blood."[96] Many antirevolutionary texts depicted France as a ferocious and blood-thirsty carnivore. A song included in a primarily nonpolitical book of sea chanteys, published in 1800, versified France as a bear that wished to crush the United States in its paws. Though "gorg'd to the full," the bear was "not yet sated with blood" and still howled for more food.[97] William Cobbett, an English expatriate who lived in the United States from 1792 to 1800, called the French bloodthirsty dogs.[98] Anti-Jacobins denounced France as a tiger or a wolf.[99] Other critics emphasized the humanness of revolutionary depravity, calling the French cannibals – human ghouls who devoured their own kind. William Cobbett translated a German book, entitled *The Cannibals' Progress*, which chronicled the French Republican atrocities committed during the invasion of the German states and attracted an enormous readership in the United States, running through ten editions and appearing excerpted in popular periodicals, including the *Philadelphia Monthly Magazine*.[100]

---

[95] Elijah Parish, "The King of Assyria," November 1798, EPP.

[96] Paine, *Works*, 245.

[97] *The Festival of Mirth, and American Tar's Delight: A Fund of the Newest Humorous, Patriotic, Hunting, and Sea Songs. With a Variety of Curious Jests, Bon Mots, Entertaining and Witty Anecdotes, &c.* (New York, 1800).

[98] William Cobbett, *Porcupine's Works; Containing Various Writings and Selections, Exhibiting a Faithful Picture of the United States of America; of Their Governments, Laws, Politics, and Resources; of the Characters of Their Presidents, Governors, Legislators, Magistrates, and Military Men; and of the Customs, Manners, Morals, Religion, Virtues and Vices of the People: Comprising Also a Complete Series of Historical Documents and Remarks, from the End of the War, in 1783, to the Election of the President, in March, 1801* (London, 1801), 1:167.

[99] *Columbian Centinel*, Mar. 4, 1795.

[100] William Cobbett and Anthony Aufrere, *The Cannibals' Progress; or the Dreadful Horrors of French Invasion as Displayed by the Republican Officers and Soldiers, in Their Perfidy, Rapacity, Ferociousness, and Brutality, Exercised Towards the Innocent Inhabitants of Germany* (New London, Conn., 1798). For more examples of the French depicted as cannibals, see Theodore Dwight, *An Oration, Spoken at Hartford, in the State of Connecticut, on the Anniversary of American Independence, July 4th, 1798* (Hartford, Conn., 1798); Francis d'Ivernois, *Authentic History of the Origin and Progress of the Late Revolution in Geneva* (Philadelphia, Pa., 1794), 17; Lowell, *Oration... 1799*, 22; Stoddard, *Oration... 1799*, 17; Cobbett, *Porcupine's Works*, 1:164, 2:21.

Clerical opponents frequently used millennialist symbolism to attack the violence of the Revolution, describing France as the terrifying beast prophesied by Daniel.[101] The French were devils or antichrists.[102] David Osgood called the Jacobins "so many infernals, broken loose from their chains in the pit below"; the Reverend Enos Hitchcock cried out against the "sanguinary demon" who had raised its "bloody standard" over France.[103] The *Christian's Monitor* named France a "pandemonium of devils"; others simply called it hell.[104] Released from the moderating controls of Christian morality, American clerics warned, man had no reason to restrain his most vicious and bestial passions. Man's depravity, left uncorrected, could only result in the most horrifying brutality. The reign of infidelity would lead to the coming of the Last Days, when the world would fill with violence.[105] For American Calvinists, the terrible violence of the Revolution was a natural and expected consequence of infidelity.

What most frightened American anti-Jacobins about the French Revolution was how swiftly the French people had degenerated into beasts and demons. The French had occupied the pinnacle of civilization prior to the Revolution, reaching literary, artistic, and scholarly heights that were the envy of all other nations. The suddenness of France's descent into anarchic violence forewarned an equal or worse fate overhanging any less accomplished people foolish enough to embrace the same disorganizing principles. "Is it not astonishing how so great a change in the morals and manners of a nation could be so suddenly effected?" David Osgood questioned congregants at his 1794 Thanksgiving sermon. How had France degenerated so precipitately from refinement to barbarity?[106] Conservative leaders explained this transformation as an "uncivilizing" process.[107] By dissolving the constraints of law and religion, the Revolution demoralized and uncivilized the French people. The denigration of Christianity and the repudiation of deference to secular or religious authorities caused the French people to cease obeying the moral injunctions that restrained men's violence. Political demagogues and ambitious men easily manipulated the brutalized people into

---

[101] Lemuel Hopkins, *Guillotina, for the Year 1799. Addressed to the Readers of the Connecticut Courant,* 1 sheet ([1] p.) vols. (Hartford, Conn., 1798); Jeremy Belknap, *A Sermon, Delivered on the 9th of May, 1798, the Day of the National Fast, Recommended by the President of the United States* (Boston, Mass., 1798).

[102] *Christian's Monitor,* May 25, 1799.

[103] Osgood, *Some Facts Evincive,* 11; Hitchcock, *An Oration... 1793,* 16.

[104] "The Religionist and Politician, No. 1," May 25, 1799, *Christian's Monitor;* Dwight, *Travels,* 4:267.

[105] Miller, *A Sermon, Delivered May 9, 1798 Recommended, by the President of the United States, to Be Observed as a Day of General Humiliation, Fasting, and Prayer.*

[106] Osgood, *Wonderful Works of God,* 23. William Cobbett made the similar claim that the French Revolution "changed the airy French into a set of the most ferocious inhuman bloodhounds." Cobbett, *Porcupine's Works,* 167.

[107] See below the use of the term *uncivilizing* in Freeman, *Sermon... 1798.*

committing acts of violence against political opponents and other unlucky victims. The republic fell prey to warring factions and civil war. In the setting of total war all moral authority crumbled and the French people reverted to the depraved condition of unredeemed humanity.[108]

Noah Webster, the educator and architect of Federalist political theory, viewed the French Revolution as a terrifying object lesson in how bloodshed could destroy civil society. Like most Americans, Webster initially praised the Revolution; however, news of the Revolution's increasing violence (and a nasty run-in with Citizen Genet at a roadside tavern) reformed the educator's opinion. In 1794, "during the heat of revolution, when [he] was frequently receiving fresh accounts of the ferocities of the violent reformers, exhibiting the appalling effects of popular factions," Webster began to write a series of anti-Jacobin essays published initially in his journal, *American Minerva*, and then reprinted in pamphlet form. Webster's essays argued that the French Revolution was the "most extraordinary experiment in government, to ascertain whether nations can exist in peace, order and harmony, without any such restraints." The results were a spectacular failure. Without the constraints of hierarchy, religion, and law, the people surrendered to their own "malignant passions" and "implacable fury." Webster conceptualized the uncivilizing process as a self-perpetuating dynamic. The demoralization of the populace enabled the political bloodshed in France, which then "accustomed great bodies of people to scenes of cruelty." Through the exercise of violence, the French lost any vestiges of civilized repugnance to bloodshed and became savages. Webster believed that the French people would be so ferocious for years to come that no government could hope to gain control there without oppression and force.[109]

Many anti-Jacobin leaders adopted Webster's notion of an uncivilizing process. The Federalist politician Oliver Wolcott Jr. wrote to Webster in May 1794 praising his pamphlet on the Revolution. If the French succeeded in their wars with other nations, Wolcott concurred, all European peoples would "revert to barbarism." The destruction, he continued, would be "signal and complete," causing Europe to lose completely the refinements that once adorned its civilization.[110] Four years later, the Reverend Jonathan Freeman sounded a very similar note: "The revolution in France, I think,

---

[108] The Reverend John Mason blamed war for nurturing man's violence and driving him "in a retrograde motion, back towards barbarism"; Mason, *Mercy Remembered in Wrath*, 20. The Reverend Samuel Kendall described how internal faction and external threat conspired to brutalize the French people and produce "horrid scenes" of "popular fury"; Kendal, *A Sermon... 1795*, 10–18. The Reverend John Andrews delineated the continuum from personal hatred to party conflict to civil war; Andrews, *A Sermon*, 7.

[109] Noah Webster, *The Revolution in France, Considered in Respect to Its Progress and Effects* (New York, 1794), 19–20; Noah Webster, *A Collection of Papers on Political, Literary and Moral Subjects* (New York, 1843).

[110] Gibbs and Wolcott, *Memoirs of the Administrations*, 1:136.

is the first *great step* towards uncivilizing Europe. Half of the nation are already barbarians."[111] In late-eighteenth-century thinking, the opposition between civilized and savage was not fixed into an unbridgeable racial dichotomy. Savagery and civilization were mutable conditions, dependent on circumstances of religion and law. And the accomplishments of nations, no matter how hoary or long established, were ever in danger of reversal. Even cannibalism, which many nineteenth-century racial thinkers identified as the archetypal savage behavior committed by nonwhites, was seen by seventeenth- and eighteenth-century writers as a learned behavior to which Europeans or Americans could sink.[112]

American anti-Jacobins feared the potential that French-style democracy had to uncivilize the United States and plunge it into murderous violence. Conservatives frequently noted how recently the "many-headed monster" of the Confederation government had caused America to "totter on the brink of the most dreadful convulsions."[113] The United States had only just ascended from terrible "scenes of horror and devastation."[114] It seemed a terrifying possibility that the French Revolution could push the United States back over the brink by inspiring attacks on hierarchy that would disorganize society to the point of bloodshed.[115] The American republic relied on the self-control of its citizens to restrain political disorder; there was no monarch or aristocracy to swiftly enforce the peaceful obedience of the people. If the spirit of radical democracy undermined the self-control of Americans, then domestic political conflicts could not be safeguarded from accelerating into faction and civil war. Soon the same spirit of bloody anarchy that had seized the French would overtake Americans. Witnesses and participants to acts of political warfare would become brutalized, blood would spill without constraint, and no one young or old would be safe from violence. Radicalism would uncivilize America, a nation that prized itself as an asylum of peace and prosperity, as surely as Jacobinism had uncivilized the refined French. Radical democracy threatened to turn Americans into savages.[116]

[111] Freeman, *Sermon... 1798.*

[112] Rosenberg, "Moral Order of Violence," 266.

[113] Osgood, *Wonderful Works of God,* 18.

[114] Parker, *A Sermon... 1793,* 28. See also references to the recent and horrifying bloodshed of the American Revolution in Samuel Spring, *A Discourse Delivered at the North Church in Newburyport, November 7th, 1793: Being the Day Appointed for a General Thanksgiving, by the Authority of Massachusetts* (Newburyport, Mass., 1794); Thacher, *A Sermon... 1794;* Tappan, *Christian Thankfulness.*

[115] The decline of deference is treated authoritatively in Gordon S. Wood, *The Radicalism of the American Revolution* (New York, 1993); Joyce Oldham Appleby, *Capitalism and a New Social Order: The Republican Vision of the 1790s* (New York, 1984); Sharp, *American Politics;* Elkins and McKitrick, *Age of Federalism.*

[116] Paine, *Works,* 326.

Noah Webster warned readers in 1794 that the rise of democratic political dissent in the United States, if agitated for a couple of more years by the crisis in Europe, would bring America to "open hostility and bloodshed." John Barent Johnson advised his listeners at an oration to the Tammany Society that the lack of political union would transform the United States from "the beauty of the whole earth" to a "scene of oppression, of slavery, of blood!" Fisher Ames wrote in May 1794 that American democrats hoped to kindle popular passions into fury, and if they managed to instigate a war "a moderate or honest man could be stigmatized, mobbed, declared a suspected person, guillotined, and his property might be taken for public purposes. France might see her bloody exploits rivaled by her pupil, emulous of her glory." *Massachusetts Magazine* warned its readers that American democrats, if given the chance, would kill their Federalist opponents, just as the Jacobins had assassinated their political rivals, the Girondins. At heart, American democrats were no different than the French "monsters," who waded "to eminence through the blood of innocent victims."[117]

The execution of Robespierre in late July 1794 and the disbanding of his Committee for Public Safety in 1795 did little to quiet anti-Jacobin fears in the United States. After the fall of the Jacobins, the new Directory government in France released graphic exposés of the Reign of Terror that flooded the American press.[118] European accounts of the Revolution – many written by survivors or political opponents who spared no words in their indictments of Jacobin violence – were published in the United States from the beginning of the decade; but the narratives became more grotesque after the fall of Robespierre.[119] Continuing news of violent disorder in Great Britain, the Caribbean, and Continental Europe, seemed to confirm American anti-Jacobins' fear that the decapitation of Robespierre still left many heads on

---

[117] Webster, *Revolution in France*, 32; John Barent Johnson, *An Oration on Union, Delivered in the New Dutch Church in the City of New-York, on the Twelfth of May, 1794. The Anniversary of the Tammany Society, or Columbian Order* (New York, 1794), 15. Ames, *Works of Fisher Ames*, 144. *Massachusetts Magazine*, Dec. 1795. See also Daniel Davis, *An Oration Delivered at Portland, July 4th, 1796. In Commemoration of the Anniversary of American Independence* (Portland, Me., 1796).

[118] Joseph Zizek, "'Plume De Fer': Louis-Marie Prudhomme Writes the French Revolution," *French Historical Studies* 26 (Fall 2003).

[119] See, for example, Assemblée Nationale Législative, *Impeachment of Mr. La Fayette Containing His Accusation, (Stated in the Report of the Extraordinary Commission to the National Assembly, on the 8th of August, 1792) Supported by Mr. Brissot of Warville; and His Defence by Mr. Vaublanc: With a Supplement, Containing the Letters, and Other Authentic Pieces Relative Thereto*, trans. William Cobbett (Philadelphia, Pa., 1793); J. P. Brissot de Warville, *J. P. Brissot, Deputy of Eure and Loire, to His Constituents on the Situation of the National Convention; on the Influence of the Anarchists, and the Evils It Has Caused; and on the Necessity of Annihilating That Influence in Order to Save the Republic* (New York, 1794); d'Ivernois, *Authentic History*.

the Jacobin hydra.[120] In the United States, the production of anti-Jacobin literature intensified, agitating readers with new information. The American anti-Jacobin campaign of the post-Jacobin era did not weaken; it gathered strength. New publications repeatedly warned American readers that the uncivilizing process would descend on them.

The Siege of Lyons (1795), an American edition of a British-translated French text, described the Jacobin suppression of resistance in the city of Lyons and viciously attacked Americans who defended the Revolution by quoting damningly from native democrats such as Benjamin Franklin Bache, as well as from the radical British exiles living in the United States.[121] Many more anti-Jacobin texts hit the bookstores in 1796 and 1797. A translation of Honoré Riouffe's *Memoires* described the author's imprisonment in the prisons of Paris during the reign of Robespierre and painted the Jacobins as "cannibals," "wolves," and "tygers" who relished in savagery (one held up a piece of meat and "devoured it raw, declaring *'that in the same manner he would eat the flesh of his enemies'*"). Riouffe's American printer warned readers that the violence in France could easily happen in the United States. "Any American supporter of Robespierre is dangerous," the introduction argued, "for if they come to power in the United States they would practice the same abuses."[122] The printer envisaged the French Revolution as an uncivilizing process that threatened every citizen of the Atlantic.

William Playfair, a Scottish writer and adventurer, made the same argument in his 1796 *History of Jacobinism*. Reprinted in the United States by William Cobbett, Playfair's *History* first described the actions of the Jacobin club during the Reign of Terror, then noted that in the United States "rebellion actually broke out" at the instigation of Jacobin clubs (the Democratic Societies).[123] The Jacobins were leading Americans down the same path of bloodshed they had carved in France. Cobbett extended Playfair's attack on American Jacobins in an appendix to the *History*, eloquently encapsulating

---

[120] See John Adams's remarks to Abigail Adams that, though Robespierre was gone, "he may however have a hydra head"; letter from John Adams to Abigail Adams, Apr. 11, 1794 (electronic edition), *Adams Family Papers: An Electronic Archive*, MHS, http://www.masshist.org/digitaladams/.

[121] *The Siege of Lyons (During the Dictatorship of Robespierre)* (Stockbridge, Mass., 1795), 15–22. The French text is Paul Émilien Béraud, *Relation du siege de Lyon, contenant le détail de ce qui s'y sous les yeux des représentans du peuple français* (London, 1794). The British text is Paul Émilien Béraud, *Narrative of the Events of the Siege of Lyons: Translated from the French* (Perth, UK, 1794).

[122] Honore Riouffe, *Revolutionary Justice Displayed; or an Inside View of the Various Prisons of Paris, under the Government of Robespierre and the Jacobins. Taken Principally from the Journals of the Prisoners Themselves*, trans. from the French (Philadelphia, Pa., 1796), 78, 24, iv.

[123] William Playfair, *The History of Jacobinism, Its Crimes, Cruelties and Perfidies... With an Appendix, by Peter Porcupine, Containing a History of the American Jacobins, Commonly Denominated Democrats* (Philadelphia, Pa., 1796).

the uncivilizing process when he stated that Democratic Societies were "familiarizing [Americans] to insurrection and blood."[124] In 1796 Cobbett's anti-Jacobin masterpiece, *The Bloody Buoy*, warned readers against dismissing the danger posed by domestic Jacobinism:

Shall we say that these things never can take place among us? Because we have hitherto preserved the character of a pacific and humane people, shall we set danger at defiance? Though we are not Frenchmen, we are men as well as they, and consequently are liable to be misled, and even to sink to the lowest degree of brutality as they have been.... And what would the reader say, were I to tell him of a member of Congress, who wished to see one of those murderous machines, employed for lopping off the heads of the French, permanent in the State-House yard of the City of Philadelphia? If these men of blood had succeeded in plunging us into a war; if they had once got the sword into their hands, they would have mowed us down like stubble."[125]

The American fear of domestic Jacobinism reached its apogee in 1798–9 when diplomatic conflicts between the United States and the French republic culminated in a naval quasi war, while thousands of United Irishmen – a French-allied nationalist movement – were fleeing to the United States to escape British repression following a failed rebellion.[126] After arriving in the United States, many escaped radicals (such as James Reynolds and William Duane) sustained their political radicalism, praising French democracy, forming Democratic Societies, and editing democratic newspapers. In Congress, in print, and in popular meetings, American, British, and Irish democrats harassed the Federalists with accusations of warmongering against the French republic. If these discontents got their way, a professor at Brown (then Rhode Island College) warned his graduating seniors, "It is reasonable to fear that 'the reign of terror and blood' would soon bound across the Atlantic, and devastate our peace."[127] The Federalists felt assaulted by Jacobins abroad and at home; they feared that the United States stood in danger of imminent conflagration.

Anti-Jacobins responded to the heightened threat with both popular and political measures. Ordinary citizens sent hundreds of petitions to President Adams expressing their opposition to the French Revolution. They also

---

[124] Playfair, *History of Jacobinism*, appendix p. 26.
[125] William Cobbett, *The Bloody Buoy: Thrown out as a Warning to the Political Pilots of All Nations: Or a Faithful Relation of a Multitude of Acts of Horrid Barbarity, Such as the Eye Never Witnessed, the Tongue Never Expressed, or the Imagination Conceived, until the Commencement of the French Revolution* (Philadelphia, Pa., 1796), 236–9.
[126] Wilson, *United Irishmen*; Twomey, "Jacobins and Jeffersonians"; Durey, *Transatlantic Radicals*.
[127] Asa Messer, *A Discourse, Delivered in the Chapel of Rhode-Island College, to the Senior Class, on the Sunday Preceding Their Commencement, 1799* (Providence, R.I., 1799).

embraced populist symbolic measures, including wearing the black cockade (a traditional Federalist adornment) and singing Federalist songs.[128] To strengthen the anti-Jacobin reaction, the Federalist-dominated Congress passed the infamous Alien and Sedition Acts, four laws designed to restrict the freedoms of presumably radical immigrants and to curb criticism of the Federalist government.[129] Last, anti-Jacobins developed a new line of attack in their anti-Jacobin literature.[130] The well-connected American democratic playwright William Dunlap wrote in his diary in November 1797 that at a dinner with the orthodox minister Jedidiah Morse (a writing collaborator of Elijah Parish), the clergyman read aloud to him letters from the 1780s that revealed France's long-standing ill designs on the United States.[131] Dunlap scoffed. But soon Morse had worse evidence of French evil to draw upon.

From Europe came two new books alleging the existence of a transatlantic conspiracy by Masonic Illuminati that had caused the French Revolution and that aimed to use Jacobin societies to destroy religion and social order throughout the Christian world. Republished in the United States in 1798, the respected Scottish academic John Robison's *Proofs of a Conspiracy against all the Religions and Governments of Europe* and the French Jesuit Abbé Barruel's *Memoirs Illustrating the History of Jacobinism* seemed to credit suspicions that a Jacobin plot existed to overthrow government and order in the United States. The conspiracy dated to the 1770s and involved such revolutionary luminaries as Mirabeau and Talleyrand, as well as the Enlightenment philosophes Voltaire, D'Alembert, and Diderot. Barruel's *Memoirs* even ended with a warning to the United States that it stood as a particular target of Jacobin conspiracy. Robison and Barruel persuaded American anti-Jacobins that an evil intelligence was at work to

---

[128] Thomas M. Ray, "'Not One Cent for Tribute': The Public Addresses and American Popular Reaction to the XYZ Affair, 1798–1799," *Journal of the Early Republic* 3 (Winter 1983).

[129] Joanne B. Freeman, "Explaining the Unexplainable: The Cultural Context of the Sedition Act," in *The Democratic Experiment: New Directions in American Political History*, ed. Meg Jacobs, William J. Novak, and Julian E. Zelizer (Princeton, N.J., 2003); Churchill, "Popular Nullification"; James Morton Smith, *Freedom's Fetters: The Alien and Sedition Laws and American Civil Liberties*, Cornell Studies in Civil Liberty (Ithaca, N.Y., 1956).

[130] Seth Cotlar, "The Federalists' Transatlantic Cultural Offensive of 1798 and the Moderation of American Democratic Discourse," in *Beyond the Founders: New Approaches to the Political History of the Early American Republic*, ed. David Waldstreicher, Andrew W. Robertson, and Jeffrey L. Pasley (Chapel Hill, N.C., 2004), 295. Cotlar dates American anti-Jacobinism to 1798 and views it as cynically timed, but the literature of 1798–9 is ethically consistent with earlier anti-Jacobinism.

[131] William Dunlap, *Diary of William Dunlap, 1766–1839; the Memoirs of a Dramatist, Theatrical Manager, Painter, Critic, Novelist, and Historian*, reissued ed., 3 vols., Collections of the New York Historical Society for the Year 1929–31, The John Watts Depeyster Publication Fund Series, 62–4 (New York, 1969), 176.

undermine American religion, order, and liberty and to reduce the nation to bloodshed.[132] During 1798 and 1799, while the nation engaged in a quasi war with France, fears of the Illuminati racked conservative minds and filled their sermons and orations.

Jedidiah Morse led the assault, first publicly attacking the Illuminati in his May 1798 Fast sermon. Many other published sermons from the 1798 Fast attacked French infidelity without making explicit references to Robison, Barruel, or the Illuminati. But the popularity of Morse's sermon among buyers may have persuaded other ministers and politicians to address the conspiracy more explicitly. By midsummer, references to the Illuminati abounded. Two of the most frightening disquisitions were made by Timothy Dwight and his brother Theodore Dwight; Elijah Parish sounded the same themes. The clamor extended into 1799, following Morse's lengthy 1798 Thanksgiving sermon, which was replete with proof of the terrible plot. Morse warned his listeners of the Illuminati's designs to instigate massacres in the United States: "France wants only a *point d'appui* upon the border, or within the United States, to make a *fourth of September* at Philadelphia."[133] The September Massacres continued to serve as a reference point for the onset of horror.

The Illuminati conspiracy frightened Federalists and Calvinists because it promised to transform American beliefs and enable the anarchists to achieve their goal of world chaos. Anti-Jacobins believed that America's strong belief in God had protected the nation, until then, from being destroyed by the disorganizing principles of French Revolutionary thought. However, the popularity of deistic texts, such as Thomas Paine's *Age of Reason* during the 1790s, seemed to undermine the strongest bulwark of social order. Christianity, insisted anti-Jacobins at every public occasion, was the foundation of American stability. If infidelity hewed that great oak, then all of the terrible enormities witnessed in France would be reproduced at home. Skepticism of religion, argued David Tappan, one of the first clerical critics of the French Revolution, "opens the floodgates to every brutal excess."[134]

---

[132] Michael Lienesch, "The Illusion of the Illuminati: The Counterconspiratorial Origins of Post-Revolutionary Conservatism," in *Revolutionary Histories: Transatlantic Cultural Nationalism, 1775–1815*, ed. W. M. Verhoeven, Romanticism in Perspective (New York, 2002); Joseph W. Phillips, *Jedidiah Morse and New England Congregationalism* (New Brunswick, N.J., 1983), chap. 3; Henry Farnham May, *The Enlightenment in America* (New York, 1976); Vernon Stauffer, *New England and the Bavarian Illuminati*, vol. 82, no. 1, Columbia University, Studies in History, Economic, and Public Law (New York, 1918).

[133] Dwight, *The Duty of Americans at the Present Crisis: Illustrated in a Discourse, Preached on the Fourth of July, 1798*, Dwight, *Oration . . . 1798*, Morse, *Sermon . . . November 29, 1798*, Morse, *Sermon . . . May 9th, 1798*; Jedidiah Morse, *A Sermon, Exhibiting the Present Dangers, and Consequent Duties of the Citizens of the United States of America. Delivered at Charlestown, April 25, 1799, the Day of the National Fast* (New York, 1799).

[134] Tappan, *Discourse . . . April 5, 1798*, 8.

The French philosophy that threatened to beguile Americans had "monstrous" and "abortive" implications. Tappan warned the graduating class of June 1798 not to be seduced by the "wrong and dangerous opinions" that the Illuminati were circulating in America. Disbelief in God would brutalize them and destroy American social order. "Behold France," Tappan instructed America's next leaders, "converted...into one great theatre...[of] unspeakable degradation and misery."[135] Who doubted that America could undergo a similar conversion?

The Illuminati crisis influenced even many who had previously held their tongues to speak out in alarm about the potential for bloodshed in America. The Reverend William Linn, an early supporter of the Revolution, apologized in his 1798 Fast Day sermon for ever having tried to "palliate" French crimes. He kept silent too long, he confessed, but now the film was lifted from his eyes: "I will be no advocate for enormities unequalled in the annals of mankind, for principles which subvert all religion, morality and order, and which threaten to involve us, with the whole human race, in the utmost confusion and misery." Democratic and atheistic principles had a "monstrous" effect on France, forcing revolution after revolution, causing "torrents of blood [to] flow after torrents," and transforming the people into "a terror to themselves and all around them." Robison's book, Linn warned, proved that America was not as far from France's "scene of blood" as she might wish. America's sins, her infidelity, inattention to family order and government, neglect of the Sabbath, and rising disunion, revealed the "accursed thing" lurking in the nation's midst; there were American Illuminati sowing the seeds of disorder, conspiring to sink the United States into the same miserable pit as France.[136]

Fear of the Illuminati soon retreated as Republicans attacked Morse's credibility, and skepticism regarding Robison and Barruel took hold.[137] The Illuminati affair may have revealed the hysteria of American anti-Jacobinism, yet it succeeded in destroying most remaining American support for the French Revolution's Jacobin phase. William Dunlap initially found the spectacle of American anti-Jacobinism so laughable that he began writing a novel in 1797 titled *The Anti-Jacobin*, which satirized the life of a narrow-minded anti-Jacobin Presbyterian minister probably modeled after Morse (or possibly after Dunlap's relation by marriage, Timothy Dwight).[138] However, Dunlap seemed to give the novel up in 1798 – perhaps because he chronically

[135] David Tappan, *A Discourse Delivered in the Chapel of Harvard College, June 19, 1798. Occasioned by the Approaching Departure of the Senior Class from the University* (Boston, Mass., 1798).

[136] Linn, *Discourse...1798.* See also Prince, *A Discourse, Delivered at Salem, on the Day of the National Fast, May 9, 1798: Appointed by President Adams, on Account of the Difficulties Subsisting between the United States and France.*

[137] Phillips, *Jedidiah Morse*, chap. 3.

[138] Dunlap, *Diary of William Dunlap*, 152–73.

left projects incomplete, or perhaps because by the end of 1798 the equation of Jacobinism and violence had become indisputably established in American political culture. Even today the idea that an atheist conspiracy was responsible for the French Revolution, and threatens the United States, still exists.[139]

The anti-Jacobin narrative of French Revolutionary violence became so dominant during the second half of the 1790s, Republicans even began adopting its terms. The shift came in 1798, when Republicans described the Alien and Sedition Acts as a "reign of terror." At a democratic gathering at Fouquet's tavern in Philadelphia on July 4, 1798, celebrators toasted "the Constitution of the United States – may it be protected against unconstitutional laws, the fatal effects of a system of alarm, and the reign of terror."[140] The term spread in influence after Representative John Randolph Jr. of Virginia complained to President Adams that a "reign of Terror" was being waged against American Republicans.[141] Although Randolph preserved his democratic identification by signing his letter from "a citizen," his adoption of anti-Jacobin rhetoric signified the extent to which the French Revolution's radical phase had been discredited. Another Republican politician went even further, drawing on Randolph's letter to accuse the Federalists of possessing a "long-known violence" that drove them to threaten their opponents by "*the reign of terror*' and a Paris '*September*'" (referring to the September Massacres).[142] No longer did Republicans celebrate, dismiss, or excuse the violence of the Jacobin era; instead, they tried to turn the anti-Jacobin brush against their political and religious enemies.[143]

American democrats were taking a page from British radicals who had labeled William Pitt's repression of republican reform in Great Britain as a "reign of terror." The British radical Francis Place first described the Pitt ministry's assault on domestic radicals as a "reign of terror," a term by which it has been known to historians for centuries since.[144] Irish radicals also used "reign of terror" to describe the British proscriptions in

---

[139] See, for example, Web sites such as http://www.masonicinfo.com/illuminati.htm, http://www.conspiracyarchive.com/, http://www.prolognet.qc.ca/clyde/illumin.htm, and http://www.illuminati-news.com/.

[140] "A Number of Members of Congress," *Time Piece*, July 16, 1798.

[141] House of Representatives, *Report of the Committee, to Whom Was Referred, on the 14th Instant, the Message of the President of the United States, Together with a Letter of John Randolph, Junr. A Member of This House, for the State of Virginia* (Philadelphia, Pa., 1800), 7.

[142] *To the Republican Citizens of the State of Pennsylvania. Lancaster, Sept. 17, 1800* (Lancaster, Pa., 1800), 2.

[143] See also Sean Wilentz, *The Rise of American Democracy: Jefferson to Lincoln* (New York, 2005), 97.

[144] Marianne Elliott "French Subversion in Britain in the French Revolution" in *Britain and Revolutionary France: Conflict, Subversion, and Propaganda*, ed. Colin Jones, Exeter Studies in History 5 (Exeter, N.H., 1983), 40.

Ireland following the 1798 rebellion.[145] American radicals picked up on this language in 1798 to counter their own persecution. In fact, James Callender, the exiled Scottish radical newspaper editor, contributed to the growing American outcry against the Federalist "reign of terror." "It is very well known," Callender argued "that such is the favorite system of the British faction." Now, he warned, "we have seen in this city a recent instance of an attempt to establish the federal *reign of terror!*"[146]

The language of anti-Jacobinism not only spread among Republicans after 1798 but also began finally to travel beyond the Northeast. Support for the French Revolution reigned in the southern states throughout the 1790s, only declining "painfully and with remorse" after a decadelong "love affair." Supporters of the French Revolution in the South initially rationalized revolutionary violence as a just reward for monarchical brutality.[147] Only the spreading influence of the Haitian Revolution seemed to turn the tide. As African Americans such as Gabriel Prosser, the leader of a planned slave revolt in Virginia in 1800, increasingly identified black freedom with France and Haiti, slaveholders were forced to repudiate the Revolution.[148] A minister in Virginia made this point to his Republican parishioners when he compared Jacobins to rebellious slaves, but he demanded that Americans not permit a "reign of terror" in the United States.[149] The diffusion of the term *reign of terror* among Republicans in the South illustrates how the American language of anti-Jacobinism took on different meanings as it spread beyond its northeastern Calvinist-Federalist origins. Southerners would embrace the terms of anti-Jacobinism during the nineteenth century, but the language fueled the development of a Burkean slaveholding conservatism radically different from the northeastern variant.

New Words, New Sounds

American anti-Jacobinism became diffused after 1798, but it did not dissipate. Americans' general terror of Jacobin violence persisted throughout the first half of the nineteenth century. As John Quincy Adams wrote to Alexis de Tocqueville in 1831, "The crimes of the French Revolution have made a strong impression upon us; there has been a reaction of feeling,

---

[145] "Ireland. Dublin. April 2," *Albany Centinel*, June 8, 1798.

[146] James T. Callender, *The Prospect before Us* (Richmond, Va., 1800), 149.

[147] Elizabeth Fox-Genovese and Eugene D. Genovese, *The Mind of the Master Class: History and Faith in the Southern Slaveholders' Worldview* (New York, 2005), chap. 1.

[148] Simon Newman, "American Political Culture and the French and Haitian Revolutions," in *The Impact of the Haitian Revolution in the Atlantic World*, ed. David Patrick Geggus (Columbia, S.C., 2001); James Sidbury, *Ploughshares into Swords: Race, Rebellion, and Identity in Gabriel's Virginia, 1730–1810* (New York, 1997), 39–40; Klein, *Unification of a Slave State*.

[149] *Address from a Minister in Virginia*, 8–14.

and this impulse still makes itself felt."[150] The rhetorical attack launched by anti-Jacobins thoroughly revisioned the Revolution from a mirror of American liberty to a theater of grotesque horrors. The term *Jacobin* became synonymous with murderer. Long after the radical political club was disbanded, associations of violence remained firmly attached to the French Revolution.

When General Napoleon Bonaparte overthrew France's Directory government and declared himself emperor, the Jacobin cloak slipped easily over his shoulders. American conservatives in the early 1800s spoke and wrote about the monster Bonaparte in violent terms strikingly similar to their descriptions of Robespierre, Danton, and Marat. Anti-Jacobin authors frequently stressed Bonaparte's membership in the Jacobin club during his youth as evidence of his violent nature. Thomas Green Fessenden, a Vermont lawyer and satirist who studied under the Federalist political theorist Nathaniel Chipman, stepped nimbly from villain to villain in his anti-Jacobin poems and verse. In 1798 during the Quasi-War, Fessenden first rallied an audience against "Bonapart come with his sans-culottes band." Eight years later, when tensions between the United States and France had again reached a critical point, Fessenden, probably delighted with his own foresight, reprinted the anti-Jacobin and anti-Napoleonic ode. Jacobinism, according to Fessenden, was as grave a threat in 1806 as it had been ten years earlier.[151]

The endurance of the imagery of Jacobin bloodshed following the French Revolution is partly attributable to the novelty and profusion of the language that described it. From 1790 to 1815, the United States was saturated in texts denouncing the French Revolution and its Napoleonic aftermath.[152] These narratives "got into every farm house" wrote one conservative commentator in 1799, and "they won't go out, till the stories of the Indian tomahawk and war dances around their prisoners do."[153] Several nineteenth-century authors recalled the significance that accounts of Napoleon's "butchery" had for their frontier childhoods.[154] Many of the anti-Jacobin narratives included detailed descriptions of torture and brutality and used shockingly explicit language. While these narratives may have recalled the anti-Indian and anti-Catholic literature of the past, the internalization of the Jacobin enemy marked a terrifying departure from those earlier literary traditions. Anti-Jacobin language was directed at an

---

[150] Quoted in Perry Miller, *The Life of the Mind in America, from the Revolution to the Civil War* (New York, 1965), 4.

[151] "An Ode," *Weekly Inspector*, Oct. 18, 1806.

[152] Miller, *The Life of the Mind in America, from the Revolution to the Civil War.*

[153] Quoted in Stauffer, *Bavarian Illuminati*, 127.

[154] Joyce Oldham Appleby, *Inheriting the Revolution: The First Generation of Americans* (Cambridge, 2000), 100; Louis C. Jones, ed., *Growing Up in the Cooper Country: Boyhood Recollections of the New York Frontier* (Syracuse, N.Y., 1965), 160.

enemy within. The domestic threat posed by transatlantic Jacobinism so disrupted American political culture that it required the invention of a new language, an American Gothic mode of writing, to accommodate its enormities.

Literary theory describes the Gothic as a dark, mysterious, and emotionally redolent genre that dates to the mid-1760s, but here the term is used in a broader and more historicist sense as an adjective to describe writing that was explicitly bloody and intended to arouse an emotional reaction. To Americans of the late eighteenth century, the term *Gothic* connoted the primitive violence that was typically associated with the Goths' sacking of the Roman Empire.[155] *Gothic* functioned as a synonym for brutality within late-eighteenth-century American public discourse. The blood spilled by the Reign of Terror, and the fear of bloodshed with American political culture, created an imperative for a new Gothic rhetoric, which would both describe the violence of the Revolution and violently disrupt American Jacobin sympathies. Influenced by the Gothic genre, Gothic narratives of the French Revolution extended beyond strictly literary productions, pervading political, religious, pedagogical, and popular discourse in the early American republic.

John Cotton Smith argued in a July 4, 1798, oration that "new words, new sounds, must be invented, if they are ever to comprehend, in any measure, the unparalleled atrocities which have marked the progress of the French Revolution." The events of the French Revolution were "written in lines of blood"; its histories would have to be so as well.[156] In similar words, another conservative critic of the French Revolution described the history of republics as "written by the hand of violence in characters of blood."[157] The first quotation suggests the Gothic image of a murder victim scrawling the name of his assailant in his own blood on the floor before painfully expiring. The second quotation suggests an image of the murderer, leaving his signature at the scene of the crime in the blood of his victim. To write in lines of blood is both to record and enact violence. Fears of the French Revolution required American anti-Jacobins to practice both types of Gothic writing in defense of the nation.

Authors of the new Gothic literature used descriptions of violence to inspire feelings of revulsion for the French Revolution. Yet conservative

---

[155] Noah Webster, *An American Selection of Lessons in Reading and Speaking. Calculated to Improve the Minds and Refine the Tastes of Youth...* (Philadelphia, Pa., 1787), 276.

[156] John Cotton Smith, *An Oration, Pronounced at Sharon, on the Anniversary of American Independence, 4th of July, 1798* (Litchfield, Conn., 1798), 5.

[157] John Ward Fenno, *Desultory Reflections on the Political Aspects of Public Affairs in the United States of America* (New York, 1800), 29. See also Azel Backus's 1798 claim that French infidelity was "writing its inferences in blood;" Azel Backus, *Absalom's Conspiracy: A Sermon, Preached at the General Election, at Hartford in the State of Connecticut, May 10th, 1798* (Hartford, Conn., 1798), 33.

critics did not want to inure their audiences to the bloodshed they reviled; they did not want to mitigate the violence by making it familiar. Authors needed to subject their audiences to accounts of violence thoroughly enough to produce feelings of revulsion, yet at the same time they needed to preserve their audiences' sense of shock. They needed both to condemn the violence as unspeakable and to repeat their accounts of these unspeakable crimes for the largest possible readerships. Authors typically reconciled these contradictory injunctions by introducing their texts with apologies for the graphic language they contained. For example, the anonymous author of a history of the Revolution published in Philadelphia in 1794 conceded that it would be "offensive to decency to depict the numerous and shocking barbarities" that had so far marked the Reign of Terror. He then proceeded to offer detailed accounts of the killing of the Swiss guards, the September Massacres, and the murder of Princess Lamballe. The latter set piece described at length how she was struck in the head and dragged, bleeding profusely, over the corpses of slaughtered prisoners, before her head was severed from her body, placed on a pike, and carried to her friend, the queen.[158]

As the years progressed, anti-Jacobin texts became more and more graphic. Rather than fading like old photographs, their colors perversely intensified. While critiques of the Revolution made during the Reign of Terror succinctly captured the bloodshed and murder in a few paragraphs, the texts that were written after 1795 could not contain the gore; they became catalogs of horror that continued for pages and chapters. *The Siege of Lyons* (1795) was a picaresque series of Gothic set pieces. It described the murder of a pregnant seventeen-year-old by three soldiers: "one of them fired upon her with a carabine. Another quartered her with his hanger, while a third held up the expiring husband to be spectator of their more than hellish cruelty." So many were killed in Lyons, according to the pamphlet, that "three times was the place of the guillotine changed, at every place holes were dug to receive the blood, and yet it ran in the gutters!" Even the bodies of those killed by other means were fed to the guillotine; when their corpses did not bleed, enraged sansculottes delivered "thousands of kicks" upon the mutilated flesh. The author demanded that readers immerse themselves in the scenes of violence. "Reader, fix your eyes on this theatre of carnage!" the text called out. These scenes of bloodshed were intended to instill a revulsion against political violence in American readers. "Can there be, a faction in America, so cruel, so bloody minded, as to wish to see these scenes repeated in their own, or any other country?" the author asked, forcing readers to rethink the proper limits of American political culture.[159]

[158] *A New and Concise History of the Revolution in France from Its Commencement to the Execution of the Gironde Party and the Death of the Duke of Orleans* (Philadelphia, Pa., 1794), 132–7.
[159] *Siege of Lyons*.

William Cobbett perfected the genre of the anti-Jacobin Gothic in his 1796 book *The Bloody Buoy*, which went through multiple American editions and was reprinted to great applause in Britain. Forsaking narrative, Cobbett organized *The Bloody Buoy* as a recitation of horrors drawn from French sources. Its central trope was cannibalism (an obsession for which his rival Philadelphia publisher, Matthew Carey, later made fun of him).[160] Examples of cannibalism listed in the table of contents included "a man tears out a woman's heart reeking hot and bites it with his teeth"; "women roasted alive, and their flesh cut off and presented to men for food"; "a woman lying dead, and a child sucking at her breast"; "one invites another to taste the brains of an aristocrat"; "Goullin beats his own father on his death-bed, and says no man ought to be accounted a good revolutionist who has not the courage to drink a glass of human blood." Other recurring tropes in the book included corpse mutilation and the slaughter of infants. These terrible deeds were described in evocative details. A passage illustrating the killing of priests drew close attention to how "the marble pavement was covered with dirt and gore and mangled carcases [*sic*], and the sides of the altar splashed with blood and brains." Familiar references to "rivers of blood," human "tigers," and the guillotine filled the book.

Images from Cobbett's *Bloody Buoy*, as well as from his translation of *The Cannibals' Progress*, circulated throughout the sermons and orations of the late 1790s. In his July 4, 1798, oration, Theodore Dwight insisted that French Revolutionary bloodshed was "too disgusting to hear, to horrid to relate," but nevertheless Dwight recounted instances "without number" in which whole families were blown from the mouths of cannon, in which innocents were torn to pieces in the streets or sacrificed to the infernal fury of cannibal fishwives. The Jacobins forced their victims to "kiss the bleeding heads of their fellow victims" (heads that had been impaled on pikes). Dwight described the "butchered bodies piled in heaps" and claimed that corpses had been flayed for boot leather to be used by the French Republican army. His narrative of French violence continued for pages – or, when he originally delivered the speech, for many many long minutes. He gave examples of victims guillotined, of mass drownings, of rapes, and of "new species of wickedness" that savage man had never before considered. In France, he argued, murder was "set so low in the scale of crimes, as almost to become a virtue."[161]

In another typical sermon from the late 1790s, David Osgood charged the French Revolution with "indescribable evils," which he then attempted to describe, because, he argued, there was no other way to prepare Americans to defend themselves against the threat of Jacobin annihilation. The "shocking catalogue of miseries and crimes" committed by France, which Osgood

[160] *Carey's United States Recorder*, July 3, 1798.
[161] Dwight, *Oration...1798*.

detailed over several pages, included "its rivers of blood, its desolation of families, its rapines, its violences, its ravages, [and] its burnings." Osgood supported his claims both with numbers, tallying the victims massacred, and with examples. He focused especially on the damage to women and children, figuring that five hundred thousand had been killed exclusive of war, and claiming that "infants were carried to be drowned, stuck on the points of spears; and the hands of mothers, stretched out for mercy to their tender babes, were chopped off."[162]

Created by the exigencies of an Atlantic political culture, American anti-Jacobinism hardly stood in isolation from European literary discourse. Gothic descriptions of French violence saturated texts authored by Frenchmen, Genevans, Irishmen, and Britons. Tales of grotesque enormities spread virally throughout the Atlantic World, carried by mailbags, newspapers, novels, histories, and word of mouth. Translated, edited, annotated, and excerpted, the anti-Jacobin Gothic crossed national borders, serving different purposes in different places. Edmund Burke's *Reflections on the Revolution in France* (1790) is described by many literary critics as a Gothic masterpiece, and its passages describing the forced removal of the royal family from Versailles in October 1789 is brightly colored with descriptions of bloodshed. The "cruel ruffians and assassins, reeking with . . . blood" left the palace "swimming in blood, polluted by massacre, and strewed with scattered limbs and mutilated carcases [*sic*]."[163] Historians have described this passage as "shamelessly rhetorical."[164] The description is certainly marked by Gothic rhetoric, but the rhetoric had meaning. Like American anti-Jacobins, Edmund Burke sought to instill readers with a sense of revulsion at political violence; yet unlike American authors, Burke used Gothic writing to support monarchy and attack Republicanism.[165] American anti-Jacobins, on the other hand, used Gothic rhetoric to paint Republicanism as the pacific middle road between the brutality of monarchy and the savagery of democracy. Elijah Parish, for example, lambasted monarchical government in Britain, where "laws are written in blood & every petty crime is

---

[162] Osgood, *Some Facts Evincive*, 6.

[163] Edmund Burke, *Reflections on the Revolution in France*, ed. J. C. D. Clark (Stanford, Calif., 2001), 232.

[164] Stuart Andrews, *The British Periodical Press and the French Revolution, 1789–1799* (New York, 2000), ix, 5. Even Ian Christie agrees that Burke "went overboard" in his emotive passages about Marie Antoinette; Ian R. Christie, *Stress and Stability in Late Eighteenth-Century Britain: Reflections on the British Avoidance of Revolution; the Ford Lectures, Delivered in the University of Oxford, 1983–1984* (Oxford, 1984), 174.

[165] Richard Slotkin argues in his massive survey of violent early American literature that anti-Jacobinism did not have a profound impact on the United States, as it never embraced Burkean conservatism. But he overlooks the American conservatism that it inspired; Richard Slotkin, *Regeneration through Violence: The Mythology of the American Frontier* (Middletown, Pa., 1973), 332–48, 395–8.

punished with death," in a November 1793 sermon that also mournfully described the French republic as "convulsed" with blood.[166]

American anti-Jacobins used Gothic imagery from European texts to their own ends, altering the intended messages of foreign authors by excerpting, annotating, and appending the original productions. Likewise, European writers adopted American anti-Jacobin texts for their own purposes. William Cobbett's *Bloody Buoy* was republished in London with a preface by John Gifford, addressed to "the people of Great Britain," insisting that the horrible deeds described within "are very little known in *England*."[167] Gifford, a passionate monarchist, hoped that the facts contained within the book would help secure the nation from domestic Republicanism. A decade later, after Cobbett had returned to his homeland, British anti-Jacobins were dismayed to witness him turn against monarchy and become a passionate republican reformer.[168] However, Cobbett's *Bloody Buoy* perhaps had the influence that Gifford hoped. In the years following, an upsurge of anti-Jacobin novels focusing on the violence of the Terror helped produce a powerful popular reaction to the French Revolution in Great Britain.[169]

Perhaps the European text that seeded the greatest number of horror stories in American Gothic discourse was *The Cannibals' Progress*. The book tallied and described the murders, rapes, and mutilations executed by the French Republican Army during the invasion of the German states in 1796. The most horrifying passages appeared in the first section, on the "hellish barbarities" perpetrated in Swabia. There, according to the author, French soldiers dragged people from their beds and gang-raped all the women, repeating their crimes on the women's murdered bodies: "even the bodies of young women, who had expired under their barbarity, and of women who but a few hours before had been in labour, were made use of to satiate the infernal lust of these monsters in human shape, degraded far beneath the beasts of the fields." The author repeated his graphic descriptions of the rapes of corpses and laboring women, of mass murder and mutilation, in many of the subsequent sections. His portrait of French Revolutionary violence assaulted his readers' senses; he suffused his description with smell, sound, color, feel. A typical passage described the soldiers "reeking with human gore, arrayed in all the bloody splendor of rapine and murder."[170]

[166] Elijah Parish, "Psalm 100.4," Nov. 1793, EPP.

[167] William Cobbett, *The Bloody Buoy: Thrown out as a Warning to the Political Pilots of All Nations: Or a Faithful Relation of a Multitude of Acts of Horrid Barbarity, Such as the Eye Never Witnessed, the Tongue Never Expressed, or the Imagination Conceived, until the Commencement of the French Revolution*, 3rd ed. with additional facts, and a preface addressed to the people of Great Britain (London, 1797).

[168] David Wilson, *Paine and Cobbett: The Transatlantic Connection* (Kingston, 1988).

[169] M. O. Grenby, *The Anti-Jacobin Novel: British Conservatism and the French Revolution*, ed. Marilyn Butler and James Chandler, Cambridge Studies in Romanticism (Cambridge, 2001). Grenby argues that the reaction became strongest after 1798.

[170] Cobbett and Aufrere, *Cannibals' Progress*.

The plentiful availability of transatlantic texts describing the horrors of the French Revolution enabled Americans to adapt the material to domestic political and cultural concerns. European texts succeeded in the United States because they answered a need in American political culture. In March 1800, the *Monthly Magazine and American Review*, a Philadelphia periodical, published a three-page register, derived from a European text, that purported to calculate the deaths and destruction caused by the French Revolution between 1789 and 1795 (the "total of the slain and banished" arrived at by the figures is 2,152,979). Like other sources, the magazine demanded that its readers "recoil from the spectacle with horror." However, the article also suggested that readers study the register and draw their own conclusions about the French Revolution as a world-historical event. As the *Monthly Magazine* succinctly stated:

The French Revolution, surely one of the most important events in human history, differs from all past transactions in the accuracy with which its origin, progress, and effects may be known to us. In consequence of taking place in an age of literature, we, though so many hundred leagues from the stage on which it is performing, are enabled to survey it minutely and comprehensively. We have memoirs, registers, and catalogues in abundance, and are able to take the length and breadth, as it were, of every motive and tendency belonging to it.[171]

Indeed, the editor of the *Monthly Magazine*, Charles Brockden Brown, a political Federalist, clearly paid close attention to such "memoirs, registers, and catalogues" before composing *Wieland, or the Transformation* (1798), the first American Gothic novel. Brown initially welcomed the French Revolution, but he became an anti-Jacobin and a Federalist during the Reign of Terror. Raised a Quaker, Brown seemed to have adopted Jonathan Edwards's Calvinist vision of man's moral nature and was deeply effected by conservative texts such as David Hume's history of the English Revolution, which disparaged its violence.[172] *Weiland* relates the tale of Carwin, a young American recently returned from Europe, where he received instruction in political radicalism and ventriloquism from a member of the Illuminati. Carwin's irresponsible use of ventriloquism destroys an American family, the

---

[171] *Monthly Magazine and American Review*, Mar. 1800. Arthur Maynard Welter also remarked on the effects of the French Revolution transpiring in an age of literature in his essay, "A Century of Literature and Revolutions," published in the *Monthly Anthology* in April 1805. His comments served to introduce a laudatory review of a newly published edition of John Adams's *Discourses on Davila*.

[172] Colin Morris, "To 'Shut out the World': Political Alienation and the Privatized Self in the Early Life and Works of Charles Brockden Brown, 1776-1794," *Journal of the Early Republic* 24 (Winter 2004), 613. Michael T. Gilmore, "Calvinism and Gothicism: The Example of Brown's *Wieland*," *Studies in the Novel* 9 (1977). For another essay connecting Calvinism and the Gothic, see Joel Porte, "In the Hands of an Angry God: Religious Terror in Gothic Fiction," in *The Gothic Imagination: Essays in Dark Romanticism*, ed. G. R. Thompson (Pullman, Wash., 1974).

Wielands, who have welcomed him into their company, by driving Theodore Wieland insane and causing him to slaughter his own wife and children. Theodore Wieland's sister Clara, the heroine and narrator of the novel, wonders how her brother descended so swiftly into murderous violence: "I wondered at the change which a moment had effected in my brother's condition.... Was I not transported to the brink of the same abyss? Ere a new day should come, my hands might be embrued in blood."[173] Clara's statement acknowledges that the depravity within any person might transform her into a murderer in the context of degrading conditions.

The novel allegorizes the bloody threat that Illuminatism–Jacobinism posed to the United States. Carwin represents the unfettered voice of the Enlightenment. He uses his knowledge without concern for the danger he causes. The Wieland family signifies America. Clara Wieland describes herself, at several points, in terms that suggest her as Columbia, the figuration of the American nation. She also describes threats against her life as "treason."[174] *Wieland* echoes the era's political and religious literature, which argued that Jacobin ideas would corrupt America from within, causing the nation to descend into domestic violence and bloodshed.[175] Toward the end of the novel, Clara is shocked to learn that Carwin is not the murderer of her family; rather, he had inspired her brother to kill his own wife and children. Carwin's voice has rapidly transformed Wieland from a peaceful man to a wrathful murderer. The novel showed that America was vulnerable to the same degenerative process. The true threat France posed was its potential to cause America to self-destruct.[176]

"How shall I support myself, when I rush into the midst of horrors such as no heart has hitherto conceived, nor tongue related?" asks Clara Wieland, when first introducing the character of Carwin to the narrative.[177] American anti-Jacobins asked themselves the same question during the 1790s, when fear of the violence of the French Revolution gripped their minds.

---

[173] Charles Brockden Brown and Caleb Crain, *Wieland, or, the Transformation: An American Tale and Other Stories*, The Modern Library Classics (New York, 2002), 172.

[174] Brown also hints that the family serves as a model for the nation in a conversation held among the Wielands; see Brown and Crain, *Wieland*, 60, 31.

[175] Tappan, *Discourse...June, 1798*; David Daggett, *Sun-Beams May Be Extracted from Cucumbers, but the Process Is Tedious. An Oration, Pronounced on the Fourth of July, 1799. At the Request of the Citizens of New-Haven* (New Haven, Conn., 1799), Stoddard, *Oration...1799*, 9; Paine, *Works*, 308; Timothy Dwight, *The Nature, and Danger, of Infidel Philosophy Exhibited in Two Discourses, Addressed to the Candidates for the Baccalaureate, in Yale College* (New Haven, Conn., 1798).

[176] Emory Elliott, *Revolutionary Writers: Literature and Authority in the New Republic, 1725–1810* (New York, 1982), chap. 6. Another critic who interprets *Wieland* in light of the dangers of the French Revolution is Larry Kutchen, "The 'Vulgar Thread of the Canvas': Revolution and the Picturesque in Ann Eliza Bleecker, Crevecoeur, and Charles Brockden Brown," *Early American Literature* 36 (2001).

[177] Brown and Crain, *Wieland*, 48.

How could they respond to the threat of democratic ideas and potential violence? Federalists and Calvinists reacted by launching a rhetorical offensive, a torrent of sermons, orations, books, newspaper copy, magazine essays, and letters that strongly condemned the Reign of Terror. Their campaign inspired a new Gothic critique of violence and a positive vision of America as an asylum of nonviolence. America needed to cultivate an antiviolent ethic in order to preserve itself from succumbing to the malignant passions that had destroyed the French republic. From attacks on French Revolutionary violence, anti-Jacobins launched into attacks on institutions of violence within the United States – most significantly, American slavery. Fears of the disorganizing potential of democracy inspired Americans to articulate an ideology opposing violence that would nourish ameliorative potentials within American political culture.

At the same time, the anti-Jacobin rhetorical initiative presented dangers that even its authors could perceive. Charles Brockden Brown terrifyingly invoked the danger of Jacobin corruption in his novel *Wieland*, yet his writings also expressed fear that anti-Jacobins themselves would dangerously manipulate the public through incendiary language.[178] When Republicans accused conservative politicians and ministers of waging a reign of terror in the late 1790s, their accusations accurately captured the violence of anti-Jacobin language. Criticisms of Jacobinism served to delegitimize political violence in the United States, but at the same time it fueled violent passions. In 1798, as the United States fought a quasi war against France, anti-Jacobin rhetoric rallied support for the war and for domestic oppression. The violence of language can be a moderate substitute for physical violence, or it can carve the path to physical violence. To pick up the pen and write in lines of blood is a violent act.

---

[178] Bryan Waterman, *Republic of Intellect: The Friendly Club of New York City and the Making of American Literature* (Baltimore, Md., 2007); Bryan Waterman, "The Bavarian Illuminati, the Early American Novel, and the Histories of the Public Sphere," *William and Mary Quarterly* 62 (2005).

3

Mortal Eloquence

From Anti-Jacobinism to Antislavery

> Mortal eloquence may attempt to depicture the horrors of slavery, but never
> will be able to succeed. They beggar description.
> – Thomas Branagan, *Political and Theological Disquisitions on the Signs
> of the Times, Relative to the Present Conquests of France, etc.*

Like many critics of the French Revolution, Thomas Branagan reviled the
cataclysmic violence of the Terror and the bloodthirsty reign of Napoleon.
Along with other American critics, Branagan, an Irish immigrant, worried
that the United States would join France on its "retrograde march to a state
of barbarism." As a Protestant millennialist, Branagan anxiously read the
"signs of the times" for portents to his adopted nation's future. And as a committed abolitionist, Branagan found the direst omen in America's national
crime of slavery. In an 1807 prophetic text, Branagan described the brutality of slavery as the providential reason that "French fraternizing violence"
threatened the United States. Branagan argued that American slaveholders caused more suffering than cannibals; cannibals consumed their victims
quickly, whereas slaveholders "murdered" their victims' bodies and souls
"by slow degrees." Such violence connected American slaveholders to French
subversion: "While these evils, while these inconsistencies prevail, shall we
wonder that anarchy begins to lift the threatening arm . . . or that deep and
dark laid conspiracies, factions and combinations of foreign spies, are organized and preparing in our country." Unless the United States eliminated
slavery, Branagan warned, God would use French spies and armies, aided
by righteously rebellious slaves, to scourge America for its crimes. Americans
had to repudiate those "ambitious men who by profession, are the votaries of
liberty, but in practice the tyrants of mankind" (southern Republican slaveholders), before French "ANARCHY" destroyed the nation. Branagan's text
conflated the violence of revolutionary France with the violence committed

by slaveholders and argued, from their combined threat, for the need to emancipate American slaves immediately.[1]

Thomas Branagan's radical abolitionist and anti-Jacobin argument represented the logical extreme of the critique of violence embedded in Federalist opposition to the French Revolution. Beginning in the early 1790s, anti-Jacobins used allegorical and allusive writing to construct a link between slaveholding violence and French violence, for example, describing southerners as "supported by the labor of slaves," which made them "necessarily in favor of domination," as well as "friends to the French Revolution," filled with "hatred to our own country" and desire for "rebellion and open insurrection."[2] As political and sectional tensions weathered the conflicts of the early nineteenth century, charges of slaveholding Jacobinism became more explicit – leading Jarvis Brewster, for example, to complain in 1815 that slavery was "a system of tyranny and persecution more horrible perhaps than was ever practiced by a Nero, or a Robespierre."[3] By the antebellum era, anti-Jacobin tropes routinely suffused abolitionist writing. Newspaper articles like "The Slaveholders' 'Reign of Terror'," printed in 1837, depicted slaveholders as Jacobins who plundered the "bones and sinews, the flesh and blood" of their bondsmen.[4] During the late eighteenth and early nineteenth centuries, anti-Jacobins articulated an attack on the violence of slavery that would, over time, jump the confines of its conservative ideological origins and became a powerful ingredient of abolitionist rhetoric.

Northeastern Federalists and their orthodox allies believed that American slavery posed multiple Jacobin threats to the nation's peace and order. Slavery was an uncivilizing institution that introduced Jacobin violence into the American political system. The southern leaders of the Republican Party (Thomas Jefferson and James Madison, in particular) were accustomed to wielding violence over their slaves and would not shy away from subverting American politics through similar means. Like Jacobins, slaveholders were willing to shed rivers of blood in order to achieve their own interests. Opponents to the French Revolution also argued that slavery made America vulnerable to an external Jacobin threat. Slavery signified a national crime that God would punish with merciless severity, by sweeping away the guilty parties. God could use France, like Assyria, as the rod of his anger to wreak righteous violence on the nation; or alternatively, God might use the bloody hand of a slave rebellion to exact his vengeance, as he had done to the planters of Saint Domingue.

[1] Branagan, *Political and Theological Disquisitions on the Signs of the Times, Relative to the Present Conquests of France, etc.*, 22–23, 26, 43, 50, 56, 89.

[2] Christopher Gore, *Manlius: With Notes and References* (Boston, Mass., 1794), 49, 51, 53.

[3] Jarvis Brewster, *An Exposition of the Treatment of Slaves in the Southern States, Particularly in the States of Maryland, Virginia, North Carolina, South Carolina and Georgia* (New Brunswick, N.J., 1815), 7.

[4] "The Slaveholders' 'Reign of Terror'." *Philadelphia National Enquirer*, Apr. 29, 1837.

Anti-Jacobins integrated attacks on slavery into their political texts at length and in brief. The conflation of Jacobin violence and the violence of slavery also became common in nonpolitical antislavery texts dedicated to the struggle for emancipation. Authors of antislavery texts struggled with the question of how to write in a language that would best convey to their audiences the horrors of slavery. In an emancipation discourse before an African American audience, the Reverend Jedidiah Morse, Elijah Parish's coauthor and a rabid anti-Jacobin, wrote of the slave trade: "How shall I describe it, when I contemplate it my heart revolts; my hand trembles."[5] He found an answer in the mode of writing that he had helped perfect in the fight against the French Revolution. From the early 1790s through the first decade of the nineteenth century, antislavery authors focused increasing attention on the brutality that defined slavery, employing many of the same tropes that figured so largely in anti-French writings. Antislavery writers used blood as a recurring symbol in their attacks on the institution, picturing its color, viscosity, and abundance. They labeled slave owners *cannibals*, and they described the slave South as a landscape of death.[6]

Between 1790 and 1815, anti-Jacobins proved to be the strongest advocates of antislavery, following slaves themselves, both in the United States and in Great Britain – a transatlantic connection that has previously escaped notice.[7] The French Revolution invigorated Federalist–Calvinist antislavery by spurring concerns about the uncivilizing potential of slaveholder violence. Historians suspicious of Federalist elitism, such as Sean Wilentz, have argued that "the Federalists did not hate the Jeffersonians out of antislavery

---

[5] Jedidiah Morse, *A Discourse, Delivered at the African Meeting-House, in Boston, July 14, 1808, in Grateful Celebration of the Abolition of the African Slave-Trade, by the Governments of the United States, Great Britain, and Denmark* (Boston, Mass., 1808), 11.

[6] Kimberly K. Smith, *The Dominion of Voice: Riot, Reason, and Romance in Antebellum Politics* (Lawrence, Kan., 1999); Winthrop Jordan, *White over Black: American Attitudes toward the Negro, 1550–1812* (Chapel Hill, N.C., 1968), 367–71; Lorenzo Dow Turner, *Anti-Slavery Sentiment in American Literature Prior to 1865* (Washington, D.C., 1929), chap. 1. Jordan describes the turn to Gothic antislavery literature as "atrocity-mongering" and a "failure of nerve," but Smith argues that sympathetic arguments corrected the overrationalized discourse of late-eighteenth-century politics. Most antislavery scholars date the Gothic strain of abolitionist literature to the antebellum era, see Richard H. Brodhead, "Sparing the Rod: Discipline and Fiction in Antebellum American," *Representations* 21 (Winter 1988); David S. Reynolds, *Beneath the American Renaissance: The Subversive Imagination in the Age of Emerson and Melville* (Cambridge, 1988); Karen Halttunen, "Humanitarianism and the Pornography of Pain in Anglo-American Culture," *American Historical Review* 100 (Apr. 1995); Elizabeth B. Clark, "The Sacred Rights of the Weak: Pain, Sympathy, and the Culture of Individual Rights in Antebellum America," *Journal of American History* 82 (1995).

[7] Ian Haywood has recently drawn interesting parallels between the "bloody romanticism" of anti-Jacobin and antislavery writings in Britain; Ian Haywood, *Bloody Romanticism: Spectacular Violence and the Politics of Representation, 1776–1832*, ed. Anne K. Kellor and Clifford Siskin, Palgrave Studies in the Enlightenment, Romanticism and Cultures of Print (New York, 2006).

conviction; rather, they sometimes took antislavery positions because they hated the 'Jacobin' Jeffersonians."[8] However, the truth lies outside this neat binary. Northeastern conservatives in the early republic shared a fear of human violence that led them both to reject the supposedly Jacobin Jeffersonians and to take antislavery positions. Anti-Jacobinism and antislavery were connected by a common concern: unrestrained violence could destroy civil society. Anti-Jacobin writings progressed from political attacks on Jeffersonians that employed antislavery imagery to fully realized emancipatory claims because the two positions shared an ethical common ground.[9]

It may seem logical to assume that the French Revolution would stifle antislavery sentiment among conservatives because it made them paranoid about disruptions to the social order.[10] But surprisingly, northeastern conservatives rarely made the seemingly obvious connection between Jacobin violence and the danger of slave violence. In fact, northeastern conservatives were surprisingly sympathetic to slave rebellion throughout the 1790s and early 1800s, even as they criticized the French Revolution. Anti-Jacobins were less fearful of the potential violence of slave rebellion in the South than of the violence that slave masters and their northern Republican allies posed to the national political scene. Southerners who feared being slaughtered by their slaves rejected the French Revolution after 1800; however, northeastern conservatives who opposed the French Revolution did not consequently turn against antislavery.[11] Anti-Jacobins blamed slaveholder violence for

---

[8] Sean Wilentz, *The Rise of American Democracy: Jefferson to Lincoln* (New York, 2005), 162. See also Sean Wilentz, "The Details of Greatness: American Historians Versus American Founders," *New Republic* 230 (Mar. 29, 2004). Other recent criticisms of Federalist antislavery include John Kyle Day, "The Federalist Press and Slavery in the Age of Jefferson," *The Historian: A Journal of History* 65 (2003); David Waldstreicher, *In the Midst of Perpetual Fetes: The Making of American Nationalism, 1776–1820* (Chapel Hill, N.C., 1997), 252. For recent histories sympathetic to Federalist antislavery, see Gary Wills, "*Negro President*": *Jefferson and the Slave Power* (Boston, Mass., 2003); Marc Arkin, "The Federalist Trope: Power and Passion in Abolitionist Rhetoric," *Journal of American History* 88 (2001); Paul Finkelman, "The Problem of Slavery in the Age of Federalism," in *Federalists Reconsidered*, ed. Barbara B. Oberg and Doron S. Ben-Atar (Charlottesville, Va., 1998). Matthew Mason's excellent recent survey of slavery and politics in the early national era takes seriously Federalist critiques of southern slavery during the War of 1812 but discounts Federalist antislavery before 1808; Matthew Mason, *Slavery and Politics in the Early American Republic* (Chapel Hill, N.C., 2006).

[9] The claim of ethical consistency challenges arguments that antislavery emerged primarily from the self-concern of abolitionists; Marcus Wood, *Blind Memory: Visual Representations of Slavery in England and America, 1780–1865* (New York, 2000), 219; Christopher Leslie Brown, *Moral Capital: Foundations of British Abolitionism* (Chapel Hill, N.C., 2006), 26.

[10] David Brion Davis, *Inhuman Bondage: The Rise and Fall of Slavery in the New World* (New York, 2006); Mason, *Slavery and Politics*, 36–40; David Brion Davis, *The Problem of Slavery in the Age of Revolution, 1770–1823* (Ithaca, N.Y., 1975), 329; Jordan, *White over Black*, 375.

[11] Elizabeth Fox-Genovese and Eugene D. Genovese, *The Mind of the Master Class: History and Faith in the Southern Slaveholders' Worldview* (New York, 2005); Simon Newman,

endangering civil society throughout the Atlantic World, and many supported antislavery as a necessary redress. Sometimes they even defended slave rebellion as a means of redress.

Thomas Branagan – who was born in Ireland, worked as a slave trader in Africa, and became an overseer in Antigua before immigrating to the United States and settling in Philadelphia – saw the violence of the French Revolution and the violence of slavery as inextricably woven into a fatal web that connected every point on the Atlantic perimeter.[12] The slave trade had "crimsoned the waves of the Atlantic with human blood," he wrote; anywhere those waves lapped ashore stood in danger of Jacobin violence. The United States and Great Britain were united by blood bonds – the blood of kinship, the blood of the slave system, and the blood of the Jacobin threat.[13] To defeat Jacobinism both America and Britain would have to abolish their violent slave systems. And yet despite his apparent antipathy toward bloodshed, the violence of Thomas Branagan's language opened up the possibility that if slaveholders did not renounce the institution by choice, it would be justifiable to forcibly emancipate their slaves. Ultimately, in the hands of radicals like Branagan, the anti-Jacobin assault on slavery could become a battle cry.

The Slavery Hole of Democracy

Anti-Jacobin antislavery had roots in the northeastern Calvinist attack on slavery during the American Revolution. The New Divinity inheritors of Jonathan Edwards's theology viewed the American Revolution as a divine punishment for the national crime of slavery. Edwards's students, such as Samuel Hopkins and Levi Hart, as well as his son Jonathan Edwards Jr., attacked slavery as a sin and promoted emancipation as a religious duty. The New Divinity clerics viewed slavery as a manifestation of depravity, the human quality that posed the greatest threat to man's peaceable future existence, and argued that eliminating slavery was necessary to reestablishing civil society.[14]

"American Political Culture and the French and Haitian Revolutions," in *The Impact of the Haitian Revolution in the Atlantic World*, ed. David Patrick Geggus (Columbia, S.C., 2001).

[12] Thomas Branagan, *The Penitential Tyrant, a Juvenile Poem, in Two Cantos: To Which Is Prefixed, Compendious Memoirs of the Author* (Philadelphia, Pa., 1805).

[13] Branagan, *Disquisitions*, 187–8, 196–7.

[14] Peter Hinks, "Timothy Dwight, Congregationalism, and Early Anti-Slavery," in *The Problem of Evil: Slavery, Freedom, and the Ambiguities of American Reform*, ed. Steven Mintz and John Stauffer (Amherst, Mass., 2007); Kenneth P. Minkema and Harry S. Stout, "The Edwardsean Tradition and the Antislavery Debate, 1740–1865," *Journal of American History* 92 (2005); Davis, *The Problem of Slavery in the Age of Revolution, 1770–1823*, chap. 7. The loss of her American colonies stimulated an antislavery movement in Britain during the 1780s; Brown, *Moral Capital*.

Revolutionary-era political leaders in the United States also challenged the institution of slavery. Rising antislavery sentiment in the Northeast led to the gradual abolition of slavery everywhere north of Delaware by the turn of the century.[15] The elimination of slavery from the northeastern states owes partial credit to the "contagion of liberty" spread by republican ideology.[16] However, the idealization of freedom and the defense of slavery were remarkably compatible in American republican ideology, which defined freedom as a quality that depended on personal virtue and resistance, and thus justified the enslavement of supposedly degenerate and passive blacks. Many early national democrats embraced this understanding of freedom, including the Irish Philadelphian printer Matthew Carey, as well as the future president James Monroe and the members of the New York Democratic, Tammany, Mechanic, and Military societies.[17]

Not all early national democrats proved so sanguine about slavery. Certain northern Jeffersonians, including James Sloan and David Bard, both from Pennsylvania, introduced antislavery legislation in Congress during the early 1800s. The democratic political impulse contained a deeply egalitarian streak that led some men of conscience to advocate for emancipation and perhaps racial equality. However, most northern members of the Republican Party renounced antislavery to make common cause with the southern party leadership. James Sloan ultimately chose instead to abandon the Republicans and maintain his antislavery commitment. But persuaded that Federalist aristocrats posed the gravest threat to republican politics in the United States, many Republicans who strongly disliked slavery set aside their objections during the 1790s and early 1800s in order to present a united democratic front against the scourge of northern elitism. Some northern Republicans even argued that slaves were the enemies of freedom and in cahoots with British tyrants and Federalist elites to destroy democracy.[18]

Those northern elitists, who trembled with fear that democracy would undermine civil society in the new republic, became slavery's most strident opponents during the early national era because they viewed it as an institution of social violence that posed a threat to "liberty with order." Federalist

---

[15] Vermont 1777; Connecticut and Rhode Island, 1784; Massachusetts ca.1780–3; Pennsylvania, 1780; New Hampshire 1789; New York 1799; New Jersey 1804; Arthur Zilversmit, *The First Emancipation: The Abolition of Slavery in the North* (Chicago, Ill., 1967).

[16] Quote from Bernard Bailyn, *The Ideological Origins of the American Revolution* (Cambridge, Mass., 1992). See, for example, David Cooper, *A Serious Address to the Rulers of America on the Inconsistency of Their Conduct Respecting Slavery* (Trenton, N.J., 1783).

[17] Francois Furstenberg, "Beyond Freedom and Slavery: Autonomy, Virtue, and Resistance in Early American Political Discourse," *Journal of American History* 89 (2003).

[18] For example, William Duane, the United Irishmen refugee; see Padraig Riley, "Northern Republicans and Southern Slavery: Democracy in the Age of Jefferson, 1800–1819" (Ph.D., University of California, Berkeley, 2007). Matthew Mason, *Slavery and Politics*, dates northern democratic antislavery to the post-1815 era. For a more positive appraisal of democratic antislavery in the early national era, see Wilentz, *Rise of American Democracy*, 218–22.

antislavery in the 1790s combined partisan self-defense, virulent section-alism, and fears of violence into a consistent language of attack. When southern leaders of the strengthening Republican opposition during the early 1790s denigrated the Federalists as "aristocrats or "monocrats" who opposed the rights of man, Federalists retaliated by arguing that the Republican leaders were America's true bloodthirsty aristocrats. Jefferson and Madison, and many of their allies, owned tens or hundreds of slaves to whom they denied all rights. The Republican leaders possessed the wealth and personal power over human subjects that defined aristocracy. Alluding to the three-fifths clause, Federalists argued that the Republicans, like European aristocrats, acquired political power from their vassals. "The men...who have raised themselves to the condition of a real aristocracy; who have obtained for every five of their negro slaves an equal weight on the general scale, to that of any three substantial yeoman; – these men are now considered by the half the nation as the great bulwark of liberty, the quintessence of republican purity, while the plain farmers of New-England, who till their ground with their own hands, are called by the opprobrious name of aristocrats," complained an essay writer for the conservative periodical *The Balance*.[19]

A debate between the Federalist congressman Samuel Dexter, from Massachusetts, and the Democratic–Republican congressman William Giles, from Virginia, held in the House of Representatives in January 1795, typified these contesting claims of aristocracy. Giles first introduced an amendment to the Naturalization Act of 1790 that would require expatriate aristocrats to renounce their titles before becoming American citizens. Federalists believed that Giles had submitted the amendment in the hope of securing their negative votes, and then using the issue to publicly indict their party as elitist. Dexter retaliated by offering an amendment compelling the erstwhile aristocrats to renounce the titles to their slaves: if any "such alien shall hold any person in slavery he shall renounce it, and declare that he holds all men *free and equal*." Dexter hoped to reveal the Republicans as the true American aristocrats by forcing them to vote no on this antislavery amendment. Giles retaliated with a shrill defense of slavery and sharply rebuked Dexter for the dangerous effect his comments might have on American slaves. When the subject of slavery arose in the national legislature, southern representatives routinely threatened dire consequences to the Union. Federalists' dedication to a strong national government prevented them from frequently broaching the subject at a legislative level, but accusations of southern slaveholding aristocracy routinely filled conservative newspapers and periodicals.[20]

---

[19] "On the Moral and Political Effects of Negro-Slavery," *The Balance, and Columbian Repository*, June 7, 1803, 177.

[20] See the Federalist coverage of the Dexter/Giles debate in *Columbian Centinel*, Jan. 10, 1795. Also, John Bach McMaster, *A History of the People of the United States, from the Revolution to the Civil War* (New York, 1883), 208–12. See also the remarks in Congress of James Bayard, a Delaware Federalist, in 1798; quoted by Padraig Riley.

The Federalist *Gazette of the United States* deployed charges of southern aristocracy to great effect for many years. After the democratic *Daily
Advertiser* published a letter criticizing the Federalists as aristocrats in 1793,
the *Gazette* published a mocking retort that promised to point out the true
"dark spots of aristocracy." Satirically presented as a letter written by an
oblivious democrat, the article first claimed that slavery was "rather a mark
of modern democracy" and that emancipatory measures, such as that signed
by King Louis XVI, signified "*monarchical* conduct." Then, letting slip the
satirical democratic mask, the *Gazette* pointed out the absurdity of violent
slaveholders laying claim to the status of protectors of liberty:

Who talk most about liberty and equality – who monopolize the virtue and spirit
of America? Who are the guardians of the equal rights of man? Is it not those, who
hold the bill of rights in one hand and a whip for the affrighted slaves in the other?
Are not some of our warmest declaimers upon liberty, men who traffick in human
flesh and riot on the profits which arise from the sweat and groans of their darky
brethren?

The letter did not simply call attention to the abrogation of rights in southern slavery, it depicted slave mastery as physically violent: slaveholders held
the "whip" and trafficked in "flesh." Given the article's mocking ventriloquism, the casual racism of the phrase "darky brethren" was probably
intended to indict slaveholders of bigotry; although at the same time it
revealed the racial prejudice shared by most Federalists. The article finished by attacking the democrats' infidelity and their support for the French
Revolution.[21]

Even southern Federalists occasionally joined the assault on slaveholders'
claims of democratic spirit. A series of letters by Marcellus published in 1794
in the *Virginia Gazette* accused democrats of "more than papal tyranny."
The so-called southern democrats betrayed their true aristocratic tendencies in their self-presentation: "[those] who make the most noise about
danger of aristocracy, equality, and liberty, [are] pompous in their dress
and equipage, *luxurious* in their tables, *fastidious* in their deportment, and
tyrants in every circumstances." And that critique, the author conceded, did
not take into account "our slaves (who in violation of the doctrine of equality, are deprived of every social rights)." Marcellus condemned immediate
emancipation as a grave danger to the safety of southern society, yet even
the cautious antislavery of Virginia Federalists like himself spurred Virginia
Republicans to position themselves in opposition as the "bulwark against
slavery's critics."[22] Virginia Federalists responded by accusing the Republicans of Jacobinism. Marcellus connected southern slaveholding aristocracy

[21] "For the Gazette of the United States," *Gazette of the United States*, Feb. 23, 1793.
[22] Anthony Alfred Iaccarino, "Virginia and the National Contest over Slavery in the Early
Republic, 1780–1833" (Ph.D., University of California, Los Angeles, 2000).

to violent support for the French Revolution; among Republicans "*violence is regarded as patriotism*," Marcellus bemoaned. He warned Americans to avoid military alliance with France and to remain a neutral party in the European war.[23]

The Federalist attack on southern opposition leaders as aristocratic slave owners resonated with attacks on southern Republicans as Jacobins and partisans of violence, despite the seeming incongruity of the two charges. Charges of slaveholding aristocracy did not undermine the Federalist argument that southerners were Jacobins, because the Federalists did not define Jacobinism by its democratic ideals. American anti-Jacobins redefined the French Revolution as a cataclysm of anarchic violence and the Jacobins as "men of blood." Conservative propagandists argued that the high-flying southern rhetoric of rights and freedom was as false as the Jacobins' claim to upholding the Rights of Man. Neither sanguinary French Jacobins nor slave-holding southern "democrats" promoted true liberty. American democrats and the French Jacobins they idealized were all demagogues who talked about liberty to disguise their violent pursuit of private interests.

The Federalists' identification of Jacobinism as a form of violent dema-goguery similarly disrupted any tendency by conservatives to label the slaves themselves as Jacobins. Fear of slave Jacobinism is little evident in north-eastern writings. A great deal of historical argumentation to the contrary has been based on the remark by the South Carolinian Edwin Holland, following the supposed Vesey slave conspiracy of 1822, that slaves were "truely the Jacobins of the country."[24] Yet even this southern remark is hardly a transparent assertion of slave Jacobinism. The quotation closes a book-long "refutation" by Holland of northern charges that southern-ers treated their slaves with violence and inhumanity, most recently exem-plified in their execution of the Vesey conspirators. Holland's use of the modifier *truely* in his assertion that slaves were "truely the Jacobins of the country" suggests that he was refuting the decades-old discourse that described slaveholders as Jacobins by displacing the critique onto their chat-tel. Holland intended his remark less to convict American slaves than to

23 Marcellus, *Marcellus: Published in the Virginia Gazette, November and December, 1794* (Richmond, Va., 1794), 8, 2, 29. John Quincy Adams used the nom de plume Marcellus for a well-known series of Federalist essays that appeared in the *Columbian Centinel* in 1793; the Virginia author may have assumed the same pseudonym in order to indicate his Federalist politics.

24 Wilentz, *Rise of American Democracy*, 239; Steven Hahn, *A Nation under Our Feet: Black Political Struggles in the Rural South, from Slavery to the Great Migration* (Cambridge, Mass., 2003), 13, 484; Robert L. Paquette, "Jacobins of the Lowcountry: The Vesey Plot on Trial," *William and Mary Quarterly* 59 (Jan. 2002), 185; Larry E. Tise, *Proslavery: A History of the Defense of Slavery in America, 1701–1840* (Athens, Ga., 1987), 52; Duncan J. MacLeod, *Slavery, Race, and the American Revolution* (New York, 1974), 157. For an article that questions whether there was a Vesey conspiracy, see Michael P. Johnson, "Denmark Vesey and His Co-Conspirators," *William and Mary Quarterly* 58 (2001).

exculpate their white southern masters from a set of oft-repeated charges against them.[25]

Federalist critiques that allegorized southern slaveholding Republicans to Jacobins gained credence from the tactics of demonstrative disorder used by the Jeffersonians against the presidential administrations during the 1790s, as well from the Republicans' advocacy for involving America in the war between revolutionary France and its European enemies. The riotous opposition to the Jay Treaty in 1795 sealed the connection between the Republicans' pro-French and proslavery violence, as for southern Republicans one of the treaty's main failures was its lack of compensation for runaway slaves whom the British had helped relocate to freedom in Canada and elsewhere after the Revolution.[26] Northeastern Federalists saw the demonstrations against the Jay Treaty as uncivilized southerners guillotining effigies in order to protect their property in slaves.

Christopher Gore, a Massachusetts Federalist who began his political career in opposition to Shays's Rebellion and was later appointed as a commissioner under the Jay Treaty, published a series of essays in 1794 that connected a critique of democratic violence to a critique of opposition slave owning. The essays identified the American opposition as "desperadoes of faction and anarchy" and "lovers of war." Gore reviled the violent tactics of his political enemies, then admonished his readers, "Be not astonished, freemen of *New-England*! for in that land whence you hear the greatest bellowings about liberty a great proportion of the people are slaves." Gore's comment recalled Samuel Johnson's famous attack on the American Revolution, that the "loudest yelps for liberty [come from] the drivers of slaves." In the final essays of his series, Gore developed the connection between opposition violence and opposition slaveholding, concluding that men of the South were not true republicans: "they are supported by the labor of slaves; their habits and manners, from this circumstance, are necessarily in favor of domination; and against equal liberty or equal rights." Slaveholding habituated masters to the use of violent domination and led them to a hatred for the United States that they disguised as a zeal for the French Revolution.[27]

Federalist critics argued that slavery, like democracy itself, represented an uncivilizing process that reduced both masters and slaves to savages. Noah Webster, the original theorist of the uncivilizing process, first described its workings in an attack on slavery that predated his 1794 essay criticizing the

---

[25] Edwin C. Holland, *A Refutation of the Calumnies Circulated against the Southern and Western States, Respecting the Institution and Existence of Slavery* (New York, 1822; repr. 1969), 86.

[26] *Connecticut Courant*, Aug. 3, 1795; Henry Wilson, *History of the Rise and Fall of the Slave Power in America* (New York, 1969), chap. 9.

[27] Gore, *Manlius*, 6, 49, 51. The South Carolina proslavery Federalist William Loughton Smith similarly described democrats as men "who delight in war." William Loughton Smith, *An Address from William Smith, of South-Carolina, to His Constituents* (Philadelphia, Pa., 1794).

French Revolution. In a 1793 oration to a Connecticut emancipation society, Webster argued that slavery impeded "the public happiness of man"
because of its ill consequences on men's characters. It produced villainy and
indolence among slaves (an effect also observable in the peons of Poland,
Scotland, Russia, and Greece), and it brutalized masters. "Men who from
their infancy *hold*," Webster argued, "and those who *feel*, the rod of tyranny
become equally hardened by the exercise of cruelty." Despotism, continued Webster, "converts the civilized man into a savage." Webster warned
that slave owners were "haughty, capricious, and cruel" as well as "rough,
boisterous, [and] irritable." Webster's language clearly drew from Thomas
Jefferson's lament in *Notes in the State of Virginia* that slavery was the
"perpetual exercise of the most boisterous passions, the most unremitting
despotism on the one part, and degrading submissions on the other."[28] However, unlike Jefferson, Webster argued that slaveholders' faulty characters
endangered American politics. In a republic, Webster argued, men needed
to "moderate their passions." But slave owners wanted to draw blood at
every perceived offense to their dignity. For example, Webster offered the
flourishing practice of dueling among southern elites. Although Webster also
worried about the uncivilizing impact slavery had on African Americans, he
strongly supported their emancipation. In his 1793 oration he objected to
colonization as cruel and instead designed a graduated plan to meliorate the
condition of American slaves and slowly raise them to freedom.[29]

Another founding member of Connecticut's abolition society, the prominent Federalist and vitriolic anti-Jacobin Theodore Dwight, revisited Webster's argument in his own oration to its members the following year. Dwight
condemned slavery as an institution of violence without moral justification.
Slavery was "tyranny," "torture," "evil," "death," and "barbarity and murder." Dwight voiced the standard natural rights arguments against slavery
that had developed during the revolutionary era; then he shifted to the
awful consequences of slavery on the character of slave owners. Slavery
gave children the "disposition to cruelty and injustice." It left their characters untrained; they were taught to give "implicit obedience to the dictates
of passion." As adults, southern men raped their slaves and sold their children. Even southern women "indulge themselves in the paroxysms of rage
and . . . seize the engines of torture." They were possessed with the "spirit
of domination." For this reason, Dwight continued, they could not be "true
republicans," and their claims to support the Rights of Man were hypocritical.[30]

---

[28] Thomas Jefferson, *Notes on the State of Virginia*, ed. William Harwood Peden (Chapel Hill,
N.C., 1954), 162.

[29] Noah Webster, *Effects of Slavery, on Morals and Industry* (Hartford, Conn., 1793).

[30] Theodore Dwight, *An Oration, Spoken before "the Connecticut Society, for the Promotion of Freedom and the Relief of Persons Unlawfully Holden in Bondage": Convened in
Hartford, on the 8th Day of May, A.D. 1794* (Hartford, Conn., 1794). See also George

The concept of the uncivilizing process bridged the gap between slave-holder violence and democratic violence by revealing both to stem from a common source – the individual's failure to control his or her depraved passions and be obedient to moral authority. Theodore Dwight masterfully used antislavery to condemn southern politics by arguing that the violence of slave masters would cause the Jacobin destruction of the United States. Dwight concluded his 1794 oration with a warning that American slavery would reduce America to the same violence as seen in France, where "the government was seized by a profligate and bloodthirsty junto." The *Connecticut Courant*, a newspaper to which Theodore Dwight frequently contributed and that he later edited, published a series of letters from "Pelham" in 1796, probably written by Dwight, which also linked southern slavery to Jacobin destruction. According to Pelham, the northern states were at a point of crisis and faced the choice between breaking from the South or suffering "confusion and slavery." Pelham pictured southern slavery as a grotesquely violent institution. "Is there much probability," Pelham asked, "that a system so inhuman and discordant, so violent and bloody as that of Slavery, can possibly be kept in order?" It was inevitable, Pelham argued that the South would enter "that state which France and her colonies have been forced to realize," total bloody anarchy.[31] Again, in his July 4, 1798, oration, Dwight characterized Thomas Jefferson as a slave owner who wished to cut the bonds of the Constitution to free his hands for Jacobin bloodshed.[32]

The uncivilizing thesis enabled anti-Jacobin leaders like Noah Webster and Theodore Dwight to undermine slave owners' most important self-justification – that they were not active commissioners of injustice but merely its unfortunate inheritors. Revolutionary-era antislavery had largely confined criticisms of violence to the slave trade; a humane view of slave-holders' behavior could coexist with arguments that the slave trade violated natural rights. The anti-Jacobin sensibility supported a new argument, that

---

Buchanan's argument that the slave trade made "monsters" of its practitioners; George Buchanan, *An Oration upon the Moral and Political Evil of Slavery: Delivered at a Public Meeting of the Maryland Society, for Promoting the Abolition of Slavery, and the Relief of Free Negroes, and Others Unlawfully Held in Bondage. Baltimore, July 4th, 1791* (Baltimore, Md., 1793), 9, 15.

[31] *Connecticut Courant*, Dec. 12, 1796; May 22, 1797.

[32] Theodore Dwight, *An Oration, Spoken at Hartford, in the State of Connecticut, on the Anniversary of American Independence, July 4th, 1798* (Hartford, Conn., 1798). In an ironic counterpoint, Dwight's democratic relative William Dunlap argued that slaveholder violence necessitated the continuance of slavery, so that owners would not "become enraged or desperate" causing "devastation, misery, & murder"; William Dunlap, *Diary of William Dunlap, 1766–1839; the Memoirs of a Dramatist, Theatrical Manager, Painter, Critic, Novelist, and Historian*, 3 vols., Collections of the New York Historical Society for the Year 1929–31, The John Watts Depeyster Publication Fund Series, 62–4 (New York, 1969), 118–22.

the violence of slavery was an evil for which present-day owners could not be exculpated. Slaveholders were not innocents struggling under the burden of a system of slavery unfortunately passed down from their fathers, but active promoters of a terrible American sin for which they bore responsibility each day that they starved, whipped, and tortured their chattel.[33]

Many northeastern Calvinist leaders seconded their Federalist allies' concerns that slaveholding violence would uncivilize American political leaders and destroy the nation. In the very first annual oration to Connecticut's emancipation society, its founder Jonathan Edwards Jr. argued that slavery's cruelties, including kidnapping, the Middle Passage, torture, suicide, starvation, overwork, and the whip, were "exceedingly hurtful to the state which tolerates them." Edwards explained, they were hurtful:

As they deprave the morals of the people. – The incessant and inhuman cruelties practiced in the trade, and in the subsequent slavery, necessarily tend to harden the human heart against the tender feelings of humanity in the masters of vessels, in the sailors, in the factors, in the proprietors of these slaves, in their children, in the overseers, in the slaves themselves, and in all who habitually see those cruelties.

Less clearly partisan than his Federalist allies, Edwards did not confine his critique of slaveholder violence to domestic politics. Unafraid to appear a friend to England, Edwards enlisted himself in the transatlantic antislavery movement, quoting from the British abolitionist Thomas Clarkson to argue that slaveholding violence threatened Britain as well as the United States. A second edition of Edwards's sermon was published in the United States with an appendix made up of extracts from evidence against the slave trade delivered before the British House of Commons in 1791. Edwards's sermon suggests the ethical consistency of the Federalist antislavery argument with a transatlantic religious ideology that transcended American partisanship.[34]

---

[33] Tyrannical Libertymen: *A Discourse upon Negro-Slavery in the United States: Composed at –, in Newhampshire; on the Late Federal Thanksgiving-Day: Four Lines of Quotation* (Hanover, N.H., 1795); Philanthropos, *The African Miscellanist, or, a Collection of Original Essays on the Subject of Negro Slavery* (Trenton, N.J., 1802), 23–4; John Phillips, *An Appeal to Matter of Fact & Common Sense Recommended to the Serious Consideration of the Inhabitants of Charleston, South Carolina, &c.* (New York, 1798), 6; David Humphreys, *A Valedictory Discourse, Delivered before the Cincinnati of Connecticut in Hartford, July 4th, 1804, at the Dissolution of the Society* (Boston, Mass., 1804), 33.

[34] Jonathan Edwards, *The Injustice and Impolicy of the Slave Trade, and of the Slavery of the Africans: Illustrated in a Sermon Preached before the Connecticut Society for the Promotion of Freedom, and for the Relief of Persons Unlawfully Holden in Bondage, at Their Annual Meeting in New Haven, September 15, 1791* (Providence, R.I., 1792), 10. The Reverend Charles Backus, another member of the abolition society, similarly joined an attack on the violence of the French Revolution with a deep antislavery plea in his 1793 election sermon; Charles Backus, *A Sermon Preached before His Excellency Samuel Huntington . . . Governor . . . Of the State of Connecticut. May 9, 1793* (Hartford, Conn., 1793).

British antislavery authors also drew suggestive connections between the violence of slavery and French violence. Prior to the Revolution, abolitionists like Thomas Clarkson and Granville Sharp argued that slavery was incompatible with the ideal of British liberty and allegorized slaveholder violence to aristocratic violence in France. In a few chapters of his 1768 novel *A Sentimental Journey*, Laurence Sterne progressed rapidly from a meditation on the Bastille to a brief against enslavement.[35] Following the Revolution, anti-Jacobins shifted their allegory to draw a connection between revolutionary violence and slavery. Hannah More revised her famous poem "Slavery" after the Revolution to make it assertively anti-Jacobin.[36] John Somers Cocks began a 1791 anti-French pamphlet with a stinging attack on slavery and the slave trade, arguing that slavery pointed to the despotic hearts of men that made restraints on liberty necessary.[37] The great anti-Jacobin illustrator James Gillray showed French revolutionaries as "Negro drivers" in a 1798 print.[38] Granville Sharp included pages of anti-Jacobin conspiracy theory in his 1797 *Serious Reflections on the Slave Trade*.[39]

The Boston minister John S. J. Gardiner attributed British reformers' combined antislavery and anti-Jacobinism to their love of "benevolence and humanity."[40] Perhaps Gardiner's well-known Anglophilia distorted his vision. More accurately, the ethical core of both British and Federalist–Calvinist opposition to Jacobinism and slaveholding lay not in love but in its opposite emotion, fear – the fear of human depravity. Elijah Parish eloquently articulated this transatlantic antislavery argument in an undated sermon promoting Britain's closure of the Atlantic slave trade. The sermon opened with the argument "that human nature is in a lapsed, depraved state" and that governments had emerged "to restrain and govern this deplored waywardness of mankind." In a subtle dig at the French Revolution, Parish argued that humanity was so depraved that "the vilest despotism is better than licentious anarchy." However, government was only a secondary mode of retraining human violence. The best means to restrain mankind was through the Gospel. Would the world accept Jesus Christ and be enlightened? Prophesizing the arrival of an enlightened world, Parish used antislavery imagery to illustrate the promise of global salvation. "Are the sons of

35 Marcus Wood, *Slavery, Empathy, and Pornography* (New York, 2002), 13–18; Prince Hall, *A Charge, Delivered to the African Lodge, June 24, 1797, at Menotomy* (Boston, Mass., 1797).

36 Robert Hole, "Hannah More on Literature and Propaganda, 1788–1799," *History [GB]* 85 (2000), 617.

37 John Somers Cocks, "Patriotism and the Love of Liberty Defended: In Two Dialogues (1791)," in *Political Writings of the 1790s*, ed. Gregory Claeys (London, 1995), 3–5, 17.

38 David Bindman, ed., *The Shadow of the Guillotine: Britain and the French Revolution* (London, 1989), 62.

39 Granville Sharp, *Serious Reflections on the Slave Trade and Slavery* (London, 1805).

40 John Sylvester John Gardiner, *A Sermon Preached before the African Society on the 14th of July 1810 the Anniversary of the Abolition of the Slave Trade* (Boston, Mass., 1810), 17.

Canaan, the children of Africa, to be delivered from the miseries of slavery? Is the land of Ham to burst her chains?" Parish's answer located the promise of global redemption in the transatlantic antislavery movement: "the spirit of God shall come on a Clarkson, a Wilberforce, and a holy brotherhood of worthies, who shall move the British nation, who shall move all the nations of Christendom, who shall persuade the world, to unite in the benevolent design of suppressing the traffic in human blood." Like Jonathan Edwards Jr.'s sentiments, Parish's antislavery sentiments stemmed from a deep-felt fear of human depravity and a transatlantic dream of a future without brutality. In the following decade, Parish would incorporate antislavery into his fiercely partisan sermons opposing the War of 1812, but his later partisan outpourings made arguments against violence that were consistent with his earlier sermons.[41]

Federalists often used antislavery to strengthen sectional or partisan attacks on political enemies, yet even texts in which slavery was a secondary concern could give way to powerful direct arguments for emancipation. Arguments opposing slavery qua violence flowed naturally into arguments opposing slavery for its own sake. Oliver Whipple's 1802 poem dedicated to John Adams, "The Historic Progress of Civil and Rational Liberty," demonstrates the progression. Whipple began by attacking Jeffersonian political violence for endangering civil society. In rhyming couplets, Whipple described the destruction of earlier republics by factional fighting. In a passage describing Caesar's assault on the Roman republic, Whipple compared Caesar's actions to the Jacobin Reign of Terror, then celebrated the momentary restoration of freedom following the ides of March in antislavery terms:

> Again the fire of Freedom glows,
> No fear, but thine and virtue's foes,
> The reign of terror now is o'er,
> And slav'ry's bound to *Afric's* shore.
> May Freedom's beams forever shine,
> And *Afric's* sable sons be thine,
> May Man's rude heart absorb the ray,
> Where Phebus pours a dawn of day.

In the first four lines, the poem used slavery as a counterpoint to freedom: by killing Caesar, Brutus and Cassius had cast political slavery to Africa's shore. Yet the following four lines shifted to a more fully realized antislavery

---

[41] "Sermon XIV," in Elijah Parish, *Sermons, Practical and Doctrinal with a Biographical Sketch of the Author* (Boston, Mass., 1826), 281–91. Parish's War of 1812 sermons will be addressed in the following chapter. In one of his earliest anti-Jacobin sermons Parish compared the violence in revolutionary France to violence in Africa, although it is unclear whether he was referring to the violence produced by the slave trade; Elijah Parish, "Psal. 92.1," Thanksgiving, Feb. 1795, EPP.

position, as Whipple prayed that *"Afric's* sable sons" also experience the beam of freedom. The poem moved from using slavery as a signifier of violence to directly imploring the abolition of slavery. The use of the present tense suggests that the line could be read to address the present day – and the poem ended with a plea to abolish the slave trade in the United States. Whipple's poetic dream of emancipation stemmed from the hope that human depravity could be tamed, that "man's rude heart" could be healed and violence be abolished from the world. Concerns about human violence led Whipple from political invocations of antislavery to assertive arguments for emancipation.[42]

Early national political antislavery reached its fullest flower in the attacks on Thomas Jefferson made throughout the 1790s and early 1800s. In the Jeffersoniad essays published during the presidential campaign of 1800, the author warned that Jefferson's goals were "to Jacobinize, revolutionize and of course, demoralize the people of these United States." The essays indicted Jefferson as an atheist, a charge that connoted the stain of depraved violence – as atheism in France had produced "acts of the most brutal ferocity." The Jeffersoniad essays also condemned their target as chief among a party of "bastard children owners," "bastard children starvers," "Negrostealers," and "man-slayers," a party that "knashes its teeth for rage and feels a thirst that nothing will slake but the blood of proscriptions." In twice-weekly essays published throughout June, July, and August, the Jeffersoniad expounded on the dangers that the presidential candidate posed to the republic. If elected to the nation's highest office, "nothing short of the revival of the sanguinary scenes which so desolated the great city of Lyons, during the reign of Robespierre" would come to pass in America.[43] (Accounts of the siege of Lyons contained many of the most blood-saturated descriptions of the French Revolution produced in the 1790s.)

Antislavery Federalists sealed southern democracy and violent slavery into a moral equivalency, which anti-Jacobin authors found easy to incorporate into their rhetoric. Many northeastern orators and authors integrated pithy remarks attacking slavery into orations or sermons that criticized the French Revolution, making slavery a common component of the Federalist–Calvinist attack on institutions of violence abroad and at home.[44]

---

[42] Oliver Whipple, *The Historic Progress of Civil and Rational Liberty, and Order, Triumphant over Faction* (Portsmouth, N.H., 1802), 12–13, 44–5; George L. Roth, "Verse Satire on 'Faction,' 1790–1815," *William and Mary Quarterly* 17 (1960).

[43] "The Jeffersoniad," Nos. 1–16, *Columbian Centinel and Massachusetts Federalist.* They were reprinted in *Newburyport Herald, Gazette of the United States,* and *Philadelphia Gazette,* among other journals.

[44] Samuel Deane, *A Sermon, Preached February 19th, 1795: Being a Day of National Thanksgiving, Appointed by the President of the United States* (Portland, Me., 1795); Ashbel Green, *A Sermon, Delivered in the Second Presbyterian Church in the City of Philadelphia: On the 19th of February, 1795. Being the Day of General Thanksgiving throughout the*

Antislavery was a staple of Federalist electioneering materials, alongside the critique that democratic leaders wished to establish a reign of terror in the United States.[45] Anti-Jacobins also pictured the French as would-be enslavers of America, thus completing the parallel between Jacobins and American democrats.[46] Although these references may have been brief, they typically drew on the same core ethical concerns about depravity and violence that motivated longer attacks. For example, the Boston minister and scholar Jeremy Belknap preached a Fast Day sermon in 1798, at the outset of the Quasi-War with France, which attacked the "revolutionary phrenzy" and "wonton despotism" of the French Revolution, as well as the influence of the French party in the United States. The sermon accused French leaders and their American minions of wishing to "enslave" America, and ended with the hope that religious enlightenment would abolish all "war, slavery, oppression, tyranny, superstition and bloodshed."[47] Although the mentions of slavery in this sermon are brief and may be seen to serve the anti-Jacobin cause, Belknap had in fact sustained an active antislavery commitment throughout his life. His typically Calvinist concerns about human depravity led him both to an early opposition to slavery and to a firm Federalist hatred of the French Revolution.

While Federalist–Calvinist critics of southern slavery demonstrated an ethical opposition to the violence of slavery, this ethic had limits. For one, the critique rarely acknowledged the history or presence of slavery in the North. On the few occasions that New Englanders acknowledged slavery in their own region they differentiated it as less violent than the southern variant. The Reverend Timothy Dwight's poem "Greenfield Hill" (1794), which celebrates Connecticut yeoman farming culture, condemns West Indian slavery

United States (Philadelphia, Pa., 1795); Daniel Davis, *An Oration Delivered at Portland, July 4th, 1796. In Commemoration of the Anniversary of American Independence* (Portland, Me., 1796); Abiel Abbot, *A Discourse, Delivered at North-Coventry, July 4th, 1799 Being the Twenty-Third Anniversary of American Independence* (Hartford, Conn., 1799). For an example of this critique in periodical literature, see "The Versifier – No. II," *Connecticut Courant*, Apr. 1, 1793.

45 Federal Party (N.J.), *Address to the Federal Republicans of Burlington County Recommending to Them to Support the Present Members in the Legislature from That County, at the Ensuing Election, as Friendly to the Re-Election of President Adams and Governor Howell* (Trenton, N.J., 1800); Federal Party (N.J.), *Address to the Federal Republicans of the State of New Jersey Recommending the Choice of Aaron Ogden, William Coxe, Jun., James H. Imlay, Franklin Davenport & Peter D. Vroom, Esqrs. For Representatives in the Seventh Congress of the United States* (Trenton, N.J., 1800).

46 Josiah Quincy, *An Oration Pronounced July 4, 1798, at the Request of the Inhabitants of the Town of Boston in Commemoration of the Anniversary of American Independence* (Boston, Mass., 1798); John Lowell, *An Oration, Pronounced July 4, 1799, at the Request of the Inhabitants of the Town of Boston in Commemoration of the Anniversary of American Independence* (Boston, Mass., 1799).

47 Jeremy Belknap, *A Sermon, Delivered on the 9th of May, 1798, the Day of the National Fast, Recommended by the President of the United States* (Boston, Mass., 1798).

in a gory passage capturing "the shrieks of tormented slaves"; but Dwight apologizes for the institution in his own state. Although it is a terrible sin – the North's "chief curse" that must be abolished – slavery is not violent in Connecticut, the land of "mild manners." In the idyllic town of Greenfield Hill, the slave "shares his master's toil" and "takes his portion of the common good."[48] While recent statistical scholarship suggests that slavery in fact was less abusive and homicidal in the North than in the South, Dwight's apology for Connecticut slavery nonetheless indicates the unwillingness of conservative northeastern antislavery writers to acknowledge the injustices of their own racial hierarchy.[49]

The rise of the Federalist–Calvinist critique of Jacobin slavery coincided with an upsurge of racial prejudice in the North, produced in part by postemancipation anxieties. This increasing racial prejudice erected an enormous obstacle to improving the lives of African Americans in the North.[50] Most Federalist and Calvinist critics of slavery believed it consistent both to condemn southern violence against blacks and to demand social subordination from northern blacks.[51] Federalist antislavery writings often balanced awkwardly between using racial prejudice to advance their attacks and indicting southern racism as part of their attacks. Firm believers in hierarchy, the Federalists' dominant racial attitude seems to have been that blacks deserved a place within the social and political system, but that place should be primarily subordinate to whites. The early national era constituted a racial "middle-ground," when conservative white antislavery advocates supported a deferential and yet humanitarian vision of social "uplift" for black people.[52] They criticized racist ideas that removed blacks from human brotherhood, but they treated social integration as a privilege to be awarded only the most accomplished black candidates rather than to African Americans as a whole. Anti-Jacobin antislavery was not egalitarian; it did not germinate contemporary ideals of racial equality. However, it had a consistent ethical core that carried ameliorative potential.

The popular political satire *Remarks on the Jacobiniad* (1795), by John S. J. Gardiner, neatly captures how Federalists used attacks on slaveholder

---

[48] James D. Essig, *The Bonds of Wickedness: American Evangelicals against Slavery, 1770–1808* (Philadelphia, Pa., 1982), 100–2. Also, Turner, *Anti-Slavery Sentiment*, 9. Peter Hinks offers a much more sympathetic reading of *Greenfield Hill* than Essig; see Hinks, "Timothy Dwight."

[49] Randolph Roth, "Twin Evils? Slavery and Homicide in Early America," in *The Problem of Evil: Slavery, Freedom, and the Ambiguities of American Reform*, ed. Steven Mintz and John Stauffer (Amherst, Mass., 2007).

[50] Paul Goodman, *Of One Blood: Abolitionism and the Origins of Racial Equality* (Berkeley, Calif., 1998); Joanne Pope Melish, *Disowning Slavery: Gradual Emancipation and "Race" in New England, 1780–1860* (Ithaca, N.Y., 1998).

[51] See Morse, *Discourse...1808*; Gardiner, *Sermon...14th of July 1810*.

[52] James Brewer Stewart, "The Emergence of Racial Modernity and the Rise of the White North, 1790–1840," *Journal of the Early Republic* 18 (Summer 1998).

violence to strengthen arguments against domestic Jacobinism, even while they reinforced racial hierarchy. This series of satiric essays, first published in the *Federal Orrery* in late 1794, purported to review a poem celebrating the triumph of the Jacobin spirit in the United States. However, the title's suffix signaled to audiences that they were actually reading a satiric attack modeled after Alexander Pope's *The Dunciad* (1725).[53] In the first numbers of the *Jacobiniad*, Gardiner describes the Jacobin spirit as a vision of violence. Her hair is fashioned of snakes, she wears a funereal robe, her hands are stained with blood, and she is rousing the populace to war. The spirit instructs her followers to be strong in the cause of murder and not to allow the "milder dictates of humanity" to triumph. The first half of the essay deploys all the standard anti-Jacobin tropes to demonstrate the danger that French Revolutionary violence poses to the United States.

Then halfway through the review, in the fifth essay, an African American democrat petitions for admission to the Jacobin club. For the subsequent five essays, the *Jacobiniad* becomes a diatribe against democratic hypocrisy and the crime of slavery. Members of the club argue against admitting the applicant because the leaders of their movement, Jefferson, Madison and Giles, are slaveholders:

> Those loved confederates deem all Negroes, dogs –
> Creatures almost beneath the rank of hogs.
> Soon as *Aurora* leaves her saffron bed,
> The *Ethiop* to his daily task is *led*;
> Or, rather, like the brutes, is *driven* along,
> Forced by the threatening curse, and scourging thong-
> If, worn with toil, his 'whip-galled' limbs should fail
> Through pained ear, is driven the vengeful nail.

Gardiner punned on the title of Benjamin Franklin Bache's "Jacobin" news-paper the *Aurora*, to argue that Jacobinism and slavery arose together: "Soon as *Aurora* leaves her saffron bed / The *Ethiop* to his daily task is *led*." By describing the brutal techniques that democratic leaders used to control their slaves (the "scourging thong" and "vengefull nail"), Gardiner con-nected the violence of Jacobinism with the violence of slavery, reviling both spirits as inimical to the peace of the United States.[54] The poem encapsulated the antislavery sentiments of many conservative readers like Abigail Adams

---

[53] This satirical form had been used with great success against Shays's Rebellion, and it was also used by British anti-Jacobins to fight the French Revolution; David Humphreys, *The Anarchiad: A New England Poem, 1786–1787*, ed. Luther G. Riggs (Gainesville, Fla., 1967); William Gifford, *The Baviad, and Maeviad* (London, 1797).

[54] John Sylvester John Gardiner, *Remarks on the Jacobiniad: Revised and Corrected by the Author; and Embellished with Carricatures* (Boston, Mass., 1795), 43.

and John Adams, who speculated on its authorship with great interest.[55] John Adams frequently referred to Jefferson and his fellow Republicans as Jacobins, and Abigail called the Republicans both "Jacobines" and "a packe of Negro-drivers."[56] Both found the *Jacobiniad* a keen and severe indictment of their enemies.

Yet Gardiner's *Jacobiniad* shares the same limitations as Dwight's "Greenfield Hill." In the last verses of Gardiner's *Jacobiniad*, when the Jacobins finally admit the black applicant to their club, Gardiner satirizes the intimate welcome that the Jacobins extend to their new member as sexual and revolting: "each member gave the cordial, close embrace / And smacked, with many a kiss, his ebon face."[57] Northern conservatives were not integrationists, preferring to see blacks freed from slavery but confined to a separate social category. Suggestions of interracial sexuality especially offended conservatives like Gardiner. Nonetheless, northeastern anti-Jacobins harshly criticized the racist fulminations of Jefferson and other slaveholders. They found the bigotry of the slave system distasteful and viewed southern racism as perversely hypocritical for a faction that laid claim to the democratic spirit; moreover, they feared the violent effects that southern racism had on American politics and society.

Thomas Green Fessenden's satiric writings negotiated the same ambiguous space between condemning southern racism and rejecting racial integration. Fessenden, the son of an anti-Jacobin Calvinist minister, began his writing career publishing anti-Jacobin materials in the late 1790s and routinely attacked the French Revolution and its American supporters in Gothic anti-Jacobin terms. "While Marat, Danton, and Robespierre, were wading in human blood," a typical Fessenden essay argued, "they received the applause and acclamations of millions."[58] Fessenden's masterpiece was "Democracy Unveiled" (1805), a two-hundred-page poem in rhyming

[55] Letter from Abigail Adams to John Adams, Dec. 12, 1794; letter from John Adams to Abigail Adams, Dec. 23, 1794; letter from Abigail Adams to John Adams, Dec. 26, 1794; letter from Abigail Adams to John Adams, Jan. 16, 1795; letter from John Adams to Abigail Adams, Jan. 27, 1795 (electronic edition), *Adams Family Papers: An Electronic Archive*, Massachusetts Historical Society (MHS), http://www.masshist.org/digitaladams/.

[56] Letter from John Adams to Abigail Adams, Dec. 28, 1792; letter from Abigail Adams to John Adams, May 23, 1794 (electronic edition); *Adams Family Papers: An Electronic Archive*, MHS, http://www.masshist.org/digitaladams/.

[57] Gardiner, *Jacobiniad*, 49. William Cobbett also made political hay out of the episode of a "Negro man" seeking entry to a Democratic Society and encountering rejection. Like Gardiner, Cobbett used slavery to indict southern democrats of racial bigotry and violent hypocrisy, while at the same time Cobbett's writings revealed his own bigotry; see William Cobbett, *History of the American Jacobins, Commonly Denominated Democrats. By Peter Porcupine, Philadelphia. Being a Supplement to the History of Jacobinism* (Edinburgh, 1797); William Cobbett, *Porcupine's Political Censor, for March 1797*, vol. 1797 (Philadelphia, Pa., 1797).

[58] *Weekly Inspector*, Dec. 6, 1806, 121.

A PHILOSOPHIC COCK

FIGURE 3. "A Philosophic Cock." This print from Newburyport, Massachusetts, the town where Elijah Parish's sermons were published and William Lloyd Garrison began his printing career, depicts a rooster with the head of Thomas Jefferson standing by a hen with the face of a black woman, presumably intended to represent Sally Hemings. The image conflates Jefferson's Jacobin radicalism (the cock was a symbol of revolutionary France, and the adjective *philosophic* was used by conservatives as a synonym for French revolutionary ideology) with his slaveholding. This image calls attention to the common indulgence of sexual passions, rather than violent passions, within each system. *Courtesy of American Antiquarian Society.*

couplets that attacked democratic politics. Canto 4, "The Jeffersoniad," criticized the president for his demagoguery, his violent support of the French Revolution, his atheism, his slaveholding, and his relationship with Sally Hemings. In fifty-five lines of verse, Fessenden scurrilously implied that the three-fifths clause enabled slaveholders like Jefferson to increase their political power through reproduction:

> Great men can never lack supporters;
> Who manufacture their own voters;
> Besides, 'tis plain as yonder steeple,
> They will be *fathers* to *the people.*

Fessenden's attack criticized Jefferson's slaveholding as sexually immoral. On the one hand, this attack clearly identified slaves as exploited subjects (manufactured to serve their owners). However, it also implicitly assumed that conservative readers would be repulsed by interracial sexuality.[59]

Yet many antislavery Calvinists condemned racial prejudice, and Jefferson's racial prejudice in particular, without caveats. Orthodox theologians viewed the president's racism as indicative of his religious infidelity, which in turn made the nation vulnerable to Jacobin anarchy. In another passage from *Notes on the State of Virginia*, Jefferson had theorized that blacks constituted an inferior race, somewhere between orangutans and humans on the scale of existence. Orthodox ministers reacted with revulsion to this early articulation of American racial theory. In the New Testament, Paul preached, "God hath made of one blood all nations of men" (Acts 17:26). Jefferson's racial theory degraded blacks, in Jefferson's own quasi-apologetic words from "the rank in the scale of beings which their Creator may perhaps have given them."[60] Jefferson's opponents reacted bitterly not only to his profane views on race but also to his use of the modifier *perhaps* in a clause concerning the acts of God. "Sir, we excuse you not!" wrote the anti-Jacobin minister William Linn in an 1800 election pamphlet encouraging readers not to vote for Jefferson. "You have degraded the blacks from the rank which God hath given them in the scale of being! You have advanced the strongest argument for their state of slavery!" A country that would elect an infidel for president would suffer the same punishment that France had, after it abolished Christianity. "No colours can paint the horrid effects of such a principle, and the deluge of miseries with which it would overwhelm the human race," warned Linn.[61] Jefferson's skepticism regarding the flood, his opposition to the use of the Bible in schools, his failure to attend church

---

[59] Thomas Green Fessenden, *Democracy Unveiled, or Tyranny Stripped of the Garb of Patriotism, by Christopher Caustic* (Boston, Mass., 1805), 99–125.

[60] Jefferson, *Notes on the State of Virginia*, 143.

[61] *Connecticut Courant*, Feb. 11, 1793; William Linn, *Serious Considerations on the Election of a President Addressed to the Citizens of the United States* (New York, 1800), 13. See also Clement Clarke Moore, *Observations upon Certain Passages in Mr. Jefferson's Notes on Virginia, Which Appear to Have a Tendency to Subvert Religion, and Establish a False Philosophy* (New York, 1804); Branagan, *Disquisitions*, 117; John M. Mason, *The Voice of Warning, to Christians, on the Ensuing Election of a President of the United States* (New York, 1800).

regularly, and his supposed denigration of Jesus, also contributed to his reputation for atheism.[62] In punishment for Jefferson's irreligious denigration of black people, God would subject the United States to Jacobin violence and dissolution.

Despite its limitations, many free blacks saw political promise in Federalist–Calvinist antislavery. Free blacks appear to have supported the Federalist Party at the polls, when given the opportunity to vote.[63] An 1809 campaign speech delivered by the African American leader Joseph Sidney, on the one-year anniversary of the end of the American slave trade, demonstrates how blacks put Federalist antislavery language to use. Sidney instructed his audience in New York City to vote for the Federalists because the party represented liberty and prosperity. He then attacked southern democrats using precisely the same rhetoric that conservative critics had first voiced in the early 1790s. Although southern democratic leaders frequently spoke about the Rights of Man, Sidney argued that "there is not a spot in the United States where oppression reigns with such unlimited sway." Southern elites ruled with the lash. Their "mad democracy" would destroy the United States. For black voters, it was a simple choice between slavery and freedom. "Will you flock to the *slavery-hole* of democracy?" Sidney challenged.[64] Rather than identifying democracy as a liberating ideology, Sidney saw it as a negative force sucking up the rights of black men. Canny observation would confirm this belief, as the democratic expansion of white voting rights in the early nineteenth century was accompanied by the disenfranchisement of free blacks. In New York, most African Americans lost the vote in 1821, the same year that all white men gained it.[65]

Black religious leaders also employed Calvinist–Federalist antislavery language to seek their rights. The late-eighteenth- and early-nineteenth-century tradition of Africanist Calvinism was personified by the Reverend Lemuel Haynes, a biracial New Divinity minister in Vermont.[66] Alive from 1753 to 1833, Haynes bridged the emancipatory fervor of the age of revolution to the abolitionist era and devoted the years in between to formulating a

---

[62] Samuel Hopkins, *A Discourse upon the Slave-Trade, and the Slavery of the Africans: Delivered in the Baptist Meeting-House at Providence, before the Providence Society for Abolishing the Slave-Trade, &c. At Their Annual Meeting, on May 17, 1793* (Providence, R.I., 1793); Amynto, *Reflections on the Inconsistency of Man, Particularly Exemplified in the Practice of Slavery in the United States* (New York, 1796), 19.

[63] Paul Finkelman, "The Problem of Slavery in the Age of Federalism," Barbara B. Oberg and Doron S. Ben-Atar, eds., *Federalists Reconsidered* (Charlottesville, Va., 1998).

[64] Joseph Sidney, *An Oration Commemorative of the Abolition of the Slave Trade in the United States Delivered before the Wilberforce Philanthropic Association, in the City of New-York, on the Second of January, 1809* (New York, 1809).

[65] Jeffrey A. Mullins, "Race, Place and African-American Disenfranchisement in the Early Nineteenth-Century American North," *Citizenship Studies* 10 (Feb. 2006).

[66] The term comes from John Saillant, "'Wipe Away All Tears from Their Eyes': John Marrant's Theology in the Black Atlantic, 1785–1808," *Journal of Millennial Studies* 1 (Winter 1999).

FIGURE 4. The biracial Congregationalist minister Lemuel Haynes (1753–1833) is portrayed on this serving tray preaching before his white congregation in Rutland, Vermont. A committed Federalist, strongly supportive of the reform efforts that constituted the Benevolent Empire, Haynes demonstrates the appeal of anti-Jacobin antislavery to certain northeastern African Americans. *Published by permission of the Museum of Art, Rhode Island School of Design. Bequest of Lucy Truman Aldrich. Photography by Erik Gould.*

Calvinist–Federalist critique of slavery. The illegitimate son of an African father and a white mother, Haynes was abandoned in his infancy and indentured to a pious white family in western Massachusetts who raised him as a foster son and gave him a strong education in the "dreadful state of the damned," as well as other Calvinist doctrines. In 1775 Haynes enlisted as a minuteman, then volunteered for the Fort Ticonderoga expedition. After his service, he returned to his foster family (having completed his indenture) and began to preach, before departing to study for the ministry. His religious outlook throughout his life emphasized the absolute government of God and the sinfulness of man. In 1788 he accepted a ministry in Rutland, Vermont, where he embarked on a public career battling infidelity, Jacobinism, Jeffersonian democracy, and slavery. When he died in 1833, the abolitionist movement celebrated him as a hero.[67]

---

[67] Timothy Mather Cooley, *Sketches of the Life and Character of the Rev. Lemuel Haynes, A.M., for Many Years Pastor of a Church in Rutland, Vt., and Late in Granville, New York*

Haynes's first antislavery work, an unpublished essay titled "Liberty Further Extended" (ca. 1776), drew on the revolutionary ideal of liberty as well as the Calvinist conception of sin to forge an attack on slave keeping. The essay strongly condemned slavery's violence, frequently calling upon bloody imagery, for example addressing slave traders and slaveholders as cannibals: "ye that have made yourselves Drunk with human Blood!"[68] Five more references to blood followed in as many sentences. This Gothic imagery suggested Haynes's dark view of man, which led him to embrace strong government as necessary "to curb the passions of men." Naturally, Haynes became a Federalist in the 1790s. In the years following he preached support for the Alien and Sedition Laws, opposition to the Jeffersonian party, and resistance to the War of 1812. Haynes wielded Federalist political theory against the violence of Jacobinism and of slavery. His sermons frequently employed France as an example of the horrible violence to which men who escaped the control of religion and political deference succumbed. He castigated enemies as Robespierres and drew from the gothic anti-Jacobin narrative *The Cannibals' Progress* to illustrate his sermons. In a typical invocation of the uncivilizing process, Haynes warned his congregation that men who degraded authority and supported the French Revolution were at risk "to imbibe the ferocity of warriors; [and to] become inhuman." The slaveholding of the Virginia party revealed that the Jeffersonians had already begun the dangerous path to barbarism. Haynes's anti-Jacobin and antislavery preaching strongly resembled the opinions of his religious and political friends and allies (among them Timothy Dwight).[69]

Haynes may appear to be a unique case – a singular "black preacher to white America" – but he was not the only African American to embrace religiously conservative antislavery language. John Marrant, the loyalist New Divinity antislavery leader, corresponded with the anti-Jacobin ministers Samuel Hopkins and Samuel Stillman, and his antislavery rhetoric bore the stamp of New Divinity concerns about human depravity.[70] Prince Hall, the Boston-based Calvinist founder of African American Freemasonry, also joined Haynes in mixing conservative political attitudes and antislavery views. Hall volunteered a black regiment to aid the Massachusetts government in suppressing Shays's Rebellion in 1787. The next year, the

(New York, 1837; repr. 1969); Rita Roberts, "Patriotism and Political Criticism: The Evolution of Political Consciousness in the Mind of a Black Revolutionary Soldier," *Eighteenth-Century Studies* 27 (Summer 1994); John Saillant, *Black Puritan, Black Republican: The Life and Thought of Lemuel Haynes, 1753–1833* (Oxford, 2003).

[68] Lemuel Haynes, "Liberty Further Extended"; Lemuel Haynes, *Black Preacher to White America: The Collected Writings of Lemuel Haynes, 1774–1833*, ed. Richard Newman (Brooklyn, N.Y., 1990), 23.

[69] Lemuel Haynes, "The Nature and Importance of True Republicanism"; Haynes, *Black Preacher to White America*, 79.

[70] Saillant, "John Marrant's Theology." Marrant died in 1791, before the violent turn of the French Revolution, but his theological conservatism and connection to Hopkins among other anti-Jacobins suggests that he would not have approved.

Federalist antislavery scholar Jeremy Belknap aided Hall in petitioning for the release of three free blacks kidnapped from Boston for sale into slavery. Hall positioned his cause – improving civil rights for Boston's black population – alongside the Federalist interest in preserving order and maintaining a peaceable civil society.[71] Later, in a 1797 oration before the African Lodge, Hall used typically Federalist language to bemoan the "bloody wars" in Europe, and he encouraged his black audience to "weep with those that weep." Hall posited a connection between the sufferings of Europeans touched by the revolutionary wars abroad and blacks hurt by white violence at home. At a time when Americans strongly associated mobs with Jacobinism, Hall castigated the "mob" in Boston for "shamefully abusing" black citizens. Sounding very much the Federalist, Hall described the mob as comprising lower-class sorts: "low-lived" former domestic servants and hostlers. Asserting the superiority of the African American community to mobbish whites, Hall declared that blacks "had rather suffer wrong than to do wrong, to the disturbance of the community and the disgrace of our reputation: for every good citizen doth honor to the laws of the State where he resides." Standing firmly for the principle of submission to the laws, Hall mixed support for the rights of African Americans with a conservative political perspective in a seemingly smooth emulsion.[72]

Typical Calvinist–Federalist antislavery views also appear in an 1808 essay by an anonymous member of the African Society of Boston. The unknown author began his essay with a strong statement of human depravity. Because humanity had eaten the forbidden fruit, the human race had been afflicted with sin, expressed through human violence in "the spirit of an oppressor, the spirit of tyranny, and the spirit of a murderer!" Most especially, man displayed his sinfulness by the "capital . . . abomination" of human bondage. The author mourned the bloody impact that bondage had wreaked on his people by the lashing whip. Borrowing a phrase from Samuel Hopkins, the author argued that men of "disinterested benevolence" could not support a government that tolerated keeping or trafficking in slaves. He praised the government of Massachusetts, positioning it in stark contrast to the southern states that permitted slavery. How "criminal" it was for those "who love freedom themselves, to prevent any from its enjoyment," the author argued, recapitulating the Federalist critique of southern politicians. Sounding much like any New England chauvinist of the day, the author returned again and again to the privilege of living in Massachusetts, where the air was free and the rights of Africans were respected.[73]

---

[71] Joanna Brooks, "Prince Hall, Freemasonry, and Genealogy," *African American Review* 34 (2000), 200.

[72] Hall, *A Charge*, 10–11.

[73] Member of the African Society, *The Sons of Africans: An Essay on Freedom with Observations on the Origins of Slavery by a Member of the African Society in Boston* (Boston, Mass., 1808).

When the author of "The Sons of Africans" quoted St. Paul that all men were created "of one blood," he had the support of orthodox anti-Jacobin Calvinists like Jedidiah Morse, who made the same remark in an address to Boston's African Meeting House the following year.[74] Yet the subordinate circumstances of free blacks in the Northeast during the early nineteenth century suggests that Paul's hierarchical teachings had wider currency among whites than did his assertions of universal human brotherhood. Jedidiah Morse and most other white conservatives who preached antislavery also preached black submission to the social order. The fact that free blacks in the North like Haynes, Sidney, Hall, and the anonymous author of "The Sons of Africans" used Federalist antislavery to advance the interests of African American people does not indicate that the ideology was color blind. Lemuel Haynes was frequently on the receiving end of racist stares and remarks. He achieved influence over his congregants by demonstrating a soul purely "white" like the Lamb of God. Nonetheless, after thirty years in the Rutland pulpit, Haynes lost his position when – according to his own witticism – the "sagacious" congregation "found out he was *a nigger.*"[75] Racial prejudice was a constitutive factor of the northeastern sensibility in early American republic. Despite that prejudice, Federalist antislavery had ameliorative potentials that attracted African Americans in their search for social justice.

During the early national era, Federalist antislavery served the political purpose of discrediting Jeffersonians. But acknowledging the political utility of the anti-Jacobin critique of slavery does not undermine its significance. Rather, the rhetoric's political utility reveals its power to influence people's minds; political utility is a sign of the effectiveness of a rhetorical trope. While anti-Jacobin antislavery may have had antidemocratic roots, we cannot assume that its conservative origins effectively limited the rhetoric's reception. To the contrary, the anti-Jacobin critique of southern slaveholding violence attracted black authors and ultimately invigorated the abolitionist effort to change American popular sentiment. Antislavery proved useful for the partisan purposes of American anti-Jacobins, but the ethical core of the critique expanded its application beyond the confines of electoral battles.

The Horrors of Slavery

The language of anti-Jacobinism proved as useful for the dedicated opponents to slavery as the language of antislavery did for anti-Jacobins. During the 1790s antislavery discourse turned increasingly to Gothic descriptions

---

74 Morse, *Discourse . . . 1808.*
75 Richard Brown, "'Not Only Extreme Poverty, but the Worst Kind of Orphanage': Lemuel Haynes and the Boundaries of Racial Tolerance on the Yankee Frontier, 1770–1820," *New England Quarterly* 61 (Dec. 1988).

of physical violence, sometimes inflected by overt anti-Jacobin references, which enlarged and transformed earlier antislavery rhetoric. Before the late eighteenth century, concerns about the violence of slaveholding had sounded a minor note in antislavery. Soon after the Chesapeake and the West Indies transitioned from reliance on white indentured servitude to African slavery in the late seventeenth century, religious figures including Richard Baxter, George Fox, and Morgan Godwyn criticized the cruel disciplinary practices used against the slaves. The Puritan Baxter, anticipating Thomas Branagan and many other antislavery writers, went so far as to describe West Indian planters as the "veriest Cannibals." Some early Anglophone abolitionists specifically linked critiques of slavery's violence to attacks on French colonial violence. In 1684, the mystic vegetarian London merchant Thomas Tryon, who had lived in Barbados during the 1660s, published attacks both on the violence of Caribbean slaveholders and on the violence of French Catholic colonialism; the two tracts were linked by a shared "ethical core concerned with the subjective experience of violence."[76] In New England in 1700, in the midst of a three-decade wave of new importations that more than doubled the African population in Massachusetts from 200 to 550, the Massachusetts Puritan Samuel Sewall authored an antislavery text accusing slave traders of "murder." Sewall also wrote in the midst of an influx of refugees from French Catholic violence.[77] Throughout the northern Atlantic, the brutality of slavery and French Catholic bloodshed appeared linked by the problems that violence posed to civil society.

Yet men like Tryon and Sewall represented a few lonely voices waging a minority reaction to the rapidly expanding British slave system. Not until the second half of the eighteenth century did wartime tribulations heighten Anglo-American concerns about the violence of slavery. During the 1750s Quaker reformers identified slavery as the cause of the tribulations they experienced at the onset of the French and Indian War in Pennsylvania; the sect's antislavery turn emerged from its wartime efforts to purify the community and appease God.[78] While Quaker reformers such as Benjamin Lay and Anthony Benezet used evidence of slavery's violence to criticize the institution, many Quakers' pacifist desire not to give voice to violence limited the virulence of their critiques.[79] Most early national Quakers probably

---

[76] Philippe Rosenberg, "Thomas Tryon and the Seventeenth-Century Dimensions of Antislavery," *William and Mary Quarterly* 61 (2004).

[77] Samuel Sewall, *The Selling of Joseph a Memorial* (1700), 2; Mark A. Peterson, "The Selling of Joseph: Bostonians, Antislavery, and the Protestant International, 1689–1733," *Massachusetts Historical Review* 4 (2002), 3.

[78] Sydney V. James, *A People among Peoples: Quaker Benevolence in Eighteenth-Century America* (Cambridge, Mass., 1963).

[79] Benjamin Lay, *All Slave-Keepers That Keep the Innocent in Bondage Apostates Pretending to Lay Claim to the Pure & Holy Christian Religion, of What Congregation So Ever, but Especially in Their Ministers, by Whose Example the Filthy Leprosy and Apostacy Is Spread*

identified with their coreligionist Elias Hicks when he confessed that discussing the tortures used by slave owners was "too much for my nature."[80]

Concerns about the violence of slavery continued to play a secondary role in the antislavery of the 1770s and 1780s. Not until the 1790s did Gothic language begin to dominate antislavery because of a fortuitous coincidence: emancipationist strategy began shifting from politics to persuasion and looking for new rhetorical techniques at precisely the moment when anti-Jacobin discourse was flooding American literature. By the mid-1790s, most of the northern states were advancing toward emancipation by constitutional provision, legal statute, or judicial decision. However, in the South where the cotton gin drove an expansion of slavery after 1793, any progress toward emancipation had ceased. The Constitution secured slavery from national interference, and southern representatives made clear to northern politicians that any attack on slavery at the federal level would precipitate disunion.[81] Although antislavery advocates pushed for the end of the slave trade in 1808 (as soon as the Constitution allowed for the ban), little change could otherwise be made at the political level.

Abolitionists of the early republic who hoped to avoid civil war decided that the best strategy for antislavery progress was to effect a change in national sentiments through the use of propaganda. Yet many abolitionists worried about the inadequacy of language to forward their goals. Revolutionary-era antislavery texts relied primarily on natural rights arguments to convey their message; earlier texts mostly employed biblical objections to the institution. Neither rhetoric had yet persuaded American slaveholders to give up their human property. By 1793, antislavery rhetoric seemed to have become stagnant, leading the Reverend Samuel Hopkins to mourn that "nothing new can be said of slavery."[82] At precisely that moment, anti-Jacobinism arose to supply the abolitionists with a violent new mode of language. Gothic attacks on the French Revolution and the southern Jacobins who supported it pointed the way for American

---

Far and Near (Philadelphia, Pa., 1737); David Crosby, "Anthony Benezet's Transformation of Anti-Slavery Rhetoric," *Slavery and Abolition* 23 (Dec. 2002).

[80] Elias Hicks, *Observations on the Slavery of the Africans and Their Descendants Recommended to the Serious Perusal, and Impartial Consideration of the Citizens of the United States of America, and Others Concerned* (New York, 1811), 22. Even during the antebellum era, as abolitionism vastly increased in popularity, many Quaker communities avoided expressing outright support for abolition because they did not wish to contribute to the violence of social upheaval. Ryan Jordan, "Quakers, 'Comeouters,' and the Meaning of Abolitionism in the Antebellum Free States," *Journal of the Early Republic* 24 (Winter 2004).

[81] Paul Finkelman, "Slavery and the Constitutional Convention: Making a Covenant with Death," in *Beyond Confederation: Origins of the Constitution and American National Identity*, ed. Richard Beeman, Stephen Botein, and Edward C. Carter II (Chapel Hill, N.C., 1987).

[82] Hopkins, *A Discourse . . . 1793*, 3.

abolitionists to attack slavery by publishing extensive accounts of slave-holder violence peppered with anti-Jacobin allusions.

The American Convention for Promoting the Abolition of Slavery announced the shift in strategy toward using violent language to influence American minds at its second annual meeting, in 1795. The representatives of state abolitionist societies who gathered in Philadelphia early that year outlined an ambitious plan to collect and publish information regarding the history and legal frameworks of slavery in their states. American slavery had survived thus far, the minutes concluded, because of a "want of reflection." Americans, especially slave owners, needed to be awakened through "force of reason, and the persuasion of eloquence" into a state of *"horror at the enormity* of their conduct."[83] Many state antislavery societies embraced this change in strategy during the last decade of the eighteenth century.[84] In a 1798 address to the New-York Society for Promoting the Manumission of Slaves, founded by the anti-Jacobins John Jay and Alexander Hamilton, the New York doctor Elihu Smith instructed his audience about the need to shift to a rhetorical strategy for fighting slavery. Smith argued that abolitionists had a duty "to preserve the vivid recollection of the enormities which mark the reign of oppression [slavery]" in order to fight the willful blindness of American slaveholders.[85]

At a time when the enormities of the French Revolution filled American newspapers, preceding even domestic news, abolitionists decided to high-light "enormities" in their antislavery rhetoric. The connection was not coincidental; Elihu Smith embraced Gothic antislavery language after years of reading violent accounts of the French Revolution. Although Smith largely eschewed politics 'and broke with the religious orthodoxy of his child-hood to embrace deism, he nonetheless was embedded in Federalist family and social networks, and the members of his literary salon, the Friendly Club, were almost entirely Federalists. As Elihu Smith, Charles Brockden Brown (the anti-Jacobin author of America's first Gothic novels), William Woolsey (Timothy Dwight's brother-in-law), James Kent (the Federalist

---

[83] American Convention, *Minutes of the Proceedings of the Second Convention of Delegates from the Abolition Societies Established in Different Parts of the United States Assembled at Philadelphia, on the Seventh Day of January, One Thousand Seven Hundred and Ninety-Five, and Continued, by Adjournments, until the Fourteenth Day of the Same Month, Inclusive* (Philadelphia, Pa., 1795). My italics.

[84] Zilversmit, *First Emancipation*, chap. 7.

[85] E. H. Smith, A Discourse, *Delivered April 11, 1798, at the Request of and before the New-York Society for Promoting the Manumission of Slaves, and Protecting Such of Them as Have Been or May Be Liberated* (New York, 1798), 5. Samuel Miller also delivered an antislavery discourse to the New-York Society; "Extract from a discourse delivered before the New-York Society for Promoting the Manumission of Slaves, April 12, 1797." Caleb Bingham, ed., *The Columbian Orator: Containing a Variety of Original and Selected Pieces; Together with Rules; Calculated to Improve Youth and Others in the Ornamental and Useful Art of Eloquence*, 2nd ed. (Boston, Mass., 1799), 293–4.

legal scholar), Samuel Miller (the anti-Jacobin minister), and William Dunlap (the playwright) met to discuss the most recent prints during their club meetings, Smith must have been struck by the persuasiveness of violent writing.

Anti-Jacobins had transformed public opinion of the French Revolution – including Brown's and Miller's attitudes – by repeatedly recounting its atrocities. Perhaps Smith even discussed the need to call similar attention to the enormities of slavery with Woolsey and Dunlap – who had both served as representatives to the national abolitionist convention in 1795. The Friendly Club was a microcosm of the early national social circles in which anti-Jacobins and abolitionists met and exchanged thoughts about language and violence. From these overlapping sensibilities emerged an abolitionist attack on the violence of slavery that self-consciously drew on anti-Jacobin language.[86]

Reflections on the Inconsistency of Man, Particularly Exemplified in the Practice of Slavery (1796), by Amynto, is one of the earliest American antislavery texts to explicitly charge slaveholders as violent Jacobins. The anonymous pamphlet, which was published in New York by a conservative printer of anti-Jacobin literature, pleaded for "total abolition" and defined slavery as an institution of violence, caused by the same human depravity that inspired wars and murder. The pamphlet raised familiar objections to the inconsistency shown by southern Republicans who advocated for the rights of man yet held Africans enslaved. But Amynto went farther than prior abolitionist authors by attacking slaveholders as violent Jacobins. *Reflections* asserted that among "the representatives of Congress from . . . the southern [states], where slavery is yet raging in all its horrors, a furious democracy copied from the Jacobin principles of France appears to be the wish of most of the southern gentry." Amynto gave credence to his claims of slaveholder violence by calling attention to the southern gentry's support for the French Revolution. "'Tis no uncommon sight," Amynto wrote, "to see children, with whips and cudgels, striking and mauling poor old decrepid Negroes," while men raped their slaves and sold their own children. Readers might be tempted to dismiss such extraordinary tales of children torturing elders, and parents selling their children; but by aligning slaveholders with Jacobins, Amynto made his antislavery charges more persuasive.

Reflections suggested that Jacobins and slaveholders were alike because neither would submit to legal or moral limits on their power. Slaveholders

---

[86] Catherine O'Donnell Kaplan, *Men of Letters in the Early Republic: Cultivating Forms of Citizenship* (Chapel Hill, N.C., 2008), chap. 2; Bryan Waterman, *Republic of Intellect: The Friendly Club of New York City and the Making of American Literature* (Baltimore, 2007); James E. Cronin, "Elihu Hubbard Smith and the New York Friendly Club, 1795–1798," *PMLA* 64 (June 1949). Bryan Waterman argues against consensus readings of Charles Brockden Brown's *Wieland* as an anti-Jacobin novel, emphasizing instead the novel's antipathy to religion; Waterman, *Republic of Intellect*, 73–85.

were so accustomed to wielding absolute authority, even to the point of murdering their human property, that they could not govern their passions in the political sphere. The blood spilled by the slave master's whip and the blood spilled by the guillotine flowed into a common pool. In both lands "the voice of brothers blood crieth unto me from the ground." Relief from both nightmares would only come through releasing men from civil and moral bondage:

if we seriously regret those horrid scenes of violence which have been perpetrated by those villains, and cut-throats who have desolated France: If we mourn at the tragic tale, of those multitudes of innocent lives, who have bled under the awful blade of the guillotine... [we] hope that the revolutions of America and France are but introductory movements towards a general emancipation of human nature.[87]

Readers of anti-Jacobin texts who had repudiated the French Revolution after its "horrid scenes of violence" became exposed were compelled by the same logic to repudiate the horrors of American slavery and pray for a "general emancipation." *Reflections* used the language of anti-Jacobinism to recapitulate the audience's rejection of the French Revolution and redirect the sentiment against American slavery.

A similar antislavery title published seven years later, *Reflections on Slavery* by Humanitas, also used anti-Jacobin language to make a radical argument for black racial equality and immediate emancipation. Both titles (as well as a similar magazine essay published in 1796), likely paid tribute to the 1778 antiwar and antislavery pamphlet *Serious Reflections*, by Anthony Benezet.[88] *Reflections on Slavery* told the gothic story of Romain, a Saint Dominguan slave-refugee living in New Jersey who killed himself rather than be forced to return to the West Indies. Stories of slave suicide appeared frequently in late-eighteenth-century abolitionist literature to invoke the innate nobility of the slave.[89] The trope of suicide was associated with Roman virtue, and thus also suggested that black people possessed

---

[87] Amynto, *Reflections on the Inconsistency.*

[88] "Reflections on the Slavery of the Negroes," *The Rural Magazine, or Vermont Repository*, June 1796. Anthony Benezet, *Serious Reflections Affectionately Recommended to the Well-Disposed of Every Religious Denomination Particularly Those Who Mourn and Lament on Account of the Calamities Which Attend Us; and the Insensibility That So Generally Prevails* (Philadelphia, Pa., 1778).

[89] "The Desperate Negroe," *The Massachusetts Magazine, or Monthly Museum*, Oct. 1793; "The Slave," *The Philadelphia Minerva*, Nov. 7, 1795; "Meloncholy Effects of Slavery," *The Balance and Columbian Repository*, Nov. 16, 1802, 366; U.S. Congress, *The Debates and Proceedings in the Congress of the United States; with an Appendix Containing Important State Papers and Public Documents, and All the Laws of a Public Nature*, Permanent ed., vol. 42 (Washington, D.C., 1834), 9th Session, 201; Lay, *All Slave-Keepers*; Thomas Branagan, *A Preliminary Essay, on the Oppression of the Exiled Sons of Africa Consisting of Animadversions on the Impolicy and Barbarity of the Deleterious Commerce and Subsequent Slavery of the Human Species: To Which Is Added, a Desultory Letter Written to Napoleon Bonaparte, Anno Domini, 1801* (Philadelphia, Pa., 1804), 54; Moore,

the personal qualities necessary to participate within the public sphere.[90] (The trope of suicide also exposed how slavery exceeded the violence of the French Revolution, as no one suggested that Europeans killed themselves rather than escape the Jacobins.) Sympathetic anecdotes of suicide became so common in Gothic antislavery literature that one author felt compelled to follow his contribution to the genre with a reminder that suicide was a sin.[91] Humanitas explained that he was forced chose to use suicide to make the case against slavery, because a tale of "human sacrifice" was the "only way" that he could approach a subject of "such magnitude" as human bondage.

While *Serious Reflections* included antislavery arguments based on natural rights, Humanitas described this rhetorical strategy as ineffective because it did not compel readers' attention. Instead, Humanitas offered bloodshed and gore. He described in detail Romain's suicide and the appearance of his corpse where it lay fallen. Unwilling to trust his readers' spontaneous reaction to this Gothic account, Humanitas even modeled the appropriate response through characterization of the suicide's onlookers: "the sensibility of the citizens, who viewed the breathless corse [*sic*] and bloodstained pavement, were excited; and mingled expressions of horror and compassion were mutually exchanged: and an universal sentiment of detestation, seemed to prevail against a system productive of such consequences." Humanitas used Gothic language in order to excite his readers' emotions and to persuade them to "universally" reject the institution of slavery. Later chapters of *Reflections* gave further accounts of the brutality suffered by slaves. Finally, like Amynto, Humanitas closed his *Reflections* by raising the specter of Jacobin bloodshed to drive home the brutality of slavery. Following several warnings about the providential consequences threatened against the national crime of slavery, Humanitas concluded, "We have been blesst with peace while all Europe were involved in war.... Let us then, at least, offer up the insense of gratitude for such mercies, ... by observing the command, to 'Loose the bands of wickedness, to undo heavy burdens, and let the

---

Observations, 24; John Parrish, *Remarks on the Slavery of the Black People Addressed to the Citizens of the United States, Particularly to Those Who Are in Legislative or Executive Stations in the General or State Governments: And Also to Such Individuals as Hold Them in Bondage* (Philadelphia, Pa., 1806); Boyrereau Brinch and Benjamin F. Prentiss, *The Blind African Slave, or, Memoirs of Boyrereau Brinch, Nick-Named Jeffrey Brace* (St. Alban's, Vt., 1810), 77; Thomas Branagan, *Avenia, or, a Tragical Poem on the Oppression of the Human Species and Infringement on the Rights of Man, in Six Books: With Notes Explanatory and Miscellaneous, Written in Imitation of Homer's Iliad* (Philadelphia, Pa., 1805), 267; Jesse Torrey, *A Portraiture of Domestic Slavery, in the United States: With Reflections on the Practicability of Restoring the Moral Rights of the Slave, without Impairing the Legal Privileges of the Possessor...* (Philadelphia, Pa., 1817; repr. 1970), 11.

[90] David N. Gellman, "Race, the Public Sphere, and Abolition in Late Eighteenth-Century New York," *Journal of the Early Republic* 20 (Winter 2000): 627–8.

[91] Philanthropos, *African Miscellanist*, 19–20.

oppressed free." The shadow of Napoleonic and Jacobin violence forced the conscientious to seek a general emancipation of humankind.[92]

In an oration delivered before a conservative political club in 1804, the Federalist diplomat and committed emancipationist David Humphreys also drew on his audience's anti-Jacobin sentiments to inspire disgust for slavery. Humphreys pleaded in impassioned verse:

> If we on changeful Gaul, not coldly gaz'd
> But lov'd the fair reforms by patriots plann'd
> Till, fir'd by crimes, our indignation blazed,
> That democrats enrag'd should rule the land,
> [then]
> Of every class, ye proud oppressors! hear!
> Monarchs and demagogues who realms enslave,
> Or ye who purchase bondsmen far and near,
> I hate your conduct and your anger brave.

Any person who truly loved freedom but reacted with horror at the Reign of Terror, insisted Humphreys, should similarly despise the tyranny and bloodshed of slavery. Humphreys attacked slavery as an institution of violence, which would be punished by violence. God would not permit the Africans long to suffer the whip, the fetters, and the "penal thong." He would chastise the United States for its national crime, and force slaveholders to "drink, inebriate, of the blood they spilt" until the earth would be "unburden'd of their crimes; / And Hell! rise grim, their coming shades to greet." Like many northern proponents of antislavery, Humphreys worried that direct political action taken by abolitionist societies might lead to a civil war. But he knew that calls to natural rights were not enough to persuade Americans to disavow slavery. He needed to appeal to their "sensibility as well as [their] reason." The language of anti-Jacobinism enabled Humphreys to elicit the sympathy of his audience.[93]

When British abolitionists similarly used anti-Jacobin language to foster sympathy for antislavery, American publishers sometimes adapted their arguments for domestic audiences. *The Connecticut Gazette* reprinted a 1794 article from a London paper attacking the slave trade for being written in "characters of blood," like the crimes of revolutionary France.

---

[92] Humanitas, *Reflections on Slavery, with Recent Evidence of Its Inhumanity Occasioned by the Melancholy Death of Romain, a French Negro* (Philadelphia, Pa., 1803), 14, 36. A second antislavery pamphlet was published under the pseudonym "Humanitas" in Kentucky two years later; however, the two texts probably did not share a single author; Humanitas, *Hints for the Consideration of the Friends of Slavery, and Friends of Emancipation, Containing Remarks on Mr. Conway's Investigation of Slavery, and Other Publications of the Same Nature* (Lexington, Ky., 1805).

[93] Humphreys, *Valedictory Discourse*, 31–36, 29. Humphreys antislavery commitment was longstanding, he had volunteered to captain an all-black regiment from Connecticut during the American Revolution.

"We revile the Convention of France for confiscation of property, we revile them for supporting rapine by murder, and we are shocked at their impiety. Do we not in the present instance practice what we depreciate? We confiscate property, we support rapine by murder" declaimed the author. The trade should be abolished to provide "a virtuous contrast to the crimes of France," as the two nations met on the battlefield.[94] Ten years later, still at war with France, the English anti-Jacobin Stephen Jones warned his countrymen that God would punish Britain for the injustice of the slave trade by subjecting them to devastation at the hands of Napoleon. In the late 1780s, France had tried to increase the slave trade "and to avenge devoted Africa at least, if not to save her, [God] dropped down among them the French Revolution." A conservative American religious periodical that reviewed Jones's book drew the obvious parallel to the United States. "If Great Britain had reason to tremble on account of their guilt contracted by the slave trade, so have we."[95]

At times, antislavery conservatives interpolated anti-Jacobin references into their texts to draw an implicit comparison, without making the connection explicit. Royall Tyler, an eccentric Federalist lawyer and author, used this technique in his popular 1797 novel *The Algerine Captive*, which describes the misadventures of Updike Underhill, a young New England doctor on the make who becomes involved in the slave trade. In the first chapter, Underhill traces his descent from John Underhill, the Puritan warrior who slaughtered Pequot women and children at the Mystic Fort massacre in 1637; the doctor turns out to be similarly lacking in ethical compunctions concerning violence. The novel's central chapters recall Underhill's visit to the South, where he discovers a brutal slave system dependent on the lash. Although Underhill once feels a pang of his "New England . . . conscience," the sentiment is too weak to prevent him from enlisting on a slave-trading voyage aboard the ship *Freedom*. Captured by Algerian pirates during the voyage, Underhill is enslaved by his complicity in the violent slave system. To guard his readers' consciences against the same moral failings as his character, Tyler shifts narrative gears in the midst of the book's antislavery chapters to depict the horrors of the French Revolution. Between accounts of southern slaveholding violence and the brutality of the slave trade, the reader's attention is directed to the crimes of the French Revolution, evoked by customary anti-Jacobin tropes like "Fierce Roberspierre [*sic*]," the "Moloch of the French nation," and the "reign of the terrorists." Tyler briefly inserts anti-Jacobinism into his antislavery narrative in order to heighten his readers' reaction against the violence of slavery. *The Algerine Captive* arms readers with moral approbation against Jacobin violence, then moves on to persuade readers to reject slavery's violence.[96]

94 "Slave-Trade," *Connecticut Gazette*, June 5, 1794.
95 "The Slave Trade," *Christian Disciple*, Oct. 1814, 309–11; Dec. 1814, 357–60.
96 Royall Tyler, *The Algerine Captive: Or, the Life and Adventures of Doctor Updike Underhill: Six Years a Prisoner among the Algerines*, ed. Caleb Crain, The Modern Library (New York, 2002), 79–96. For additional anti-Jacobin references, see pp. 173 and 179.

Like Tyler's *Algerine Captive*, many periodicals and newspapers suggested a similarity between French Revolutionary violence and slavery's violence through narrative proximity. Conservative editors routinely positioned antislavery essays next to anti-Jacobin texts, leaving readers to observe the similarity between the excessive violence in each. For example, *The Balance and Columbian Repository*, which started publication in January 1802, immediately began publishing both antislavery and anti-Jacobin materials. Although the two were usually kept separate, proximity and a continuity of language drew implicit connections between them. Articles throughout the first year mourned the "blood of millions of enslaved and murdered wretches" spilled by slavery. Many issues also contained jabs at the pretension of the southern Republicans who supported slavery, as well as editorial asides condemning French violence. Oftentimes, *Balance* condemned the French as especially brutal slaveholders, using the violence of the Haitian Revolution as proof of their guilt. Elsewhere the newspaper clearly attributed both revolutionary violence and slavery's violence to man's depravity.[97] Conservative British periodicals of the era also used the tactic of positioning antislavery and anti-Jacobin materials adjacently, often to highlight Britain's exemplary nonviolence in its pursuit of ending the slave trade.[98]

The antislavery author who most consistently matched the themes of Jacobinism and slavery in his gothic abolitionist writings was the ex-slave trader Thomas Branagan. In his first antislavery pamphlet, the *Preliminary Essay* (1804), Branagan explained that he chose to use the Gothic genre because "to my serious strains the ear is shut." He employed violent language because dispassionate reason could not accomplish his task. "Do I seem to treat you with uncommon asperity of language?" Branagan rhetorically asked South Carolina's slaveholder legislators in one chapter of the *Preliminary Essay*. "Scurrility of language I abhor; but, on such a topic, asperity of language is unavoidable. Nay, on such a subject we labour under a penury of language. Language fails; and it is almost unmeaning. The enormity of your conduct, I confess, I know no words sufficient to express. Conception, in this case, is too big for expression." Branagan made this point repeatedly throughout his many "bloody recitals" of slavery's crimes. "What words can possibly describe, what imagination can paint, the horrors [slavery] have occasioned?" he asked. None, he answered later: "no imagination can conceive, no tongue or pen can describe" the bloodshed he witnessed.[99]

[97] *The Balance*, especially February, March, July, and August issues. For man's depravity, see Nov. 30, 1802. Other examples of periodicals that placed antislavery sentiment near anti-Jacobin articles include *The Rural Magazine or Vermont Repository*, Mar. 1795; *Columbian Centinel*, Jan. 24, 1795; *Massachusetts Magazine*, Nov. 1795 and Oct. 1793; *American Moral and Sentimental Magazine*, 1797; *Philadelphia Monthly Magazine*, 1798.

[98] Robert R. Dozier, *For King, Constitution, and Country: The English Loyalists and the French Revolution* (Lexington, Ky., 1983), 19.

[99] Branagan, *Preliminary Essay*, 219, 169, 186.

Branagan drew frequently on anti-Jacobinism to reinforce his antislavery rhetoric, making a clear connection between slavery's violence and Jacobin violence. Although American and British readers had not yet suffered Jacobin violence at home, Branagan warned that God would soon lift his protection and use France to punish them for the crime of slavery. "You have not been reduced to the painful necessity of beholding your children dashed against the stones, or pierced through by the point of the bayonet, nor can you form a just conception of a beloved relative blown to pieces by a ball from the mouth of a cannon, burnt alive, or suspended on a gibbet," Branagan wrote, recalling the horrors described by Anthony Aufrere in *The Cannibals' Progress*. But if they continued to engage in slavery, they would learn of these crimes firsthand. Branagan imagined a scenario in which the French army invaded New York and kidnapped ten thousand people to serve as slaves in the West Indies. God would have punished the United States for slavery with violence that was "Jacobin" either in its form or its actors.[100]

If God did not punish the United States with violence at the hands of the French themselves, Branagan persisted, then the slaveholding southern Jacobins would destroy the nation. Like Theodore Dwight and Noah Webster, Branagan pictured slavery as an uncivilizing institution that degenerated men and led inevitably to civil collapse and anarchy. As an institution of violence, slavery was inconsistent with civil government. If slaveholders were permitted "to put their principles to practice," a footnote to his antislave-trading poem "Avenia" warned, it "will give the death blow to liberty." Slave owners were "cruel, ambitious, interested men, who would wade through seas of the blood of their fellow men, to exalt themselves." Slaveholders were aristocrats, morally incapable of preserving the republic. They had no sense of justice, but were merely wolves, and the greater control they gained in the United States, the increasing likelihood that the nation would be "rent asunder," like the French Republic.[101]

Warnings about the dangers that French or southern Jacobins posed to the American republic were only a secondary concern for Branagan, however. His main "painful task" was to describe "the cruelties and barbarities" of slavery. Branagan depicted his suffering African subjects as not merely enslaved, "they are, in instances innumerable, oppressed, and starved, and tormented, and murdered... [suffering] shocking barbarities, barbarities which debase human nature far beneath the brute." Slaves suffered a lifetime of tortures so brutal that when Branagan recalled them, it caused his soul to recoil and "tremors seize my whole frame; I can hardly restrain

---

[100] Branagan, *Preliminary Essay*, 170, 186; Branagan, *Penitential Tyrant*, 227.

[101] Branagan, *Avenia*, 311–12, Thomas Branagan, *Serious Remonstrances, Addressed to the Citizens of the Northern States, and Their Representatives Being an Appeal to Their Natural Feelings & Common Sense: Consisting of Speculations and Animadversions on the Recent Revival of the Slave Trade in the American Republic* (Philadelphia, Pa., 1805).

my knees from smiting one against another, while my blood hangs shivering in my veins." It was precisely this physical effect that Branagan hoped to achieve in his readers. By exploiting the conventions of Gothic literature, familiarized in America through the anti-Jacobin reaction, he hoped to seize his readers by the guts, to cause their stomachs to twist, and to physically impel them to act in support of his cause.[102]

Branagan described his narrative in the *Preliminary Essay* as a "catalogue" of terrors.[103] The word *catalogue* or the phrase "catalogue of horrors" recurred frequently in anti-Jacobin literature, where it was often followed by serial accounts of atrocities.[104] Branagan's catalog supplied innumerable examples of the terrible tortures that slaveholders used to control their chattel. These practices included not just whippings and mutilations but also practices such as dripping hot lead on slaves, scalding them with boiling water, filling slaves' wounds with salt and pepper, weighing them down with heavy chains, forcing slaves to eat their own cutoff ears, holding their feet to a slow fire until their bodies roasted, and throwing slaves into pots of boiling cane juice. Ostensibly directing his comments toward slaveholders, Branagan instructed his readers to look on the wretched scenes he described: "Go, thou wretch, view thy hungry, naked, bleeding, groaning, expiring slaves; all raw with fresh wounds."[105] Earlier antislavery authors such as Sewall, Benezet, or Hopkins used accounts of violence as evidence to support arguments against slavery. Branagan transcended argumentation and used violence to induce pure horror. Readers need not be reasoned toward an understanding of the injustice of slavery; it was enough for them to reject slavery out of revulsion.

The substitution of horror for reason is emblematically captured in the descriptions and pictures of a torture device known as the slave's muzzle, which Branagan included in many of his books. The slave muzzle was an iron face mask that projected into the subject's mouth, preventing the person from eating, drinking, or speaking. An article in *American Museum* first described the slave's muzzle in 1789, but the device gained traction in the public imagination during the late 1790s, after an illustrator named Alexander Anderson pictured it in an iconic set of wood engravings. Anderson's image, along with others of his woodcuts, was used to illustrate an abolitionist broadside entitled *Injured Humanity*, published in New York

---

[102] Branagan, *Preliminary Essay*, 22–30.
[103] Branagan, *Preliminary Essay*, 68.
[104] *Western Star*, May 14, 1793; *Columbian Centinel*, Feb. 28, 1795; *Monthly Magazine and American Review*, Mar. 1800; David Osgood, *Some Facts Evincive of the Atheistical, Anarchical, and in Other Respects, Immoral Principles of the French Republicans Stated in a Sermon Delivered on the 9th of May, 1798, the Day Recommended by the President of the United States for Solemn Humiliation, Fasting, and Prayer* (Boston, Mass., 1798), 6.
[105] Branagan, *Preliminary Essay*, 84.

FIGURE 5. "Injured Humanity" (ca. 1805–8). This engraving by Alexander Anderson depicts the violence of slavery. The picture of a torture device that physically restrains its victims from speech is especially effective at capturing the early national trope of slavery's unspeakable violence. Anderson's evocative imagery was widely reprinted in nineteenth-century antislavery literature. *Collection of the New York Historical Society.*

in 1802, which depicted slavery as a catalogue of horrors.[106] It appeared again in Thomas Branagan's *Penitential Tyrant* (1805) and *Avenia* (1805). Two years later, Anderson's image of the slave muzzle was reprinted in the Gothic abolitionist print *The Mirror of Misery, or Tyranny Exposed* (1807), along with other iconic images such as the schematic of a packed slave ship that recurred throughout antislavery literature. The image of the slave's muzzle was powerful because it showed the subjectivity of the slave victim, eyes gazing out from within the torture device. And yet the image precluded the possibility of hearing the slave's voice; the slave's words were silenced, and only the visual impression of violence gave testimony to his suffering. The popularity of descriptions and images of the slave's muzzle in the 1790s witnesses the transition to a Gothic language of antislavery, which substituted horror and revulsion for reason and empathy. The violence of slavery was so appalling that only Gothic narrative devices could convey the horror by reducing its onlookers to bodily mortification.[107]

Violence came to predominate over all other critiques of slavery during the 1790s and early 1800s; what had previously figured as a proof of injustice developed into slavery's only meaning. Violent tropes that had flourished in anti-Jacobin literature bloomed anew in antislavery texts. Sometimes Jacobin violence served as a quick reference point to judge the horrors of slavery. Jarvis Brewster complained that slavery was "a system of tyranny and persecution more horrible perhaps than was ever practiced by a Nero, or a Robespierre."[108] More commonly, antislavery texts adopted writing techniques and specific images from anti-Jacobin literature. No longer was it sufficient to mention the shedding of blood in antislavery materials; now authors pictured it in stomach-wrenching detail. "And oft our gore hath crimson'd thy green serge, / Pour'd copious from our purpling tort'ring wounds," complain the "shades of Afric's slaughter'd millions" in an antislavery poem published in *Rural Magazine* in 1796.[109] In a poem relating the tale of a slave who committed suicide, the author envisioned how "his mangled carcass floated on the flood, / and stained the silver winding stream with blood."[110] *Avenia* imagined bloodied slaves "their bodies scourg'd, and stiff with clotted gore." Many other texts described blood as

---

[106] "The Gleaner of Scraps. No. I," *The American Museum, or, Universal Magazine, Containing Essays on Agriculture*, Nov. 1789, 408. See also "The Slave's Muzzle," *The American Moral and Sentimental Magazine*, Sept. 11, 1797. Wood, *Slavery, Empathy, and Pornography*, 224.

[107] *The Mirror of Misery, or, Tyranny Exposed: Extracted from Authentic Documents, and Exemplified by Engravings* (New York, 1807), 19.

[108] Brewster, *Exposition*, 7. Jesse Torrey also compared slaveholders to Nero; Torrey, *Portraiture of Domestic Slavery*, 11.

[109] "Reflections on the Slavery of the Negroes," *The Rural Magazine: or Vermont Repository*, June 1796.

[110] "The Slave," *Philadelphia Minerva*, Nov. 7, 1795.

"flowing" from the marks of the lash. The imagery of slave bloodshed calls to mind the poetic descriptions of the Reign of Terror found in many of the same Federalist periodicals that published antislavery materials.

Accusations of cannibalism, the ultimate indicator of Jacobin savagery, recurred frequently in Gothic antislavery writings. A poem published in the *Connecticut Courant* in 1793 suggested facetiously that slavery could supply the cannibalistic appetite of the Jacobins. Early verses of the poem described the violence of the French Revolution, and the execution of King Louis XVI: "blood-stain'd trophies from his reeking gore, the savage mob in savage triumph bore!" A later verse suggested that southern Republicans would be most helpful to the French cause if they sent them slaves to eat, rather than rolls of tobacco: "A score of Negroes sent over for feed, / Would much improve the present patriot-breed."[111] The poem linked Jacobinism, slavery, and cannibalism by their common core of violence. Abolitionist authors also accused American slaveholders of possessing cannibalistic desires. In Pelham's first letter to the *Connecticut Courant*, he argued that if slaves were good for food, their southern masters would undoubtedly eat them.[112] *Balance* described slave owners as the "wolves of Adam's race" who "gorge themselves with the spoils and blood of their species."[113] Other antislavery materials condemned the consumption of sugar as a form of cannibalism, because its cultivation involved the destruction of so many lives: "Oh guilty sweet seducing food, / Tainted by streams of human blood!"[114] This image resonated with the anecdotal accounts often repeated in abolitionist literature of masters murdering their slaves, or slaves committing suicide, by being boiled alive in vats of cane juice.

Taking a page straight out of *The Cannibal's Progress*, the archetypal anti-Jacobin narrative, the *United States Gazette* suggested that southerners were skinning slaves for shoe leather.[115] The popular anti-Jacobin image of the landscape of death also appeared in abolitionist literature. John Kenrick's *Horrors of Slavery* included an extract from a British source implying that if "human blood was the best manure for the land," planters would justify killing their slaves to feed the crops.[116] Black abolitionist Peter Williams pictured the slave trade's disfiguration of the African landscape, "these fair fields are now bedewed with blood, and covered with mangled carcasses."[117] Philanthropos, the author of an 1802 antislavery pamphlet published in

---

[111] "The Versifier – No. II," *Connecticut Courant*, Apr. 1, 1793.

[112] "Pelham," *Connecticut Courant*, Nov. 21, 1796.

[113] *The Balance*, Mar. 9, 1802.

[114] "On Sugar," *The American Moral and Sentimental Magazine*, Aug. 28, 1797.

[115] *United States Gazette*, Aug. 17, 1814; quoted in Mason, *Slavery and Politics*, 47.

[116] John Kenrick, *Horrors of Slavery: In Two Parts* (Cambridge, Mass., 1817), 26.

[117] Peter Williams, *An Oration on the Abolition of the Slave Trade; Delivered in the African Church, In the City of New-York, January 1, 1808. By Peter Williams, Jun. A Descendant of Africa* (New York, 1808), 17–19.

New Jersey, argued that slavery had caused "the plains of African [to be] deluged with blood."[118] Philanthropos also deployed the anti-Jacobin description of slavery as a "catalogue of crimes," as did George Ritter, the member of a Philadelphia debating society that took up the subject of slavery in 1802.[119] Echoing another anti-Jacobin formulation, several antislavery texts quoted William Wilberforce's description of slavery's history as "written throughout in characters of blood."[120] The same phrase was also used to describe the violence of Jacobinism.[121] The African American abolitionist Henry Sipkins echoed the Gothic trope of linguistic inability by describing the "sanguinary massacres" committed in the slave trade that had cause the shores of Africa to "be drenched with human blood," then asking "why attempt to portray in their true colors, scenes of oppression, which language the most descriptive is inadequate to delineate?"[122] Other familiar elements of anti-Jacobin literature that figure heavily in Gothic antislavery texts include the violence of rape and the figuration of slave owners as monsters or beasts.[123]

Antislavery texts published in the United States during the early 1800s increasingly forsook narrative or argument in exchange for cataloging brutality. Publications such as *The Mirror of Misery* (1807) and *Horrors of Slavery* (1817) presented serial extracts of the most violent elements from longer works. *Horrors of Slavery* included passages describing the prolonged torture and murder of a ten-month-old child during the Middle Passage, a female slave tortured with a blazing torch, the cruel murder of a runaway slave, and a slow death by gibbeting. In the preface to his Gothic exposé of southern cruelty, Jarvis Brewster apologized for its rhetorical violence but complained that natural rights language had not abolished slavery. "Liberty is a soft and pleasing sound," he wrote; it had led Americans to fight for independence, but it also permitted the victors to extend dominion over

---

[118] Philanthropos, *African Miscellanist*, 5. This pseudonym had been used in 1798 by the radical Baptist antislavery preacher, Morgan John Rhees.

[119] George Ritter, *A Speech Delivered on the 13th January, 1802, before the Society Called the Proficuous Judicatory, Concerning the Advantages That Would Be Derived from a Total Abolition of Slavery* (Philadelphia, Pa., 1802), 11.

[120] "Slave-Trade," *Connecticut Gazette*, June 5, 1794; "Slavery," *Philadelphia Repository, and Weekly Register*, Aug. 18, 1804; Edwards, *Injustice and Impolicy*, 56; Humanitas, *Reflections on Slavery*, 37.

[121] Jedidiah Morse, *A Sermon, Exhibiting the Present Dangers, and Consequent Duties of the Citizens of the United States of America. Delivered at Charlestown, April 25, 1799, the Day of the National Fast* (New York, 1799), 18.

[122] Henry Sipkins, *An Oration on the Abolition of the Slave Trade; Delivered in the African Church, in the City of New-York, January 2, 1809. By Henry Sipkins, a Descendant of Africa* (New York, 1809), 14, 19.

[123] David Rice, *Slavery Inconsistent with Justice and Good Policy, Proved by a Speech, Delivered in the Convention, Held at Danville, Kentucky* (New York, 1804); Alexander McLeod, *Negro Slavery Unjustifiable: A Discourse* (New York, 1802); Smith, *Discourse ... 1798*.

a million American slaves. The failures of natural rights language drove Brewster to dip his pen in blood. He apologized for upsetting readers but reminded them that "those instances of cruelty which I have enumerated, are but a drop in the bucket."[124] The reservoir of blood would fill the pen of antislavery writers for many decades to come. The Gothic critique of slavery as an institution of violence strengthened calls for immediate emancipation. Every day, new crimes of violence were committed against slaves; they were whipped anew, starved anew, raped anew. Unlike the religious and natural rights arguments, which criticized slavery as an unjust condition, the new abolitionism criticized slavery as comprising brutal actions that multiplied in number every day. The author of *Tyrannical Libertymen* (1795) scorned the gradualists who believed that "there shall be an abolition but it shall begin moderately, and proceed leisurely." He was joined by many Gothic antislavery authors in demanding an immediate end to the national evil.[125]

In 1872, when American slavery had been thoroughly destroyed and Reconstruction still seemed plausible, the Republican political leader Henry Wilson published a history of abolitionism that marked the movement's 1795 decision to focus attention on slavery's horrors as a significant turning point.[126] Graphic descriptions of bloodshed, tortures, murders, and rapes served as critical tools to arrest the attention of the public. The uneasy political union between free and slave states made many Americans resistant to antislavery speech. They disregarded the classic political and religious arguments against slavery, because those arguments threatened to unleash civil war. Antislavery authors adopted the violent language of anti-Jacobinism for its power to demand attention by inducing a physical reaction in a resistant audience. Logic could be dismissed, but a hyperaccelerated heartbeat or a gag reflex was harder to ignore. Anti-Jacobinism enabled early national abolitionists to expand the general indictments of violence that had been made before and to transform antislavery texts into catalogs of horror that violently repulsed their readers and compelled a reaction. Violent language, abolitionists hoped, could create a bipolar reaction, both of humanitarian concern for the slaves and of anger at slave masters. Wilson and his allies would ultimately need to cultivate both reactions in order to destroy the slave power.

The Horrors of Saint Domingue

The dual functions of violent language, its ability both to turn the reader against violence and to raise the reader's desire to commit violence, are set in relief by American abolitionists' writings about slave rebellion. During

---

[124] Brewster, *Exposition*, iv–6.
[125] *Tyrannical Libertymen*, 4–5; Rice, *Slavery Inconsistent*; Dwight, *An Oration . . . 1794*; Humanitas, *Reflections on Slavery*.
[126] Wilson, *Slave Power*, chap. 2.

the 1790s and early 1800s, the techniques of Gothic literature developed in a transatlantic context to describe not only the enormities of the French Revolution but also the horrors of the slave rebellion in the French colony of Saint Domingue. A slave revolt that began in 1791 roiled the island in transracial and transnational bloodshed for twelve years until the establishment of the Republic of Haiti in 1803. While France, the United States, Great Britain, and Spain repeatedly intervened in the island's affairs, refugees fled to neighboring Caribbean islands, the United States, and Europe, spreading accounts of Dominguan bloodshed throughout the Atlantic by conversation, correspondence, and reportage.[127] Many of these accounts employed the same techniques of Gothic literature popularized in anti-Jacobin literature. Professing the inability of their pens to account for the "horrors" in Saint Domingue, authors filled pages with gory descriptions of tortures, murders, cannibalism, mutilation, and ever-flowing blood.[128] These accounts should have produced revulsion in conservative anti-Jacobins fearful of bloodshed, but violent language's bipolar powers to seduce as well as to repel readers produced a more surprising reaction.

While southern slaveholders reacted with predictable horror to the Haitian Revolution, many northeastern antislavery authors expressed sympathy for the rebels and used violent language about the rebellion to threaten slaveholders rather than to condemn their victims. Some celebrated the Revolution as a glorious cause, akin to the American Revolution. A 1796 essay titled "Reflections on the Slavery of the Negroes" called on Vermont readers to rethink their initial reactions to the seemingly frightful reports coming from the former French colony:

> The fierce revolt of Afric's tortur'd tribes,
> which now wide rage around Carribbean isles,
> Our half reflecting minds too quick condemn.
> Were we in dire captivity and chains,
> Oppresst, degraded, as they've been for ages,
> We would revolt, had we the means and pow'r
> Strowing our way with carcasses and blood,
> And deem it justice, reason, noble virtue.
> Whips, chains, swords, so long in tyrants' hands
> Are now destroying ———— is this more than just?[129]

The poem uses Gothic description to engage the complicity of the reader; we are incited to strow "our way with caracasses and blood." Here bloody

---

[127] For recent overviews, see Robin Blackburn, "Haiti, Slavery, and the Age of Democratic Revolution," *William and Mary Quarterly* 63 (Oct. 2006); Laurent Dubois, *Avengers of the New World: The Story of the Haitian Revolution* (Cambridge, Mass., 2004).

[128] Matt Clavin, "Race, Rebellion and the Gothic: Inventing the Haitian Revolution," *Early American Studies* 5 (Spring 2007).

[129] "Reflections on the Slavery of the Negroes," *The Rural Magazine, or Vermont Repository*, June 1796.

language is used to seduce the reader to acts of violence rather than to repulse readers from the cause.

American antislavery authors inverted typical tropes of anti-Jacobin writing into words of support for the black rebels of Saint Domingue. Echoing every conservative who had ever criticized the French Revolution as written in words of blood, the Virginia-born Presbyterian minister David Rice praised the "brave sons of Africa" for waging a "noble" rebellion that was "written with the blood of thousands." These violent deaths were pictured as heroic sacrifices rather than as meaningless bloodshed. Like other early national abolitionists, Rice condemned slavery as an institution of violence; it was a constant state of war between master and servant. Yet rather than revile the bloody outcome of the war in Saint Domingue, Rice cheered the violence of the slaves, who were finally wreaking their righteous vengeance. In Rice's formulation, bloody language became a call to arms rather than a prompt for disgust.[130]

Abolitionists used Haiti to condemn slaveholder violence, which they blamed for initially causing the rebellion. In Saint Domingue, "the consequent atrocities, most unquestionably resulted from the remembrance of the former barbarity of masters," argued the colonizationist Jesse Torrey in 1817. Although Torrey did not praise the Haitian Revolution outright, he glossed over its violence quickly and reserved his Gothic rhetoric for the French. Torrey quoted from a speech delivered by Mirabeau to illustrate French violence: "it was a white, who first plunged a negro into a burning oven, – who dashed out the brains of a child in the presence of its father, – who fed a savages with his own proper flesh. These are the monsters that have to account for the barbarity of the revolted slaves." By comparison, he remained vague about the horrors of slave rebellion, alluding to but not detailing one atrocity as "too horrible to describe."[131] More radical abolitionists exceeded Torrey, not only blaming slaveholder violence for the rebellion but also describing the massacres of whites as sanctified. Extracts from a Saint Dominguan travelogue that were published in a New York periodical in 1802 related horrifying stories of the arbitrary violence committed upon slaves by their owners and concluded with the "hope that Divine Justice will hear the cries of the sufferer, and sooner or later accumulate on the tyrant's head all the weight of its vengeance."[132] The violent practices of slave owners justified their sufferings. In the Haitian Gothic, horror was sometimes a fantasy, not always a nightmare. Harkening back to revolutionary understandings of freedom as an obligation to resist tyranny, northern supporters of the Haitian Revolution depicted the violence as legitimating, not delegitimating, emancipation in the Caribbean.[133]

---

[130] Rice, *Slavery Inconsistent*, 9.
[131] Torrey, *Portraiture of Domestic Slavery*, 13.
[132] "Slavery," *The Balance and Columbian Repository*, July 13, 1802, 221.
[133] Furstenberg, "Beyond Freedom and Slavery."

Anti-French sentiments inflected this warm-blooded literature. The arch-conservative author of *The Jacobiniad* published an antislavery sermon in 1810 that condemned French planters for treating their slaves with "the greatest barbarity." Combining praise for the Haitian Revolution with Francophobic enmity, John S. J. Gardiner argued that "In St. Domingo, [the French] have exposed [slaves] to be torn to pieces by bloodhounds, and you all know the perfidy and cruelty they displayed towards the gallant Toussaint."[134] Anti-French enmity also seeped through a sympathetic account of a slave revolt at the French slave-trading Fort of Gorée.[135] George Ritter, the Philadelphia debater, tied the violence of the French Revolution and the violence of the Haitian Revolution together in order to justify emancipating slaves in the United States.[136] Ultimately, the threat of foreign slave rebellions did not deter abolitionists of the late 1790s and early 1800s from promoting emancipation; rather, it served them as a tool to scare a national audience into supporting their cause.

Abolitionists used sympathy for the Haitian Revolution by extension to excite sympathy for slave rebellion in the United States. Antislavery authors blurred the lines between slave uprisings in the Caribbean and slave uprisings at home, suggesting that both were righteous violence. In 1795, an English translation appeared in Philadelphia of Louis-Sébastien Mercier's futuristic 1770 short story "Memoirs of the Year 2500," about a man who arose from a deep sleep to discover a remarkable monument to humanity, which included a statue of a fierce-eyed "Negro," named as "the Avenger of the New World." Readers of the story, also excerpted that year in the *Massachusetts Magazine*, were astounded by the prescience of Mercier's tale, which seemed to predict the slave rebellion in Saint Domingue. Beneath the statue of the avenger was an inscription that celebrated the figure's leadership of his fellow slaves in a war that poured forth the blood of their oppressors and caused the "soil of America" to "drink with avidity that blood for which it had so long thirsted." The geographic ambiguity of the inscription's reference to the "soil of America" revealed the danger that the United States stood in as well.[137]

Throughout early national antislavery literature, slave rebellion is frequently treated as a sign of the Last Days, which – though bloody – will precipitate the reign of God on Earth. Slave rebellion is seen as containing the power to birth, in blood, a regenerate world capable of elevating humanity to new heights.[138] American abolitionists did not shy away from

---

[134] Gardiner, *Sermon... 14th of July 1810*, 17.
[135] "Account of a Plot," *New York Magazine, or Literary Repository*, Apr. 1796, 207.
[136] Ritter, *Speech*, 10–11.
[137] Louis-Sébastien Mercier, *Memoirs of the Year 2500*, trans. M. A. W. Hooper (Philadelphia, Pa., 1795). Also "A Remarkable Monument: Memoirs of the Year 2500," *Massachusetts Magazine*, Nov. 1795.
[138] See, for example, "The Death of Alice," *Philadelphia Minerva*, Sept. 20, 1795; "Pelham" and "Gustavus" letters, *Connecticut Courant*, Dec. 12, 1796, and Jul. 3, 1797; "The Negro

directly threatening the United States with providential slave violence. Early national antislavery texts sometimes followed lengthy Gothic expositions on the dangers of slave rebellion at home with the vicious kicker that the bloodshed would be well deserved. Thomas Branagan excelled at this rhetorical technique. The "penitential tyrant" focused most attention to the danger of slave rebellion in his *Serious Remonstrances* (1805). The text seemed to conform to proslavery warnings about the horrors of slave rebellion, until Branagan reached the application of his argument: the need for immediate emancipation and the establishment of a black republic in the American West. Masters, not slaves, bore responsibility for the present and potential violence within the system of slavery, and everyday they risked the just consequences.[139] Ultimately, if American slaves massacred their southern masters, it would "not be so tragical." While Branagan indulged freely in slave rebellion Gothic, he also insisted that "we must applaud and not censure [rebels], and the forebearance they have already manifested, does them eternal honor."[140] Early national texts warning of the potential for slave rebellions cannot necessarily be read as anti-emancipationist. Slaveholders' complaints that northeastern abolitionists were agitating for slave rebellion had validity.

Even the most politically conservative abolitionists, such as the rabid anti-Jacobin Theodore Dwight, showed surprising sympathy for slave rebellions. In a 1792 oration delivered to the Society of the Cincinnati, Dwight applauded the expansion of independence to enslaved Africans: "even the miserable victims of slavery have themselves aroused from the abyss of injury, and in some parts of the world made a noble, vigorous, and manly attack on their oppressors.... Justice must behold with a smile of approbation, the rapid progress of the slaves to triumph and independence." Dwight praised the justice of slave rebellion even while he decried other manifestations of violent disorder and warned the French against succumbing to bloodshed (the oration was delivered several months prior to the September Massacres). He treated the violence of slave rebellion with an exceptional sympathy because he believed that the slaves' "injuries exceed[ed] computation, conception, or credulity."[141] Slaves had it so bad that Dwight swallowed his fear of disorder in support of their emancipation. Dwight's ferocity on behalf of slaves emerged again during the 1807 antislave-trade debates in Congress, when he suggested that the penalty for slave smuggling should be death.[142]

Boy," *Philadelphia Monthly Magazine*, Jan. 1798; Humanitas, *Hints for the Consideration*; Parrish, *Remarks on the Slavery*; Branagan, *Preliminary Essay*.

[139] Branagan, *Serious Remonstrances*.

[140] Branagan, *Disquisitions*, 67–70, 55–56.

[141] Theodore Dwight, *An Oration, Spoken before the Society of the Cincinnati, of the State of Connecticut: Met in Hartford, on the 4th of July, 1792* (Hartford, Conn., 1792), 16–17.

[142] Riley, "Northern Republicans and Southern Slavery," chap. 5.

To committed abolitionists, the violence of slavery overshadowed the horrors of slave rebellion. A satirical poem published in the Federalist *Gazette of the United States* in 1802 eulogized several slaves who were hanged for participating in a rebellion in Virginia. A mocking adaptation of "Gray's Elegy," the poem diverted attention from the violence threatened by the slaves to the violence exacted on the slaves by white southerners. The poem's supposed narrator, Thomas Jefferson, looks on as "the gaping crowd without one sigh or sob; / ruthless plod onward to the fatal tree" to hang the conspirators. When two of the rebels receive a stay of execution from Governor Monroe, the narrator explains that their redemption strengthens the power of their Republican white masters:

> Yet e'en such slaves from justice to protect,
> Of all philanthropists be still the plan,
> And keep as make-weights for our favor'd 'sect'
> These glorious champions of the Rights of Man.
> The name of slaves on Jacobinic poll
> The place of freemen aptly will supply,
> 'Tis thus, Virginia will defy control,
> And perch'd on Negro-Backs to greatness fly.

"Philanthropically" preserving the lives of the rebels would strengthen Jefferson's political position, because the "make-weight" slaves would add numbers to the "Jacobinic poll" (through the Constitution's three-fifths clause), thereby enabling Virginia to increase its strength on the "backs" of the slaves.[143] With hardly a concern for the inciting episode of slave rebellion, the poem made clear that the violence of the hapless slave captives was completely outmatched by the power of their Jacobinical slave masters, who could perform the satanic miracle of turning benevolence into oppression.

Ultimately, northern antislavery advocates in the late eighteenth and early nineteenth centuries were not deterred by the specter of slave rebellion because they saw it as the South's problem, not as their own. Jonathan Edwards Jr. acknowledged that many proslavery advocates brandished the violent danger posed by black people as a reason to keep them enchained. However, Edwards argued that the North had nothing to fear because of the small size of its black population. Encouraging Connecticut to follow the example of Massachusetts, he pointed out that no bloodshed had followed the judicial decisions that rendered slavery unconstitutional in the Bay State. Edwards acknowledged that the southern states had good reason to fear their slaves, as the black population was both numerous and deeply resentful of the injustices perpetrated against them. But even if whites feared their slaves, justice still demanded their release from bondage. In fact, Edwards argued that whites who feared their chattel should themselves quit the South

---

[143] "Ode," *Gazette of the United States*, June 28, 1802.

and turn over their wealth to the black men and women who built it in the first place. This strategy was far cheaper, Edwards reasoned, than the alternative – giving all their sons and daughters to black spouses and thereby producing a population all of the same brown color. The small African American population made intermarriage nothing to fear in the North, according to Edwards, because it would have no effect on the general complexion. Edwards shrugged his shoulders at southern fears of black violence and interracial marriage because the North was safe from both.[144]

However, the North was not safe from the dangers posed by southern whites. Fears of retaliation by irate slaveholders exerted a strong repressive force on northern antislavery during the late eighteenth and early nineteenth centuries. Federalist–Calvinist critics of slavery avoided pursuing political antislavery not because of the dangers posed by the slaves, but because southern political representatives and social elites threatened disunion or civil war as a consequence. Northeastern antislavery was hampered more by a fear of white Jacobins than of black Jacobins. The conservative dedication to preserving social order that underlay early national antislavery limited its efficacy because most sympathizers shied away from pressing their argument to the point of engendering a violent sectional conflict. Federalist and Calvinist leaders used antislavery language to inculcate revulsion against violence, not to promote it. Even committed antislavery leaders who willingly supported slave rebellion felt constrained from promoting violence between the states. Yet violent language is invariably itself an act of violence. Despite their initial intentions, early national antislavery authors used a Gothic rhetoric that exacerbated American sectionalism. Northern conservatives added antislavery to their anti-Jacobin critique in a bid to restrain violence in the national political sphere. Antislavery advocates followed course from the desire to restrain the violence of slavery. Yet both parties used violent language in ways that prepared the ground for future battles.

[144] Edwards, *Injustice and Impolicy*, 37.

4

Fighting the War of 1812

Was there *ever* a war so unreasonable, so wicked, so abominable?
– Elijah Parish, *A Discourse, Delivered at Byfield,*
on the Annual Fast, April 8, 1813

In 1812, the Jacobin, slave-owning, warmongering democrats who controlled the government plunged the United States into a murderous offensive war on the side of the great Antichrist, Napoleon Bonaparte. Or so
said dissenters such as Elijah Parish, the short, loud, and morbid minister
of Byfield, Massachusetts, who for two decades prior had been preaching
passionate sermons against the depravity of democratic bloodshed. As the
spiritual leader of a small agricultural village near the commerce-oriented
coastal community of Newburyport, Parish raised early objections to the
national government's restrictive commercial policies that preceded the War
of 1812. In an 1808 sermon opposing President Jefferson's first embargo
on trade with Britain, Parish accused the administration of conspiring with
France – a nation that had "beheaded, and drowned, and butchered" millions of its own citizens.[1] After the 1809 Non-Intercourse Act, Parish warned
the Massachusetts legislature that yoking the United States to Napoleon
would cause a regression to the warlike past, when "the earth was ... filled
with violence" and "the fields were red with blood."[2] The renewal of non-
importation in February 1811 prompted Parish to revisit the butchery of
the French Revolution in his sermons, by describing how its victims were

---

[1] Elijah Parish, *Ruin or Separation from Anti-Christ; a Sermon Preached at Byfield, Apr. 7,*
1808, on the Annual Fast in the Commonwealth of Massachusetts (Portland, Me., 1808),
7–8.
[2] Elijah Parish, *A Sermon, Preached at Boston, before His Excellency Christopher Gore,*
Governor, His Honor David Cobb, Lieut. Governor, the Council and Legislature, Upon the
Annual Election, May 30, 1810 (Boston, Mass., 1810), 13.

slaughtered like cattle.[3] After the United States declared war against Great Britain in June 1812, thus seemingly entering a de facto alliance with France, the irate cleric compared the United States' invasion of Canada to "the lawless attack of Goths and Vandals" – Gothic rhetoric at its most elemental.

The Republican rebuttal against Parish proved similarly extreme. A contemporary letter writer to the Republican *Northern Centinel* accused Parish of "diabolical slander of your rulers" as well as "atrocious villainy," and labeled him a "wretched, lying, libeller."[4] A letter writer to the *New-Hampshire Gazette* called Parish "a foe to his country," "a zealous British partisan," and a "miserable man."[5] An article titled "Prostitution of the Pulpit," which circulated through several Republican newspapers, back-handedly praised Parish for "excelling all his fellow laborers, in virulence, outrage, sedition, and projected treason."[6] And all these projectiles were lobbed in the year before the war began. Since then, Parish has been pilloried, if remembered at all, as a "secessionist," "a virtual dictator," and a "vituperative" hypocrite.[7] While the bitterness of Parish's antiwar writings can hardly be disputed, the question of their consistency with his prewar ideological positions deserves further examination. Rather than accept the terms of his opponents, this chapter seeks to place Parish, and the broader antiwar opposition he represented, within a framework of ethical continuity and transatlantic anti-Jacobinism.

Elijah Parish was singled out for attack in his own time, and has been in ours, because of the quality of his language. His sermons evince a talent for violent locutions that commanded the attention, often negative, of an audience. In his words, the War of 1812 became a monster, bearing down hungrily on the American people; readers could smell the stench of death rising from its jaws. For latter-day readers unfamiliar with the Gothic context of Parish's rhetoric, his speeches demonstrate an unjustifiable paranoia and point to the unreasonableness of the war's opposition. Parish's allies in the opposition did not possess his virtuoso abilities and have not attracted the same attention, but their speeches and writings drew from

---

[3] Elijah Parish, *A Sermon Preached at Byfield, on the Annual Fast, Apr. 11, 1811*, 3rd ed. (Newburyport, Mass., 1811), 11.

[4] "Fellow Citizens," *Northern Centinel*, May 30, 1811.

[5] "To Elijah Parish, D.D.," *New-Hampshire Gazette*, Jun. 11, 1811.

[6] "Prostitution of the Pulpit," *American Watchman*, Jul. 27, 1811.

[7] "Did the Federal Party," *Eastern Argus*, Dec. 12, 1828; William Gwyer North, "The Political Background of the Dartmouth College Case," *New England Quarterly* 18 (Jun. 1945): 184. There is no published biography of Parish. An unpublished article on Parish's opposition to the War of 1812, by Matthew Mason, provides a nuanced study of Parish's antislavery discourse but generally agrees with the common assessment of Parish's "vituperation"; Matthew Mason, "'Infuriate Ravings': The Reverend Elijah Parish and Federalist Antislavery," (unpublished paper, 2006).

the same pool of imagery. Opponents condemned the war as murderous and uncivilizing, and its advocates as Jacobins, slave owners, and cannibals. They attacked the war for activating the violent passions of the citizens, which they argued threatened republican politics and undermined national stability. Dissenters also articulated commercial and political reasons for opposing the war. Parish gladly marshaled economics to his cause, claiming that war would mean commercial ruin for New England.[8] Opponents loudly praised the golden age of Washingtonian neutrality, mourned the day their Jeffersonian rivals took power, and demanded that citizens vote against the Republicans.[9] Dissenters felt no compunction about disclosing their worldly stakes in the question of war. But what makes the dissent remarkable is that commonplace criticisms of the war's inexpediency, likelihood of failure, and costliness were overshadowed by an enormous and consistent ethical antiwar argument. The great body of the published opposition reviled the war for exposing the United States to the problem of violence in republican political life.

The extensive political, clerical, and popular opposition to the War of 1812 rose on thick ideological foundations. The war reignited conservative American fears, first catalyzed by the French Reign of Terror, that democratic violence would destroy the young republic. According to Federalists and orthodox ministers, the War of 1812 exposed the republic not only to physical destruction at the hands of Great Britain, but also to moral destruction under the influence of France, and through the experience of warfare. Opposition politicians and ministers rallied the rhetorical tools with which they had battled earlier violent threats, delivering and publishing hundreds of sermons, orations, discourses, and addresses condemning the war as inexpedient and unjust. These critiques often employed familiar anti-Jacobin images of illegitimate bloodshed, democratic anarchy, and violent slaveholding to rally citizens against the war.

Critics of the war also reached beyond those familiar rhetorical tools, to attempt organizational solutions to the problem of violence. Federalist politicians, almost entirely limited to the northern states by then, reached out to northern Republicans, inviting them to combine in a new sectional "peace party" to defeat the war hawks in the 1812 national and state elections. Additionally, outside the formal halls of government, critics of the war reshaped national political culture by crafting persuasive arguments against war as an institution and by establishing the nation's first nonsectarian peace societies. Through their work for these peace societies, orthodox religious leaders extended their ties with the transatlantic reform communities that

---

[8] Elijah Parish, *A Protest against the War; A Discourse Delivered at Byfield, Fast Day, Jul. 23, 1812*, 2nd ed. (Newburyport, Mass., 1812), 13.

[9] Humphrey Moore, *A Discourse Delivered at Milford, Aug. 20, 1812, the Day Recommended by the President, for National Humiliation* (Amherst, N.H., 1812).

had successfully agitated in 1807 to ban the Atlantic slave trade, and that would press for total abolition in the following decades.

Last, in pursuing their antiwar course, both politicians and ministers extended the boundaries of legitimate opposition to war in the United States. Dissenters rejected Republican arguments that the war necessitated domestic political unity. Antiwar leaders were forced by a decade in the minority to reverse their earlier condemnations of dissent. Timothy Dwight, the so-called pope of Connecticut who had railed against Republican traitors during the quasi war of 1798–9, now argued to Yale students that "men are not bound to obey magistrates acting contrary to the will of God and the Scriptures." While freedom of the press entailed dangers, Dwight began to insist that restrictions on the press caused even greater evils.[10] In the context of an unjust war, antiwar leaders argued that citizens had a moral duty to voice opposition not only to the masters of war but also to the minions as well. In their crusade against the War of 1812, ministers pilloried common soldiers as murderers and warned that the soldiers' "moral putrefaction" would destroy the United States.[11] By extending their attacks to ordinary soldiers, opponents to the War of 1812 pushed the legitimacy of opposition speech beyond not only contemporary standards but also the boundaries that restrain many commentators today.

To Express Their Opinions

The opposition to the War of 1812 outmatched any antiwar sentiment that has since followed. When the war bill came before the Congress of the United States in June 1812, 40 percent of federal legislators voted against it. In the House of Representatives, the vote was 79 to 49, with 20 percent of Republicans joining a unified Federalist opposition. The resolutions passed in the Senate by only 19 to 13.[12] Outside of the halls of government, Americans opposed the war with their feet, their pocketbooks, their speech, and their suffrage: refusing to enlist, resisting orders to march into Canada, failing to subscribe to government loans, publishing opposition tracts in vast number, turning state governments from Republican control over to the Federalists, and returning increasing numbers of peace candidates to national office. In New England, discussion of disunion reached such a peak that moderates in state government called a convention at Hartford to defuse the tension. The convention, which demanded national political changes to adjust the

[10] Timothy Dwight, *President Dwight's Decisions of Questions Discussed by the Senior Class in Yale College, in 1813 and 1814* (New York, 1833), 170, 27–31.

[11] Parish, *Sermon... 1811*, 30.

[12] Donald R. Hickey, *The War of 1812: A Forgotten Conflict* (Urbana, Ill., 1989), chapter 2. For comparison, consider that more House Democrats voted for the Oct. 11, 2002, joint resolution to use force against Iraq than voted against it. The House approved the resolution by 296 to 133 (69 percent in favor); the Senate voted 77 to 23 (77 percent in favor) (H.J.R. #114, Oct. 12, 2002).

regional balance of power in New England's favor (or face secessionist consequences), initially earned strong approval from Federalists as well as from some northern Republicans.[13] Only the fortuitous coincidence of the Treaty of Ghent and the magnificent American victory at New Orleans washed the war clean of its disastrous unpopularity and secured its hazy yet positive reputation in U.S. history.

Despite its extraordinary magnitude and richness of language, opposition discourse against the War of 1812 has been little studied.[14] Overall, the War of 1812 has received such limited attention that the author of the most recent synthetic history of the war subtitled his book "a forgotten conflict."[15] Studies of the war are mostly limited to narratives of military campaigns and debates over the war's true causes.[16] Guided by a nationalist telos that treats disunion as unforgivable, many historians have been reluctant to invest work in the war's opponents, who flirted with secession. The bias against the antiwar movement has resulted in its strange exclusion from narratives of the origin of America's first peace societies following 1815. Although these societies were established by Federalist and Calvinist opponents to the War of 1812, historians have looked instead for liberal-enlightenment or Quaker roots.[17]

---

[13] James M. Banner, *To the Hartford Convention: The Federalists and the Origins of Party Politics in Massachusetts, 1789–1815* (New York, 1970); Samuel Eliot Morison, *Harrison Gray Otis, 1765–1848: The Urbane Federalist* (Boston, Mass., 1969).

[14] Exceptions include Lawrence Delbert Cress, "'Cool and Serious Reflection': Federalist Attitudes toward War in 1812," *Journal of the Early Republic* 7 (Summer 1987); Harvey Strum, "New Jersey Politics and the War of 1812," *New Jersey History* 105 (1987); Ellen Dana Hoffman, "'Unnecessary,' 'Unjustified' and 'Ruinous': Anti-War Rhetoric in Massachusetts Federalist Newspapers, 1812–1815" (Ph.D., University of Massachusetts, 1985); Harvey Strum, "The Politics of the New York Antiwar Campaign, 1812–1815," *Peace and Change* 7 (Winter 1981); D. R. Hickey, "The Federalists and the War of 1812" (Ph.D., University of Illinois, 1972); Sarah McCulloh Lemmon, "Dissent in North Carolina During the War of 1812," *North Carolina Historical Review* 49 (1972); William Gribbin, "The Covenant Transformed: The Jeremiad Tradition and the War of 1812," *Church History* 40 (Sept. 1971); Myron F. Wehtje, "Opposition in Virginia to the War of 1812," *Virginia Magazine of History and Biography* 78 (Jan. 1970); Samuel Eliot Morison, "Dissent in the War of 1812," in *Dissent in Three American Wars* (Cambridge, Mass., 1970).

[15] Hickey, *War of 1812*.

[16] Samuel Eliot Morison went so far in 1970 as to argue that nothing "of any consequence on political, economic, or other internal matters" during the War of 1812 had yet been written; Morison, "Dissent in the War of 1812." More recent political and cultural histories of the war include Richard Buel Jr., *America on the Brink: How the Political Struggle over the War of 1812 Almost Destroyed the Young Republic* (New York, 2005); Steven Watts, *The Republic Reborn: War and the Making of Liberal America, 1790–1820* (Baltimore, 1987); William Gribbin, *The Churches Militant: The War of 1812 and American Religion* (New Haven, Conn., 1973); Roger Hamilton Brown, *The Republic in Peril: 1812* (New York, 1964).

[17] Valarie H. Ziegler, *The Advocates of Peace in Antebellum America* (Bloomington, Ind., 1992). Ziegler avoids the political context of the antebellum peace movement, focusing instead on the biographies of its founders. Peter Brock attributed opposition to the War of

Antipathy to the secessionist strains of the Federalist opposition has led historians to describe antiwar sentiment as "strange and subversive,"[18] "rancorous," "secessionist," and "negative obstructionism,"[19] "near-hysterical" "self-indulgent" and "avaricious,"[20] and a "whining litany of complaints, despair, bitterness, and self-pity."[21] Purely materialist motivations are often ascribed to the Federalist opposition.[22] Antiwar authors' tendency to attack the war in terms derived from the French Revolution has led to criticisms of their "hypocrisy," "inconsistency," and "purple prose."[23] Yet viewed through a transnational lens, their opposition appears not inconsistent but evidence of an Atlantic counterrevolutionary ideology. Recontextualizing opposition to the War of 1812 within a history of transatlantic anti-Jacobinism revises our understanding of early national attitudes toward violence, war, and political opposition.

The opposition began long before the war. Starting in 1806, the United States floundered through a series of restrictive laws intended to discipline the British and French navies that were interfering with its neutral carrying trade. American shipping had become tangled up in the Napoleonic Wars. From the outset, Federalists representing northern commercial interests disliked the restrictive system, as well as the southern-controlled national government's seeming bias toward France. Rumors of an imminent war

---

1812 to "economic interests" rather than "moral repugnance" and disassociated it from the peace societies that followed; Peter Brock, *Pacifism in the United States: From the Colonial Era to the First World War* (Princeton, N.J., 1968), 1: 449. The progressive historian Merle Curti's foundational text *American Peace Crusade* (1929) attributed the first peace societies to the spirit of Thomas Jefferson, peppered with a dash of Quakerism; Merle Eugene Curti, *The American Peace Crusade* (Durham, N.C., 1929), 19. Amos Hovey, a contemporary of Curti's, also declined to study the antiwar movement of 1812–5 because "one is led to conclude that it was motivated probably not so much by a conscientious objection to war as by certain ulterior motives"; Amos Hovey, "A History of the Religious Phase of the American Movement for International Peace to the Year 1914" (Ph.D., University of Chicago, 1930), 30. An exception to the preceding trend is Clyde Macdonald, "The Massachusetts Peace Society, 1815–1828: A Study in Evangelical Reform" (Ph.D., University of Maine, 1973).

[18] George Dangerfield, *The Era of Good Feelings* (New York, 1952), 87–8. Dangerfield argues of the Hartford Convention that "disunion is disunion, however mildly asserted."

[19] Roger H. Brown, *Republic in Peril: 1812*, 158.

[20] Steven Watts, *Republic Reborn*, 276, 292. In the introduction, Watts states his intention to exclude the opposition to the war from consideration (xvii).

[21] Len Travers, *Celebrating the Fourth: Independence Day and the Rites of Nationalism in the Early Republic* (Amherst, Mass., 1997), 194.

[22] Dangerfield, *Era of Good Feelings*, 39. S. E. Morison refuted this argument: "there was no 'economic influence' on the New Englanders' opposition – even the late Charles A. Beard could find none." Morison, *Harrison Gray Otis*, 326. Norman Risjord similarly refuted the argument that Republicans fought the war from economic motivations; Norman K. Risjord, "1812: Conservatives, War Hawks, and the Nation's Honor," *William and Mary Quarterly* 18 (1961): 196.

[23] Richard Buel Jr., *America on the Brink*, 175. Buel cites an 1813 newspaper article that compared the war to the times of "Danton and Anarchsis Clootz," or "the maddest moments of the French [Revolution]."

against Britain circulated in newspapers and conversations in the summer of 1807, after the HMS *Leopard* fired on the USS *Chesapeake*, in an attempt to recover British deserters from the American ship. Britain later apologized for the attack, returned three of the seized sailors, and agreed to pay reparations, but the affair remained a topic of vitriol among Republicans. Federalists believed that the Republicans, who had long despised the former mother country, wanted to go to war against Britain in aid of France. In religious and political discourses, conservatives warned that Napoleon was the Antichrist, a despotic tyrant who had killed millions of his own people and who would infect the United States with "the gangrene of moral death."[24]

Despite France's shift in government from the First Republic to the Napoleonic Empire, transatlantic opponents continued to assault French Jacobinism in the early nineteenth century. Napoleon's personal history played into this rhetoric; he had once been a member of the Jacobin club, and his willingness to sacrifice massive casualties in the pursuit of power signified the continuity of his bloodthirstiness. Anti-Napoleonic literature from the early 1800s deployed such familiar anti-Jacobin tropes as cannibalism, bloodiness, bestial savagery, the landscape of death, slavery, and barbarism to describe Napoleon. Just as ceaselessly, critics made overt comparisons between the emperor's brutality and "the frightful crimes of a Robespierre."[25] Alexander Hanson, the editor of the rabidly antiwar *Federal Republican* (Baltimore), instructed readers in 1809 that

they who have witnessed or read of the horrors of the French Revolution; who are acquainted with the history of a Robespierre a Carrere, a Danton and a Marat, and the prodigal effusion of human blood to gratify the vengeance of those revolutionary bloodhounds, will not think it incredible that a wretch of Bonaparte's character could butcher prisoners in cold blood and poison his own soldiery.[26]

As diplomatic tensions arising from the Napoleonic Wars engrossed the United States, transatlantic conservative authors continued to rely heavily on anti-Jacobinism to rally their readers.

[24] See, for example, Isaac Braman, *Union with France a Greater Evil Than Union with Britain; a Sermon Preached in Rowley, West-Parish, at the Annual Fast, Apr. 5, 1810* (Haverhill, Mass., 1810); Parish, *Ruin or Separation;* John Sylvester John Gardiner, *A Sermon Preached at Trinity Church Apr. 6, 1810, Being the Day of Publick Fast* (Boston, Mass., 1810); John Lowell, *Peace without Dishonour, War without Hope: Being a Calm and Dispassionate Enquiry into the Question of the Chesapeake, and the Necessity and Expediency of War* (Boston, Mass., 1807); John Park, *An Address to the Citizens of Massachusetts on the Causes and Remedy of Our National Distresses* (Boston, Mass., 1808). Quotation is from Parish, *Ruin or Separation.* 11.
[25] *The Anti-Gallican; or, Standard of British Loyalty, Religion and Liberty. Including a Collection of the Principal Papers, Tracts, Speeches, Poems, and Songs That Have Been Published on the Threatened Invasion; Together with Many Original Pieces on the Same Subject* (London, 1804), 10.
[26] "Corrupt-Divide and Terrify," *Federal Republican and Commercial Gazette,* Nov. 15, 1809.

The threat of war peaked and subsided, then rose again in the fall of 1811. In a November speech, President Madison requested the Twelfth Congress to begin preparing for war against Great Britain. A Federalist leader in the House, Josiah Quincy encouraged his party allies to maintain a strategy of silence – believing that the Republicans would never follow through on their threats. If the Federalists objected to the war preparations, Quincy feared, they would be castigated as lovers of Britain; better to leave the Republicans to their own devices.[27] In June 1812, Madison sent a message to Congress urging the nation to go to war. The House Foreign Relations Committee introduced a war bill; the Republican majority imposed secrecy over the debate. Prevented from making a public opposition, the Federalists refused to debate the bill, and it passed in only two days. Immediately following the declaration of war, the Federalists in the House of Representatives released an address to their constituents, laying out the case against the war. Written by Josiah Quincy and signed by nearly every Federalist congressman, the address was published in newspapers across the country as well as in twenty independent editions.[28]

An explosion of protest followed. Local representatives in New England assembled and released their own addresses against the war.[29] At July 4 celebrations, Federalist leaders criticized the war. Caleb Strong, the Federalist governor of Massachusetts, called for a special Fast on July 23, 1812, to bemoan the sinful course that the nation had taken. Across the state, ministers answered in bleak terms; more than twenty of their sermons were published. When President Madison declared a national Fast on August 12 to implore God's blessing on the armies, more than thirty dissenting ministers seized the opportunity to condemn the war once more – three times as many who gave it praise. Rather than pray for American soldiers, the ministers labeled them murderers and warned that the guilt of blood would be on their hands. Fall election pamphlets sustained the drumbeat of opposition,

---

[27] Primary accounts of the Federalist strategy can be found in the published letters of two Federalist congressmen: "Letters of Abijah Bigelow, Member of Congress, to His Wife, 1810–1815," *Proceedings of the American Antiquarian Society* 40 (1930): 318, 323; "Letters of Samuel Taggart," *Proceedings of the American Antiquarian Society* 33 (1924): 371, 399.

[28] Hickey, "Federalists"; Hickey, *War of 1812*.

[29] See, for example, Federal Party (N.J.), *Proceedings and Address of the Convention of Delegates to the People of New Jersey* (Trenton, N.J., 1812); James Prescott, *Address to the Friends of Independence, Peace, and Union in the County of Middlesex* (Middlesex County, 1812); Federal Party (Mass.), *Proceedings of a Convention of Delegates from Forty One Towns, in the County of Worcester, Holden at Worcester, the 12th and 13th of August, 1812* (Worcester, Mass., 1812); William Crosby, *An Address to the Electors of the County of Hancock with the Resolutions Adopted at the Convention, Held at Buckstown, Sept. 15, 1812* (Castine, Me., 1812); George Sullivan and Daniel Webster, *Speech of the Hon. George Sullivan, at the Late Rockingham Convention with the Memorial and Resolutions, and Report of the Committee of Elections* (Concord, N.H., 1812).

winning the Federalists more seats in Congress, turning over state governments to their control, and nearly unseating President Madison (if Madison's
opponent DeWitt Clinton had won the very close race in Pennsylvania, he
would have become president).[30] Addresses, orations, discourses, and sermons opposing the war continued to be published throughout the following
two years, until finally the government, hurried by the opposition pressure,
made peace with Britain.[31]

At the heart of this great body of opposition lay the allegation, made by
religious and political speakers alike, that the United States was waging an
offensive war. According to the dissenters, no transgression committed by
Great Britain justified the Republicans' decision to declare war. The United
States was not defending itself from invasion. The Orders in Council –
British trade laws restricting neutral shipping, which were the primary cause
for war cited by President Madison – were objectionable, yet a necessary
retaliation to the similar French Continental Decrees that had come first.
Unless France repealed its decrees (the Republicans were desperately seeking
evidence that they had done so), Britain's Orders in Council could not justify
a war against her alone. Opponents likewise questioned impressment as a
rationale for the war. True, Great Britain had taken sailors from American
commercial ships, but those sailors – argued the dissenters – were deserters
from the British navy who owed their service to the Crown. Any American
citizens accidentally caught up in British raids had been returned or were
in the process of being returned. Ultimately, Britain had harassed American
shipping with little regard to her sovereignty, but Federalists believed the
conflict should have been solved through diplomacy, not warfare. Critics
blamed the Madison administration for the inadequacy of its negotiations
with Britain. (And, in fact, the Republicans did fail to perceive a softening
of the British attitude during the spring of 1812, which led to a repeal of the
Orders in Council only days before America's declaration of war.) To the
minds of the dissenters, the United States bore the burden of responsibility
for the war.

The United States' complaints against Britain may have adequately justified a limited naval defense in the minds of some dissenters. But the Orders in
Council, impressments, and sundry minor complaints against Britain could
not possibly support the actual Republican war strategy, which combined

---

[30] Examples of antiwar election pamphlets are James Sloan, *An Address to the Citizens of the United States, but Particularly Those of the Middle and Eastern States* (Philadelphia, 1812); Isaiah L. Green, *Barnstable Congressional Nomination and Statement of Votes in Congress* (Boston, Mass., 1812); Friends of Peace and Federal Party (N.J.), *Proceedings and Address of the Delegates of the Friends of Peace Convened at Salem on the 16th Day of December A.D. 1812* (N.J., 1812).

[31] Both scholars of dissent in the War of 1812, Donald Hickey and S. E. Morison, agree that the opposition helped shorten the war; Morison, "Dissent in the War of 1812"; Hickey, "Federalists."

naval warfare with a land invasion of neighboring Canada. Canada had committed no offenses against the United States invasion of its territory did not constitute just war as defined by popular political authorities such as Hugo Grotius, Emerich de Vattel, and Samuel Puffendorf.[32] Opponents branded the War of 1812 as offensive. Consequently, the blood shed in its cause could not be excused as instrumental. The aggressions of the American armies were merely depraved violence. On the first Sunday following the declaration of war, David Osgood – who had long warned his parishioners about man's depravity and had been among the earliest to oppose the violence of the French Revolution – preached "a solemn protest" that called the war to the standards set by Emerich de Vattel.[33] Failing to find sufficient rationale for the war, Osgood described it as merely "violence against the lives and properties of our fellow-beings." Quoting from Vattel, Osgood reproved the Republicans who had voted for the declaration: "those who run to arms without necessity, are the scourges of the human race, barbarians, enemies to society, and rebels to the law of nature."[34]

To that list of execrations, Osgood added murder. The logic of labeling the war offensive led inexorably to this damning charge. If the laws of just war could not sanction the killing done by American soldiers and sailors during battle, then the killing had to be called by its proper name, *murder*. To arraign the nation's soldiers as murderers, during a time of war, was shocking. Yet it is a measure of the strength of the opposition that many of Osgood's colleagues joined him in this argument. On the national Fast Day that President Madison called to encourage Americans to pray for the success of their armies, the Reverend Samuel Mead instead delivered

---

[32] Moore, *Discourse . . . 1812*; William Ellery Channing, *A Sermon, Preached in Boston, Mass., Jul. 23, 1812, the Day of the Publick Fast, Appointed by the Executive of the Commonwealth of Massachusetts, in Consequence of the Declaration of War against Great Britain* (Boston, Mass., 1812).

[33] David Osgood, *A Sermon, Preached at the Request of the Ancient and Honourable Artillery Company, in Boston, Mass., Jun. 2, 1788 Being the Anniversary of Their Election of Officers* (Boston, Mass., 1788); David Osgood, *The Wonderful Works of God Are to Be Remembered: A Sermon, Delivered on the Day of Annual Thanksgiving, Nov. 20, 1794* (Boston, Mass., 1794).

[34] David Osgood, *A Solemn Protest against the Late Declaration of War in a Discourse Delivered on the Next Lord's Day after the Tidings of It Were Received*, 2nd ed. (Exeter N.H., 1812), 8–10. This passage is also quoted in three other protest sermons; Jonathan French, *Sermons, Delivered on the 20th of August, 1812, the Day Recommended by the President of the United States for Public Humiliation and Prayer to Which Are Added, Observations on the Propriety of Preaching Occasionally on Political Subjects* (Exeter, N.H., 1812); Nathan Perkins, *The National Sins and National Punishment in the Recently Declared War Considered in a Sermon, Delivered Jul. 23, 1812, on the Day of the Public Fast . . . In Consequence of the Declaration of War against Great Britain* (Hartford Conn., 1812); John Smith, *An Apology for the Friends of Peace in Two Discourses Delivered Aug. 20, 1812, Being the Day Appointed for Fasting and Prayer Throughout the United States on Account of the War with Great Britain* (Haverhill, Mass., 1812).

an unforgiving indictment. You are called upon to pray for our soldiers' success, Mead acknowledged, but you must first inquire about the justice of this war. "What is a war, when chosen and offensive, and no imperious necessity compels a nation to it? – What is it but plunder and murder on their part who commence it?" he asked. God would not forgive Americans who participated in the war; their hands would not be cleansed of innocent blood. They would come before God guilty of murder. "I said murder," Mead repeated for the benefit of disbelieving listeners. "I know the difference between killing and murder. But I say, that every unjustifiable war is a system of national murder."[35]

The Reverend Noah Worcester – future founder of the Massachusetts Peace Society – committed his 1812 national Fast sermon, "Abraham and Lot," to developing this argument. His title page epigraph, "whosoever hateth his brother, is a murderer" (1 John 3:15), previewed the subject of his discourse. Worcester related the biblical story of Abraham and Lot to demonstrate how governments could resolve their problems bloodlessly, then he enumerated the evils of war. "*First . . .* War always implies *murder* on the one side or the other, if not on both," Worcester began, "Unjustifiable or aggressive war is always *murder* on the part of the *aggressor*." In the passages that followed before item two, the minister repeated the word *murder* or one of its variants (*murderous, murdering*) seventeen times. In the published text, murder is almost always italicized, suggesting that Worcester vocally stressed the word during the sermon's delivery. Worcester was battling the numbness to killing that he believed war engendered. "People lose sight of the *murderous* nature of war," he bemoaned. People felt the death of one person more acutely than they did the deaths of many. Through some mysterious alchemy, the battlefield transformed murder into honor. War leached killing of its sinfulness. Worcester used a Gothic rhetorical style, relentlessly returning to the word *murder*, to shock people and ensure that they do not leave his church that day without a sense, however fleeting, of the moral stakes of an unjust war.[36]

Labeling common soldiers as murderers transgressed the limits of legitimate opposition. Supporters of the war reacted with expressions of terrible

[35] Samuel Mead, *A Sermon on the War Delivered in Amesbury, Aug. 20, 1812, on the General Fast* (Newburyport, Mass., 1812), 5–12.

[36] Noah Worcester, *Abraham and Lot: A Sermon, on the Way of Peace, and the Evils of War: Delivered at Salisbury, in New-Hampshire, on the Day of the National Fast, Aug. 20, 1812* (Concord N.H., 1812), 8–11. Also Reuben Holcomb, *A Discourse in Two Parts; Delivered at Sterling, Massachusetts, Thursday, Jul. 23, 1812 at the State Fast* (Worcester, Mass., 1812); Parish, *Protest against the War, French, Sermons . . . 1812*; Smith, *Apology for the Friends of Peace*; Perkins, *National Sins and National Punishment*; Francis Brown, *The Evils of War: A Fast Sermon Delivered at North-Yarmouth, Apr. 7, 1814* (Portland, Me., 1814). For a political text that makes this charge, see James Sloan's accusation that prowar politicians were leading American sailors and soldiers to "murder their fellow-mortals"; Sloan, *Address to the Citizens*, 4.

outrage against antiwar speakers. A writer for the Boston *Yankee* in 1813 took such great offense at Parish's accusations of murder that he reversed the charges, declaring to the minister, "Your own tremendous sentence falls on your own head."[37] The New York *Public Advertiser* rebuked the Reverend John Mason on similar grounds, but in far more passionate terms, by painting a picture of "Doctor Mason with his pistol cocked against the union, and on his right hand, a brawny Indian with a white-woman's scalp, a tomahawk, and a scalping knife."[38] The resonance of the conservatives' antiviolent critique of the war is laid bare by the incendiary language that war hawks were willing to use for rebuke. Describing opponents as secessionists and abettors of rape and murder were heady charges but not enough. Because the accusations of murder had a meaningful ethical consistency, supporters of the war worked hardest to tear down the reputations of their opponents. By labeling Osgood, Parish, Mason, and others as hypocrites – the most common charge against the men – war hawks sought to disarm their opponents' ability to make ethical arguments against the war.

Typically, Republicans fueled accusations of hypocrisy by pointing to the antiwar faction's prior agitation for war against France or to the faction's support for Great Britain, despite Britain's aggressive attacks on other nations. The protestors, Republicans argued, did not oppose war; they supported an alliance with Great Britain.[39] These charges have been reproduced by historians critical of the Federalist opposition. Yet equating Federalist partiality toward Britain with ethical inconsistency assumes a nationalist ethos that obscures more than it illuminates. Federalist–Calvinist fears of political violence did not originate in isolation; they emerged in response to the challenges posed by transatlantic Jacobinism in the post-Bastillian world. Prior to the end of the War of 1812, conservative early national leaders rarely articulated an abstract pacifist rejection of violence per se. Instead, they distinguished legitimate forms of force that upheld state power and civil society from illegitimate violence that disabled the state and civil society. This ethical distinction, formed in the context of the wars spawned by the French Revolution, remained consistent from the early 1790s through the War of 1812. American conservatives of the early nineteenth century did not view themselves as an isolated nation free to choose among different potential European allies. Rather they viewed the United States as an inextricable participant in an Atlantic World that was divided between two political–ideological clusters, roughly approximating good and evil. In the eyes of the anti-Jacobins, the War of 1812 dislocated the United States from its political history, identity, and intended future by placing the nation in an unnatural and corrupting connection with France.

[37] "Political Miscellany. For the Yankee, to Elijah Parish, D.D.," *Yankee*, Aug. 27, 1813.
[38] "Brief Summary," *Public Advertiser*, Aug. 26, 1812.
[39] "The Way the Junto Work It," *Baltimore Patriot and Evening Advertiser*, Oct. 21, 1813.

After the offensive nature of the conflict, no aspect of the War of 1812 aroused greater dissent than the suggestion of an American alliance with Napoleonic France. The war linked France and the United States through a common enemy; by engaging Great Britain on yet another front, the United States distracted it from the fight against Napoleon. Since the late 1790s, millennialist sermons and writings had argued that revolutionary France fit the New Testament prophecies of the reign of the Antichrist. Napoleon's ascendancy during the first decade of the nineteenth century reinforced this understanding. Elijah Parish titled his 1808 sermon opposing the prospect of war against Great Britain "Ruin or Separation from Anti-Christ." Parish could not forgive any aid given, however indirectly, to a nation he considered to be the Antichrist; he blamed the Republicans' corrupt servility to France for America's blustering war threats against Britain. Quoting from the book of Revelation, he demanded that the United States "come out" from association with France, before American citizens imbibed the Jacobin spirit of depraved violence. The nation's leaders were already corrupted. President Jefferson had led the United States, "like moles and bats, [to] crawl at the feet of the Conqueror; like serpents eat the dust of his feet."[40] The Congregationalist minister and Federalist congressman Samuel Taggart referred to the war hawks as the "violent party," using the same shorthand that had earlier been applied to the Jacobins.[41]

After the war began, calls for the United States to "come out" from France redoubled.[42] The war gave proof that America's leaders had indeed formed a sinful and traitorous alliance with the unholy power. New England Calvinists worried that God would permit America's violent destruction, to punish her for cooperating with France. The Reverend Nathan Strong of Hartford, Connecticut, warned his parishioners in the summer of 1812 that they faced a choice. They could either come out, by resisting the war, or die by the sword; for God says: "they have shed blood, and I will give them blood to drink."[43] The war itself portended violence. God could punish the United States by awarding Great Britain success in battle. Alliance with France also made the United States vulnerable to Jacobin treachery. Every nation that ever joined her cause, the French had "trampled in the dust, together with

[40] Parish, *Ruin or Separation*, 21. Also Braman, *Union with France*, Parish, *Sermon . . . 1811*; Otis Thompson, *Signs of the Times; a Sermon, Preached in Attleborough, West Parish, on the Annual Fast in Massachusetts, Apr. 9, 1812* (Providence, R.I., 1812).

[41] "Letters of Samuel Taggart," 394.

[42] Thomas Snell, *Repentance with Prayer . . . Praying for Rulers a Christian Duty* (Brookfield, Mass., 1812); Winthrop Bailey, *National Glory: A Discourse, Delivered at Brunswick, on the Day of the National Fast, Aug. 20, 1812* (Portland, Me., 1812); Eliphalet Gillet, *A Discourse Delivered in the Forenoon at Hallowell and in the Afternoon at Augusta on the Day of the National Fast Aug. 20, 1812* (Hallowell, Me., 1812).

[43] Nathan Strong, *A Fast Sermon, Delivered in the North Presbyterian Meeting House, in Hartford, Jul. 23, 1812* (Hartford, Conn., 1812).

the blood and mangled carcasses of millions of their slaughtered citizens!"[44] At a July 4 oration in Fryeburg, Maine, William Barrows articulated this danger in classic Gothic language: France was "more to be dreaded as an *ally*, than feared as an *enemy*! . . . [France] snuffs for blood like the vulture – like the panther and tyger, destroys when she is full, and gorg'd with flesh – and tears and mangles what she cannot devour!"[45]

Even more threatening than French armies was the influence of her Jacobin political culture. Dissenters feared that alliance with France would make American citizens violent, causing worse damage than any foreign force could wreak. In one of the memorable turns of phrase that made Timothy Dwight, like Elijah Parish, a magnet for Republican hatred, the venerable Yale president aphorized: "To ally *America* to *France* is to chain living health and beauty to a corpse dissolving with the plague. . . . The touch of *France* is pollution. Her embrace is death."[46] If America did not "come out" from France, her citizens would sicken, and the republic would dissolve "in violent threatenings; in tumults; in quarrels; and in death."[47] Dwight objected to the War of 1812 because alliance with France would hasten the moral destruction of American citizens, release their potential for depraved violence, and wound the republic at its core. The American republic depended upon its citizens to preserve the social order; French moral degeneration threatened civil society. Dwight so despised France that he had endorsed a war against the republic in 1798, and he would likely have approved an anti-Napoleonic war a decade later. Yet his support for war against France was not an ethical lapse from his antiwar position in 1812.

The consistency of Timothy Dwight's antiwar position is eloquently captured by a published collection of moral teachings he delivered between 1812 and 1815. As president of Yale, Dwight had a special responsibility to instruct the senior class of the college. He accomplished this pedagogical task by hosting a twice-weekly "disputation" among his students on significant moral, societal, and political questions such as, "Has Christianity been a temporal benefit?" "Would a Division of the Union be beneficial?" and "Are Wars beneficial?" During 1813 and 1814, the president's nephew, Theodore Dwight Jr., who was serving as his amanuensis (Dwight

---

44 Braman, *Union with France*. 12. For more warnings of French perfidy, see Bailey, *National Glory*; Samuel Worcester, *Calamity, Danger, and Hope; a Sermon, Preached at the Tabernacle in Salem, Jul. 23, 1812: The Day of the Public Fast in Massachusetts, on Account of the War with Great-Britain* (Salem, Mass., 1812).

45 William Barrows, *An Oration, Pronounced at Fryeburg, Maine, on the 4th Day of July, 1812 at the Request of the Federal Republicans of Fryeburg and the Adjacent Towns* (Portland, Me., 1812), 16.

46 Timothy Dwight, *A Discourse, in Two Parts: Delivered Jul. 23, 1812, on the Public Fast, in the Chapel of Yale College* (Utica, N.Y., 1812), 52.

47 Timothy Dwight, *A Discourse, in Two Parts: Delivered Aug. 20, 1812, on the National Fast, in the Chapel of Yale College* (Utica, N.Y., 1813), 34, 41.

had cripplingly weak eyesight), recorded the president's decisions on each of forty-one disputations. These seemingly verbatim transcriptions of the incidental comments and deeply pondered judgments delivered by Timothy Dwight reveal a well-developed ideology that repudiated violence, promoted the integrity of the Union, and opposed France at all costs.

The president's antipathy toward violence is evident throughout the book. In his instructions to the senior class, Dwight promoted a nonviolent character formation, emphasizing self-restraint and moderation over more conflictive qualities such as honor or dominance. For example, to demonstrate Christianity's temporal benefits, Dwight praised its cultivation of an antiviolent ethic evident in the social movements against war, the slave trade, and blood sports. Dwight's concerns about violence also commanded his political decisions; a question concerning whether representatives ought to be bound by the will of constituents prompted Dwight to express fear of the "jealousies, passions and violence" that people would release in a direct democracy. Forced to convene and discuss every political question, Americans "would use fists and clubs," if not pistols, to settle their differences. The principle of restraining humanity's injurious passions guided Dwight's answers to all questions religious, societal, political, and personal.[48]

The president's attitudes toward war are especially revealing of his concerns about violence. Regardless of the cause at stake, he flatly declared that war damaged people more than any other situation by familiarizing them to death and brutality. As a chaplain during the Revolution, he had heard patriot soldiers "talk of butchering men, as if they had been butchers, talking about slaughtering an ox." Dwight's account of the War of Independence, while deeply nationalistic, nonetheless bemoaned the brutalizing impact of warfare. While Dwight praised the political goals and consequences of the American Revolution, he expressed horror at its moral cost. In statements such as "the soldiers of that period were patriots, though bad men," he combined a moral critique of warfare with political support of war in a way unfathomable by contemporary standards. His attitude toward the War of 1812 similarly expressed a nationalist sensibility that was furrowed by deep concerns about the impact of violence upon the American character. While Dwight expressed strong commitment to the union in his decisions (at a time when many of the young men in his classes may have been gearing up for sectional war), he agonized that America's involvement with France would destroy national character. Throughout the *Decisions*, France served as a frequent bête noire, a point of violent comparison to the moral order he sought to praise. And thus Dwight's moral concerns about violence led him to both repudiate war and seek the destruction of France.[49]

---

[48] Dwight, *President Dwight's Decisions*, 77–82, 130.
[49] Ibid., 7, 27, 73–7, 95–104, 335.

Dwight's beliefs were typical of many conservative orators who warned about the political hazards of allying the United States to France. John Wallace, who addressed the Washington Benevolent Society (a Federalist political club) in Newbury, Vermont, in 1812, delivered a history lesson to his audience, recalling the differences between the American and French revolutions, and reminding listeners of the horrors of Jacobinism and the perfidies of Napoleon. Once before, in 1794, French influence had instigated a rebellion in the United States. According to the Federalists, Jacobin-controlled Democratic Societies had seduced western Pennsylvania farmers into violently opposing the new excises on whiskey. Now the greatest threat facing the United States was neither British conquest nor French betrayal, but the *"French Alliance,"* which Wallace described as the "chill embrace of the grisly messenger of death."[50] True patriots needed to rise in opposition and break the alliance, before the French system of "guillotines" and "midnight murders" spread at home. The War of 1812 threatened to unleash the potential for political violence that had worried American conservatives since the beginning of the postrevolutionary period.

Ultimately, the dissenters would not require past examples to be made aware of the prowar party's potential for political violence. The rising tide of opposition during June and July 1812 greatly angered Republican leaders and members, creating a spirit of intolerance that led to multiple outbreaks of violence. Many prowar orators and writers made incendiary suggestions for punishing the opposition. In a letter to James Madison, Thomas Jefferson expressed a typical Republican viewpoint on the matter, advising the president to send a "barrel of tar to each state South of the Potomac," and in the North to "apply the rougher drastics of Govr. Wright, hemp and confiscation" in order to silence the opposition.[51] The cerebral Madison did not take Jefferson's advice to tar, or even worse to hang, dissenters; however, others proved more agreeable to the task. The Federalists' long-standing concern that democracy encouraged a violent temper bore out in the antidissenter bloodshed of 1812, when Republican partisans made threats against Federalist editors in Savannah, Alexandria, Richmond, Baltimore, Elizabethtown,

---

[50] John Wallace, *An Oration, Delivered before the Washington Benevolent Society in Newbury, Vermont, on the Fourth of July, 1812* (Windsor, Vt., 1812). For more July 4 orations that warn about American political enslavement to France, see Daniel Webster, *An Address Delivered before the Washington Benevolent Society at Portsmouth, Jul. 4, 1812,* 2nd ed. (Portsmouth, N.H., 1812); Samuel Prentiss, *An Oration, Pronounced at Plainfield, July 4, 1812, before the Washington Benevolent Societies of Montpelier, Calais, Plainfield, and Barre: Being the Thirty-Seventh Anniversary of American Independence* (Montpelier, Vt., 1812); Peter Kean, *An Oration, Delivered in the First Presbyterian Church at Elizabeth-Town, N.J. On Saturday, Jul. 4, 1812* (Morristown, N.J., 1812).

[51] Quoted in Hickey, *War of 1812,* 56. Hickey claims, in his footnotes, that this letter has been "discretely omitted" from published works of Jefferson and Madison (345).

and New York City.[52] Most editors left town; however, Alexander Hanson, the editor of the Baltimore *Federal Republican*, was foolish enough to remain in place.

Since having established his newspaper in 1808, Alexander Hanson had taken pride in defying Baltimore's democratic populace by publishing highly critical articles about the Madison administration, and the restrictive system in particular. In 1812, Baltimore was a boomtown populated by many young male immigrants from France, Scotland, Ireland, and the German states, a population that leaned decidedly toward the Republicans. As the likelihood of war against Britain increased during the spring of 1812, threats against Hanson became more common. Two days after the war was declared, Hanson published a searing editorial condemning the vote. On June 22, the angered Republicans of Baltimore destroyed the *Federal Republican* printing office. Hanson initially fled to nearby Georgetown. Less fortunate targets of Republican hatred in Baltimore, including the city's black population as well as Protestant Irishmen, continued to suffer mob violence in the subsequent weeks. Local government failed to intervene in any meaningful manner. On July 25, 1812, Hanson returned to Baltimore with a small group of supporters – including the revolutionary hero, General "Light Horse Harry" Lee – determined to renew printing of the *Federal Republican* there. The evening of July 27, a mob gathered outside the home Hanson had rented and began to throw stones. By that time, Hanson and his friends had been joined by numerous local Federalist supporters. The new printing office was swiftly becoming a garrison.[53]

General Lee organized the defense. The Federalists planned to deter the crowd by demonstrating their willingness to use violence, if needed, to defend the building. They fired shots into the air from an upper window, but their actions only angered the men below. A local doctor, Thadeus Gale, led the mob in a charge on the house, bursting through the barricade of furniture that Lee had placed against the front door. As Gale rushed the stairs to the upper story, the gathered Federalists fired; the doctor was fatally hit. The mob retreated and the Federalists retrenched, hoping that the mob would

[52] Wehtje, "Opposition in Virginia," 83–4, Strum, "New Jersey Politics," 42; Strum, "The New York Antiwar Campaign," 9. Sean Wilentz argues that the antiwar resistance "sporadically turned violent," but his footnotes provide a citation to only one incident; see Sean Wilentz, *The Rise of American Democracy: Jefferson to Lincoln* (New York, 2005), 163.

[53] Alexander C. Hanson, *An Exact and Authentic Narrative, of the Events Which Took Place in Baltimore, on the 27th and 28th of July Last Carefully Collected from Some of the Sufferers and Eyewitnesses: To Which Is Added a Narrative of Mr. John Thomson, One of the Unfortunate Sufferers, &c.* (1812); Hickey, *War of 1812*, chapter 3; Paul A. Gilje, "The Baltimore Riots of 1812 and the Breakdown of the Anglo-American Mob Tradition," *Journal of Social History* 13 (Summer 1980); Frank A. Cassell, "The Great Baltimore Riot of 1812," *Maryland Historical Magazine* 70 (1975).

remain intimidated long enough for the civil authorities to restore order. However, the mayor and the local militia were either unwilling or unable to disperse the crowd. By the early morning, the mob had swelled to almost two thousand men, and they had dragged a cannon to the scene to destroy the home and the Federalists inside it. The editor of the rival Republican newspaper, the *Baltimore Sun*, stood at the head of the cannon urging his fellow rioters to ignite it. General Lee then decided to accept an offer from city officials to lead the Federalists from the house, under the protective custody of the militia, to the local jail. Members of the mob remained behind to destroy the house.

The militia deflected attacks against the Federalists en route, but once they had arrived at the jail, the troops disassembled. The militia leader, General Stricker, would issue the men only blank cartridges for their guns. Many in the militia were Republicans and unwilling to protect Hanson, Lee, and their friends. Throughout the day, the mob rejoined outside the jail. They sent in an emissary to identify the Federalists harbored inside. When evening came, the mob attacked the jail (being admitted by the turnkey) and invaded the cell where the Federalists were hiding. The victims swiftly put out the gaslights and attempted to flee in the confusion. Nine or ten of the men escaped. Twelve more, having been identified by the daytime visitor, were captured by the mob, severely beaten, and tortured. One defender, General James M. Lingan – another revolutionary hero – was stabbed to death by a crowd shouting, "Tory!" Both Hanson and Lee were so badly injured that neither ever fully regained his health, and both died within the decade. John Thompson was beaten, gouged, stripped, tarred and feathered, set on fire, extinguished, beaten with clubs and an iron bar, and stabbed with rusty swords, and yet he lived. When the beaten men played dead, the rioters dripped candle grease on them or stabbed them, for signs of life. Only after the victims lost consciousness completely, were local doctors able to remove the "corpses" from the crowd.

Even before the lynching of Hanson and his protectors, Federalists had warned that the Republicans intended to deploy Jacobin-style violence against the opposition. The burning of the offices of the *Federal Republican* in late June frightened opponents to the war sufficiently to inspire allusions to the French Revolution. William Barrows warned in his July 4, 1812, oration that the time was coming when the Republicans would persecute their opposition with violence, and Federalists would suffer "their tongues torn out by the roots...their heads elevated on poles at the corners of the streets...grinning forth a horrid memento."[54] Only days before Hanson returned to Baltimore, the Reverend Kiah Bayley described Baltimore as a "horrid, barbarous, and bloody scene" that would bring European

---

[54] Barrows, *Oration... 1812*, 6.

"revolution and blood" to America.[55] It is little surprise that the immediate witnesses to and victims of the riots, as well as secondhand commentators, compared the violence perpetrated in Baltimore to Jacobin enormities.

One eyewitness remarked: "All I have ever read of the French [Revolution] does not equal what I saw and heard last night. Such expressions as these were current – 'We'll root out the damn'd tories.' 'We'll drink their blood.' 'We'll eat their hearts.'"[56] Hanson's narrative claimed that the violence of the Baltimore Republicans had exceeded even that of the Jacobins, "The blood hounds of republican France, massacred by thousands those obknoxious [*sic*] to their vengeance, but they despatched their victims quickly, rarely ever resorting to such lingering tortures as the exclusive republicans of this boasted land of liberty and happiness have the credit of inventing."[57] (A similar argument had been made to discredit slaveholders as worse than Jacobins.) A later pamphlet titled *A Portrait of the Evils of Democracy*, which supplied the definitive Federalist view of the Baltimore riot, returned over and over again to the example of French violence as a comparison point. The Baltimore mob had attempted to "imitate the example set by the bloodthirsty Parisians"; in fact, it had even exceeded the French example; the Baltimore mob "outstripe[d] the sanguinary acts of the Jacobins of France, when in the maturity of crime."[58] Even after the Maryland countryside had been invaded by British soldiers, and Baltimore itself threatened, the author of *Portrait* turned to the imagery of anti-Jacobinism as a standard of horror. In 1815, the *Federal Republican* was still attacking American Republicans as devotees of Jacobinism and its tyrannical Napoleonic offshoot.[59]

Baltimore gave evidence to conservative fears that the War of 1812 made the American republic vulnerable to French corruption. The Reverend Otis Thompson warned his congregants that the events in Baltimore, as well as lesser episodes of Republican violence in Savannah and Charleston, proved "that the reign of terrour is to commence!"[60] A reaction meeting held in

---

[55] Kiah Bayley, *War a Calamity Greatly to Be Dreaded; the Substance of Two Discourses Delivered . . . Jul. 23, 1812 . . . A Day of Fasting, Humiliation, and Prayer* (Hallowell, Me., 1812), 2. Elijah Parish also decried the violence in Baltimore at his Jul. 23, 1812, sermon; Parish, *Protest against the War*, 9.

[56] Quoted in Hickey, *War of 1812*, 66.

[57] Hanson, *Exact and Authentic Narrative*, 35.

[58] *A Portrait of the Evils of Democracy; Submitted to the Consideration of the People of Maryland* (Baltimore, 1816), 14, 82.

[59] "Speaking Facts," *Federal Republican*, Jul. 14, 1815. See also "From the Same," *Dedham Gazette*, Sept. 15, 1815.

[60] Thompson, *Signs of the Times*, 9. Also Worcester, *Abraham and Lot*, 19. More examples of the Baltimore riots described as a reign of terror include (Mass.), *Proceedings of a Convention* (Worcester, Mass., 1812), 8, 16–17; Sloan, *Address to the Citizens*, 8; James M. Broom, *Address of the Committee Appointed by the Friends of Liberty, Peace, and Commerce of New-Castle County, at a Meeting on the 29th Ultimo to the Citizens of the State of Delaware* (Wilmington, Del., 1812), 6.

Faneuil Hall, Boston, directly attributed the Baltimore riots to the new "alliance" between France and the United States.[61] The effectiveness of the language of terror is captured in the diary of a young Republican lawyer, John Gallison, who attended the Boston meeting. Although he stood politically on the other side of the fence, Gallison experienced a deep wave of paranoia that "some violence should take place" during the meeting, and he joined the Federalists in thinking it "not absurd to suppose that the democrats, in imitation of their French brethren, might by a previous concert have come armed into the hall, & would upon a signal given fall upon their unarmed rivals."[62] Gallison's fright suggests that the Baltimore riots really did create a reign of terror in the souls of many antiwar sympathizers.

Twenty years after the September Massacres, anti-Jacobinism continued to supply a vocabulary and an ideological paradigm for describing America's vulnerability to transatlantic violence. Thus, it is unsurprising that accusations of violent slavery also played a central role in the opposition to the War of 1812. As they had since the early 1790s, American anti-Jacobins linked the violence of the Republican war hawks to their temperaments as slave owners. American historians have traditionally been dismissive of Federalist–Calvinist antislavery rhetoric during the War of 1812, seeing it as an indication of sectionalist hatred rather than ethical commitment.[63] Looking beyond the national sphere, however, reveals the significance of slavery within a transatlantic struggle over violence, social order, rights, and equality. Far from being symptomatic of a solely internal conflict, disputations about slavery during the War of 1812 involved the United States in a heated international conversation.[64] Conservative attacks on Republican slave mongering during the War of 1812 emerged from a well-developed argument against the violence of slavery and would contribute to an assertive antislavery movement in the decades to follow.

The grounds of the argument connecting slavery to the war were simple. Many in the Republican leadership, including the president, James Madison, were southern slaveholders. Western war hawks such as Henry Clay and Andrew Jackson were equally dedicated to slaveholding interests. Slavery could be blamed for the War of 1812 not only because it gave the war hawks a political advantage by awarding them additional representation on the basis of their slave property (the three-fifths clause). Slavery was also to

---

[61] John Bach McMaster, *A History of the People of the United States, from the Revolution to the Civil War* (New York, 1883), 3:555; Morison, *Harrison Gray Otis*, 330.

[62] Padraig Riley, "Northern Republicans and Southern Slavery: Democracy in the Age of Jefferson, 1800–1819" (Ph.D., University of California, Berkeley, Calif., 2007).

[63] Most recently, Wilentz, *Rise of American Democracy*, 163–4.

[64] Matthew Mason, *Slavery and Politics in the Early American Republic* (Chapel Hill, N.C., 2006), chapter 2; Matthew Mason, "The Battle of the Slaveholding Liberators: Great Britain, the United States, and Slavery in the Early Nineteenth Century," *William and Mary Quarterly* 59 (2002).

blame because the institution made masters dangerously violent. Dissenters argued that slavery had made the Republicans "warrish"; slavery developed the violent passions that drove men to fighting rather than diplomacy.

The violent temperament of slaveholders could also be witnessed in their proclivity toward Indian killing. Critics of the war often lumped together slavery and Indian killing in their criticisms of the war hawks' savagery; an association advanced by the very real violence of slaveholder expansion in the southwest during the war.[65] According to antiwar speakers, slavery and Indian killing revealed the leaders of the War of 1812 to be murderers. Drawing on a deep-rooted political-cultural tradition that identified human depravity as an ever-threatening proclivity toward violence, opponents blamed the war on southern-democratic indulgence of the passions. The Reverend Thomas Andros, a veteran of the War of Independence who turned to the ministry after experiencing the horrors of war, preached that the depravity exemplified by the war hawks had "filled the earth with violence" since the beginning of humanity. "Pause and reflect," Andros commanded the audience at his 1812 Thanksgiving sermon, "of the boast, in southern papers, of the number of scalps we take in an Indian expedition – to say nothing of advertising for sale, buying and selling men, as we buy and sell horses and cattle." Violent passions drove both Indian killing and slavery, and it explained the Republicans' passion for war.[66]

Andros spoke from personal experience of war, and his sermon unquestionably represented more than a mere flash of sectional hatred. Nonetheless, Andros's argument, and those of his many compatriots, proved an especially effective means of disarming the Republicans' claims that the war operated from humanitarian motivations. Advocates of the war often painted the endeavor in a positive light, as a blow against the injustice of impressment. By making war against Britain, Republicans argued that they were freeing American sailors (and the nation at large) from slavery at the hands of their old colonial masters. Richard Rush, the son of Benjamin Rush, went so far as to deliver a prowar oration before the U.S. Congress on July 4, 1812, in which he argued that British impressment was harsher and more brutal than southern slavery.[67] Most references to southern slavery, however, were used by opponents to counter the war hawks' ethical claims. According to Thomas Andros, "Virginia infidelity and love of domination, regards not the wailings of humanity. To authenticate this charge its thousands of wretched

---

[65] Adam Rothman, *Slave Country: American Expansion and the Origins of the Deep South* (Cambridge, Mass., 2005), 11–13.

[66] Thomas Andros, *The Grand Era of Ruin to Nations from Foreign Influence: A Discourse, Delivered before the Congregational Society in Berkley, Nov. 26, 1812* (Boston, Mass., 1812), 14–15; Joseph Estabrook White, "Thomas Andros: Captive," *New England Quarterly* 10 (Sept. 1937).

[67] Richard Rush, *An Oration, Delivered in the Hall of the House of Representatives, at the Capitol, Washington, Jul. 4, 1812* (Concord, N.H., 1812).

DEATH OF THE EMBARGO, WITH ALL ITS " RESTRICTIVE ENERGIES."

A wit first celebrated this great event in the FEDERAL REPUBLICAN, in the manner to be seen below ; but he has had the politeness to revise and correct the article for the Evening Post, with additions : in this improved state it is now presented to our readers, aided by an appropriate engraving devised by the author and admirably executed by one of our fellow-citizens. Here it comes—

" TO THE GRAVE GO SHAM PROTECTORS OF " FREE TRADE AND SAILORS' RIGHTS"—AND ALL THE PEOPLE SAY AMEN !"

FIGURE 6. "Death of the Embargo," *Evening Post*, April 25, 1814. This newspaper illustration by Alexander Anderson, engraver of the slave muzzle, depicts James Madison as a "sham protector" of sailors' rights, desperately trying, and failing, to free himself of the failed 1813 Embargo Act (represented by the terrapin "Ograbme" – *embargo* backward). The illustration celebrates the figurative death of the embargo and Madison as the key to restoring true freedom. From *Early American Newspapers, an Archive of Americana Collection. Published by Readex (Readex.com), a division of NewsBank, Inc.*

slaves will appear as swift witnesses." Northern critics argued that southern slaveholders by definition could not represent the cause of freedom.[68] "Does your President wage war from this humane motive of regaining seamen?" Elijah Parish asked his congregants. "If he is so humane, why does he continue the lash of oppression on the slaves, which blacken his fields?"[69] Dissenters attacked Republican slaveholding to reveal the prowar party as dangerously violent, and moreover to undermine the supposed humanitarian rationales for the war.

[68] Andros, *Grand Era of Ruins*, 14–15.
[69] Parish, *Discourse . . . 1813*, 13.

Despite the obvious one-upmanship of cross-sectional claims to be protecting freedom against slavery, the arguments were not confined within a national framework. When Thomas Andros criticized the war hawks for slaveholding, he joined British critics of the United States, many of whom had been allies in transatlantic anti-Jacobin and antislavery sentiment during the previous two decades. During the concurrent British and American movements against the slave trade in 1807, transatlantic anti-Jacobins had banded together to stress the dangers of the "barbaric traffic." The English antislavery barrister Stephen James published a pamphlet entitled *Dangers of the Country* in 1807, which warned that God was using the French Revolution and Napoleon to punish Europe for the crime of slave trafficking. In 1814, the American Evangelical periodical the *Christian Disciple*, published by the antiwar leader Noah Worcester, printed a review of *Dangers* that extended James's logic to the United States, warning that the ongoing crime of slavery in the United States was being avenged by war.[70] Since the early 1790s, Anglophone antislavery advocates throughout the Atlantic had been exchanging texts and visits, and forming a common language of struggle that highlighted the brutal violence of the slave trade. Britain used this language to criticize the United States during the war and backed its rhetoric with action by freeing thousands of American slaves. American opponents to the war, loyal to what they viewed as the United States' true path – not its criminal seduction by France – echoed these complaints, remaining in step with British critics throughout the war years.

In both the United States and Great Britain, accusations of Jacobinism served as a central element of the antislavery critique during the War of 1812. In a classic anti-Jacobin trope, used very effectively by Theodore Dwight in the 1790s, a Federalist newspaper writer in 1814 fantasized that southern slaveholding was so brutal that masters would produce "shoes made of 'biped skin leather' obtained by skinning slaves."[71] Similar anti-Jacobin tropes appeared in British charges against American slaveholding.[72] Connecting antislavery arguments to the Francophobic arguments against the war, the Connecticut minister Nathan Strong argued that the violence of war making and the violence of slavery both signified the kingdom of the beast, and northerners needed to "come out" before they were reduced to slavery. Attached by multiple points of connection, the antislavery argument during the War of 1812 emerged from twenty years of transatlantic counterrevolutionary political culture, not simply local imperatives.[73]

The tarring brush of slavery reappeared throughout American antiwar sources in many iterations. Critics warned that the war, waged by slave

---

[70] "The Slave Trade," *Christian Disciple*, Oct. 1814, 309–11; Dec. 1814, 357–60.
[71] Quoted in Mason, *Slavery and Politics*, 47.
[72] Mason, "The Battle of the Slaveholding Liberators: Great Britain, the United States, and Slavery in the Early Nineteenth Century."
[73] Strong, *A Fast Sermon... 1812*, 15–16.

owners, would lead to America's enslavement by France.[74] They complained that the "national hatred" of Great Britain, encouraged by Republican speakers, enslaved the nation.[75] Dissenters charged the South with the desire to make northerners into slaves – a charge that was meant to evoke chattel slavery as well as political slavery. Elijah Parish rallied his parishioners to resist southern enslavement with the call: "Let your puissant lords be satisfied by inflicting the bloody lash on more than ten hundred thousand *African* slaves."[76] John Lowell, an incendiary and radical critic of the war who favored New England secession, argued that the masterly desire to dominate was the real, sinister, source for the war. He charged the aristocratic, slave-owning, "warm-bloods of the south," with making war as an excuse to subdue the North by sword.[77] Josiah Dunham fulminated that the "Virginia Influence" wanted to compel northerners "to be substituted, perhaps, in process of time, for African slaves, and *to serve the same masters.*"[78] Other critics accused the South of attempting to destroy commerce in order to force all men of capital to become slaveholding landowners.[79] They implicated President Madison personally as a slave owner.[80] They compared British impressment to the far greater evil of southern slavery.[81] They described human bondage as a national sin, which God was punishing by subjecting the United States to a bloody war.[82]

---

[74] Bayley, *War a Calamity*; John Sylvester John Gardiner, *A Discourse, Delivered at Trinity Church, Boston, Mass., Jul. 23, 1812; on the Day of Publick Fast in Massachusetts, Upon the Declaration of War against Great-Britain* (Boston, Mass., 1812).

[75] William Ladd, *An Oration, Pronounced at Minot, Maine, on the Fourth Day of July, 1814* (Portland, Me., 1814).

[76] Parish, *Protest against the War*, 17.

[77] John Lowell, *Perpetual War: The Policy of Mr. Madison: Being a Candid Examination of His Late Message to Congress, So Far as Respects . . . The Pretended Negotiations for Peace – . . . A Conscript Militia – and the Establishment of an Immense Standing Army of Guards and Spies, under the Name of a Local Volunteer Force* (Boston, Mass., 1812), 77. For similar remarks by Lowell in other pamphlets, see John Lowell, *Mr. Madison's War: A Dispassionate Inquiry into the Reasons Alleged by Mr. Madison for Declaring an Offensive and Ruinous War against Great Britain: Together with Some Suggestions as to a Peaceable and Constitutional Mode of Averting That Dreadful Calamity* (New York, 1812), 3, 16. Also Sloan, *Address to the Citizens*; Friend to Freedom, *Southern Oppression an Address to the People of the Eastern States, Developing the Causes of Their Oppression* (New York, 1813).

[78] Josiah Dunham, *An Oration, in Commemoration of the Birth of Our Illustrious Washington: Pronounced at Windsor, Feb. 22, 1814, before the Washington Benevolent Society* (Windsor, Vt., 1814), 30.

[79] "Letters of Samuel Taggart," 368.

[80] Worcester, *Abraham and Lot*, 25; Parish, *Discourse . . . 1813*, 13.

[81] French, *Sermons . . . 1812*, 5–6.

[82] Perkins, *National Sins and National Punishment*, 16; Lewis Mayer, *The Crisis: A Sermon, Preached at Shepherd's-Town, Virginia, on Thursday, Aug. 20, 1812: The Day Appointed by the President of the United States, to Be Observed as a Day of Humiliation and Prayer* (Martinsburgh, Va., 1812).

For some critics who had long been committed to anti-Jacobinism and antislavery, the War of 1812 provided an opportunity to threaten the South again with the possibility of slave rebellion. The bipolar qualities of violent language made it paradoxically possible to oppose violence with threats of violence, a dynamic frequently at work in abolitionist remarks about slave rebellion. Lemuel Haynes, Vermont's biracial Congregationalist minister and Federalist partisan, brilliantly finessed his antiwar rhetoric against southern slaveholding into an ambiguous endorsement of the justice of slave rebellion abroad and at home. In an 1813 sermon, Haynes questioned President Madison's humane rationale for the war against Britain in light of the number of slaves then living in Virginia. If it was just to pursue a war to free impressed seamen, Haynes asked, was it "the duty of these slaves to rise and massacre their masters?" The question expressed a subtle ambivalence about the justice of slave rebellion. The clearly intended, yet unspoken, answer to Haynes's question was no – slave rebellion was a violence that could not be justified, and therefore the War of 1812 was a violence that could not be justified. However, by posing the parallel between slave rebellion and the War of 1812 as a question, Haynes implicitly encouraged his audience to consider the alternative answer: yes, slave rebellion might be legitimate violence.[83]

Many opponents went beyond questioning whether slave rebellion might be legitimate to making outright threats of imminent slave rebellion within the United States. The war, according to its critics, made the South more vulnerable to slave revolt. While some dissenters whispered their prognostications with fearful reluctance, others loudly suggested that such a revolt would be well deserved.[84] Elijah Parish, in yet another remark that provoked his opponents to rage, chastised: "let the southern *Heroes* fight their own battles, and guard their slumbering pillows against the just vengeance of their lacerated slaves, whose sighs and groans have long since gone up to the court of the Eternal, crying for the full viols of his incensed wrath."[85] Southern Republicans rightly interpreted Parish's remarks as more threat than warning. Even more frightening to southerners during the war years, Parish's remarks did not represent the frothing of one extremely vitriolic individual. Even the most pacifistic critic of the war, the Reverend Noah Worcester, published threats of slave rebellion.[86]

As with antislavery rhetoric in general, remarks connecting slave rebellion to the War of 1812 took many forms. The radical secessionist John Lowell

[83] Lemuel Haynes, *Black Preacher to White America: The Collected Writings of Lemuel Haynes, 1774–1833*, ed. Richard Newman (Brooklyn, N.Y., 1990), 67–9, 83, 153, 157.

[84] For a fearful warning against slave rebellion, see Samuel Austin, *A Sermon, Preached in Worcester, Massachusetts, on the Occasion of the Special Fast, Jul. 23, 1812* (Worcester, Mass., 1812), 13.

[85] Parish, *Protest against the War*, 16.

[86] "The Slave Trade," *Christian Disciple*. Dec. 1814, 359–60.

attacked Republican commercial policies against Haiti during the buildup to the war and wrote approvingly of Haiti's "great, bloody, and savage struggle to regain their natural rights," concluding that "no man in a Christian or a free country can question the justice of their cause."[87] More than a short aside, Lowell developed his brief in favor of the Haitian revolutionaries over four well-argued pages. After the war began, congressman Abijah Bigelow (Massachusetts) complained that fear of rebellion weakened the southern states' ability to wage a military defense, and thus increased their reliance on northern aid.[88] Timothy Dwight warned that Great Britain might foment a slave rebellion.[89] Robert Kennedy compared slave "insurrection" to the "insurgency" in Baltimore; both were evidence of God's displeasure at the United States for declaring an offensive war.[90] Noah Worcester argued that the logic justifying America's declaration of war against Britain could equally teach slaves to slaughter their masters. And, in unforgiving judgment, Worcester asked "why may we not accuse every slaveholder in the United States with *murder*, with as much propriety as we have accused the British government of *making war*?" Worcester's pacifism led him to "shudder" at the thought of a slave rebellion, though he believed the cause to be just.[91] Yet even when opponents to the war forswore slave rebellion, one can detect a certain schadenfreude shading their remarks.

At its Gothic height, opposition rhetoric charged the entire prowar party with the crime of cannibalism. Alexander Hanson described his Baltimore attackers as men who "tortured in a manner until now unknown in the annals of all time, to satiate the bloody appetite of cannibals and tigers in human form."[92] Francis Blake expanded this indictment to include all the members of Congress who supported the war. In a July 4 oration, he accused the war hawks of preparing a "Feast of War" whose participants would be "regaled, by quaffing blood in the skulls of their enemies!"[93] Josiah Quincy, the Federalist opposition leader, delivered this verdict on congressional Republicans to their face, in a January 5, 1813, speech, when he charged that his colleagues had "rushed upon Canada. Nothing would satisfy them but blood. The language of their conduct is that of the giant in

[87] John Lowell, *The New-England Patriot Being a Candid Comparison, of the Principles and Conduct of the Washington and Jefferson Administrations: The Whole Founded Upon Indisputable Facts and Public Documents* (Boston, Mass., 1810), 53–6.

[88] "Letters of Abijah Bigelow," 392–4.

[89] Dwight, *Discourse...Jul. 23, 1812*, 50.

[90] Robert Kennedy, *A Fast-Day Sermon, Preached at Greencastle, on the Last Thursday of July 1812* (Hagerstown, Md., 1812), 8.

[91] In Worcester's words, "If we 'reflect, that God is just,' must we not expect that there will be a day of retribution to the Southern States." Worcester, *Abraham and Lot*, 25–8.

[92] Hanson, *Exact and Authentic Narrative*, 25.

[93] Francis Blake, *An Oration, Pronounced at Worcester (Mass.) on the Thirty-Sixth Anniversary of American Independence, Jul. 4, 1812* (Worcester, Mass., 1812), 24.

children's stories: 'Fee, faw, fum, / I smell the blood of an Englishman; / Ded or alive, I will have some.'"[94] The accusation of cannibalism recalled centuries of English discourse about cruelty and questioned the war hawks, very right to claim a place in civilized society.[95]

Aspersions on the civilized status of the war hawks were not merely rhetorical fodder to heighten the flames of opposition. The accusation of savagery reveals what dissenters believed to be at stake in the War of 1812 and explains why many waged such a fervent opposition. Since the mid-1780s, conservatives had argued that man's innate tendency toward violence would undermine the new Republican state. The Revolution had overthrown traditional standards of deference, deposed the colonial power elite, and placed the government in the hands of the people. The new politics depended upon the citizens' own virtue and self-control to secure the social order. If Americans were to lose control of their violent passions, the nation could swiftly degenerate into bloodshed and anarchy. The War of 1812 posed a potentially mortal danger to the United States because it threatened to release Americans' savage potential. The war had generated from the violent passions of "the semi-barbarians of the southern states."[96] Antiwar believers feared that the experience of warfare threatened to reduce all the citizens who joined the battle to the same depraved condition.

In a telling phrase that echoed throughout the opposition rhetoric, dissenters criticized war as a "school of depravity" that would corrupt American citizens and undermine the state.[97] This formulation encompassed a broad range of meaning. In his 1812 national Fast sermon, Noah Worcester described army camps as "schools of depravity" because they habituated men to gambling, idleness, dissipation, excessive drinking, and other disorderly habits.[98] But Worcester and his allies intended more by the phrase than those common sins. War was a mode of education that made men violent. The anonymous author of a long essay defending the opposition clergy against accusations of treachery explained that, "by familiarizing a people to scenes of violence and slaughter, [war] produces a savageness of feeling and manners."[99] In the words of the Reverend Samuel Walker, "War turns men into ferocious beasts, and teaches them to delight in blood and

[94] Edmund Quincy, *Life of Josiah Quincy of Massachusetts* (Boston, Mass., 1867), 281.

[95] Philippe Rosenberg, "The Moral Order of Violence: The Meanings of Cruelty in Early Modern England, 1648–1685" (Ph.D., Duke University, 1999), chapter 3.

[96] Gardiner, *A Discourse, Delivered at Trinity Church, Boston, Mass., Jul. 23, 1812; on the Day of Publick Fast in Massachusetts, Upon the Declaration of War against Great-Britain*, 9.

[97] See, for example, Noah Worcester, "A Solemn Review of the Custom of War; Showing That War Is the Effect of Popular Delusion, and Proposing a Remedy," in *The Friend of Peace* (Boston, Mass., 1822); Brown, *Evils of War*, 11.

[98] Worcester, *Abraham and Lot*, 13. See also Bayley, *War a Calamity*, 6.

[99] *A Defence of the Clergy of New-England, against the Charges of Interfering in Our Political Affairs, and Condemning the Policy of the Present War* (Concord, N.H., 1814), 35.

carnage."[100] The Reverend Nathan Beman – who, like Worcester, quoted from the story of Abraham and Lot to introduce his national Fast sermon – described the demoralizing effects of warfare at greater length. In war,

the most base and depraved passions of the heart are called into action, and the most awful *expressions* of them are daily witnessed in the camp and the field of battle. The conflicting armies breathe the spirit of *murder* and *revenge*, and exult with satanic triumph at the wounds they inflict on each other.... The scenes which are witnessed in war have a deleterious influence on the heart. They obliterate serious impressions; destroy the principles of responsibility to God, and degrade *men* to *monsters*.[101]

The experience of slaughtering soldiers in the field of battle released men's violent passions and transformed them into murderous monsters unfit for civic life. War initiated an uncivilizing process that would undermine the state. Even a just war, like the American Revolution, had destroyed the morals of its soldiers according to many ministers of the postrevolutionary era.[102]

Political antagonists, as well as their ministerial allies, made this ethical critique of war. Joel Linsley, who delivered an antiwar oration at Middlebury College in 1814, identified the American Revolution as a turning point in America's moral decline. He also blamed America's moral declension and its political consequences on the crime of slavery.[103] The War of 1812, political opponents agonized, would sink the nation's morality into a dark abyss from which it would never rise. A Federalist convention that gathered in New Jersey on July 4, 1812, insisted that its members band together to stop the war "before its corruptions, its passions, and its violence" made the warfare perpetual. If fighting is "permitted to flourish over peace and social habits," they warned, "all history proves that war becomes the *predominant* passion" and "civil liberty" is yielded.[104] Another convention, held in New Castle, Delaware, warned that "war demoralizes the nation; [and] gives vent to lawless passions."[105] The Delaware convention pointed to the rioting in

[100] Samuel Walker, *Two Discourses, Delivered Jul. 23, 1812; Being the Day Appointed by the Governor of Massachusetts for Fasting and Prayer* (Salem, Mass., 1812), 16–17.

[101] Nathan S. S. Beman, *A Sermon, Delivered at the Meeting House of the Second Parish in Portland, Aug. 20, 1812, on the Occasion of the National Fast* (Portland, Me., 1812), 6–7. See also Nathaniel Thayer, *A Sermon Delivered Aug. 20, 1812, the Day of Publick Humiliation and Prayer Appointed by the National Government* (Worcester, Mass., 1812), 12; Bayley, *War a Calamity*, 6.

[102] Jeremy Belknap, *An Election Sermon: Preached before the General Court, of New Hampshire, at Portsmouth, Jun. 2, 1785* (Portsmouth, N.H., 1785); Jabez Chickering, *An Oration Pronounced at Dedham on the Anniversary of American Independence, Jul. 4, 1812* (Boston, Mass., 1812), 7; David Low Dodge, *Memorial of Mr. David L. Dodge: Consisting of an Autobiography* (Boston, Mass., 1854).

[103] "An Oration: On the Moral History of the United States," *The Adviser: or Vermont Evangelical Magazine*, Jan./Feb. 1815, 33–42.

[104] (N.J.), *Proceedings and Address of the Convention*, 10.

[105] Broom, *Address of the Committee*, 6.

Baltimore as an example of how war, by corrupting citizens, destroyed the institutions of civic life.

The opponents to the War of 1812 retained the revolutionary-era belief that Republican governments were inherently fragile. A quarter century of constitutional government had not yet proved the durability of the national experiment. The republic remained susceptible to the problem of violence: to passionate bloodshed that the state – a creature of the people – might not have the power to control. Clement Clark Moore, a passionately anti-Jeffersonian Federalist minister from New York, remarked in an 1813 political pamphlet that the greatest evil arising from the war was its "tendency to render passion predominant over reason. In our country, this should be particularly avoided, and this consideration alone should, at all times, render our government very cautious of declaring war. A people that governs itself ought, if possible to be always calm and temperate."[106] Federalists drew the lesson from reading history that the spirit of war had ultimately pushed every republic into despotism.[107] The Reverend Jacob Catlin explained: "by war is erected and supported a terrific power, able and disposed to influence the civil concerns of the state; and every exertion of that power saps the foundation of republicanism."[108] Remarks like Moore's and Catlin's demonstrate how Federalist–Calvinist opposition to the War of 1812, grounded in a history of transatlantic anti-Jacobinism as well as contemporary political-economic interests, overflowed the bounds of the partisan and entered the realm of political ethics.

The War of 1812 generated an outpouring of opposition speech that moved swiftly from the local to the national, from the particularistic to the general, and from the political to the ethical. The citizens of Georgetown captured the logic of opposition speech in a complaint they authored following the 1812 riots in nearby Baltimore. Whereas the American Revolution had been fought to "protect the lives, liberties, and properties of their countrymen, equally against unbridled licentiousness and individual violence," and whereas recent "outrages [had] been committed against the lives, liberties, and properties of the citizens," the citizens of Georgetown wished "to express their opinions, and let their determination be known, so that practices big with danger to every thing man holds dear in life may be arrested in their progress."[109] Antagonism to the War of 1812 swiftly transformed into antagonism toward war at large. The ethical arguments sparked by the war would not be contained by the conflict. Rather, the antiwar leaders' failure

---

[106] Clement Clarke Moore, *A Sketch of Our Political Condition: Addressed to the Citizens of the United States, without Distinction of Party* (New York, 1813), 43.

[107] Prentiss, *Oration... 1812*, 29.

[108] Jacob Catlin, *The Horrors of War: A Sermon Delivered at New-Marlborough, Mass. At the Celebration of Independence* (Stockbridge, Mass., 1813), 7. Also "Letters of Abijah Bigelow," 326.

[109] Hanson, *Exact and Authentic Narrative*, 65.

to effect their political goals led to a social movement to rectify the problem of violence at its point of origin.

Friends of Peace

From the beginning, leaders of the political opposition to the War of 1812 complemented their political speech with political action, by attempting to wrest control of local and national governments from the war hawks. Soon after the June 1812 declaration of war, political opponents began gathering in ad hoc conventions to organize a new sectional coalition of northern Republicans and Federalists who shared a fierce antagonism to the war. The men who gathered at these meetings styled themselves the "Friends of Peace," or, more informally, the "Peace Party" – perhaps following the recommendation issued by the Massachusetts legislature, one week after Congress had declared war, to "organize a *peace party* throughout your Country, and let all other party distinctions vanish."[110] The term also had historic resonance; John Adams had used the phrase "Friends of Peace" in 1794 to describe the anti-Jacobin opponents to the Whiskey Rebellion.[111] The label identified the historical-ideological commitment shared by members of the coalition.

Although Federalists preponderated the new peace party, they distinguished "peace men" as a new political identity distinct from their partisan past.[112] Some of the Republican members of the coalition shared ethical commitments with the Federalist members that transcended the war question. For example, the New Jersey Congressman James Sloan, who wrote a strongly anti-Jacobin antiwar pamphlet in 1812, represented one of the few committed antislavery voices within the Jeffersonian party during the early national era. Sloan connected his antiwar and antislavery commitments, advising fellow northerners not to vote for the tyrannical southern slaveholders who had brought the nation to war.[113] Similar sentiments appeared in many of pamphlets published by the Friends of Peace, which supported antiwar candidates for local and national offices.[114] At the state level, this

---

[110] Morison, *Harrison Gray Otis*, 326.
[111] Letter from John Adams to Abigail Adams, Nov. 15., 1794 [electronic edition], *Adams Family Papers: An Electronic Archive*, Massachusetts Historical Society, http://www.masshist.org/digitaladams/.
[112] "Letters of Abijah Bigelow," 343.
[113] Sloan, *Address to the Citizens*. See discussion of the confusion over the date of Sloan's death in Riley, "Northern Republicans and Southern Slavery."
[114] See, for example, Republican of Norfolk, *An Address to the Citizens of Norfolk County Exposing the Absurdity of the Present War and the Great Benefits of Peace: And Showing the Absolute Necessity of Choosing a Representative to Congress Who Will Vote for a Speedy and Honourable Peace* (1812); Peace and (N.J.), *Proceedings and Address*; Broom, *Address of the Committee.*

campaign proved successful, and the election of 1812 turned many war hawks out of office in the North.

However, the defeat of the Friends of Peace coalition presidential candidate in 1812 doomed this nascent party to failure. In the summer of 1812, Federalist opponents to the war took their greatest risk by informally endorsing the New York Republican, De Witt Clinton, for the office of the presidency. Federalists knew they had no chance of electing a member of their own party, considering their vastly diminished number of supporters. Instead they supported Clinton, who assumed the mantle of the peace party. Clinton won New England (except Vermont) and New York, but Madison's close victory in Pennsylvania preserved his presidency. A victory by Clinton would have forced the northern peace coalition into formalizing and defining their new party. Instead, the coalition proved ephemeral, a marriage of convenience that did not survive the moment. By the next presidential election in 1816, the war had ceased to be an effective rallying point for any candidates except victorious Republicans. The Peace Party disappeared, and the Federalists lost their national influence (although they continued to hold power in several states).[115]

Stifled in the political sphere, committed ethical opponents to the War of 1812 sought a societal solution to the problem of violence. At the close of the war, many of its most fervent and outspoken opponents joined together to found the first two American nonsectarian peace societies. The Massachusetts Peace Society (MPS) was established in 1815 by Noah Worcester, with the help of William Ellery Channing who, like Worcester, had delivered and published prominent antiwar sermons during the previous three years. The New York Peace Society (NYPS) was also incorporated in 1815, by a deeply religious, arch-Federalist, Connecticut-born merchant named David L. Dodge, who had likewise reviled the War of 1812. The MPS and the NYPS, as well as the many local organizations that were established in their wake, dedicated their efforts to eradicating the "custom of war" (in Noah Worcester's words) from American society. The MPS attempted this goal both by enlisting members and by publishing a serial, *The Friend of Peace*, that proselytized the cause. The NYPS concentrated more exclusively on publishing antiwar materials and did little to enlist ordinary citizens.

The NYPS and the MPS reflected a range of religious and political positions within the Congregationalist–Federalist tradition. Dodge was a devout consistent Calvinist, influenced by leading anti-Jacobin ministers including Ludovicus Weld, Aaron Cleveland, and Nathan Strong. In his youth, he was a fierce Federalist partisan, whose shock at the "atheism and violence of the French Revolution" led him to contribute political essays to contemporary

[115] Steven E. Siry, "The Sectional Politics of 'Practical Republicanism': De Witt Clinton's Presidential Bid, 1810–1812," *Journal of the Early Republic* 5 (Winter 1985); Strum, "The New York Antiwar Campaign"; Strum, "New Jersey Politics."

newspapers. Up to the end of his life, he remained committed to traditional Calvinist teachings about human depravity, quoting from the prophet Jeremiah, "the heart is deceitful above all things and desperately wicked" (17:9), in letters to his children.[116] The theology of the founders of the MPS represented Congregationalism's more liberal side. Worcester and Channing were both leaders of the Unitarian split from Trinitarian Calvinism. However, the membership of the MPS were the same Federalist anti-Jacobin Evangelicals who dominated the other branches of the conservative reform movements known generally as the Benevolent Empire. Although Worcester insisted on the organization's political disinterestedness, only two known members were Republicans (the rest were confirmed, or likely, Federalists). Despite some differences in doctrine between the leaders and certain members of the MPS, they shared in common a deep-running concern with the problem of violence caused by humanity's innate depravity.

Noah Worcester first published on the subject of religion in reaction to the early Unitarian John Murray's tract on the origins of evil, which refuted the doctrine of depravity. At that time, Worcester embraced a Hopkinsian theology with its strong emphasis on depravity. In 1809, Worcester's faith shifted toward Unitarianism; however, his views on human depravity remained traditional. In his best-known antiwar essay, "A Solemn Review of the Custom of War," Worcester attributes war to the "basest passions of human nature." He begins his essay, much as Elijah Parish began a sermon published in 1797, with an evocation of child sacrifice and slavery, two horrid examples of men's depravity. Worcester believed that Christianity could civilize man and the state, and abolish those evils, as well as the custom of war, with which he was most concerned. He had great faith in the power of Christian education to make people less violent. Yet even Worcester's final writings revealed the persistence of his belief in man's innate sinfulness as a fact "too obvious" to be questioned. Worcester never accepted the doctrine of universal redemption, and throughout his life, he remained politically committed to Federalism, with its conservative emphasis on preserving social order. Worcester's peace-reform activities represent an extension of, not a break from, the New England religious tradition.[117]

---

[116] Dodge, *Memorial*, 50–60, 308–9.
[117] Worcester, "Solemn Review." For biographical information, see Henry Ware and Samuel Worcester, *Memoirs of the Reverend Noah Worcester, D.D.* (Boston, Mass., 1844). W. E. Channing's 1812 sermons also reveal a perhaps surprising concern with violence and social order. See, for example, William Ellery Channing, *A Sermon, Preached in Boston, Mass., Aug. 20, 1812, the Day of Humiliation and Prayer, Appointed by the President of the United States, in Consequence of the Declaration of War against Great Britain* (Boston, Mass., 1812). It is interesting to observe that not only does the Unitarian reaction against Calvinism fail to explain the origin of antiwar societies but also some Unitarians from the era were busy making arguments to justify the custom of war; see Hosea Ballou, *A Sermon, Delivered at Portsmouth, N.H., Appropriate to the Occasion of a Day of Humiliation and*

The evolution from Federalist–Congregationalist opposition against the War of 1812 to general antiwar sentiment is unsurprising when one considers the substance of many opposition texts. Embedded within numerous dissenting sermons and orations is a general argument against the institution of war. For example, the Reverend Reuben Holcomb divided his Massachusetts 1812 special Fast sermon into two parts, the first laying out the case against war in general and the second attacking the War of 1812 in particular.[118] Such general antiwar sentiment may have served a partisan purpose during the war years, but its usefulness did not diminish its strength. The typical structure of a strong antiwar text enumerated a series of reasons why war was immoral and detrimental to society. These reasons included war's bloodshed, high cost, uncivilizing effect, injury to Christianity, injury to commerce, impediment to knowledge, and tendency toward despotism.[119] At the end of a July 4, 1813, antiwar sermon, the Reverend Jacob Catlin asked his audience what remedy could end the terrible custom. War would only cease, he argued, if the Friends of Peace joined together in profession of their benevolence. This solution was both partisan (he delivered his oration to the Federalist Washington Benevolent Society) and humanitarian, as it pointed the way to dissenters' involvement in general peace societies following the war.[120]

While the peace societies proved an innovative approach to the problem of violence, a glancing knowledge of nineteenth-century history will expose their failure to eliminate war from American society. For a while, the societies flourished, acquiring new branches, members, and moneys before their momentum dissipated. In 1828, William Ladd (also an opponent of the War of 1812) revitalized the movement, organizing the many local groups into the new American Peace Society (APS).[121] Ten years later, the APS fractured between the radical New England Non-Resistant Society, led by William Lloyd Garrison and Henry Clarke Wright, and the more sober APS. Neither group maintained the integrity of their peace testimony; however, when faced with the challenge of the Civil War – which promised

Prayer... On the 20th of August, 1812 (Portsmouth, N.H., 1812). William Gribbin also notes that Universalists "were emphatic in their support for the war"; Gribbin, *Churches Militant*, 98.

[118] Holcomb, *Discourse... 1812*. Also Walker, *Two Discourses*.

[119] Brown, *Evils of War*; French, *Sermons... 1812*; Huntington Porter, *Peace and War, and Duties of People under These Different Events Considered in a Sermon, Delivered at Rye, 1812, after President Madison's Declaration of War* (Portsmouth, N.H., 1812).

[120] Catlin, *Horrors of War*.

[121] Ladd, *Oration... 1814*. Ladd's opposition to the War of 1812 was as political as other antiwar speakers. In an 1814 opposition oration, Ladd criticized the war hawks in strongly partisan terms: "the rise and progress of that political party, which... has been kept alive by the stimulation of the most baneful passions, has corrupted our body politic, and if not speedily remedied will end in its entire and everlasting destruction" Ladd, *Oration... 1814*, 12.

to achieve the abolition of slavery, a more important cause to many of both societies' members. The APS openly approved the Civil War, as did many Non-Resistants.[122] The bipolar power of the violent language that the peace groups used to criticize violence prepared them for the fight, as seduction overpowered the revulsion generated by images of horrific bloodshed. Far from ending the custom of war, the anti-Jacobin tradition ended up feeding into the deadliest conflict in American history.[123]

Constitutional Resistance

While politically progressive historians have overlooked the role that conservative opponents to the War of 1812 played in the formation of the nation's early peace societies, nationalist historians have similarly overlooked the positive impact that the quasi-seditious opposition had on the realm of free speech. The antiwar leaders' tendency toward disunionism pushed the boundaries of legitimate opposition to a new extreme. Prior to 1812, no popular or legal consensus had established an acceptable range for free speech in wartime. During the American Revolution, dissenters including loyalists and religious pacifists were tarred and feathered, imprisoned, deprived of their property, and sometimes killed extrajudicially.[124] The civil dimensions of the Revolution, which divided communities and families into polarized antagonists, could not confer any legitimacy to dissent against the war. Even the Quakers, whose peace testimony predated the conflict by a century, suffered persecution for their refusal to join the war. Later, America's entry into a quasi war with France spurred the Federalists to pass the Sedition Act of 1798, but that unpopular legislation did not forge a consensus as to the limits on dissension. The "Revolution of 1800" that brought Jefferson into the presidency signified in part a rejection of the Sedition Act; however, the Republicans did not generate a consistent standard for free speech when they came to office. The Sedition Act expired in 1800, but Republican state officials prosecuted numerous Federalist editors for seditious libel in the years following.[125]

Republican persecution of opposition opinion during the first decade of the nineteenth century was not intensive, but this was probably attributable to the declining popularity of the Federalist party – which made them unthreatening – rather than to any profound acceptance of opposition. Thomas

[122] Ziegler, *The Advocates of Peace in Antebellum America.*
[123] This point is explored more fully in chapter 6.
[124] Wayne E. Lee, *Crowds and Soldiers in Revolutionary North Carolina: The Culture of Violence in Riot and War* (Gainesville, Fla., 2001).
[125] James Morton Smith, *Freedom's Fetters: The Alien and Sedition Laws and American Civil Liberties*, Cornell Studies in Civil Liberty (Ithaca, N.Y., 1956), 418.

Jefferson, for example, never accepted the legitimacy of the Federalist opposition, and he always hoped to eliminate the supposedly corrupt faction from national politics.[126] When the War of 1812 erupted, the provisional goodwill of the Republicans dissipated under the weight of crisis. The war hawks swiftly challenged the opposition to the war as treasonous and demanded that opponents be quiet and compliant. Behind these demands lay threats of violence.

In terms ranging from gentle to abrasive to incendiary, war hawks rejected the legitimacy of voicing dissent against the war. At their most generous, the war's supporters censured party divisiveness during a time of national conflict. In this soft critique, the particularities of the opposition went unremarked in favor of paeans to American unity.[127] More aggressive attacks on the dissenters discounted the ethical arguments against the war as hypocritical and motivated by love for Great Britain over the United States. For example, John Giles denigrated the war's ministerial opponents for using religion as a "trumpet of sedition."[128] The harshest criticism employed Gothic rhetoric to describe opponents to the war as a violent threat to the nation. The Reverend Titus Barton attributed dissent to the "depravity of man" and warned that the opposition faction would unleash "quenchless violence" upon the land. They had "set themselves in the most violent opposition to the government," and were their plans to be carried out, "the land must be stained with the blood of its inhabitants."[129] Another supporter of the war charged the dissenters with guilt for the "horrid crime of suicide." He claimed that their opposition made the nation vulnerable to old Tories from Canada who wished to cross the border and slaughter Americans.[130] By 1812, Gothic rhetoric had transcended its

[126] Richard Hofstadter, *The Idea of a Party System: The Rise of Legitimate Opposition in the United States, 1780–1840* (Berkeley, Calif., 1969). See also Padraig Riley's discussion of Levi Lincoln's criticism of dissenting speech; Riley, "Northern Republicans and Southern Slavery."

[127] Gershom C. Lyman, *A Sermon Preached at Marlborough on the Public Fast Aug. 20, 1812* (Brattleborough, Vt., 1812); Conrad Speece, *A Sermon Delivered at Peterville Church on Thursday, Aug. 20, 1812: Being the Day Appointed by the President of the United States for Public Humiliation and Prayer, on Account of the War with England* (Richmond, Va., 1812).

[128] John Giles, *Two Discourses Delivered to the Second Presbyterian Society in Newburyport, Aug. 20, 1812*, 3rd ed. (Newburyport, Mass., 1812), 14. See also Ferdinand Ellis, *A Discourse Adapted to the Present Situation of Our National Concerns; Preached at Marblehead, Mass., Jul. 23, 1812, Appointed... A Day of Fasting, Humiliation and Prayer* (Salem, Mass., 1812). Also Dangerfield, *Era of Good Feelings*, 86.

[129] Titus Theodore Barton, *A Fast Sermon, Preached at Fitchburg, Jul. 23, 1812* (Leominster, Mass., 1812).

[130] Henry Greene, *An Oration Delivered at Shoreham to a Numerous Collection of Citizens of Addison County on the Anniversary of American Independence Jul. 4, 1812* (Rutland, Vt., 1812), 12.

anti-Jacobin origins to become a generalized element of American partisan politics.[131]

Prowar assaults on clerical opposition often questioned the ministers' right to speak on a political subject at all. In response, ministers justified their freedom to opinion by distinguishing between their moral opposition to the war and others' (equally valid) political arguments against the war. They insisted on their duty to address any moral question affecting their congregations. They were speaking out against the war because it broke God's laws.[132] Other ministers conceded that their opposition had political dimensions, but they defended political sermons as appropriate in extremis; the nature of the situation justified their vocal opposition to the national government.[133] A few ministers refused to accept the proscription on political preaching at all. Such avowed partisans as Jonathan French and Samuel Mead defended their right to speak on political subjects.[134] Last, William Ellery Channing transcended the question of ministerial politics to get to the real question raised by the war hawks. Did American citizens have the right to freedom of speech even during a war, when external dangers seemed to demand domestic unity? His eloquence demands a lengthy extract from his answer:

The cry has been, that war is declared, and all opposition should therefore be hushed. A sentiment more unworthy of a free country can hardly be propagated. If this doctrine be admitted, rulers have only to declare war and, they are screened at once from scrutiny. . . . Admit this doctrine, let rulers once know that by placing the country in a state of war, they place themselves beyond the only power they dread, the power of free discussion, and we may expect war without end. Our peace and all our interests require, that a different sentiment prevail. We should make our present and all future rulers feel, that there is no measure, for which they must render so solemn an account to their constituents, as for a declaration of war; that no measure will be so freely, so fully discussed; and that no administration can succeed, in persuading this people to exhaust their treasure and blood in supporting war, unless it be palpably necessary and just. In war then, as in peace, assert the

[131] For uses of anti-Jacobin rhetoric to attack the Federalists during the War of 1812, see "Here Follows," *Northern Whig*, May 30, 1815; "To the Republicans of Essex!" *Essex Register*, Mar. 16, 1816; "Reign of Terror," *Western Monitor*, Jun. 14, 1816.

[132] Joseph Clark, *A Sermon, Delivered in the City of New-Brunswick, on Thursday, Jul. 30, 1812 Being the Day Set Apart by the General Assembly of the Presbyterian Church, for Fasting, Humiliation and Prayer* (New Brunswick, N.J., 1812); Beman, *A Sermon . . . 1812*; Austin, *A Sermon . . . 1812*; Strong, *A Fast Sermon . . . 1812*.

[133] Benjamin Bell, *The Difference between the Present and Former Days Shown in a Discourse Upon Eccles. Vii. 10. Delivered at Steuben, Aug. 20, 1812* (Utica, N.Y., 1812); Jedidiah Morse, *A Sermon, Delivered at Charlestown, Jul. 23, 1812; the Day Appointed by the Governor . . . To Be Observed in Fasting and Prayer . . . In Consequence of a Declaration of War with Great Britain* (Charlestown, Mass., 1812).

[134] French, *Sermons . . . 1812*; Mead, *Sermon on the War*.

freedom of speech and of the press. Cling to this, as the bulwark of all your rights and principles.[135]

Political dissenters defended themselves from Republican censure by defining public speech and writings as constitutional opposition, then situating their own dissent within its limits. They argued that war did not weaken the Constitution's guarantees to freedom of speech and of the press. As early as 1807, during the war crisis caused by the Chesapeake affair, the Massachusetts lawyer John Lowell refuted a local Republican editor who had argued that "it is treason to question the justice or expediency of a war." This doctrine, Lowell wrote, would make the Constitution into a "dead letter."[136] As dissenters first organized their resistance against the war during the summer of 1812, they premised their harsh criticisms of the national government on powerful assertions of their civil rights. An antiwar convention that gathered in Worcester, Massachusetts, during August, 1812, prefaced the report it released to Federalist newspapers by declaring not only the right but also the *"duty"* to gather and discuss the war. Sounding very much like Republicans, the conventioneers argued that American citizens, as members of the civil compact, were required to watch over their public agents. Conversely, they recognized no duty to support the war. "We consider a declaration of war, like every other act of government, a proper subject of public animadversion," the report declared.[137]

Religious and political dissenters differentiated their constitutional resistance from sedition on the basis of its nonviolence. Physically attacking the national government or its agents, as opposition Republicans had done during the 1790s, was unlawful. Only spoken dissent that did not incite violence fell within the constitutional guarantee of free speech. Accordingly, antiwar speakers repeatedly pledged to limit their opposition to speech and suffrage, and not to use force. In a July 4 oration delivered in Fryeburg, Maine, William Barrows promised that "no violent measures will be resorted to – no popular insurrections excited, to lacerate those ties, which bind the union of the states."[138] On the same day in Greenfield, Massachusetts, Samuel Allen pledged, on behalf of the local Washington Benevolent Society that "we disclaim all violence and artifice. We invade no man's rights, and we endanger no man's safety."[139] Also speaking on the Fourth of July, Daniel Webster

---

[135] Channing, *Sermon... Aug. 20, 1812,* 11.
[136] Lowell, *Peace without Dishonor,* 7.
[137] (Mass.), Proceedings of a Convention (Worcester, Mass., 1812), 10. More examples of convention arguments for free speech include Prescott, *Address to the Friends* (N.J.), *Proceedings and Address of the Convention;* Crosby, *Address to the Electors.*
[138] Barrows, *Oration... 1812,* 19.
[139] Samuel C. Allen, *An Oration, Delivered at Greenfield, Jul. 6, 1812, in Commemoration of American Independence at the Request of the Washington Benevolent Societies, of the County of Franklin* (Greenfield Mass., 1812), 20.

assured his New Hampshire audience that the dissenters would obey the laws of the nation; "resistance and insurrection form no part of our creed."[140] Throughout New England and the mid-Atlantic states, conservative politicians and ministers forswore the use of force in effecting domestic political change, remaining ideologically committed to "order" above all.[141]

By 1812, New England conservatives had thoroughly integrated an antiviolent sensibility into their regional identity. Shortly after the war was declared, the Reverend Freeman Parker asked his New Hampshire congregation, "Is there one man in *New-England*, who can make war his sport and pastime?" Passions and bloodthirst, he answered, were reserved for southern, barbarian, Jacobin slaveholders. New England conservatives rejected violence as a means of pleasure. The Reverend John Lathrop similarly lamented that there were some men in the nation who "engage in war, as 'their sport and pastime.'" He insisted that true Americans (such as numbered his Massachusetts congregation) "cannot delight in blood."[142] Bloodlust subjected the fragile republic to its greatest challenge. And so even when the War of 1812 seemed to threaten the very survival of the republic, dissenters could not resist the war with force. Parker directed his congregants to obey the government, even at this moment of crisis: "for if a violent resistance of law should once become general it would soon end in the destruction of rational freedom, and the introduction of anarchy and confusion."[143] The antiwar party claimed to be restrained by the cardinal virtue of political order.

Opponents to the War of 1812 defended their speech in constitutional terms that appealed to a broad audience in the past and continue to have broad appeal today. Yet in practice, their remarks carved a far more radical niche for opposition speech. Antiwar language between 1812 and 1815 was marked not only by the measured rationalism of constitutional arguments but also by a blood-soaked intensity intended to terrify, repulse, upset, and

---

[140] Webster, *Address... 1812*, 21.

[141] For more examples of July 4 orators who disavowed violence for "constitutional" means, see Blake, *Oration... 1812*, 24; Prentiss, *Oration... 1812*, 32. This promise is also contained in the July 4 address issued by a meeting of the Federal party in New Jersey, *Proceedings and Address of the Convention*. Sermons containing nonviolent dissent include Parish, *Ruin or Separation*, 11; Huntington Porter, *The Present Distressed Situation of Our Country, and the Duty of Ministers and People in Such a Time as This Considered in a Sermon, Preached at Rye, Aug. 20, 1812, the Day Recommended by President Madison for a National Fast* (Portsmouth, N.H., 1812).

[142] John Lathrop, *The Present War Unexpected, Unnecessary, and Ruinous; Two Discourses Delivered in Boston: The First on the 23rd of July 1812, the Fast Appointed by the Governor of Massachusetts: The Second on the 20th of August, the Fast Appointed by the President of the United States in Consequence of the Present War* (Boston, Mass., 1812).

[143] Samuel Parker, *A Sermon Preached before His Honor the Lieutenant-Governor... And House of Representatives of the Commonwealth of Massachusetts, May 29, 1793, Being the Day of General Election* (Boston, Mass., 1793), 7, 15.

enrage. Drawing on traditions in New England rhetoric dating back to the Puritan Jeremiad, antiwar leaders used speech to produce an intense emotional reaction in their audiences. Abjuring traditional standards of loyalty and deference, opponents labeled the nation's soldier murderers. Even more shockingly, extremist antiwar newspaper editors, political essayists, and local leaders began to call loudly for disunion. If the national administration would not end the war, then the radicals desired to withdraw from the nation. At an 1814 oration, Josiah Dunham made the constitutional argument that the war hawks wished "TO SILENCE OPPOSITION, TO SUBVERT OUR LIBERTIES!" and then shifted immediately into a clarion call for battle: "We must resist unto blood!"[144] The violence of the opposition to the War of 1812 contained tendencies toward bloodshed that nearly led to civil war.

The pressure toward violent rejection of the war is evident in the juvenile writings of William Cullen Bryant, the future antislavery editor of the *New-York Evening Post*. Bryant, whose first published writing was a poem attacking Thomas Jefferson published in 1808 when he was only fourteen, opposed the War of 1812 with a passionate vehemence. Writing home from his law studies in 1814, Bryant asked his arch-Federalist father, Peter Bryant, for permission to join the Massachusetts militia in order to prepare for civil war against the southern states – a fight against "an intestine foe in the defense of dearer rights than those which are endangered in a contest with Great Britain." Bryant tried to reassure his father that by joining the militia, he would be creating a formidable defense that would dissuade the national government from risking war to protect the union. Yet the bloody-mindedness of his thinking is evident from scraps of a Byronic poem on battle that he included in his next letter: "The only heart, the only eye / Had bled or wept to see him die, / Had seen his mangled limbs composed –, / And mourned above his turban-stone." Violent writing in this case fed a violent ambition.[145]

Despite the violent tendencies within the antiwar opposition, historical contingency ultimately guaranteed a nonviolent path of resistance. In fall 1814, after several false starts and much politicking, the Massachusetts legislature issued an invitation to the other states of New England to meet in a convention to be held in December at Hartford for the purpose of discussing the region's suffering. The Connecticut and Rhode Island legislatures sent delegates to meet the Massachusetts men. New Hampshire and Vermont declined, but counties in both states did send representatives. While radical secessionists may have urged the Massachusetts legislature to call the meeting, the delegates appointed to attend promoted constitutional

---

[144] Dunham, *An Oration... 1814*, 31.
[145] William Cullen Bryant to Peter Bryant, Oct. 10, 1814; William Cullen Bryant to Peter Bryant, Oct. 18, 1814; Bryant-Godwin Papers, New York Public Library, Box 1.

means of resistance, which did not include threats of force or disunion. The preamble of the report issued by the convention clarified this commitment to all readers. Its very first sentence recognized the difficulty of answering the needs of the people of New England "without violating constitutional principles, or disappointing the hopes of suffering or injured people." The preamble acknowledged the sentiment among some citizens that the Constitution was defective beyond repair, but the delegates restated their own faith in that document and proposed "a course of moderation and firmness," which might save the nation from "the regret incident to sudden decisions."[146] At the time of its publication, newspapers and politicians throughout the country recognized the temperance of the report. Leaders of the antiwar party had used the Hartford Convention to vent the steam of the most enraged dissenters, without, in fact, threatening the union. Unfortunately, news of the Treaty of Ghent and the victory at New Orleans, which swiftly followed the release of the report, soon supplanted the Hartford Convention in the public's attention. Its characteristics grew as hazy in the nation's memory as would the war itself.

Afterward, the participants – and later their sympathetic historians – struggled to correct the belief that the Hartford Convention was treasonous.[147] But arguments that the convention was disunionist are not entirely groundless. The meeting's moderation was predicated on calls to meet again with a more radical agenda if New England's demands were not met. In other words, the meeting was not secessionist, but it threatened secession in the future. If the confluence of the Treaty of Ghent and the Battle of New Orleans had not disarmed the opposition, there is no saying what would have transpired in the spring of 1815. The convention's members and their descendants described the meeting as testimony to the level of commitment that New England conservatives felt to the U.S. Constitution. Edmund Quincy, the abolitionist son of Josiah Quincy, claimed in his 1868 memoir of his father that only New England's "settled habits of order and obedience to law" had prevented the region from rebelling. Edmund Quincy praised the "moral influence of [Federalist] resistance" against the "men of violent temper and malignant passions" who controlled the nation after 1800, even though he conceded that the Federalists' "settled habits"

---

[146] Hartford Convention (1814), *The Proceedings of a Convention of Delegates from the States of Massachusetts, Connecticut and Rhode Island, the Counties of Cheshire and Grafton in the State of the New Hampshire and the County of Windham in the State of Vermont: Convened at Hartford in the State of Connecticut, Dec. 15, 1814* (Hartford, Conn., 1815), 3–4.

[147] For participants' defenses, see Theodore Dwight, *History of the Hartford Convention with a Review of the Policy of the United States Government, Which Led to the War of 1812* (New York, 1833); Harrison Gray Otis, *Otis' Letters in Defence of the Hartford Convention, and the People of Massachusetts* (Boston, Mass., 1824). For historical exculpations, see Banner, *Hartford Convention*; Hickey, "Federalists"; Morison, *Harrison Gray Otis*.

had rendered the party archaic and impotent.[148] Quincy captures half the picture. Certainly opposition to the war, peace societies, and the repudiation of physical means of civil resistance all furthered the conservative ideological commitment against bloodshed that had been strengthening since the 1780s. However an undercurrent also ran through the network of opposition, a violent language of resistance, which could have led to a far bloodier outcome.

---

[148] Quincy, *Josiah Quincy*, 326. See also Lucius Manlius Sargent, *Reminiscences of Samuel Dexter. Originally Written for the Boston Evening Transcript* (Boston, Mass., 1857), 86.

5

Disciplining the "Wild Beast"

Violence and Education

> To remedy the evils of the fall, is the proper design of education.
> – *The Panoplist*, April 10, 1810

On July 18, 1796, a procession of students, instructors, trustees, clergy, literary gentlemen, and proud parents filed into the Taunton, Massachusetts, meetinghouse for the dedication of the town's new secondary school, the Bristol Academy.[1] The Reverend Simeon Doggett, its young principal, stood before the assembly to deliver an oration in celebration of the town's good fortune. Only thirty-one, Doggett seemed to represent the optimism of the postrevolutionary generation; he was a religious liberal and a standard-bearer for the democratization of education and literacy that helped to empower American expansion in the early nineteenth century.[2] However, his oration eschewed the exuberant pieties in celebration of learning that had typified educational discourse since the American Revolution.[3] Instead of listing the wonderful advantages of education, Doggett envisaged the violent world from which education preserved the community. After a brief acknowledgment that on this celebratory day some joy had penetrated his normal feelings of anxiety, Doggett turned immediately to a survey of human violence:

While some of our fellow creatures are roaming in the gloomy forest as beasts of prey; or, in wild enthusiasm and dark superstition, celebrating the rites of idol and unknown gods; or exulting, with barbarous pleasure, in the excruciating torture of captive enemies: while millions are dragging out a miserable existence in the dreary countries of ignorance and despotism, or more awfully bleeding under the

---

[1] "Bristol Academy," *Columbian Centinel*, Aug. 10, 1796.
[2] Joyce Oldham Appleby, *Inheriting the Revolution: The First Generation of Americans* (Cambridge, Mass., 2000).
[3] Allen Oscar Hansen, *Liberalism and American Education in the Eighteenth Century* (New York, 1926).

cursed lash of slavery; and others, with unfeeling hearts, wantonly rioting upon these sufferings of their brother creatures and the bounties of Heaven: while thousands are armed with the implements of death in order to cut and mangle the bodies of their fellow men and to shed each other's blood, and whole nations are experiencing all the horrors of war, we . . . are this day convened by an occasion connected with everything great and valuable to man.[4]

Doggett's Gothic catalog of human violence evoked the terror-inducing preaching of the arch-Calvinist Elijah Parish, another strong supporter of education.[5] It was less a calming tisane than a deranging dram – hardly the welcoming talk to be expected at commencement these days.

Yet Doggett's remarks synchronized harmoniously with the expectations of his own time. Many early national speakers used descriptions of man's reversion to savagery in order to rally support for education.[6] The published reaction to Doggett's speech proved unanimously positive. "A very excellent oration," stated the *Providence Gazette*; the oration "did the speaker much honor," the *Columbian Centinel* praised.[7] The appreciative reception for Doggett's strikingly gloomy oration suggests that by the mid-1790s the specter of transatlantic revolution had cast a long shadow over the sunshiny faith in education familiar from the revolutionary era. In the words of Simeon Doggett, thousands of soldiers "armed with the implements of death in order to cut and mangle the bodies of their fellow men" were threatening to sweep away the triumphs of independence. The new school in Taunton offered parents much more than simply a place to increase their children's knowledge or to polish their manners. The Bristol Academy sought to teach children to control their violent passions, and thereby to preserve the social order from crumbling. Quoting from the British anti-Jacobin William Paley, Doggett called children who had been deprived of education "mad dogs or wild beasts." The Bristol Academy would tame them.[8]

Simeon Doggett's antiviolent pedagogy grew out of the transatlantic anti-Jacobin political culture of the 1790s. Although Doggett rejected the Calvinist doctrine of election, he saw human nature as prone to "disagreeable,

[4] Simeon Doggett, *A Discourse on Education, Delivered at the Dedication and Opening of Bristol Academy, the 18th Day of July, A.D. 1796* (New Bedford, Mass., 1797), 5–6.

[5] Elijah Parish, "Psalm 100.4," Thanksgiving (Nov.) 1793, EPP; Elijah Parish, "Psal. 92.1," Thanksgiving, Feb. 1795, EPP.

[6] For example, David Osgood, *A Sermon, Preached at the Request of the Ancient and Honourable Artillery Company, in Boston, June 2, 1788 Being the Anniversary of Their Election of Officers* (Boston, Mass., 1788); Freeman Sears, *An Oration on the Nature and Perpetuity of American Independence, Pronounced at Natick, July 4, A.D. 1809 before the Fifth Regiment of the First Brigade, and Third Division of the Militia* (Dedham, Mass., 1809), 9.

[7] "Bristol Academy," *Providence Gazette and Country Journal*, Aug. 6, 1796; "Bristol Academy," *Columbian Centinel*, Aug. 10, 1796.

[8] Doggett, *Discourse on Education*. 15. On Paley's anti-Jacobinism, see Kevin Gilmartin, "In the Theater of Counterrevolution: Loyalist Association and Conservative Opinion in the 1790s," *Journal of British Studies* 41 (July 2002).

ridiculous, and wicked," "tyrannical and overbearing," and even "insolent and cruel" behavior.[9] He did not often preach on contemporary issues, but Doggett delivered an anti-Jacobin oration on July 4, 1799, that gave full vent to his moral and political fears of man. "We live, my Friends, in an age of revolution and disorganization," Doggett bemoaned. The anarchy in France had released "the most corrupted passions of the human heart." His audience could "read in letters of blood" about the "vile excesses and awful enormities" of the Revolution: three million people had perished as a consequence of French rule "by guillotine and sword," the spread of "Jacobinic poison" within Switzerland had left "the Alps reddening with human blood," and in the United States Jacobinism was spreading atheism and rebellions against the government. Doggett concluded his oration by stressing the imperative to combat "the awful torrent of licentiousness that is flowing across the Atlantic" with a strong education of the sort offered by the Bristol Academy.[10] Transatlantic counterrevolutionaries like Doggett believed that education would erect a crucial bulwark against the Jacobin horde.

Historians have long recognized that "no theme was so universally articulated during the early decades of the Republic as the need of a self-governing people for universal education."[11] But they have repeatedly based their interpretations on a limited canon of early national educational texts, including works by Thomas Jefferson and Benjamin Rush, which are far more democratic, secular, nationalistic, and optimistic than the general tenor of the era's pedagogical literature.[12] While some canonical texts democratically

9 Simeon Doggett, *Concerning the Way to Eternal Life. A Discourse, Preached to the Congregational Society in Norton, on the Third Sabbath in March, and Also to the First Congregational Society in Providence, on the First Sabbath in April, A.D. 1796* (Providence, R.I., 1796), 18–19.

10 Simeon Doggett, *An Oration, Delivered at Taunton, on the 4th of July, 1799. By Simeon Doggett, Jun. A.M. Preceptor of Bristol Academy* (New Bedford, Mass., 1799), 13–20.

11 Lawrence Arthur Cremin, *American Education, the National Experience, 1783–1876* (New York, 1980), 2:103. See also republican interpretations by Gail S. Murray, *American Children's Literature and the Construction of Childhood,* Twayne's History of American Childhood (New York, 1998); Jacqueline Reinier, *From Virtue to Character: American Childhood, 1775–1850* (New York, 1996); Gail S. Murray, "Rational Thought and Republican Virtue: Children's Literature, 1789–1820," *Journal of the Early Republic* 8 (Summer 1988); Jacqueline Reinier, "Rearing the Republican Child: Attitudes and Practices in Post-Revolutionary Philadelphia," *William and Mary Quarterly* 29 (Jan. 1982).

12 Allen O. Hansen selected this canon in his 1926 classic *Liberalism and American Education*. An influential edited collection from 1965 reinforced Hansen's choices; Frederick Rudolph, *Essays on Education in the Early Republic* (Cambridge, Mass., 1965). Scholars influenced by Hansen and/or Rudolph include Holly Brewer, *By Birth or Consent: Children, Law, and the Anglo-American Revolution in Authority* (Chapel Hill, N.C., 2005), 124–8; Carl F. Kaestle, *Pillars of the Republic: Common Schools and American Society, 1780–1860* (New York, 1983); Rush Welter, *Popular Education and Democratic Thought in America* (New York, 1962); Lawrence Arthur Cremin, *The American Common School,*

advocated education as a means to arm the people against the rise of tyranny, they were far outnumbered by conservative educational tracts like Simeon Doggett's, which advocated training children to restrain their passions in order to save the nation from violent disorder.[13] Education history, which has been written predominantly by people seeking to praise or interrogate the origins of nonsectarian public schooling, has left Christian pedagogical theories largely unexamined.[14] Meanwhile, a nationalist paradigm has biased the search to recover what defined American pedagogy in the early republic by disregarding the British children's literature that sold in vast numbers in the United States and thus overlooking the profound impact of the Atlantic context, and in particular transatlantic anti-Jacobinism, on early national society.[15]

Finally, the optimism of the canonical texts is profoundly misleading. Historians of childhood have commonly argued that John Locke's theory that the infant's mind was a tabula rasa undermined the traditional orthodox belief in infant depravity and increased republican support for education.[16] Expanded support for education during the early national era has been attributed to optimistic notions of childhood that superseded the negativism of the past. Actually, orthodox believers in child depravity found a lot of common ground with Locke, and melded his ideas with earlier biblical

an Historic Conception, Teachers College Studies in Education (New York, 1951). Siobhan Moroney makes this historiographical argument in "Birth of a Canon: The Historiography of Early Republican Educational Thought," *History of Education Quarterly* 39 (Winter 1999).

[13] Examples of the democratic argument include Asterio, "On Education," *New-York Magazine,* Mar. 1794, 146–8; Thomas Jefferson, "Bill for the More General Diffusion of Knowledge" (1779), in *Education in the United States: A Documentary History,* vol. 2, ed. Sol Cohen (New York, 1974); Richard Beresford, *Aristocracy the Bane of Liberty; Learning the Antidote. Designed to Recommend the General Establishment of Free Schools and Colleges in Republicks* (Charleston, S.C., 1797); Alexander C. McWhorter, *An Oration Delivered on the Fourth July, 1794, to a Numerous Audience, Assembled in the Presbyterian Church of Newark: To Celebrate the Eighteenth Anniversary of American Emancipation* (Newark, N.J., 1794). See also Harold Hellenbrand, *The Unfinished Revolution: Education and Politics in the Thought of Thomas Jefferson* (Newark, N.J., 1990).

[14] Milton Gaither, *American Educational History Revisited,* ed. Barbara Finkelstein and William J. Reese, Reflective History Series (New York, 2003); Michael B. Katz, *The Irony of Early School Reform: Educational Innovation in Mid-Nineteenth Century Massachusetts* (New York, 1968); Jonathan Messerli, "The Columbian Complex: The Impulse to National Consolidation," *History of Education Quarterly* 7 (Winter 1967); David B. Tyack, *Turning Points in American Educational History* (Waltham, Mass., 1967); Bernard Bailyn, *Education in the Forming of American Society: Needs and Opportunities for Study* (Chapel Hill, N.C., 1960).

[15] 1830 serves as the turning point at which historians begin their study of American children's literature; the Atlantic literature of the era from 1790–1830 often receives little attention; Murray, "Rational Thought and Republican Virtue," 160.

[16] Ibid.

understandings of childhood plasticity, as found in Proverbs 22:6: "Train up a child in the way he should go, and when he is old, he will not depart from it." Another favored biblical quote combining negativity and malleability came from Psalm 144: "Rid me, and deliver me from the hand of strange children," King David sang, "That our sons may be as plants grown up in their youth."[17] Religious pessimism about human nature and biblical ideas of childhood malleability meshed with Lockean theories to generate a transatlantic, negativistic, and Christian argument for education in the early republic.

In his optimistic moments, Doggett agreed with democrats that education was a defense against despotism: "The throne of tyranny is founded on ignorance," the young principal told his audience at Bristol Academy; education would arm the students against tyrants. But Doggett dwelled in far greater detail on education's power to correct barbarism. Taking his epigraph ("'Tis education forms the common mind: / Just as the twig is bent, the tree's inclined") from the biting satirist Alexander Pope, Doggett and other anti-Jacobins argued like Pope that man's passions compelled the need for education.[18] Doggett described education as a means to discipline humanity's anarchic tendencies and shore up republican government. Men's "passions undisciplined are ungovernable, impetuous, and awful," Doggett preached. The United States needed schools in order to make its children governable. In a corrupt world education could restrain men's passions and guard against the excesses of democracy by preparing citizens to obey the authority of law. Schools were so essential to secure governance that government, said the new principal, should pay for schools. In fact, the pessimistic Christian rationale for education proved far more effective at rallying state support for common schools than did republican exuberance.[19] In the first half of the nineteenth century, Anti-Jacobins became the nation's most consistent advocates of common schooling. The problem of violence in the early republic found a solution in the promise of education; and the problem of establishing public education in America found its answer in the ideological imperatives of the Christian social order.

---

[17] Psalm 144, 11–12, *King James Version*. Jeremy Belknap used this quote in his educational discourse, *An Election Sermon: Preached before the General Court, of New Hampshire, at Portsmouth, June 2, 1785* (Portsmouth, N.H., 1785), 8.

[18] John E. Sitter, "The Argument of Pope's Epistle to Cobham," *Studies in English Literature, 1500–1900* 17 (Summer 1977).

[19] D. W. Howe, "Church, State, and Education in the Young American Republic," *Journal of the Early Republic* 22 (Spring 2002); Peter S. Onuf, "State Politics and Republican Virtue: Religion, Education, and Morality in Early American Federalism," in *Toward a Usable Past: Liberty under State Constitutions*, ed. Paul Finkelman and Stephen E. Gottlieb (Athens, Ga., 1991); Timothy L. Smith, "Protestant Schooling and American Nationality, 1800–1850," *Journal of American History* 53 (1967).

To Remedy the Evils of the Fall

The assumed connection between the education of children, broadly speaking, and the governance of the state dates back in Western thought to at least the time of Aristotle.[20] The family both has been viewed as "an imaginative construct of power relations," and the family has been an actual site of political struggles for power, no more "idealist" than Samuel Johnson's rock.[21] Children have repeatedly been employed to symbolize the people of a nation, and the household has served to represent the state – an analogy that naturally stresses the significance of training children to be governable. Moreover, philosophers and theologians have argued that the state originated historically in family order (which again suggests the need to discipline children). These multiple yet disparate iterations of the connection between children and the state suggests why so many historical attempts to reshape society, no matter how different their guiding visions, have centered in the family.

In the seventeenth century, the family-state analogy figured large in Anglo-American political theory. King James I, and later Robert Filmer's *Patriarcha* (1680), used the family analogy to support claims to absolutist government by describing the king as the parens patriae, or political father of his people. John Locke rejected Filmer's argument, instead describing government as a contract, in which authority came with duties and subjects had the right to consent.[22] In New England, the Puritans applied contract theory to the family, both recognizing the rights of children and strengthening negativist arguments for their education. In his *Magnalia Christi Americana* (1702), Cotton Mather described the failure to properly educate children as a violent threat to political order: "where *schools* are not vigorously and honorably encouraged, whole *colonies* will sink apace into a degenerate and contemptible condition, and at last become horribly *barbarous*."[23] Mather's remarks fit within a historic tradition of support for schooling in New England. Puritan settlers established a university at Cambridge during the Massachusetts Bay Colony's first decade; the colony's charter required each new town in the years following to establish a school. A similar tradition of education existed in the neighboring colonies of Connecticut, Rhode Island, and New Hampshire. This history suggests a regional explanation

[20] Constance Jordan, "The Household and the State: Transformations in the Representation of an Analogy from Aristotle to James I," *Modern Language Quarterly* 54 (Sept. 1993).

[21] Lynn Hunt, *The Family Romance of the French Revolution* (Berkeley, Calif., 1992), 196, Linda Gordon, *Heroes of Their Own Lives: The Politics and History of Family Violence: Boston, 1880–1960* (New York, 1988), 3.

[22] Locke's theories, while liberating for adult men, may in some ways have weakened the political and labor autonomy of children in Great Britain and its North American colonies; see Brewer, *By Birth or Consent*, chap. 1.

[23] Gaither, *American Educational History*, 14.

for the predominantly northeastern anti-Jacobin faction's proeducational bent.[24] However, the tradition underwent important disruptions in the revolutionary era. Puritan support for education did not blend seamlessly into anti-Jacobin thought.

During the American Revolution, the family served as the most characteristic image in the struggle to justify the colonies' independence from Britain, their political parent. The colonists represented themselves as children who had reached maturity and were ready for self-governance, while Britain assumed the parental duty to discipline its wayward children, advancing a military solution in conformity with the biblical proverb "Spare the rod, spoil the child." America's revolutionary victory, which delivered power into the hands of metaphorical children, increased domestic pressure to train American youth for self-governance.[25] The establishment of the new government did not lessen the political valence of child rearing; rather, the assumed fragility of republican politics heightened the pressure to establish order in the family.[26] As the externalized hierarchical authority that had maintained social order during the colonial era was dismantled and replaced by a more egalitarian democratic society, conservative Federalists and their ministerial allies perceived an increased need to instill in children an internalized voice of restraint.[27] The revolutionary overthrow of political authority increased concern for family order by seeming to discredit disciplinary practices at the same time that it increased the burden on individuals to practice self-governance.

Immediately following the victory of the Revolution, when patriots looked forward to a golden age of peace and stability, early nationalists such as Benjamin Rush sought to design a system of education that would create

[24] M. L. Counts offers a useful list of New England clergy who had a strong influence on education; Martha Louise Counts, "The Political Views of the Eighteenth Century New England Clergy as Expressed in Their Election Sermons" (Ph.D., Columbia University, 1956), 188. For Federalists, see David Hackett Fischer, "The Myth of the Essex Junto," *William and Mary Quarterly* 21 (1964).

[25] Shirley Samuels, *Romances of the Republic: Women, the Family, and Violence in the Literature of the Early American Nation* (New York, 1996); Jay Fliegelman, *Prodigals and Pilgrims: The American Revolution against Patriarchal Authority, 1750–1800* (New York, 1982); Edwin G. Burrows and Michael Wallace, "The American Revolution: The Ideology and Psychology of National Liberation," *Perspectives in American History* 6 (1972).

[26] This imperative also fueled the demand for a new mode of republican motherhood during the early republic; Rosemarie Zagarri, "Morals, Manners, and the Republican Mother," *American Quarterly* 44 (1992); Linda K. Kerber, *Women of the Republic: Intellect and Ideology in Revolutionary America* (New York, 1986); Ruth H. Bloch, "American Feminine Ideals in Transition: The Rise of Moral Motherhood, 1785–1815," *Feminist Studies* 4 (1978).

[27] For arguments regarding the extent of colonial deference see Michael Zuckerman, "Tocqueville, Turner, and Turds: Four Stories of Manners in Early America," *Journal of American History* 85 (June 1998); Gordon S. Wood, *The Radicalism of the American Revolution* (New York, 1993), part 1.

perfect republican citizens by instilling in children both patriotism and virtuous obedience.[28] However, concerns about the violent threat (rather than potential benefit) that children posed to the state became more pronounced during the disorderly 1780s. The seemingly increased laxity in childrearing standards, and the rapid decline of the apprenticeship system that had traditionally subjected young men to the authority of masters, made formal modes of education increasingly important to the stability of early national society.[29] "All government originates in families, and if neglected there, it will hardly exist in society," Noah Webster wrote in 1790, "but the want of it must be supplied by the rod in school, the penal laws of the state, and the terrors of divine wrath from the pulpit."[30] Three years later, when Webster wrote his passionately anti-Jacobin essay "The Revolution in France," he returned enthusiastically to the cause of education. If natural or foster families could not discipline American youth, then institutions had to be established that would. Webster insisted that these institutions be formed especially to the task of offering a *republican* education.

When anti-Jacobins like Webster wrote of the need to match American education to republican politics, they had in mind the need to train children to be governable. Early national conservatives who believed that liberty equaled obedience defined republican education as a means to teach future citizens how to be orderly. William Tudor, a Federalist intellectual, explained that because the Christian education disseminated by New England schools was "given under a government, whose leading principle is the *minimum* of restraint, its object is to avoid rashness and violence, and to make the citizens deliberate and orderly." Representative government demanded an emotional style that enshrined restraint. The danger of this style of education was that it made people dull, overly serious, reflecting, and cold (common stereotypes of New Englanders during the eighteenth and nineteenth centuries). However, William Tudor believed that its advantages were evident in the Northeast: "there is throughout these states a general abhorrence of violence, a submission to the laws, a gentleness of demeanour, [and] a

---

[28] Benjamin Rush, "A Plan for the Establishment of Public Schools and the Diffusion of Knowledge in Pennsylvania; to Which Are Added, Thoughts upon the Mode of Education, Proper in a Republic," in *Essays on Education in the Early Republic*, ed. Frederick Rudolph (Cambridge, Mass., 1965), 12, 3; Messerli, "Columbian Complex"; Hyman Kuritz, "Benjamin Rush: His Theory of Republican Education," *History of Education Quarterly* 7 (Winter 1967).

[29] W. J. Rorabaugh and Roger Levenson, *The Craft Apprentice: From Franklin to the Machine Age in America* (New York, 1986); W. J. Rorabaugh, "'I Thought I Should Liberate Myself from the Thraldom of Others': Apprentices, Masters, and the Revolution," in *Beyond the American Revolution: Explorations in the History of American Radicalism*, ed. Alfred F. Young (DeKalb, Ill., 1993).

[30] Noah Webster, "On the Education of Youth in America," in *Essays on Education in the Early Republic*, ed. Frederick Rudolph (Cambridge, Mass., 1790), 57, 65.

FIGURE 7. "Infant Liberty Nursed by Mother Mob." This illustration included within Richard Alsop's 1807 collection of conservative satiric poems and essays, *The Echo*, paints an alarming picture of the dangers that Jacobin child rearing posed to the new republic. Likely drawn in reaction to the Whiskey Rebellion, the picture shows mother mob, with breasts marked *Whiskey* and *Rum*, nursing infant liberty. A mother's helper wearing the French Revolutionary bonnet rouge warms the infant's diaper by a fire built from burning "statute" books, while in the background a mob pulls down a building marked the "pinnacle of liberty." The picture suggests the need for an anti-Jacobin education to produce orderly citizens. *Courtesy of American Antiquarian Society.*

deference to talent" that guaranteed the perpetuity of freedom.[31] Training children to "abhor violence" became central to the anti-Jacobin educational project.

The rise of the Jacobin threat in the 1790s reinforced conservatives' focus on education's disciplinary functions. The arch-Federalist lawyer David Daggett complained in an anti-Jacobin oration in 1799 that contemporary child rearing inverted the proverb "Train up a child in the way he should go" to "Let a child walk in his own way." Ridiculing the new pedagogical theories of "Gallic" democratic visionaries, Daggett argued for a model of child rearing that balanced love and discipline to teach children self-restraint.[32] Anti-Jacobins feared that lack of family discipline in the revolutionary era had given rise to the Jacobin host. Judge Jacob Rush, the vehemently

---

[31] William Tudor, *Letters on the Eastern States*, 2nd ed. (Boston, Mass., 1821), 385–406.

[32] David Daggett, *Sun-Beams May Be Extracted from Cucumbers, but the Process Is Tedious. An Oration, Pronounced on the Fourth of July, 1799. At the Request of the Citizens of New-Haven* (New Haven, Conn., 1799).

anti-Jacobin brother of Benjamin Rush, blamed the increasingly lax standards of childrearing for encouraging the internal "disorganizers" who spread moral disorder throughout the United States, and threatened to "overwhelm" the nation "by waves of popular fury and violence." In a speech from the bench, Rush confessed that "it has long been my concern that the relaxation of domestic authority is one of the most alarming symptoms both of the degeneracy and the dangerous situation of our country. Parents and masters seem to have abandoned all control over those that Providence has placed under their care and guardianship."[33] At just the moment when children were most in need of discipline, American parents seemed to be renouncing that obligation. Judge Rush's complaint was widely shared by contemporary observers, both domestic and foreign.[34]

Anti-Jacobins embraced education in the 1790s as a solution to the challenge that human depravity posed to preserving republican government. Children were a natural target for correcting the problem of depravity, as children often served to illustrate arguments for the doctrine. Throughout the eighteenth century, religious authorities had secured American orthodoxy from the incursions of English arminianism by calling upon the evidence of infant depravity. Jonathan Edwards in his great 1758 defense of the doctrine of original sin used the sinfulness of infants to make his point.[35] The new republic's seemingly heightened dependence on the orderly behavior of children elevated the problem of infant depravity from the spiritual to the political. For those who believed in the doctrine of infant depravity, nothing could be more worrying than society's abnegation of the responsibility to discipline children. The child, born into the world a violent and savage beast, posed a threat not only to his own salvation and to the peace of his family but also to the order of the nation that contained him.

Crispin, the author of an 1815 essay on education published in an evangelical periodical, struggled to impress upon his readers a true sense of their children's sinfulness, and the consequent obligation to educate them. He began by decrying the new laxity of discipline in America: "complaint is very frequently made, that habits of obedience and decorous behavior are at the present day, less observable in children than they were in the days of our fathers." This declension troubled Crispin not because it made society less genteel, or the household less pleasant, but because the vicious and evil

[33] Jacob Rush, *Charges, and Extracts of Charges, on Moral and Religious Subjects* (Philadelphia, Pa., 1803), 36–8, 66.

[34] Peter Gregg Slater, *Children in the New England Mind: In Death and in Life* (Hamden, Conn., 1977), 108. This complaint was frequently made by European visitors to the United States during the early nineteenth century; see Alexis de Tocqueville, *Democracy in America*, ed. Henry Reeve et al., 2 vols. (New York, 1990); Frances Milton Trollope, *Domestic Manners of the Americans; Edited, with a History of Mrs. Trollope's Adventures in America*, ed. Donald Arthur Smalley and Irving Stone (New York, 1949), 213.

[35] H. Shelton Smith, *Changing Conceptions of Original Sin* (New York, 1955).

nature of children made the failure to discipline a catastrophic danger. "The root and foundation of misconduct in children is human depravity," Crispin warned his readers. "We often hear parents calling their children 'harmless creatures,' 'pretty innocents,' and other fond and endearing names which *figuratively* denote the same thing, such as 'little doves,' 'harmless birds,'" but in truth children were "birds of evil omen, if not birds of prey." Children are born to sin, Crispin argued. Children wished to gratify themselves, and "everything in opposition to this is assaulted with violence. . . . Were infants from the birth endowed with strength and activity like the young of some animals, the most fatal effects would follow. Give the child the strength of manhood without abating ought from the violence and perverseness of his temper" and parents would be compelled to resort to "chains and fetters" for discipline. The physical weakness of children permitted parents to use more gentle techniques to secure their infants' obedience. But the urgency of subjecting children to law was not lessened by their physical immaturity. According to Crispin, a child was never too young for his parents to begin teaching obedience.[36]

Crispin's remarks represent the depth of early national conservatives' fear of their children's destructive potential. In the northeast, the doctrine of infant depravity remained powerful within Protestant religious culture until the mid-nineteenth century. The New School theology of the 1820s that sought to reconcile Calvinism with the rationalism of the nineteenth century did not abandon its commitment to the doctrine.[37] Even Horace Bushnell, the author of the best-selling child-rearing volume *Christian Nurture* (1847), which is commonly credited with softening Americans' attitudes toward children, did not completely disassociate himself from the doctrine of depravity.[38] Yet early national conservatives blended their traditionalist belief in the doctrine of infant depravity with Lockean notions of the child's adaptive qualities; they argued that infants possessed a vicious nature but were highly receptive to improvement. A Christian education could easily rescue the child from his native wildness.[39]

Early national ministers and moralists credited Adam's fall as the ultimate cause for man's violence but argued that the proximate cause was the failure of education. Why did so much of humanity suffer in barbarism? "The immediate cause is their neglect of education," pontificated the rabid anti-Jacobin David Osgood.[40] Depravity explained human violence but did not exculpate it. Humans were differentiated from other animals by their ability to improve. This belief in the malleability of children leavened the

---

[36] Crispin "On the Education of Children," *The Adviser; or Vermont Evangelical Magazine*, May/June 1815, 162–71.

[37] Leo P. Hirrel, *Children of Wrath: New School Calvinism and Antebellum Reform* (Lexington, Ky., 1998).

[38] Smith, *Changing Conceptions*.

[39] Reinier, "Rearing the Republican Child."

[40] Osgood, *Sermon . . . June 2, 1788*, 10.

deterministic tendencies of early national orthodoxy. While only God could be the author of human redemption, He had made it the duty of parents to prepare their children through education. Parents could not hide from their responsibilities by blaming Adam for their children's sins. The Reverend Noah Worcester, the anti-Jacobin founder of the Massachusetts Peace Society, scolded any parents who used the fall to deflect their personal responsibility for the redemption of their children. "Among the consequences of the apostacy of Adam, one of the most deplorable is this – that his posterity are disposed to excuse their own depravity and guilt... and to neglect the means which God has appointed for their own recovery and the salvation of their children." Worcester instructed his readers that God commanded parents to educate their children: "*virtuous education is ordained by God, as the ordinary means of saving our children from sin and misery, vice and ruin.*"[41]

Anti-Jacobins believed that Christian education provided the remedy to the political problems posed by human depravity. They coupled premodern negativism about human nature with Enlightenment optimism about the power to reform humanity. Worcester blamed parents as the "principal" corrupters of their children because children absorbed the example of human violence from their parents. If parents could provide a better example, Worcester believed it possible to excite in children an "abhorrence of all sanguinary customs – all acts of violence and revenge."[42] Worcester used the Quakers and the Shakers (both pacifist sects) to serve as examples of "the power of religious opinions over the passions of *anger* and *revenge*; and [to] show the possibility of producing self-government in these particulars." Education, he believed, held the promise to lead people "to *abhor* every species of violence towards fellow beings." Although Worcester's humanitarianism has been depicted by historians as an outgrowth of the new liberal theology that arose in nineteenth-century New England, his motivations for advocating education emerged from a negative, not a positive, sense of human nature.

Osgood, Worcester and other anti-Jacobins adopted Enlightenment assumptions about child development without breaking from their negativist outlook on human nature. Their pessimism about humanity did not hamper their commitment to education. As dismal as the doctrine of depravity appears to modern eyes, in practice during the early republic it added a sense of urgency to humane schemes for man's improvement. Mixing the activist sensibilities of the new age with premodern assumptions about human sinfulness created a potent rationale for education. Before the shift toward a more romantic conception of childhood innocence – which has

---

[41] "On the Importance of Christian Education," *Christian Disciple* 3, no. 2–3 (1815) (original italics).

[42] "On the Importance of Christian Education," *Christian Disciple* 3, no. 5 (May 1815): 146; 3, no. 7 (July 1815): 198–202; 3, no. 8 (Aug. 1815): 231–4.

typically been assigned credit for bettering the treatment of children in America – depravity served as a powerful driving force behind the movement to educate the nation's youth.[43]

Discipline of the Heart

If Americans failed to educate the nation's youth properly, conservatives argued, the dire consequences it would face were clearly represented by the violence in France.

From the beginning, pedagogues blamed the Revolution's acts of violence on the inadequacy of French education, which had not properly prepared the people for democracy. "Humanity is wounded by the outrages of the mob in France, but what better can be expected from *ignorance*, the natural parent of enormity?" asked Robert Coram in 1791.[44] By spring 1793, remarks bemoaning the failure of education in France became a standard element of the anti-Jacobin reaction. Enos Hitchcock censured the French people because "unprepared for the enjoyment of [free government] by a previous course of education, of intellectual improvement, and moral discipline, they have tarnished their glory by excesses, and, in the paroxysms of their zeal, have carried excess to outrage."[45] David Tappan, Hollis Professor of Divinity at Harvard College, called the French Revolution:

a solemn and instructive spectacle; a spectacle, which like a warning voice from heaven, inculcates upon us the unspeakable importance of an enlightened and virtuous education; by which rising sons and daughters of America may, under the concurring influence of heaven, early acquire such sentiments and habits as are congenial to a great and free, a confederate and Christian republic.[46]

[43] Historians who have connected the declining belief in depravity to increased concern for children include Myra C. Glenn, *Campaigns against Corporal Punishment: Prisoners, Sailors, Women and Children in Antebellum America* (Albany, N.Y., 1984); Bernard Wishy, *The Child and the Republic: The Dawn of Modern American Child Nurture* (Philadelphia, Pa., 1968); Anne L. Kuhn, *The Mother's Role in Childhood Education: New England Concepts, 1830–1860* (New Haven, Conn., 1947), chap. 2.

[44] Robert Coram, "Political Inquiries: To Which Is Added, a Plan for the General Establishment of Schools Throughout the United States (1791)," in *Essays on Education in the Early Republic*, ed. Frederick Rudolph (Cambridge, Mass., 1965), 124.

[45] Enos Hitchcock, *An Oration, in Commemoration of the Independence of the United States of America: Delivered in the Baptist Meeting-House in Providence, July 4th, 1793* (Providence, R.I., 1793), 13.

[46] David Tappan, *A Sermon, Delivered to the First Congregation in Cambridge, and the Religious Society in Charlestown, April 11, 1793; on the Occasion of the Annual Fast in the Commonwealth of Massachusetts* (Boston, Mass., 1793). 28. British anti-Jacobins also made this argument; see Hannah More, *Considerations on Religion and Public Education with Remarks on the Speech of M. Dupont, Delivered in the National Convention of France. Together with an Address to the Ladies, &C. Of Great Britain and Ireland*, (Boston, Mass., 1794).

Anti-Jacobins identified education as the factor that differentiated the outcomes of the French and American revolutions.[47] The tradition of education in the United States had constructed a cool American temperament that did not disintegrate when loosed from the constraints of monarchical law.[48] The absence of such a tradition in France, exacerbated by the Jacobin laws and rhetoric opposing parental authority, had transformed America's sister republic into "bedlam" and "war."[49] The French Revolution proved that education was necessary to preserve the United States from future democratic bloodshed.[50]

In the past, education had helped to preserve the United States from succumbing to military despotism. In the future, education would have to prevent the United States from succumbing to transatlantic Jacobinism. Education served as a central element in the anti-Jacobin movement to secure American social order from French Revolutionary violence. Essayists called upon the national government, state governments, and their fellow citizens to support education for the benefit of political stability. Throughout the early national era, every instance of Federalist–Calvinist public expression – including Fast Day sermons, Thanksgiving sermons, election sermons, funeral sermons, militia sermons, and Fourth of July orations – became an opportunity to praise education as the best means to secure the state from the threat of a vicious yet empowered citizenry.[51] Despite their predictability, these remarks rose above the level of generalized abstractions. Anti-Jacobin

---

[47] McWhorter, *An Oration ... 1794*.

[48] Elisha Lee, *An Oration Delivered at Lenox, the 4th July, 1793, the Anniversary of American Independence* (Stockbridge, Mass., 1793).

[49] John Lowell, *An Oration, Pronounced July 4, 1799, at the Request of the Inhabitants of the Town of Boston in Commemoration of the Anniversary of American Independence* (Boston, Mass., 1799); Daggett, *Sun-Beams May Be Extracted from Cucumbers, but the Process Is Tedious. An Oration, Pronounced on the Fourth of July, 1799. At the Request of the Citizens of New-Haven.*

[50] Charles Backus, *A Sermon Preached before His Excellency Samuel Huntington ... Governor ... Of the State of Connecticut. May 9, 1793* (Hartford, Conn., 1793); John Thornton Kirkland, *A Sermon, Delivered on the 9th of May, 1798. Being the Day of a National Fast, Recommended by the President of the United States* (Boston, Mass., 1798).

[51] For examples from each of these genres, see Nathaniel Thayer, *A Sermon, Delivered on the Day of Fasting, Humiliation & Prayer, April 2, 1795* (Boston, 1795); Eli Forbes, *The Importance of the Rising Generation. A Sermon, Preached at the Desire of the Selectmen, and the Committee for Inspecting the Town Schools: Occasioned by the Dedication of a New and Very Commodious Grammar School House, Lately Erected in the First Parish of the Town of Gloucester, on the 5th of March, 1795* (Newburyport, Mass., 1795); Aaron Bancroft, *The Importance of a Religious Education Illustrated and Enforced. A Sermon: Delivered at Worcester, October 31, 1793, Occasioned by the Execution of Samuel Frost, on That Day, for the Murder of Captain Elisha Allen, of Princeton, on the 16th Day of July, 1793* (Worcester, Mass., 1793); Frederick William Hotchkiss, *On National Greatness: A Thanksgiving Sermon, Delivered to the First Society in Say-Brook, November 29th, 1792* (New Haven, Conn., 1793); Backus, *A Sermon ... 1793*; William Emerson, *A Discourse, Delivered in Harvard, July 4, 1794, at the Request of the Military Officers in That Place,*

FIGURE 8. Enos Hitchcock, 1744–1803. The Reverend Enos Hitchock, a Congregationalist minister and critic of French Revolutionary violence, was devoted to numerous benevolent causes, including antislavery and public education. Hitchcock's pedagogical vision emphasized training children to restrain their violent passions and be orderly participants in the "governmental machine." *Courtesy of American Antiquarian Society.*

tributes to education articulated a consistent pedagogical approach that focused attention on instructing children how to control their passions.

The title of a well-known mid-eighteenth-century advice book by the British author Lord Kames had described genteel child rearing as the "culture of the heart." In 1802, Senex, an essayist for the Federalist newspaper *The Balance and Columbian Repository*, tellingly recast Kames' term for his anti-Jacobin audience: a good republican education should entail the *"discipline of the heart."*[52] The shift from culture to discipline suggests that early national conservative pedagogues worried less about polishing youths' bourgeois manners than about the need to prepare youth for the heightened self-control required by republican governance. Other American commentators described the distinction between traditional European pedagogy and the new approach as a shift from informing the mind to shaping the emotions.[53] In the United States, Noah Webster explained, "The *heart* should be cultivated more than the *head*."[54] Through education, American

Who, with the Militia under Their Command, Were Then Assembled to Commemorate the Anniversary of the American Independence (Boston, Mass., 1794).

[52] Italics in original. Senex, *The Balance and Columbian Repository*, May 18, 1802.

[53] Ezra Sampson, *The Sham Patriot Unmasked, or an Exposition of the Fatally Succesful Arts of Demagogues* (Conn., 1802), 102.

[54] Webster, "Education," 67.

youth would learn self-disciplinary strategies to control the selfish human desires that were known as passions. Any human appetite left unrestrained might ultimately lead to bloodshed. American anti-Jacobins developed a disciplinary pedagogy that would prepare citizens to control their violent passions.

This pedagogy had begun to develop even before the Reign of Terror, in reaction to the domestic disorder of the 1780s. Congregationalist minister Enos Hitchcock (who later became an avowed anti-Jacobin), published a two-volume epistolary novel in 1790 on the subject of education that outlined this disciplinary model of education. Hitchcock followed in the footsteps of tradition by arguing that that the family was a "miniature of society and government," but he cast a disparaging eye over the British style of education that the United States had inherited. Historically, education had taught young elites "WHAT TO THINK, rather than HOW TO THINK." In America, Hitchcock wrote, *all* children had to be rendered into "moral agents." America needed to develop a domestic education that supported its republican government by preventing civil discord and encouraging obedience to lawful authority.[55] Education had to prepare children to restrain "the indulgence of passions," because "those who are accustomed, in their youth, to the restraints of domestic discipline . . . are suited to the government of the commonwealth." The argument that obedience to parents prepared children for obedience to the state recurred in anti-Jacobin pedagogy throughout the 1790s.[56]

In order to produce disciplined children, Hitchcock instructed parents to "acquire an entire authority over their children." Parents needed total authority in order to avoid "having recourse to any violence" when disciplining their children. To pedagogues for whom education represented a panacea against bloodshed, the use of physical violence in child rearing proved troubling. Hitchcock stressed the significance of establishing authority over children, but anxiously warned against using physical force to acquire this authority. "If you are angry with a child for its faults and rave at it, you excite the same passion in the child," Hitchcock warned; he advised hiding parental anger from children, although he conceded that at times this duty could be so challenging that it forced parents to "do violence" to themselves. Yet equanimity was necessary to the task of child rearing. The purpose of accustoming children to authority, Hitchcock explained, was to prepare them for "self command."[57] If children obeyed their parents

[55] Enos Hitchcock, *Memoirs of the Bloomsgrove Family in a Series of Letters to a Respectable Citizen of Philadelphia* (Boston, Mass., 1790), 1:15, 48, 23.

[56] For example, Thomas Snell, *Repentance with Prayer . . . Praying for Rulers a Christian Duty* (Brookfield, Mass., 1812), 13. Also John Drayton, *Letters Written During a Tour through the Northern and Eastern States of America* (Charleston, S.C., 1794), 110.

[57] Hitchcock, *Bloomsgrove*, 1:107, 55–7, 232.

from fear of violence they would have no reason to exercise self-discipline when freed from oversight, and they would not become obedient citizens. Conversely, if parents tyrannically broke their children's wills, these future citizens would later be unable to resist the blandishments of demagogues.

Having achieved authority over their children, Hitchcock directed parents to focus their energies on teaching the "regulation of passions," which he described as "the most difficult, and, at the same time, the most important part of education." The primary tool for the restraint of passion was piety, which held the power to "restrain those passions which are the principal occasion of discord." Hitchcock turned to Christian education as the solution to the problem of taming human passions because he shared the same religious conceptualization of human passions that provoked so many other conservatives of the early national era. Belief in a fallen world of human depravity grounded Hitchcock's enlightened enthusiasm for a new style of education. In "a world like this and with passions like ours," Christian education was essential; children's "angry passions" and "disposition to cruelty" needed to be addressed early in their lives.[58] Drawing on a long Christian tradition with origins in the confessions of St. Augustine, Hitchcock warned parents to monitor children's tendencies to commit acts of cruelty against animals, such as pulling the heads off sparrows or kicking puppies. He instructed parents to teach their children to feel "ashamed of themselves, if at any time they gave way to a fit of anger." Displays of anger disqualified people for society. Children were also to be protected from sights such as animal butchery "which brutalize the mind," and from reading "histories of war and carnage," which made murderers appear as heroes. Ultimately, Hitchcock believed that piety combined with well-developed feelings of "shame and disgrace" would build a person's "conscience" and prepare him or her for self-government.[59] Hitchcock's proscription of violent children's games had roots in Lockean child-rearing theory. Locke even put his theory to practice in the education of the young Third Earl of Shaftesbury, whom many historians credit as an intellectual progenitor of eighteenth-century humanitarianism (perhaps testifying to the theory's efficacy).[60] The historic tradition of restricting children's exposure to physical violence had deep roots, which supported its new prominence in the critical decade following the French Revolution.

As the rise of transatlantic radicalism made the problem of self-government appear more acute, many anti-Jacobins embraced Hitchcock's disciplinary pedagogy in their own writings. Anti-Jacobins shared the belief that the main purpose of education was to train children away from violence.

---

[58] Ibid., 1:106, 69, 216; 2:202, 206.
[59] Ibid., 1: 206–79.
[60] G. J. Barker-Benfield, *The Culture of Sensibility: Sex and Society in Eighteenth-Century Britain* (Chicago, Ill., 1992), 105.

Thomas Snell, a Calvinist minister from Massachusetts and a virulent opponent to the French Revolution, praised Christian education for restraining
children "from much of the evil and violence to which they are prompted
by their natural passions."[61] In an anti-Jacobin sermon delivered during the
height of the 1798–1800 Quasi War against France, the Reverend Nathan
Strong distinguished the importance of Christian education from secular
education as a means to restrain "the selfish heart of man."[62] In an apocalyptic sermon directed against French democracy, the Reverend John Smalley
warned that only Christian education could prevent people from succumbing to the deranged brutality of "the fiercest animals, under the operation of
the hydrophobia [rabies]."[63] Philoteknon, writing in the *Connecticut Evangelical Magazine* in 1806, warned that as a consequence of failing to provide
a religious education to youth, "the whole world would become one vast
field of blood."[64] Senex advised Bible reading and pious instruction "to teach
youth to govern their passions and appetites."[65] Timothy Dwight wrote that
if children were not educated, "they would evidently become mere beasts of
prey; and make the world a den of violence and slaughter."[66] In the absence
of a Christian education, another magazine essayist warned, children would
grow up to be passionate savages who indulged in vicious cruelties such as
torture and human sacrifice.[67]

Teaching children to resist anger, anti-Jacobins insisted, was the most
important means to prevent their transformation into violent savages. Timothy Dwight admonished parents that "children should regularly be checked,
and subdued, in every ebullition of passion; particularly of pride and
anger."[68] To achieve that end, parents had to vigilantly guard against any
elements of cruelty in children's play. Like Enos Hitchcock, Noah Worcester
warned parents in 1815 that "the practice of teasing and torturing animals
should never be countenanced."[69] Similar advice appeared in the pages of
a short-lived conservative New England periodical in 1802; nestled among

[61] Snell, *Repentance with Prayer*, 13.
[62] Nathan Strong, *A Sermon, Preached on the State Fast, April 6th, 1798. Published at the Request of the Hearers* (Hartford, Conn., 1798), 12.
[63] John Smalley, *On the Evils of a Weak Government: A Sermon, Preached on the General Election at Hartford, in Connecticut, May 8, 1800* (Hartford, Conn., 1800).
[64] Philoteknon, "On a Religious Education," *Connecticut Evangelical Magazine*, Apr. 1806, 386.
[65] Senex, *The Balance*, May 18, 1802. See also Sampson, *Sham Patriot*, 102.
[66] Slater, *Children*, 132–6.
[67] "On Education," *New-Star*, May 9, 1797, 36. See also Clark Brown, "The Importance of the Early and Proper Education of Children, Both as It Respects Themselves and Mankind in General: Considered in a Sermon Preached at Wareham, March 31st, 1795" (New Bedford, Mass., 1795).
[68] Slater, *Children*, 105.
[69] Noah Worcester, "On the Importance of Christian Education, Part VII." *Christian Disciple* 3, no. 7 (July 1815): 198–202.

articles praising the anti-Jacobin writings of John Sylvester John Gardiner and Hannah More, appeared advice from a physician warning parents not to let a child indulge in "torturing birds, dogs, cats, and such-like domestic animals" or "to sport with the lives of little buzzing insects" at the window.[70] While antipathy against children's cruelty to animals predated the French Revolution, the rise of transatlantic Jacobinism reinforced the emphasis that parents in the United States placed on avoiding animal cruelty.[71]

Anti-Jacobins took their message of kindness to animals directly to children themselves, in the extensive anti-Jacobin children's literature published on both sides of the Atlantic in the late eighteenth and early nineteenth centuries. Sarah Trimmer, a British conservative whose fear of the spread of Jacobinism among children led her to establish a periodical review of juvenile literature, published a children's book in 1786 preaching kindness to animals that became perhaps the most popular juvenile book in the United States in the following decades.[72] *Fabulous Histories* described the adventures of Harriet and Frederick Benson, a brother and sister whose mother taught them kindness to animals. The Bensons are contrasted to another brother and sister, the thoughtless Lucy Jenkins and her sadistic brother Edward, whose crimes of animal torture no doubt provided much of the book's interest to younger readers. Edward's creative ideas for tormenting pets include tying a cat and dog together to see "how nicely they would fight"; tying bladders to cats and throwing them from the housetop; instigating villagers to beat and ultimately kill a dog; tying the legs of roosters together and setting them to fighting; picking the feathers off a live chicken; and pulling the legs and wings off flies. (Edward is ultimately punished for his crimes when a horse he is beating kicks back fatally. Edward's death again suggests the bipolarity of violent language: its power both to anathematize bloodshed and to stimulate revenge fantasies.) *Fabulous Histories* was republished in multiple American editions after the French Revolution and proved enormously popular among conservative anti-Jacobins.

Transatlantic anti-Jacobins published the most popular children's books of the 1790s and early 1800s, often weaving their political views and

---

[70] Hugh Smith, "The Necessity of Cultivating the Dispositions of Children," *New England Quarterly Magazine; Comprehending Literature, Morals and Amusements*, Apr.–Jun. 1802, 141–6.

[71] Hugh Smith's advice had first been published in Britain in the 1780s but was frequently reprinted in the United States after 1790. Editions of Smith's work include Hugh Smith, *Letters to Married Women, on Nursing and the Management of Children* (Philadelphia, Pa., 1792); Hugh Smith, *Letters to Married Women, on Nursing and the Management of Children* (Philadelphia, Pa., 1796).

[72] M. O. Grenby, "'A Conservative Woman Doing Radical Things': Sarah Trimmer and 'The Guardian of Education,'" in *Culturing the Child, 1690–1914: Essays in Memory of Mitzi Myers*, ed. Donelle Ruwe (Lanham, Md., 2005).

antipathy toward physical violence into their works. The British evangelical Hannah More, a religious and political ally of Sarah Trimmer, published an anti-Jacobin chapbook series known as *The Cheap Repository Tracts* during the mid-1790s that was designed to appeal both to children and uneducated adults. The tracts' simple narratives, which encouraged readers to resist the allure of Jacobinism and submit obediently to authority, often featured children as characters. The books sold very well in the United States as well as in Britain, and formed a mainstay of children's reading during the early nineteenth century.[73] In typical *Cheap Repository* tales like "Tom White, the Postillion," religious skepticism, moral degeneracy, and animal cruelty all contribute to personal and political downfalls. Tom White, a post driver, is led from tavern culture to drunkenness, to abusing his horses, which results in him being thrown "violently" from his cart and breaking his leg, leading nearly to his death. The crisis forces Tom to acknowledge the lessons of "sober education" and reform into a moral man.[74]

American-born anti-Jacobins also appealed directly to children through juvenile texts. The geography primers coauthored by the Massachusetts anti-Jacobins Jedidiah Morse and Elijah Parish, which were perhaps the most commonly used pedagogical texts in the early national era after the Bible and Noah Webster's spelling primers, introduced the basic elements of the anti-Jacobin narrative to thousands of children. From the 1794 edition onward, the entries on France as well as the timelines presented at the back of the book highlighted well-known French Revolutionary excesses such as the imprisonment of Lafayette, the executions of King Louis XVI and Marie Antoinette, and the guillotining of Robespierre. "Many changes in the government of this unhappy country have since taken place, and it may still be considered as established on a very precarious foundation," read the 1800 edition's entry on France, perhaps suggesting to school children that their own proper education could provide a firmer foundation for government in the United States.[75] These early lessons in anti-Jacobinism did not represent a sharp break from the past, but an updating of the historic anti-French sentiment that had infiltrated New England primers in the eighteenth century.[76]

---

[73] M. O. Grenby, "Politicizing the Nursery: British Children's Literature and the French Revolution," *Lion and the Unicorn* 27 (2003).

[74] Hannah More, *The History of Tom White, the Postillion Afterwards Called Farmer White; to Which Is Added, the History of Charles Jones, the Footman* (Philadelphia, Pa., 1811).

[75] Jedidiah Morse, *Geography Made Easy: Being an Abridgment of the American Universal Geography...To Which Is Added, an Improved Chronological Table of Remarkable Events, from the Creation to the Present Time.*, 7th ed. (Boston, Mass., 1800), 352–5; Martin Brückner, "Lessons in Geography: Maps, Spellers, and Other Grammars of Nationalism in the Early Republic," *American Quarterly* 51 (1999): 319.

[76] Kerry Arnold Trask, "In the Pursuit of Shadows: A Study of Collective Hope and Despair in Provincial Massachusetts during the Era of the Seven Years War, 1748 to 1764" (1971), 252.

For parents and teachers, introducing anti-Jacobin rhetoric into their history and geography lessons would have felt natural.

Ezra Sampson, the anti-Jacobin minister and editor of the New York Federalist newspaper *Balance*, published both anti-Jacobin materials calling for education and educational materials that taught anti-Jacobinism. His extended 1802 essay "The Sham-Patriot" made repeated arguments for the need to establish common schools to educate children and inoculate them against Jacobin demagoguery.[77] Proving his commitment to pedagogy in the battle against transatlantic radicalism, five years later Sampson published *The Youth's Companion*, a history and geography textbook that proselytized virulent Francophobia to its juvenile audience. In the entry "France," Sampson wrote that "torrents of blood" had been shed since the siege of the Bastille, because the nation's citizens had lacked any moral discipline. The French "shook off at once all civil, moral, and religious restraints," and to praise God between the years 1792 and 1796 condemned the speaker to "death as a fanatic." Multiple entries reinforced this Gothic message. A definition of the term *proscription* described the practice's Roman origins before commenting that it had been "copied by Marat, Robespierre, and some other bloody Jacobins of France, who seemed ambitious to exceed all preceding usurpers and murderers in deeds of cruelty." An entry on the bloody suppression of the Huguenots likewise helped children forge the link between historic French brutality and the modern era.[78]

Children also received indoctrination in anti-Jacobinism from American political primers, such as Elphanan Winchester's *A Plain Political Catechism intended for the Use of Schools* (1796) – which warned youth that the enemies of religious education sought to follow Robespierre's example and destroy American liberty.[79] Caleb Bingham's popular *Columbian Orator* included speeches recounting the bloody history of revolutionary France in its later editions.[80] The dramatic events of the French Revolution lent themselves easily to public oration, a major element of nineteenth-century pedagogy. The suitability of Jacobinism as a subject of oration is evident from a review of programs for commencement-day speeches in American colleges

[77] Sampson, *Sham Patriot*.

[78] Ezra Sampson, *The Youth's Companion, or, an Historical Dictionary Consisting of Articles Selected Chiefly from Natural and Civil History, Geography, Astronomy, Zoology, Botany and Mineralogy Arranged in Alphabetical Order by Ezra Sampson* (Hudson, N.Y., 1807), 134–5.

[79] Elhanan Winchester, *A Plain Political Catechism Intended for the Use of Schools, in the United States of America: Wherein the Great Principles of Liberty, and of the Federal Government, Are Laid Down and Explained, in the Way of Question and Answer* (Philadelphia, Pa., 1796), 62–9.

[80] Caleb Bingham, ed., *The Columbian Orator: Containing a Variety of Original and Selected Pieces; Together with Rules; Calculated to Improve Youth and Others in the Ornamental and Useful Art of Eloquence*, 2nd ed. (Boston, Mass., 1799), 82–8.

during the first half of the nineteenth century. Harvard, Middlebury, Bowdoin, and Trinity all organized commencements featuring speeches with anti-Jacobin titles such as "The Death of Robespierre," "Against Robespierre," "The Reign of Terror," and "Portrait of Robespierre."[81] This tradition continued into the 1860s. S. O. Frye participated in the "Junior Prize Declamation" for the Bowdoin class of 1864, by delivering "Robespierre's Last Speech" to an enthusiastic audience.[82] Even after the Civil War, the French Revolution continued to serve as a subject for college orations.[83]

Anti-Jacobin elements within children's literature, as well as anti-Jacobin arguments for education, shared common concerns about physical violence that led to a developing argument against the corporal punishment of children in both literatures. To prevent children from indulging their brutal passions, many anti-Jacobins followed Enos Hitchcock by insisting that parents and teachers had to restrain their own brutality. Nothing trained children in violence as effectively as experiencing corporal punishment at the hands of adults. Anti-Jacobin child-rearing sources from the 1790s and early 1800s criticized physical discipline for its brutalizing effects. Senex, who had termed education the "discipline of the heart," stated that in a good home there hung "no terrific rod," and he called violent discipline in the classroom "a disgusting sight" not suited to raising republican children.[84] Even those conservative pedagogues who supported the use of physical discipline, like Noah Webster, expressed anxiety about overreliance on the rod, lest a parent or teacher instilled a "slavish fear" in a child.[85] Anti-Jacobin education sought to use discipline to foster obedience without instilling meek dependence or an aggressive temperament.

Theodore Dwight Jr., son of the anti-Jacobin Theodore Dwight and nephew of the anti-Jacobin Timothy Dwight, published a child-rearing manual in the early 1830s that indicated the persistence of concerns about child depravity and their link to sentiment against corporal punishment. Dwight, like his progenitors, argued strongly that children were born

---

[81] A brief sample includes: Middlebury College. "Exhibition. Afternoon – Junior Class" (Middlebury, Vt., 1809); Harvard University, "Harvard University, Cambridge. Order of performances for exhibition, Monday, Jul. 18, 1831" (Cambridge, Mass., 1831); "Trinity College, Junior exhibition. April 1st, 1852" (Hartford, Conn., 1852).

[82] Bowdoin College, "Junior prize declamation, Class of '64. Monday evening, August 3, 1863. Committee: O. W. Davis Jr. S.O. Frye. C.F. Libby" (Boston, Mass., 1863).

[83] Bowdoin College, "Bowdoin. Senior and Junior Exhibition. April 5, 1875" (Boston, Mass., 1875).

[84] Senex, *The Balance and Columbian Repository*, Sept. 28, 1802; July 13, 1802. See also "On Instruction and Good Education," *South-Carolina Weekly Museum*, Jan. 28, 1797; Hugh Smith, "The Necessity of Cultivating the Dispositions of Children," *New England Quarterly Magazine: Comprehending Literature, Morals and Amusements*, Apr.–June 1802, 145; Pater "On the Religious Education of Children," *Christian Evangelical Magazine*, Nov. 1806.

[85] Webster, "Education," 59.

innately depraved; "no child has ever been known since the earliest period of the world, destitute of an evil disposition." Education had to correct for children's natural dispositions by training youth in nonviolence. Dwight advised parents to encourage "proper submission to authority" but warned that "corporal punishments" should seldom be imposed because they would teach children to indulge their violent passions. A child had to be taught to be "his own chief disciplinarian" through lessons in "self-government," not by brute force.[86]

Conservative pedagogues who advised against the use of corporal punishment linked their opposition to familiar sentiments against animal torture, revealing a consistent concern about the demoralizing effects of violence. Theodore Dwight Jr. warned against permitting children to go fishing or shooting, or to do anything "connected with the destruction of life." Dwight assumed that all parents would share his concerns about the "demoralizing amusements connected with cruelty to animals," but he also warned against permitting children to use military toys. "The principles of peaces should be early and deeply implanted," Dwight argued, by avoiding corporal punishment, animal cruelty, and any celebration of war.[87] Dwight's remarks were in line with the advice from his own childhood in the early nineteenth century. An 1802 children's book containing brief moral lessons in obedience and Christian piety argued that the use of spurs on horses was a "national disgrace," and stated that "a spur stands in the same predicament with me as a rod; and of that you know my sentiments." Conservative pedagogues connected violence against animals to violence against children because both exposed society to the destructive passions.[88]

Antipathy to the physical discipline of children is frequently seen as an antebellum break from earlier orthodox styles of childrearing.[89] The famous scene in Louisa May Alcott's *Little Men* in which a lying student is punished by being forced to beat his teacher rather than have his teacher beat him has been used repeatedly to illustrate how antebellum pedagogy turned against conventional corporal punishment. Alcott based her tale on the actual classroom practices of her transcendentalist father, Bronson Alcott, at his progressive Temple School in Boston during the 1830s. Yet Bronson Alcott's rejection of corporal punishment can be traced to the anti-Jacobin

---

[86] Theodore Dwight, *The Father's Book, or, Suggestions for the Government and Instruction of Young Children, on Principles Appropriate to a Christian Country* (Springfield, Mass., 1835), 108–16.

[87] Ibid., 43, 88–94.

[88] *The Mother's Remarks on a Set of Cuts for Children* (Philadelphia, Pa., 1803), 59. This may have been the reprint of a British publication.

[89] Glenn, *Campaigns against Corporal Punishment*; Philip J. Greven, *The Protestant Temperament: Patterns of Child-Rearing, Religious Experience, and the Self in Early America* (New York, 1977).

milieu of his childhood in New England during the first decades of the nineteenth century.[90] The radical and innovative element of Alcott's pedagogy was his willingness to have the rod turned against himself, thus completely overturning the social order. Early national pedagogy did not advocate any such reordering of social hierarchy; rather, it sought to preserve hierarchy by eliminating violent challenges. Avoiding all physical discipline was important because the quality of self-control had to be instilled through the soul rather than the body. The model republican child was neither out-of-control nor controlled by others; he was self-controlled.

Michel Foucault has famously argued that the eighteenth-century transition from the physical punishment of criminals to prolonged imprisonment exchanged one variety of violence for another. The shift away from corporal punishment conveyed the illusion of humanitarianism but in fact created violent new technologies of power (discipline).[91] Similarly, the shift away from bodily punishment of children toward "discipline of the heart" may be seen as creating a new form of violence against the soul. Certainly, anti-Jacobin pedagogy viewed education as a medium of control, which suggests a violence against personal freedom. However, that argument assumes a model of freedom as personal autonomy that is neither temporally nor geographically universal. Early national conservatives who intended to use education to teach obedience and secure social order did not believe that their pedagogy repressed human freedoms.[92] Quite the contrary, advocates of education believed that establishing social order would provide the only context in which individuals could achieve freedom.

Most advocates of education in the early national era shared a belief in the social construction of human freedom. They rejected the Rousseauian doctrine that men sacrificed a degree of liberty when they joined society. Instead they argued that society created liberties for its members. A secure social order and the freedom of individual citizens were mutually defining values; neither could be realized without the other, and both relied entirely on education. The emphasis on subordination in early national pedagogy

---

[90] Frederick C. Dahlstrand, *Amos Bronson Alcott, an Intellectual Biography* (Rutherford, N.J., 1982).

[91] Michel Foucault, *Discipline and Punish: The Birth of the Prison*, trans. Alan Sheridan (New York, 1979).

[92] Many progressive historians, as well as the neoprogressives of the 1960s and 1970s, read late-eighteenth- and early-nineteenth-century calls for education to guarantee obedience and social order as veiled manifestoes of oppression. Merle Curti, *The Social Ideas of American Educators*, Report of the American Historical Association Commission on the Social Studies in the Schools (New York, 1935), xvi; John R. Bodo, *The Protestant Clergy and Public Issues, 1812–1848* (Princeton, N.J., 1954); Clifford Stephen Griffin, *Their Brothers' Keepers; Moral Stewardship in the United States, 1800–1865* (New Brunswick, N.J., 1960); Messerli, "Columbian Complex," 426; Katz, *Irony*; Stephen E. Berk, *Calvinism versus Democracy: Timothy Dwight and the Origins of American Evangelical Orthodoxy* (Hamden, Conn., 1974).

may be off-putting to modern ears, which interpret obedience as inherently repressive. But proponents of education in the early republican era believed that acquiring obedience was the key to achieving personal liberty; liberty without obedience was nothing more than anarchy. Education initially trained children to be obedient to their parents and instructors, but this represented only a passing stage in children's progress to self-control. The goal of education was to teach children to subordinate their passions to their own reason.[93] If a person failed to subordinate his own passions, he would fall prey to dissolution and ruin – a state the very opposite of freedom. In this view, arguments that education would secure social order by making children obedient were commensurate with arguments that education would heighten freedom.

Nathaniel Chipman devoted the final pages of his influential political treatise *Sketches of the Principles of Government* (1793), a foundational text in the development of American conservative political theory, to the role of education as a means to secure political stability and increase human liberties. Chipman struggled in his *Sketches* to identify how a republican government could maximize human liberties. He defined a true republic as a state in which the laws reflected the will of the people and were not applied by force. Chipman argued that education, by taming the violent passions, would secure a nonviolent form of governance that did not impinge on human freedom. "The violence of government, and the violence of the people," he wrote, "proceeded from a want of knowledge, from the violence of the passions and appetites, [and] the weakness of the moral sense."[94] Education could restrain human passions and thereby secure a humane nonviolent government and personal freedoms. So important was education to Chipman's dream of political progress that he chose to end his nearly three-hundred-page book with a sentence invoking its promise: "Let us endeavor to diffuse, extensively, the principles of useful knowledge." By training the "rising generation" to restrain their passions, the republic could continue creating freedom for years to come.[95]

The belief that education would free Americans from violent government and further their individual liberties also served as a central tenet of Timothy Dwight's most thoughtful discourse on political theory: "The True Means of Establishing Political Happiness" (1795). Like Chipman's *Sketches*, Dwight's inquiry focused on discovering how to secure a "free government" in America "without force and violence." Dwight believed the answer to be "the formation of a good personal character" in the nation's

[93] Jonathan Maxcy, *An Address* (Providence, R.I., 1794).

[94] Nathaniel Chipman, *Sketches of the Principles of Government* (Rutland, Vt., 1793), 136. For a similar theory of education, see James Cutbush, *An Oration on Education Delivered before the Society for the Promotion of a Rational System of Education ... November 7th, 1811* (Philadelphia, Pa., 1812).

[95] Chipman, *Sketches*, 292.

citizens. "Good citizens," he preached, "will not necessitate the adoption of force and oppression." Dwight defined good character as self-control; he described virtue as being "principally employed in regulating and confining within due bounds our appetites and passions." The key to forming a virtuous citizenry lay in a Christian education. As president of Yale, Dwight took seriously the question of the types of knowledge and the style of pedagogy best suited for training the republican citizen. He privileged study of the Bible. He discredited philosophy. He favored useful knowledge. Ultimately, Dwight promised that if children received proper early training it would "preclude the necessity of most political restraints, and of all political violence."[96] Through Christian education Americans would gain individual freedoms never before realized in human society.

Early national pedagogues argued that education provided a remedy to the potential violence of an enfranchised citizenry; that education precluded the necessity of political violence against the citizenry; and – at their most extreme – that the failure to provide an education itself constituted an act of violence against children. "Those parents who deny their children the means of knowledge," preached David Tappan, "are guilty in some important sense, of the blood of their offspring; for they murder THEIR MINDS, their nobler and better parts." Fears of violence transformed the cause of education from a wishful element of republican fantasies about human progress into a necessity driven by the possibility of direful consequences. Education signified both a force for order and for freedom. According to David Tappan, Christian education would make children into "future pillars of American order, freedom, and glory."[97] The belief that education would be an antidote to human violence motivated early national pedagogues not only to lobby for publicly financed education but also to make new arguments about government's right to educate youth, setting the stage for the future passage of compulsory schooling laws.

Children Belong to the State

During the 1780s and 1790s, the question of public education received the creative attention and rethinking that was directed at all social institutions

[96] Timothy Dwight, *The True Means of Establishing Public Happiness: A Sermon, Delivered on the 7th of July, 1795, before the Connecticut Society of Cincinnati, and Published at Their Request* (New Haven, Conn., 1795), 6, 12, 14, 37.

[97] David Tappan, *Christian Thankfulness Explained and Enforced: A Sermon, Delivered at Charlestown, in the Afternoon of February 19, 1795. The Day of General Thanksgiving through the United States* (Boston, Mass., 1795), 24. Also Pitt Clarke, *On the Rise and Signalized Lot of the United Americans: A Sermon, Delivered, February 19, M,Dcc,Xcv, on Occasion of a Thanksgiving Throughout the United States, to the Congregational Society, in Norton* (Boston, Mass., 1795); Joseph Dana, *A Sermon, Delivered February 19, 1795: Being a Day of General Thanksgiving, Throughout the United States of America* (Newburyport, Mass., 1795); Tappan, *A Sermon . . . 1793*, 27.

in the new republic. In popular magazines, orations, and pamphlets, pedagogues debated the subject. Sometimes authors made arguments critical of
popular education. An anonymous contributor to the democratic *American Museum* argued against providing poor boys with a literary education
because it would instill them with unrealizable expectations and cause them
to resent the toil that society required them to provide.[98] Many more democratic authors wrote to support the diffusion of knowledge as a means to
guard American liberties from tyrannical infringement. But democratic commitment to public education did not prove strong enough to counterbalance
Jeffersonian arguments for low taxation, and to secure adequate financing of
schools. Instead, sustained political advocacy and financial commitment to
free education came primarily from orthodox ministers and their Federalist
political allies.[99]

While democratic enthusiasts supported education, their dedication to
minimal government and low taxes prevented any effective public school
policy. State governments exclusively dominated by the Republican Party
(mostly in the South) were the least likely to pass public school laws during
the early national era.[100] An 1797 article published in *American Universal
Magazine* provides a fascinating example of the small-government argument,
decrying state education as an "infringement of personal liberty, which no
plea of expediency can justify."[101] Federalist politicians were more willing
than Republicans both to raise taxes to pay for common schools and to
construct a political argument for the state's right to provide education.
In an artillery oration delivered in 1797, John Russell expressed concern
that the United States would succumb to anarchy and argued that "public
education" should be "immediately the object of government."[102] Senex
argued that because the public interest depended on the proper education of
children, "it is a propitious subject of legislation, and requires the vigorous
attention of government."[103] Fear elevated the urgency of conservatives'
belief in education.

Some conservative pedagogues considered education so important to
national stability that they argued that the state had the right to force children to be educated. American legal tradition had traditionally privileged
the privacy of the family, limiting governmental interference in domestic

---

[98] "An examination of the question, whether the children of the poor should receive a literary
education or not?" *American Museum*, Sept. 1789, 249.

[99] Howe, "Church, State, and Education."

[100] Cremin, *American Education*, part 2: chap. 5.

[101] "The Enquirer – No. II," *American Universal Magazine*, Jan. 9, 1797, 44–50.

[102] John Miller Russell, *An Oration, Pronounced at Charlestown, July 4, 1797. At the
Request of the Selectmen, Artillery Company, and Trustees of the School in Said Town.
In Commemoration of the Anniversary of American Independence* (Charlestown, Mass.,
1797), 8.

[103] Senex, *The Balance and Columbian Repository*, Oct. 12, 1802.

questions. During the early republic, family law grew more protective of domestic privacy in many respects.[104] However, education seemed such an important cause that its proponents challenged the trend toward the exclusivity of parental rights. The origins of compulsory schooling in America lay in conservative anxieties about popular government. Jeremy Belknap, a New England Congregationalist minister who became a fervent anti-Jacobin, quoted the Spartan lawgiver Lycurgus's argument that "children belong to the State more than to their Parents," to justify the state's right to educate youth.[105] The significance of education produced such remarks from commentators more than once. Manasseh Cutler also used Lycurgus's axiom in a 1788 sermon on education.[106] William Bradford praised Connecticut's public school tradition in very similar terms: public schools were "in the pure spirit of a republic, which, considering the youth as property of the state, does not permit a parent to bring up his children in ignorance and vice."[107] Likewise, John Drayton praised Massachusetts public schools for assuming responsibility as a "political parent" for the state's children and for educating them "not as may suit the whim of their relations, but as may tend most to their country's good."[108] Because the state depended for its survival on the proper education of children, advocates were willing to extend state interference in the family far beyond its typical limit. Historians have argued that the American "family ideal" shielded abusive parents or guardians from governmental interference until the late nineteenth century. But concern for the security of the state elevated the importance of education above family privacy during the late eighteenth century.[109]

Assertions that American children should be compelled to attend public schools originated in traditional New England political arguments that the state should use force to help build a civil society safe from lawless violence. Conservative fears of the democratic pressures of the revolutionary era led the Massachusetts minister Belknap to worry that "with regard to civil society, the prospect is truly alarming." Only education could uphold the fragile social order. According to Jeremy Belknap, "our notions of liberty, if they are not guided and limited by good education, degenerate into a savage independence." Without education the rising generation would not submit to the reign of law. Belknap emphasized the state's need to provide education to poor children who had limited resources, because "there are

---

[104] Michael Grossberg, *Governing the Hearth: Law and the Family in Nineteenth-Century America* (Chapel Hill, N.C., 1985).

[105] Belknap, *Election Sermon . . . 1785.*

[106] Quoted in Onuf, "State Politics and Republican Virtue," 104.

[107] William Bradford, *An Enquiry How Far the Punishment of Death Is Necessary in Pennsylvania. With Notes and Illustrations* (Philadelphia, Pa., 1793), 43.

[108] Drayton, *Letters Written*, 50.

[109] Elizabeth Hafkin Pleck, *Domestic Tyranny: The Making of Social Policy against Family Violence from Colonial Times to the Present* (New York, 1987).

as many good capacities among the children of the poor, who are not able to give them a good education, as of the rich who are, and if it is the duty and interest of the State to avail itself of the capacities of all its citizens, it is then their duty and interest to cultivate those capacities." Belknap's argument for state-provided education emerged from his concern that without proper training "strange children" would rise up and threaten the land with violence. Interestingly, his fears – like his hopes – distributed equally among rich and poor. Belknap not only worried about uneducated lower classes threatening the social order; he agonized about the danger that privately educated (rather than state-educated) upper class youths would develop into tyrants:

If town schools be not encouraged, if education be not laid open and common to every family of whatever estate and condition, the rich only will be able to cultivate the minds of their children by sending them to distant academies or universities; the learning of the country will then be only among men of property, and the rest being ignorant, may be easily deceived. How favorable such a circumstance may prove to usurpation and tyranny, I dread to think![110]

Because orthodox ministers and conservative politicians in the 1790s believed that a state-protected civil society was necessary to preserve the social order, they promoted the power of the state to educate children. Republicans, who believed in an individuated civil society created outside the control of the state, could not justify compulsory public schools. Republicans' more humane view of children and humanity made it less possible to demand public support for their education.

After 1792, arguments that civil society required public schooling proliferated in anti-Jacobin discourses, sermons, and orations. Often speakers included a reference to the need for education during their closing remarks, perhaps a single sentence expressing support. Other authors devoted substantial time to developing the argument for education. Many focused attention specifically on the needs of the poor. In his series of articles "The Sham Patriot," Ezra Sampson argued that "there should be free schools. At the public expense, for the education of the children of the poor."[111] On a practical level, state-financed education mattered most to the poor because they were otherwise unable to pay for private instruction. Elitist intentions to discipline a potentially rebellious underclass also contributed to the focus on poor children. The Reverend Joseph Dana bemoaned the "want of knowledge generally diffused" in France that had led to the horrible bloodshed of the Terror. He thanked God that America had not suffered a similar fate, because "America is the poor man's country. Here the children of the poor

[110] Belknap, *Election Sermon ... 1785*, 19–20.
[111] Sampson, *Sham Patriot*, 102.

are instructed at the public expense."[112] Many pedagogues also hoped that education would preserve civil society against criminal violence committed by the poor.[113]

While advocates for education welcomed the disciplinary effects of education on the poor, they also stressed the importance of disciplining the master class. Native son William Tudor praised New England's "discipline for the young" because it "turned principally on two points – the subjugation of the passions, and a perfect equality of standing – giving to seniority the chief and almost exclusive claim to deference."[114] Common schools served as an effective counter to social deference. Mixing social ranks within a single classroom diminished the mystique of authority that had attached to elites in colonial society. Anti-Jacobin Ezra Sampson praised Massachusetts's free schools in his 1807 *Youth's Companion*, because within them "the children of every class of citizens may freely associate together."[115] In the common school, authority was supposed to be earned through age or merit rather than inherited status.[116]

Outsiders also admired New England common schools for mixing rich and poor students together and subjecting all classes to the same treatment. Marcellus, a Federalist commentator in Virginia, praised New England because "there schools are spread over the country, and teachers provided at the public expense; and all the citizens are obliged to send their children to these schools for instruction. The rich and poor are mingled in one undistinguished mass and nothing like distinction is permitted or countenanced."[117] Northeastern advocacy for free education challenged Jeffersonian rhetoric about Federalist aristocracy, with evidence that egalitarian pedagogy reigned in the states where the Federalists held most power. "Who better represents liberty and equality," Federalist Christopher Gore asked, "a land where

---

[112] Dana, *A Sermon … 1795*, 9. Also Ashbel Green, *A Sermon, Delivered in the Second Presbyterian Church in the City of Philadelphia: On the 19th of February, 1795. Being the Day of General Thanksgiving throughout the United States* (Philadelphia, Pa., 1795), 35.

[113] Noah Webster, "The Importance of Accommodating the Mode of Education to the Form of Government," *American Magazine*, Apr. 1788, 312; "Address of the Trustees," *Evening Fire-Side*, Aug. 24, 1805; "An Address of the Charitable Society for the Education of Indigent Pious …" *Utica Christian Magazine*, Sept. 1815, 55; Massachusetts, *Resolves of the General Court of the Commonwealth of Massachusetts: Begun and Held at Boston, in the County of Suffolk, on Wednesday the Twenty-Ninth Day of May, Anno Domini, 1793; and from Thence Continued by Adjournment and Proclamation, to Wednesday, the Fifteenth Day of January Following* (Boston, Mass., 1794); Timothy Dwight, *President Dwight's Decisions of Questions Discussed by the Senior Class in Yale College, in 1813 and 1814* (New York, 1833), 11; Bradford, *Enquiry*.

[114] Tudor, *Letters on the Eastern States*, 385.

[115] Sampson, *The Youth's Companion*, 233.

[116] Dwight, *President Dwight's Decisions*, 37–40.

[117] Marcellus, *Marcellus: Published in the Virginia Gazette, November and December, 1794* (Richmond, Va., 1794), 23. A very similar observation was made of New England schools by the South Carolinian visitor John Drayton; Drayton, *Letters Written*, 50.

slavery is unknown, where religion and learning are generally diffused, and where the poor are taught equally with the rich; or ... that land where the poverty of the poor is their curse."[118] Education played into partisan battles over which faction, the Federalists or the Democratic-Republicans, more accurately represented aristocracy.

Elitist Federalists who argued that a "natural aristocracy" should guide the nation's politics praised education as a means for children to transcend the accident of-birth status. Many remarks drew attention to the justice of providing an opportunity for all children to excel, regardless of the circumstances into which they were born. Jedidiah Morse spoke warmly about establishing a school plan "providing equally for the poor and the rich" in order to draw "genius" from the "abodes of poverty."[119] The Reverend Isaac Story beseeched his congregants for alms so that "the beggar-children of the street" could be educated to become the nation's future leaders.[120] As early as 1793, the Federalist congressman Elias Boudinot praised public education as a means of enabling even "the child of the poorest laborer" to become president.[121]

Alongside their advocacy for state-financed common schooling, Federalist politicians and Congregationalist and Presbyterian ministers poured their energies into private fundraising for education. Private charity represented another strategy to achieve the public-oriented goal of securing the state from the consequences of moral degeneration. The needs of the state figured foremost in Lyman Beecher's 1815 address promoting a new organization, the American Society for the Education of Pious Youth for the Gospel Ministry, which was established to support the education of poor young ministerial candidates. Beecher warned, "If knowledge and virtue be the basis of republican institutions, our foundations will soon rest upon the sand, unless a more effectual and all-pervading system of religious and moral instruction can be provided." Beecher, a protégé of Timothy Dwight, recapitulated the educational theories of many earlier conservatives. He supported obedience to authority as a means to further personal freedom. "Are you friends to civil liberty?" Beecher asked potential supporters of the American Society, then "give, that it may be rescued from a violent death, and a speedy one, by the hands of ignorance and irreligion." Beecher and his allies believed

---

[118] Christopher Gore, *Manlius: With Notes and References* (Boston, Mass., 1794), 52.

[119] Jedidiah Morse, *A Sermon, Delivered before the Ancient & Honourable Artillery Company, in Boston, June 6, 1803, Being the Anniversary of Their Election of Officers* (Charlestown, Mass., 1803), 14.

[120] Isaac Story, *A Discourse, Delivered February 15, 1795, at the Request of the Proprietor's Committee: As Preparatory to the Collection, on the National Thanksgiving, the Thursday Following, for the Benefit of Our American Brethren in Captivity at Algiers* (Salem, Mass., 1795).

[121] Elias Boudinot, *An Oration, Delivered at Elizabeth-Town, New-Jersey, Agreeable to a Resolution of the State Society of Cincinnati, on the Fourth of July, M.Dcc.Xciii: Being the Seventeenth Anniversary of the Independence of America* (Elizabethtown, N.J., 1793), 11.

that education would protect Americans' civil liberties from violent over-throw by securing the social order. "The right of suffrage in the hands of an ignorant and vicious citizenry, such as will always exist in a land where the Gospel does not restrain and civilize, will be a sword in the hand of a maniac," he threatened his audience.[122]

Northeastern conservatives responded to his message with enthusiasm and open pockets. Beecher's charity, renamed the American Education Soci-ety (AES) in 1820, rapidly expanded in size and scope becoming in effect "the first widespread scholarship program in American higher education." By the late 1830s, the AES was supporting almost one out of six New Eng-land college students, including 16 percent of students at Yale and 20 percent of students at Amherst.[123] The AES strongly influenced the development of American pedagogy both through direct intervention and by publishing its educational journal, the *Quarterly Register*. Moreover the AES set an organizational example for the many other Protestant reform organizations established in the following decades, which together comprised the Benev-olent Empire.[124] Educational reform became a common entry point to the world of Protestant reform. It is especially interesting to note how many ante-bellum abolitionists began their reform careers as educational reformers – including Henry Clarke Wright, Robert Rantoul, and Theodore Dwight Weld, to name just a few.[125]

One link between the worlds of education reform and abolition that enabled these figures to cross over was the long rhetorical tradition that pin-ioned slavery as bad education. As early as 1713, the Quaker London Yearly Meeting criticized slavery because it might corrupt slaveholders' children by "learning them a domineering spirit" and enabling them to "extend cruelty to [slaves] at their pleasure."[126] Concern that slavery instructed Ameri-can children in violence and cruelty became an important component of

---

[122] Lyman Beecher, "An Address of the Charitable Society for the Education of Indigent Pious..." *Utica Christian Magazine*, Sept. 1815. Eliphalet Pearson introduced the Society's mission in similar nationalist terms at the sermon he delivered at its first organizational meeting; see Natalie A. Naylor, "'Holding High the Standard': The Influence of the Amer-ican Education Society in Ante-Bellum Education," *History of Education Quarterly* 24 (1984): 479. See also David F. Allmendinger Jr., "The Strangeness of the American Educa-tion Society: Indigent Students and the New Charity, 1815–1840," *History of Education Quarterly* 11 (1971). There are also chapters dealing with the AES in Bodo, *Protestant Clergy*; Griffin, *Brothers' Keepers*.

[123] Naylor, "Holding High."

[124] John Bodo labeled the AES the "co-ordinating agency of the theocrats"; Bodo, *Protestant Clergy*, 14.

[125] Robert Rantoul and Luther Hamilton, *Memoirs, Speeches and Writings of Robert Rantoul Jr* (Boston, Mass., 1854); Robert H. Abzug, *Passionate Liberator: Theodore Dwight Weld and the Dilemma of Reform* (New York, 1980); Lewis Perry, *Childhood, Marriage, and Reform: Henry Clarke Wright, 1797–1870* (Chicago, Ill., 1980).

[126] David L. Crosby, "Anthony Benezet's Transformation of Anti-Slavery Rhetoric," *Slavery and Abolition* 23 (2002): 44.

abolitionist rhetoric in the mid-eighteenth century. John Woolman repeated this charge in his influential 1754 essay, "Some Considerations on the Keeping of Negroes."[127] Thomas Jefferson's *Notes on the State of Virginia* (1787), while hardly an antislavery manifesto, very effectively makes the same point. Jefferson's description of the child slave master as "nursed, educated, and daily exercised in tyranny" made a strong impression on antislavery authors and served as a frequent point of reference.[128] Children's books published in England and the United States during the first half of the nineteenth century frequently linked the discipline of slaves to the torture of animals and strongly protested both forms of violence as destructive of good character.[129]

An alternative theme connecting slavery to bad education warned that the practice of using slaves as teachers had corrupted the people of ancient Rome, and that the use of slave caregivers would corrupt American republicans.[130] David Cooper, a New Jersey Quaker, combined the Jeffersonian critique of slavery as bad education with the critique of slaves as bad educators, in a remark included in his "Serious Address" against slavery published in 1783: "No marvel then if slaveholders are often scourged by the vices of their own offspring, which their untutored slaves have been a means of inflicting – children who instead of being educated in nurture and admonition of the Lord, are too often nurtured in pride, idleness, lewdness, and the indulgence of every natural appetite." The misbehavior of slaveholders' children could be blamed both on the models provided by their slaves, and on the instruction the children recieved from having slaves.[131] Early national pedagogues defined slavery and education as opposing categories.

Many advocates of education during the early national era insisted on the need to end American slavery. In "Letter LXXXI" of *Memoirs of the Bloomsgrove Family*, Enos Hitchcock quoted from Jefferson's *Notes* to make the argument that the interests of American education demanded the abolition of slavery. Hitchcock developed at length Jefferson's argument that slavery educated whites to be passionate and tyrannical. "It hence appears," he concluded, "that true policy and domestic education, as well as religion and morals, loudly plead against a practice, which has no other

---

[127] John Woolman, *Some Considerations on the Keeping of Negroes Recommended to the Professors of Christianity of Every Denomination* (Philadelphia, Pa., 1754).

[128] Thomas Jefferson, *Notes on the State of Virginia*, ed. William Harwood Peden (Chapel Hill, N.C., 1954), 162. Interestingly, Holly Brewer suggests that the ultimate impact of Jefferson's pedagogy may have been to justify slavery, as he equated slaves to children as irrational beings unequipped to play a civic role; Brewer, *By Birth or Consent*, 357.

[129] Marcus Wood, *Blind Memory: Visual Representations of Slavery in England and America, 1780–1865* (New York, 2000), 271–80.

[130] "Education," *Evening Fire-Side*, Sept. 7, 1805: 310.

[131] David Cooper, *A Serious Address to the Rulers of America on the Inconsistency of Their Conduct Respecting Slavery* (Trenton, N.J., 1783), 21.

than interested and avaricious motives to plead in its favor." Hitchcock's solution to the problem of slavery in the early republic? Of course, it could be remedied by education. Might "the evil not be radically cured, by making it a part of domestic education?" he asked. "It were to be wished that short dialogues, and other pieces, suitable for schools and academies were offered to the public by some able hand, in which the injustice and inhumanity of the practice may be properly exhibited." Hitchcock correctly predicted the shifting strategy of the antislavery movement at that time, which unable to prosecute a political strategy against the potentially secessionist southern states turned instead to using propaganda to persuade Americans to renounce the violent institution.

In the final pages of his letter, Hitchcock himself used the Gothic rhetoric whose ascendancy he predicted, instructing readers to imagine the suffering of slaves "mutilated in methods atrocious to humanity."[132] Such an image would disturb readers interested in the cause of education for the same reasons that it disturbed other antislavery sympathizers, because violence of that kind threatened the stability of the new republic, which depended on the restraint of men's depraved passions. Conservative support for education did not lead all anti-Jacobins to antislavery. For example, the Massachusetts minister Simeon Doggett, whose mother had been born in the South, agreed that slavery constituted a social wrong, but he warned that abolition would unleash greater ills. Anti-Jacobin fears of violence drove Doggett to worry that uncompensated emancipation could lead to a slaveholders' "reign of terror," and that continued agitation by immediate abolitionists would provoke violent slave rebellions as well as a civil war between the North and South.[133] Doggett was unwilling to embrace immediate emancipation because it agitated the fears of violent disorder that had first inspired his conservative pedagogy.

While conservative anti-Jacobins often eschewed immediatist abolition, they frequently embraced gradualist compromises such as colonization. Jesse Torrey, a leading reformer of the early nineteenth century, combined anti-Jacobinism, antislavery, and support for education in his books *A Portraiture of Domestic Slavery* (1817) and *The Moral Instructor* (1819). More conservative in his temperament than later abolitionists, Torrey shied away from immediate abolitionism. Instead he advocated extending education to slaves to lead them gradually along the path to freedom. "Intellectual and moral improvement," he argued, "is the safe and permanent basis, on which the arch of eventual freedom to the enslaved Africans may be gradually erected." At a time when slaveholders were becoming increasingly anxious about the spread of literacy among their chattel servants, Torrey advocated that "every slave, less than thirty years of age of either sex, be taught the art

---

[132] Hitchcock, *Bloomsgrove*, 2:232–43.
[133] Simeon Doggett, *Two Discourses on the Subject of Slavery* (Boston, Mass., 1835), 20–2.

of reading." Slaveholders frequently resisted calls to educate their slaves by arguing that literacy led to slave rebellion, both in the United States and in the Caribbean. Torrey retorted that education was a "pacific weapon" and that ignorance was the true root of violence. Wherever violence held sway, Torrey argued, "ignorance is the magic spell, which sustains its scepter." That observation extended from black slaves to the peasants of France. An essay Torrey included in *The Moral Instructor* (1819) blamed France's descent into "lawless and blood acts" on the absence of a system of national education. To eliminate the violence of both transatlantic radicalism and slavery, Torrey advocated systems of education that would train youths in republican character.[134]

The connection between educational reform and humanitarian reform has not previously gone unnoticed. However, historians have typically assumed that the connection between these movements lay in softening views of humanity and the abandonment of the doctrine of depravity. For example, in an essay on the history of the family, David Brion Davis argued:

Parents who became deeply involved in the welfare and the future of each child easily gravitated toward the modern ideal of developing the best potentialities of every human being. This humanitarian ideal probably originated in changing familial relations and in a growing tendency to perceive children as embodiments not of original sin but of innocence and inclinations that could be trained for good or ill.[135]

As counterintuitive as it may appear, the example of education demonstrates that dark forebodings too have been generative of progressive movements to ameliorate the condition of American society. Distrustful visions of human nature inspired early national pedagogues to advocate for education as a means to control a potentially rebellious citizenry. Yet they imagined that by controlling human violence, education would enable every person to experience his humanity most fully. This point is made plain in a sermon delivered by a young minister-teacher to introduce an "exhibition" given by his students: "Train up children in that way in which they will make valuable members of a community," he instructed his listeners, quoting from the biblical proverb, "and in that way also, which will secure to them, *joy, peace,* and *happiness* of mind as long as they continue to exist."[136] By disciplining the heart, educational reformers believed they were increasing

---

[134] Jesse Torrey, *A Portraiture of Domestic Slavery, in the United States: With Reflections on the Practicability of Restoring the Moral Rights of the Slave, without Impairing the Legal Privileges of the Possessor* ... (Philadelphia, Pa., 1817; repr. 1970), 21–4; Jesse Torrey, *The Moral Instructor, and Guide to Virtue and Happiness in Five Parts with an Appendix, Containing a Constitution and Form of Subscription for the Institution of Free Public Libraries* (Ballston Spa, N.Y., 1819), 191–6.

[135] David Brion Davis, *From Homicide to Slavery: Studies in American Culture* (New York, 1986), 178.

[136] Brown, "Importance Of ... Education," 8. Italics in original.

the powers of rationality, and thereby enabling people to fully realize their humanity.

After the fall of New England Calvinism during the antebellum era, many who had come of age suffering the torments of a theology that emphasized depravity and hell torments looked back with little fondness. Horace Mann, the Massachusetts antislavery humanitarian who is often credited with forcing through the nation's first compulsory school-attendance laws, was raised in a milieu of strident anti-Jacobinism, attending church services led by the ultra-Calvinist Francophobic minister Nathanael Emmons. Mann's biographer, his second wife, the Unitarian reformer Mary Peabody Mann, described Mann's humanitarian work as the outgrowth of his rejection of Puritanism; revolt at the human anguish immanent within Calvinist doctrine motivated Mann to seek the welfare of humanity. Yet despite Mann's rejection of the old doctrine, he admitted, "My nerves are still keenly Calvinistic." Throughout his life, he remained strongly influenced by the childhood lessons about humanity that he had received from Emmons. The impressions of Mann's childhood can be traced in the humanitarian work for which he is best remembered: his service as secretary of the Massachusetts State Board of Education, established in 1837. As secretary, Mann argued that "every child should be educated: if not educated by its own father, the State should appoint a father to it." Sounding much like the conservative pedagogues of his childhood, Mann argued that the state was the political father of the nation's youths. Concerned about the increasing violence that characterized the riotous 1830s, Mann argued that the state had to educate children before the nation "revert[ed] to barbarism." Although Horace Mann rejected the orthodoxy of his childhood religious experiences, his humanitarian support for compulsory education strongly bore their imprint.[137]

[137] Mary Tyler Peabody Mann, *Life of Horace Mann. By His Wife* (Boston, Mass., 1865), 7, 72, 86.

6

Growing Up Anti-Jacobin

The Federalist–Abolitionist Connection Reconsidered

The child heard the grown-ups talking, about the monster named embargo, and the evil Jacobins who controlled it. At church and at home, the child's father Reverend Weld told frightening stories about how the Jacobins were "assassins" who murdered people. Right now his father and Dr. Chapman were talking intently in the study, but Thoda had stopped listening to their conversation. In the hallway he had spied the visitor's gold-headed cane. The knob looked warm and shiny, would the metal feel cold to the touch? Thoda would look important walking down the street holding the shiny cane. He could use it to punt stones out of his path, or to knock on people's doors. Absorbed in his imagination, Thoda didn't notice when Dr. Chapman entered the hallway. The stern visitor caught Thoda touching the cane and sharply rebuked him. Terrified by the angry grown-up, Thoda screamed "You're a Jacobin!" then ran as swiftly as possible out the door.[1]

The fiery abolitionist Theodore Dwight Weld, born in Hampton, Connecticut, in 1803, grew up in the cultural milieu of the anti-Jacobin reaction. His grandfather the Reverend Ezra Weld, pastor of the Congregationalist church in Braintree, Massachusetts, published a sermon on the danger of the French Illuminati in 1799. Theodore Dwight Weld's father, the Reverend Ludovicus Weld, assumed the mantle of Ezra's orthodoxy, preaching his own attacks on Franco–Jeffersonian corruption. In an 1804 Fast Day sermon Ludovicus warned his parishioners against false prophets who posed as *"Friends of the People,"* yet would lead them into the violence of French anarchy. Weld's namesake, Theodore Dwight – a relation of his mother – was a leading anti-French propagandist, politician, and antislavery advocate. Theodore Dwight's popular narratives of French revolutionaries blowing bodies from cannons and skinning corpses for shoe leather helped spread Gothic anti-Jacobinism throughout the United States. Considering

---

[1] The anecdote of Theodore Dwight Weld calling Dr. Chapman a Jacobin is found in Robert H. Abzug, *Passionate Liberator: Theodore Dwight Weld and the Dilemma of Reform* (New York, 1980), 23.

this family background, it is no wonder that the worst curse little Thoda (Theodore Dwight Weld's childhood pet name) could fling at a frightening grown-up was "Jacobin."[2]

The high tide of American anti-Jacobinism, from 1790 to 1815, was also the period during which the antislavery or abolitionist leaders of the 1830s, 1840s, and 1850s were born and raised.[3] A great majority of these reformers were born into families that, like Theodore Dwight Weld's, feared the French Revolution and strongly supported Calvinist orthodoxy and Federalist politics. Anti-Jacobinism resounded in their homes and in their churches; it was the language of the abolitionists' childhoods. The moderate antislavery writer Catharine Maria Sedgwick recalled how during her childhood her father, the antislavery Federalist politician Theodore Sedgwick, "habitually" gave voice to his antidemocratic prejudices by speaking of the people as Jacobins and sansculottes. As adults, she and her antislavery brothers Theodore and Henry had far more sympathy for democratic politics than their father, yet the influence of his critique of slavery's violence imprinted them powerfully.[4] If the abolitionist children of anti-Jacobins rebelled against the elitist prejudices of their parents, they were yet influenced by their parents' Francophobic sensibility. They took to heart its Gothic rhetorical style and its testimony against anarchic violence and southern slaveholder violence in particular. Decades later, antislavery reformers' criticisms of slavery and slaveholders revealed the influence that anti-Jacobinism had on their childhoods.

Edmund Quincy, the radical abolitionist son of the antislavery and anti-Jacobin politician Josiah Quincy, drew a straight line from his father's political sentiments to the abolitionist movement. The political attitudes of his father's generation had been rooted in their understanding of "the constitution of human nature"; fears of human depravity led Josiah Quincy to repudiate the French Revolution and the slave-owning oligarchy as twin threats to the new republic. Although Edmund Quincy recognized that the

---

[2] Theodore Dwight, *An Oration, Spoken at Hartford, in the State of Connecticut, on the Anniversary of American Independence, July 4th, 1798* (Hartford, Conn., 1798); Ezra Weld, *A Discourse, Delivered April 25, 1799 Being the Day of Fasting and Prayer throughout the United States of America* (Boston, Mass., 1799); Ludovicus Weld, *A Sermon, Delivered on the Day of the Annual Fast in Connecticut, March 30, 1804* (Windham [Ct.], 1804).

[3] Common historiographical usage distinguishes between radical *abolitionists*, who advocated the immediate end to slavery in America and the restoration of black civil rights, and more conservative *antislavery reformers*, who supported gradual means to end slavery. While I have reserved the term *abolitionist* for supporters of immediate emancipation, the chapter uses the terms *antislavery* more inclusively to refer to all movements to end slavery.

[4] Mary E. Dewey, ed., *Life and Letters of Catharine M. Sedgwick* (New York, 1871), 35. In a letter Catharine Sedgwick wrote to her father in 1804, when she was only fourteen, she described a local election as a triumph of the "Jacobins" (80). A letter from her brother Robert makes the same familiar use of the term (47). Theodore Sedgwick Sr. was instrumental in establishing emancipation in Massachusetts.

Federalists' elitism made their extinction a "moral and political necessity," he praised "the moral influence of their resistance" against the violent politics of the slaveholding party. Edmund Quincy remembered his father as the first leader to divine "the fatal nature of slavery" for the republic, and he celebrated the influence that his father's opinions against slavery had on his own childhood. Although many abolitionists embraced democratic politics that clearly defined them from their politically conservative parents, abolitionists were able to use the anti-Jacobin critique of violence that they absorbed during childhood as a powerful rhetoric to attack slavery.[5]

Similarly, the abolitionist children of orthodox religious leaders often departed from their parents' theological conservatism, yet retained the ethical arguments against human violence that were embedded within it. As an adolescent, Theodore Dwight Weld followed his father and grandfather's path into religious conservatism, enrolling in the orthodox Andover Seminary when he was fifteen. However, health problems forced him to leave the seminary and he moved with his family to upstate New York, where he was converted by Charles Grandison Finney to the Arminian doctrines of the Second Great Awakening. Despite this rebellion against his family's Calvinist orthodoxy, Weld retained the concerns about human passions that figured so prominently in the religious culture of his childhood.[6] To address those concerns Weld became an educational reformer, seeking to use manual labor as a means to train young men to control their disorderly passions. In 1832, he shifted the focus of his reformist concerns to slavery, organizing the famous Lane Seminary debates of 1833 and 1834, which swept a generation of young people into the abolitionist movement. For several years, Weld worked as an itinerant antislavery lecturer, retelling cruelty stories about slave masters giving into their violent passions. Weld later collected these stories and many more in his famous abolitionist pamphlet *American Slavery As It Is* (1839), a catalog of horrors that stylistically reproduced the anti-Jacobin sensationalism of his childhood.[7]

---

[5] Edmund Quincy, *Life of Josiah Quincy of Massachusetts* (Boston, Mass., 1867), 42, 62, 70; M. A. De Wolfe Howe, "Biographer's Bait: A Reminder of Edmund Quincy," *Proceedings of the Massachusetts Historical Society* 68 (1944–7). For Josiah Quincy's anti-Jacobinism, see Josiah Quincy, *An Oration Pronounced July 4, 1798, at the Request of the Inhabitants of the Town of Boston in Commemoration of the Anniversary of American Independence* (Boston, Mass., 1798).

[6] The radical abolitionist Henry Clarke Wright also attended Andover Seminary and followed a conservative religious path into ministry and reform; but like Weld, Wright later abandoned religious orthodoxy, eventually embracing Christian anarchism and utterly repudiating organized religion; Lewis Perry, *Radical Abolitionism; Anarchy and the Government of God in Antislavery Thought* (Ithaca, N.Y., 1973); Lewis Perry, *Childhood, Marriage, and Reform: Henry Clarke Wright, 1797–1870* (Chicago, Ill., 1980).

[7] Abzug, *Passionate Liberator*. Marcus Wood suggests that *American Slavery As It Is* was modeled after a text that anti-Jacobins had modeled their literature on: John Foxe's *Book of Martyrs*; Marcus Wood, *Blind Memory: Visual Representations of Slavery in England and America, 1780–1865* (New York, 2000), 84–5.

For two hundred double-columned pages, *American Slavery* reproduced testimony after testimony of the "barbarous inhumanity" suffered by the slaves. Torture followed torture: whipped backs clotted up with gore; women whipped until they suffered miscarriages; men whipped to death; cruel punishments, murders, and rapes. At the core of the book lay Weld's concern that arbitrary power unleashed people's worst passions; slavery was the inversion of education, as it uncivilized people and developed their violent tendencies. Even the most well-intentioned person, Weld insisted, could not withstand the corrupting influence of being a slave master. In the text, Weld used the example of the French Revolution to prove his point by comparing slave masters to Jacobins: "Perhaps no man has lived in modern times, whose name excites such horror as that of Robespierre. Yet it is notorious that he was naturally of a benevolent disposition, and tender sympathies." Arbitrary power had corrupted Robespierre, and it corrupted slaveholders as well. Uncontrolled human passions produced anarchic bloodshed. Beyond such specific allusions, Weld used the example of the reaction to the French Revolution to guide his construction of the text. Rather than rely primarily on political or Christian arguments against slavery, Weld turned to the Gothic, presenting a parade of cruelties familiar from the anti-Jacobin reaction. Weld's sister-in-law Sarah M. Grimké, an abolitionist lecturer who helped Weld to compile the book's materials, defended the text by observing that torture had a "resistless power" to move audiences. Grimké and Weld had learned this axiom from Weld's progenitors.[8]

The violence of antislavery discourse such as Weld's once prompted historians to argue that abolitionists were mentally unbalanced. According to David Donald, "The historian should be alert to see in extraordinary and unprovoked violence of expression the symptom of some profound social or psychological dislocation." This argument accurately captured how violent language served as a form of assault but falsely assumed that only derangement could explain the assault.[9] Since Donald, two generations of historians have thoroughly vindicated the abolitionists as sane, forward-thinking individuals who positively addressed the most terrible injustice in American history. But little consideration has been paid to the supposition that violent language is a red flag indicating social pathology.[10] This chapter returns to

---

[8] Theodore Dwight Weld and American Anti-Slavery Society, *American Slavery as It Is: Testimony of a Thousand Witnesses* (New York, 1968), 121. *American Slavery*'s epigraph quoted the British antislavery politician Charles James Fox: "true humanity consists not in a SQUEAMISH EAR, but in listening to the story of human suffering and endeavoring to relieve it."

[9] David Herbert Donald, "Toward a Reconsideration of Abolitionists," in *Lincoln Reconsidered; Essays on the Civil War Era* (New York, 1956). The root of abolitionists' mental problems, according to Donald, lay in their status as the children of traditional elites who were being displaced by an industrializing, urbanizing society. This argument has long since been discredited.

[10] For an overview of the enormous historiography on abolitionism, see John R. McKivigan, ed., *History of the American Abolitionist Movement*, 5 vols. (New York, 1999).

the violence of expression employed by the abolitionists and seeks its origins not in the maladjustment of the speakers but in the linguistic milieu of their childhoods. The violent language of abolitionism must be understood as the cultural inheritance of the Federalist and Calvinist reaction to the French Revolution.[11]

Emphasizing the significance of anti-Jacobinism to the formation of antebellum abolitionism provides a new answer to the perennial historical riddle: why did so many abolitionists come from conservative families?[12] But identifying the connection between anti-Jacobinism and antebellum antislavery should not collapse the diversity of the abolitionist movement. Antislavery leaders demonstrated an enormous variety of reform styles, political identities, religious faiths, and even family backgrounds. Rather than provide a systematic explanation for the conversion process that privileges a single mode of abolition, this chapter brings together radicals and moderates, politicians and anarchists, sectarians and antisectarians, and blacks and whites by identifying a significant common element of their antislavery reform: the anti-Jacobin sensibility. Antebellum antislavery included a range of reform styles and personal temperaments so diverse as to defy categorization. Abolitionists shared a common legacy, but each made different use

---

[11] This thesis challenges Karen Halttunen's influential argument that a new progressive view of humanity, which emphasized sympathy for other people's pain and suffering, led to the effusion of bloody imagery in abolitionist literature during the antebellum era. Karen Halttunen, "Humanitarianism and the Pornography of Pain in Anglo-American Culture," *American Historical Review* 100 (Apr. 1995).

[12] Historians have never agreed on the answer to this question; see Matthew Mason, "Attacking the 'Covenant with Death' across the Generations: The Link between New England's Federalists and Abolitionists," (2006); Kevin Gannon, "Their Fathers' Sons; Their Fathers' Sins: New England Federalists and Radical Abolitionists" (paper presented at the Society for the History of the Early American Republic, Providence, R.I., 2004); Bertram Wyatt-Brown, *Yankee Saints and Southern Sinners* (Baton Rouge, La., 1985); Lawrence Goodheart, "Child-Rearing, Conscience, and Conversion to Abolitionism: The Example of Elizur Wright Jr.," *Psychohistory Review* 12 (1984); Abzug, *Passionate Liberator*, 105–8; David Brion Davis, *The Problem of Slavery in the Age of Revolution, 1770–1823* (Ithaca, N.Y., 1975), 296; Lois W. Banner, "Religion and Reform in the Early Republic: The Role of Youth," *American Quarterly* 23 (Dec. 1971); James M. Banner, *To the Hartford Convention: The Federalists and the Origins of Party Politics in Massachusetts, 1789–1815* (New York, 1970), chap. 3; Linda K. Kerber, *Federalists in Dissent: Imagery and Ideology in Jeffersonian America* (Ithaca, N.Y., 1970), 62; Silvan S. Tomkins, "The Psychology of Commitment: The Constructive Role of Violence and Suffering for the Individual and for His Society," in *The Antislavery Vanguard, New Essays on the Abolitionists*, ed. Martin B. Duberman (Princeton, N.J., 1965). Historians who challenge the significance of the Federalist–abolitionist connection include Sean Wilentz, "Jeffersonian Democracy and the Origins of Political Antislavery in the United States: The Missouri Crisis Revisited," *Journal of the Historical Society* 4 (2004); John Kyle Day, "The Federalist Press and Slavery in the Age of Jefferson," *Historian: A Journal of History* 65 (2003). For a more thorough review of the literature, see Rachel Hope Cleves "Mortal Eloquence: Violence, Slavery, and Anti-Jacobinism in the Early American Republic" (Ph.D., University of California, Berkeley), 212–17.

of this inheritance. Ultimately, whether antebellum antislavery advocates sought to end slavery gradually, to end slavery immediately, to end slavery expansion, or to begin a slave rebellion, they found inspiration in the ethical arguments and linguistic tropes of the anti-Jacobin reaction.

Growing Up Anti-Jacobin

Writing after the election of 1800, the Massachusetts Federalist Fisher Ames complained that many in the newly empowered Jeffersonian party "want *no* government, and are anarchists. Some plot for a revolutionary Robespierrism; they are Jacobins thirsting for blood and plunder."[13] Such comments have earned Ames the reputation as an eighteenth-century Rasputin whose "violent word-pictures of Jacobins" and "doleful prophecies... hung over the Federalist house forever." The violence of anti-Jacobin language has carried a strong measure of blame for the defeat of the Federalist Party in the early nineteenth century; bloody mutterings seem ill suited to the optimistic individualism of the new century.[14] Yet violent language did not seem archaic to many abolitionists; it represented a vital tool for fighting the scourge of slavery. In a public address that William Lloyd Garrison published on the first page of the first edition of his abolitionist journal the *Liberator*, he conceded that "many object to the severity of my language," yet he insisted, "is there not cause for severity?"[15] Garrison did not disparage Fisher Ames; he used Ames as a model.[16]

Born in 1805 in Newburyport, Massachusetts, the home of Elijah Parish and the epicenter of Essex County conservatism, Garrison apprenticed himself in 1818 to Ephraim Allen, editor of the local Federalist newspaper, the *Newburyport Herald*. At work, Garrison absorbed the political writings of Fisher Ames, Elijah Parish (printed by Allen), and Timothy Pickering by reading through Allen's extensive political library as well as back issues of the *Herald*. In addition to the frequent anti-Jacobin fulminations in these

---

[13] Fisher Ames to Christopher Gore, Dec. 29, 1800. Fisher Ames, *Works of Fisher Ames: With a Selection from His Speeches and Correspondence*, ed. John Thornton Kirkland and Seth Ames (Boston, Mass., 1854), 1:299.

[14] Shaw Livermore, *The Twilight of Federalism; the Disintegration of the Federalist Party, 1815–1830* (Princeton, N.J., 1962), 8. More recent arguments for the vitality of Federalism in the post-1815 era have focused on the young Federalists who moved beyond the "apocalyptic" language of the old guard like Ames; Marshall Foletta, *Coming to Terms with Democracy: Federalist Intellectuals and the Shaping of an American Culture* (Charlottesville, Va., 2001).

[15] "To the Public," *Liberator*, Jan. 1, 1831.

[16] Marc Arkin, "The Federalist Trope: Power and Passion in Abolitionist Rhetoric," *Journal of American History* 88 (2001). Also Mary Stoughton Locke, *Anti-Slavery in America, from the Introduction of African Slaves to the Prohibition of the Slave Trade, 1619–1808* (Gloucester, Mass., 1965), 91; Jonathan D. Sassi, *A Republic of Righteousness: The Public Christianity of the Post-Revolutionary New England Clergy* (Oxford, 2001), 186.

texts, Garrison discovered many passionate indictments of southern slaveholding violence. In Allen's home, where he boarded, Garrison received
a further literary education by reading the British anti-Jacobin antislavery
author Hannah More, whose works reinforced the connection between the
French Revolution and slave masters' violence.[17] In 1826, Garrison founded
his own Federalist newspaper in Newburyport, which he published for six
months before moving to Boston. He continued pursuing a career as an
editor and evangelical reformer, as he moved steadily toward an antislavery
commitment during the late 1820s. His first aggressive antislavery discourse,
delivered at the Park Street Church in Boston on July 4, 1829, drew on familiar Federalist–Calvinist arguments and condemned southern slaveholders for
giving way to their passions. As Garrison pursued the logic of antislavery
over the long course of his abolitionist career, he became increasingly radical – embracing an antipolitical and antisectarian philosophy of Christian
anarchism that would have horrified Fisher Ames or Hannah More. But
Garrison never renounced their anti-Jacobinism.[18]

From the very beginning of his abolitionist career through the Civil War,
Garrison continuously used anti-Jacobin language to assail slavery, slaveholders, and antiabolitionists. In articles, speeches, and pamphlets, Garrison
described slaveholding as a system of Jacobin violence. Garrison's use of
French Revolutionary imagery was not gratuitous but firmly rooted in the
anti-Jacobin ethical argument. "The tempest of human passion is raging,"
Garrison wrote in true Fisher Ames style following the antiabolitionist riots
of 1835. What is the cause of this "anarchy" and "Jacobinism" he asked:
"THE ACCURSED SYSTEM OF SLAVERY!" Like Ames, Parish, and More, Garrison argued that slavery was an uncivilizing process that transformed its
supporters into violent Jacobins.[19] The anti-Jacobin trope "reign of terror"
also figured prominently in Garrison's writings: to describe mob attacks on
abolitionists, slave hunters' pursuits of runaways, the bloody battle between
slaveholders and free settlers for the future of Kansas, and the lynching of
northern visitors and antislavery sympathizers in the South from 1859 to
1860. At a personal level, the *Liberator* labeled slavery's varied supporters

---

[17] Another antislavery leader who recalled the influence of Hannah More's writings on his
childhood was the Democratic Senator Robert Rantoul Jr. Rantoul developed such a strong
interest in French history that he not only gave anti-Jacobin speeches but also collected more
than 1,300 volumes relating to the French Revolution, from which he planned to write a
history of the "systemized carnage [that] deluged the cities with the purple blood of human
sacrifice" during the reigns of Danton, Robespierre, and Marat. Unfortunately, Rantoul's
early death from "brain fever" prevented him from accomplishing this goal; Robert Rantoul
and Luther Hamilton, *Memoirs, Speeches and Writings of Robert Rantoul Jr.* (Boston,
Mass., 1854), 186–7.
[18] Henry Mayer, *All on Fire: William Lloyd Garrison and the Abolition of Slavery* (New York,
1998); Mason, "Attacking the Covenant."
[19] "The Reign of Terror," Aug. 15, 1835, *Liberator*, 131; "Miscellaneous," Nov. 7, 1835,
Liberator, 180.

as Robespierres and Dantons. Even during the 1860s, Garrison continued
to use anti-Jacobin language in the *Liberator* to describe the violence of the
crumbling slave system.[20]

The influence of anti-Jacobinism on William Lloyd Garrison's antislavery rhetoric also extended beyond direct references to shape his writing style
overall. Garrison adopted from his models a willingness to write in a violent language that challenged genteel sensibility. Most strikingly, Garrison
demonstrated his willingness to overturn traditional barriers on antislavery speech by tackling the subject of slave rebellion. In the initial issue
of the *Liberator*, after arguing that the abolitionist cause required severe
speech, Garrison plunged into the subject of slave rebellion to demonstrate
his commitment to using violent language. "The question," he confessed,
"is whether such language can be held by a white man, having a clear view
of its results to a black. 'Grant your opinions to be just,' a slave owner
once said to me, 'if you talk so to the slaves, they will fall to cutting their
masters throats.'" Was it just to use severe language against slavery even if
it carried the danger of inciting the slaves to rebellion? Garrison answered
that the *Liberator* did not preach rebellion but, "that if any people were
ever justified in throwing off the yoke of their tyrants, the slaves are that
people." Moreover, he continued, the true inspiration of slave rebellion was
not northern abolitionism but southern abuse.[21]

Garrison defended violent language as necessary to the antislavery cause
and exculpated such language from responsibility for slave rebellions, which
had their true origins in slaveholder abuse. Over the following three decades,
Garrison never shied away from filling the pages of the *Liberator* with
notices, warnings, and general talk of slave rebellion. He committed its violent imagery, along with every other rhetorical tool, to overcoming slavery.[22]
Garrison's repeated writings on the subject of slave rebellion highlight the
double impact that anti-Jacobinism had on abolitionists. From models like
Elijah Parish, who also defended slave rebellion, Garrison both absorbed a
critique of slaveholders' Jacobin violence and learned how violent language
could become an outlet for fantasies of violent retribution.

William Lloyd Garrison represented a radical model of abolitionism,
but antislavery advocates across the broad spectrum of reform styles experienced similar influences from anti-Jacobinism. At the opposite extreme
from Garrison stood the Congregationalist minister, Whig politician, and
Amherst professor Samuel Melancthon Worcester, son of the anti-Jacobin
minister Samuel Worcester and nephew of the anti-Jacobin ministers Noah

---

[20] See citations for each usage below.
[21] "Walker's Appeal" (nos. 1 and 2), *Liberator*, Jan. 8 and May 14, 1831. See the insightful
discussion of these articles in Louis P. Masur, *1831, Year of Eclipse* (New York, 2001).
[22] Jane H. Pease and William Henry Pease, *Bound with Them in Chains: A Biographical
History of the Antislavery Movement* (Westport, Conn., 1972), 36.

Worcester and Thomas Worcester.[23] S. M. Worcester was a conservative reformer, yet his life and writings reveal a connection between intense anti-Jacobin influence and strong antislavery sentiment.

Born in Massachusetts in 1801, Worcester spent his childhood deeply steeped in the cultural reaction to the French Revolution. Later in life, Worcester recalled that the "sanguinary" events in France during the 1790s and 1800s had obsessed his father, whose opinions were "in fervid harmony with the sentiments of Fisher Ames." Letters that Worcester's father wrote during the first decades of the 1800s frequently addressed the horrors of French democracy abroad and at home, and showed the influence of books by anti-Jacobin extremists such as Abbé Barruel and John Robison. The senior Reverend Worcester also expressed his "fervid" opinions in his sermons, and no doubt in the private lessons for advanced students that he offered within the family home, thus exposing his son to the anti-Jacobin pedagogy of the age. In addition to his political conservatism, Worcester senior expressed a high level of cultural conservatism by adhering to a strict disciplinarian approach to childrearing, seeking to break each of his children's wills before they were six.[24]

In summary, Samuel Melancthon Worcester grew up in an environment of extreme political, religious, and cultural conservatism; yet that was leavened with a heady dose of humanitarian sentiment. Worcester's father and uncles founded peace societies, missionary societies, and social welfare societies, and each incorporated antislavery arguments into their political and religious outlooks.[25] This combined inheritance of cultural conservatism and social humanitarianism manifested in S. M. Worcester's antislavery writings during the antebellum era. In the mid-1820s, before Garrison "inaugurated" the abolitionist movement with his famous 1829 speech at Park Street Church, Worcester published a series of six essays repudiating slavery in the evangelical *Boston Recorder and Telegraph*. Under the pseudonym

[23] Samuel Worcester, *Calamity, Danger, and Hope; a Sermon, Preached at the Tabernacle in Salem, July 23, 1812: The Day of the Public Fast in Massachusetts, on Account of the War with Great-Britain* (Salem, Mass., 1812); Samuel Worcester, *Courage and Success to the Good: A Discourse, Delivered . . . Aug. 20, 1812, the Day of National Humiliation and Prayer . . . : Also, the Substance of a Discourse Delivered . . . August 9, 1812* (Salem, Mass., 1812); Noah Worcester, *The Substance of Two Sermons, Occasioned by the Late Declaration of War Preached at Salisbury, in New Hampshire, on Lord's Days, June 28th and July 5th, 1812* (Concord, N.H., 1812); Noah Worcester, *Abraham and Lot: A Sermon, on the Way of Peace, and the Evils of War: Delivered at Salisbury, in New-Hampshire, on the Day of the National Fast, August 20, 1812* (Concord, N.H., 1812).

[24] Samuel Melancthon Worcester, *The Life and Labors of Rev. Samuel Worcester, D.D.: Former Pastor of the Tabernacle Church, Salem, Mass.* (Boston, Mass., 1852), 150, 226.

[25] Samuel Worcester was a founder of the American Board of Commissioners for Foreign Missions (ABCFM); Noah Worcester founded the Massachusetts Peace Society (MPS). For antislavery references, see Noah Worcester, *The Friend of Peace* (Boston, Mass., 1822); Worcester, *The Life and Labors of Rev. Samuel Worcester, D.D.*, 140.

Vigorinus, Worcester attacked slavery as a moral sin and a political evil. Like Garrison and the anti-Jacobin generation before him, Worcester showed a shocking willingness to confront the question of the justice of slave rebellion, despite the anger that he knew his opinion would inspire:

> And here I would ask the liberty to suggest a few inquiries, which, I expect, will meet with a very problematical reception. I would inquire, whether the slave has not a right to resort to the most violent measures, if necessary, in order to obtain his liberty? And if he has the least chance of success, are we not, as rational and consistent men, bound to justify him? . . . While I admit, that the people of the south are authorized to adopt every reasonable measure to prevent the horrors of insurrection, I firmly believe, that the slave has a right to immediate liberty, paramount to every claim of his master.

Worcester's defense of slave rebellion echoed the furious writings of Elijah Parish and Theodore Dwight, whose opinions held sway over his childhood.

Adopting a conservative reform persona, Worcester claimed to disavow violent language, pleading "let no one accuse me of dipping my pen in gall, or of giving an expression to the ravings of an infuriated imagination." He sustained this willful conservatism throughout the 1830s by giving support to the colonization movement, which most abolitionists repudiated as an unjust fraud. Yet Worcester's conservative vision of antislavery should not obscure the extreme challenge that he posed to the institution by defending slave rebellion. Disavowals aside, Worcester's vocal sympathy for slave rebellion as well as his later willingness to cooperate with the American Anti-Slavery Society (an umbrella group for immediate abolitionists) shows him to have imbibed a strong draught of rhetorical extremism from the cultural milieu of his youth. A later antislavery reform group that Worcester founded attacked slaveholders in familiar anti-Jacobin terms, for their mobbishness, their desire to "imbrue their hands in blood," their violent suppression of free speech, and their physical cruelty toward slaves.[26] Accepting the miserable moral and practical failings of the colonization movement, Worcester's writings nevertheless suggest that the legacy of anti-Jacobin infused even conservative antislavery with a certain violent passion.[27]

Abolitionists often moved through several reform styles over the course of their antislavery careers and carried the imprint of anti-Jacobinism into each branch of the movement. Like Samuel Melancthon Worcester, Joshua Leavitt was a young Congregationalist minister and conservative political

---

[26] Ethan Allen Andrews, *Slavery and the Domestic Slave-Trade in the United States. In a Series of Letters Addressed to the Executive Committee of the American Union for the Relief and Improvement of the Colored Race* (Boston, 1836), 17–19, 28–9, 98, 101–3.

[27] Vigorinus, "Slavery, No. V," *Boston Recorder and Telegraph*, July 22, 1825, 120. Curiously, while the first four essays of the series are signed "Vigorinus," the fifth and sixth essays are signed "Vigornius." For the complete Vigorinus/Vigornius essays, see *Boston Recorder and Telegraph* (1825), 104, 108, 112, 116, 120, 124.

partisan when he embarked upon his antislavery career in 1825 by publishing a series of antislavery articles in a Christian periodical. Like Worcester, he also showed a willingness to confront the specter of slave rebellion, arguing that Americans needed to engage in *"immediate"* discussion of the question of slavery and of slave rebellion in particular. However, unlike Worcester, Leavitt embraced increasingly political means and radical rhetoric to fight slavery over the next fifty years of his life.[28]

Leavitt was born in 1794 to a prominent orthodox family in western Massachusetts; both his grandfathers were patriots and religious conservatives (one a Congregationalist minister and the other a deacon), and his father was a Federalist state politician. He grew up in an atmosphere of vigorous antisouthern, anti-Jacobin sentiment and Hopkintonian "disinterested benevolence." At thirteen Leavitt professed his faith, then went to study at Yale where he protested the War of 1812 and supported the Hartford Convention. After a period practicing law, Leavitt embraced evangelical reform, studied for the ministry, became ordained in Connecticut, and embarked on a reform career strongly supported by his parents, with whom he kept in close communication. His choices were a reflection of the values that they sought to instill in him, yet he pursued his path of reform with a new willingness to challenge the standards of linguistic decorum imposed by the slave states.[29]

"Our Southern brethren are exceedingly unwilling to be reminded of their danger," Leavitt commented acerbically in his 1825 essay, but "who will say that a war of extermination will not ensue, in which the African cause may excite as much sympathy and as liberal contributions in England and the West Indies as the Greek cause has done in this country?" The peculiar construction of Leavitt's question, with its introductory clause "who will say," suggests two answers: both the obvious reply, that no one can deny the possibility of a popular slave rebellion, and a secondary reply, that Leavitt "will say" that slave rebellion is an imminent danger and a just cause. Leavitt announced his intention to attack slavery despite southern objections because slavery posed a greater threat to public safety than did southern anger. Every attempt at discussion of slavery, Leavitt complained, is always met with "a cry of danger: 'You will excite the slaves to insurrection.'...But I ask if there is now no danger?" Leavitt trumpeted the danger of slave rebellion to justify the need for immediate emancipation as well as the restoration of black civil rights.[30] Slavery would destroy the

---

[28] Joshua Leavitt, "People of Colour," *Christian Spectator*, Mar. 1, 1825, 130. Italics in original. Joshua Leavitt is identified as the author of this essay in Hugh Davis, *Joshua Leavitt, Evangelical Abolitionist* (Baton Rouge, La., 1990).

[29] Davis, *Joshua Leavitt.*

[30] Leavitt, "People of Colour," Mar. 1, 1825, 131, 136. Lemuel Haynes used a similar rhetorical technique in an 1813 sermon; Lemuel Haynes, *Black Preacher to White America: The Collected Writings of Lemuel Haynes, 1774–1833*, ed. Richard Newman (Brooklyn, N.Y., 1990), 153, 157.

United States, Leavitt warned, unless something effectual was done immediately. He dismissed the American Colonization Society (ACS) – soon to be the target of William Lloyd Garrison's wrath – as nothing but a "*safety valve.*" Abolition, Leavitt continued in his second essay, had to be "entire and speedy" and "*emancipation must take place on the spot where slavery exists.*" He insisted that the new president, John Quincy Adams, should turn the national government into an antislavery weapon. A youth spent enveloped in the anti-Jacobin sensibility prepared Leavitt to use rhetorical extremism as a weapon against his enemies.[31]

In 1828, Leavitt moved to New York to devote himself entirely to reform. Initially he worked for the American Seamen's Friend Society, while antislavery agitation played a secondary role in his reform agenda. Like Worcester, Leavitt embraced a conservative reform style during these years, publicly sympathetic to colonization but avoiding immediatism until 1833, when he "converted" and participated in establishing the American Anti-Slavery Society. Although Leavitt changed tactics, his rationale remained consistent; Leavitt attacked slavery as an uncivilizing institution that spread depravity throughout the United States. For the rest of the decade he worked with Garrison and other moral suasionists to turn American opinion against slavery, but in 1840 Leavitt again shifted gears by embracing political antislavery. Interestingly, Leavitt had carried his anti-Jacobin family along his shifting path through antebellum reform, and in the 1840s Leavitt's father served as the Liberty Party candidate for lieutenant governor of Massachusetts. Still later in his life, Leavitt progressed through Free-Soilism and Radical Republicanism; eventually he joined forces with the Democratic newspaper editor William Cullen Bryant, although he never joined the Democratic Party.

Throughout his long reform career, from 1828 until his death in 1873, Leavitt earned his living as a newspaper editor, and in each editorial position Leavitt consistently attacked slavery in anti-Jacobin terms. As the editor of the *New York Evangelist* from 1832 to 1837, as the editor of the *Emancipator* from 1837 to 1840, and as editor of the retitled *Emancipator and Free American* during the 1840s, Leavitt published articles describing proslavery violence as a "reign of terror." Events as wide ranging as riots in Boston, New York, and Philadelphia; the murder of abolitionist Elijah P. Lovejoy in Illinois; antiabolitionist mobs in Cincinnati; and the lynching of antislavery southerners added up to a reign of terror in which Jacobin slaveholders were using bloodshed to preserve their interests.[32] An article in the *Emancipator and Free American* condemning the antiblack Philadelphia riots of 1842 not only described the violence as a "reign of terror" but also integrated other

[31] Leavitt, "People of Colour," May 1, 1825, 239, 246.
[32] "The Reign of Terror," *New York Evangelist*, Oct. 8, 1835; "Reign of Terror – the Press in Danger! – American blood has flowed!!!" *Emancipator*, Dec. 14, 1837; "Southern Ideas upon the Right of Petition," *Emancipator*, Jan. 25, 1838; "Reasons for Discussing the Subject of Slavery," *Emancipator*, Feb. 1, 1838; "Old No. 9 – Hon. S. G. Goodrich," *Emancipator and Free American*, Oct. 13, 1842.

vocabulary common to anti-Jacobinism such as *cannibal* and *demoniac*. In a particularly Gothic passage, the article described how "the sight of two colored men in the streets aroused [the mob's] cannibal fury; they were set upon in the most furious manner, and barely escaped with their lives."[33] In Leavitt's newspapers, slavery's supporters took the shape of France's fishwives and sansculottes, driven by insensate fury, thirsty for blood.

Anti-Jacobin sentiments also shaped antislavery novelists of the antebellum era. Fiction served as an important venue for spreading abolitionism among the general public, a fact remarked upon by President Lincoln in his famous greeting to the author of *Uncle Tom's Cabin*, Harriet Beecher Stowe: "so you're the little woman who wrote the book that started this great war." Stowe's father, Lyman Beecher, was the protégé of the anti-Jacobin Yale president Timothy Dwight, and Beecher rooted his Christian conversion to the anti-Jacobin reaction at Yale in 1795.[34] Many of Stowe's fellow novelists came from similar backgrounds and demonstrated strong anti-Jacobin influences in their books.

Richard Hildreth, the author of the first American abolitionist novel, *The Slave; or, Memoirs of Archy Moore* (1836), emerged from the anti-Jacobin milieu and in his writings characterized slaveholders as violent Jacobins guilty of Gothic enormities. Hildreth was born in 1807, the son of Hosea Hildreth, a Congregationalist minister and pedagogue who preached anti-Jacobinism and Federalism throughout his son's youth. Hosea Hildreth viewed violent Jacobinism as an uncivilizing process that threatened to transform the United States into a pit of violence and cruelty.[35] Theophilus Parsons, the arch-Federalist jurist and rabid anti-Jacobin, also contributed toward shaping Richard Hildreth's worldview when he guided the young man's legal studies during the 1820s. The novelist inherited both men's revulsion toward "Jacobin" bloodshed, and after a visit to the South in 1834 he came to believe that southern slaveholders posed a violent Jacobin threat to the United States.

Hildreth's novel *The Slave* tells the story of Archy, the enslaved mulatto son of Colonel Moore. Moore is characterized as a "warm democrat" and sympathizer with the "French Republicans," yet when Archy seeks his own measure of autonomy, Moore responds by whipping Archy "with such violence, that the lash penetrated [his] flesh at every blow, and the blood ran trickling down [his] legs and stood in little puddles at [his] feet." Hildreth uses Gothic descriptions of slave violence to describe the injustice of the

---

33 "More of the Philadelphia Riots," *Emancipator and Free American*, Aug. 25, 1842.

34 For Beecher's recollections of the influence of the French Revolution on his youth see, Lyman Beecher and Charles Beecher, *Autobiography, Correspondence, Etc. Of Lyman Beecher, D.D.* (New York, 1866), 37, 43.

35 Hosea Hildreth, *A Discourse Delivered before the Washington Benevolent Society, in Exeter, on the Day of Their Anniversary, May 4th, 1813* (Exeter, [N.H.], 1813).

institution. Like Thomas Brangan, Hildreth envisages slavery as silencing its victims. During a torture scene, Moore stifles Archy's screams by "drawing a handkerchief from his pocket, [and] he thrust it into [his] mouth, and rammed it down [his] throat with the butt-end of his whip-handle." And like Branagan, Hildreth describes slavery's violence as akin to Jacobinism. In the voice of Archy Moore, Hildreth argues that "the authority of masters over their slaves is in general a continual reign of terror."[36] Drawing from the cultural milieu of his childhood, Hildreth used anti-Jacobin rhetorical techniques to win the sympathies of his readers.

Hildreth must have judged the tactic a success, as he returned to it several years later in a political volume titled *Despotism in America*. Hildreth's analysis of American politics repeatedly compares southern slaveholders to Jacobins. Defending the democratic rights of black people, Hildreth argues that southern slaveholders are violent despots who like the French Revolutionaries breech all law in pursuit of their violent ends; every time rumors of a slave insurrection spread, Hildreth argues, "many a rustic Danton" rise up to oversee tribunals of violence, and "hanging, shooting, and burning become the order of the day." *Despotism in America* demands racial equality and true democracy in the United States, insisting that northerners cease bowing to the "grim and bloody shrine of this political Moloch" (slavery). For Hildreth, democracy represents an ideal, which southern states stain by using despotic Jacobin measures against slaves and their defenders. While Hildreth rejected the political conservatism of the older generation by praising egalitarianism and popular politics in *Despotism in America*, he embraced their moral and political arguments against slavery, transforming early national anti-Jacobin antislavery into a radical social and political rhetoric.[37]

Hildreth, Leavitt, Garrison, and Worcester embraced four different styles of abolitionist reform (literary, political, radical, and conservative), yet each remained within the umbrella of political–cultural networks originating in 1790s Federalism. Worcester and Leavitt both belonged to political parties that had emerged from the embers of Federalism (the Whigs and the Liberty Party); Hildreth praised democracy, yet identified the Federalist tradition rather than Jeffersonianism as democracy's starting point; Garrison rejected politics altogether, but his radical beliefs nonetheless represented the logical extreme of the Federalist–Congregationalist Benevolent Empire. Yet other children of anti-Jacobinism jumped ship entirely from the Federalist

---

[36] Richard Hildreth, *The Slave, or Memoirs of Archy Moore*, 2nd ed. (Boston, Mass., 1840), 1:66; 2:75.

[37] Richard Hildreth, *Despotism in America: Or, an Inquiry into the Nature and Results of the Slave-Holding System in the United States* (Boston, Mass., 1840). For a study of how Hildreth balanced democracy and anti-Jacobinism, see Arthur Schlesinger Jr., "The Problem of Richard Hildreth," *New England Quarterly* 13 (June 1940).

tradition, by becoming Democrats in the party of Thomas Jefferson and Andrew Jackson. New Englanders' strong identification of the Democratic Party with Virginia slavery hampered many antislavery progressives from shifting political loyalties. When northern progressives did join the Democrats, they often muffled their antislavery opinions.[38] But some antislavery leaders made the leap with cultural baggage in hand: finding a way to combine the sentiments of their youth with the political progressivism of their adulthood.

William Cullen Bryant, the antislavery poet and Democratic editor of the New York *Evening Post* was born in western Massachusetts in 1794 to Peter Bryant, a Federalist doctor active in state politics, and Sarah Snell Bryant, a fierce Calvinist.[39] Peter Bryant was serving as doctor aboard a merchant vessel shortly after his son's birth, when his ship was impounded by the French at Mauritius, leaving the doctor trapped on the island for a year. When he returned home, Peter Bryant had become a "steady antagonist" of the "French influences" corrupting American society. Bryant's mother, Sarah Snell Bryant, was a strict moralist, committed to the ultra-Calvinist theology of Samuel Hopkins, from which she absorbed a "prompt condemnation of injustice" that her son recalled "made a strong impression upon [him] in early life." Cullen, as the poet was known, attributed a large measure of responsibility for his abolitionism to his mother, who taught him "never to countenance a wrong because others did." This Hopkintonian message was reinforced by Sarah Snell Bryant's ultrareligious father, with whom the family lived for several years.[40]

From a young age, Bryant adopted his parents' strong opinions. When he was only fourteen, Bryant published his first poem, a satiric assault on the 1807 embargo that perfectly reproduced the anti-Jacobin Federalist–Calvinist sensibilities that he learned from his father and from the Federalist newspapers to which he subscribed. Throughout his adolescence, Bryant traveled along the Federalist–Calvinist path. For two years he lived with his mother's brother, the Hopkintonian minister Thomas Snell, who was a

[38] Padraig Riley, "Northern Republicans and Southern Slavery: Democracy in the Age of Jefferson, 1800–1819" (Ph.D., University of California, Berkeley, 2007).

[39] Bryant was not the only son of a Federalist doctor to become a democratic antislavery leader; Hannibal Hamlin, Lincoln's first vice president, followed the same life path. Hamlin's antislavery was also strongly influenced by the Federalist–abolitionist lawyer Samuel Fessenden; see Charles Eugene Hamlin, *The Life and Times of Hannibal Hamlin* (Cambridge, Mass., 1899), 42. Fessenden's illegitimate son William Pitt Fessenden, named for the anti-Jacobin British prime minister, also pursued a political antislavery career, serving in Abraham Lincoln's war cabinet; U.S. Congress, *Memorial Addresses on the Life and Character of William Pitt Fessenden (a Senator from Maine)* (Washington, D.C., 1870); "William Pitt Fessenden," *American National Biography* 7 (1999).

[40] "W. C. Bryant's Life," Box 10, Bryant-Godwin Papers, New York Public Library (NYPL). Parke Godwin, *A Biography of William Cullen Bryant, with Extracts from His Private Correspondence* (New York, 1883), 1:55, 4.

fierce critic of Napoleon and French Revolutionary violence.[41] More poems followed: in 1810 a lengthy attack on Napoleon, and in 1812 a fierce condemnation of the War of 1812. That much-despised war radicalized Bryant, who wrote letters home to his Federalist father begging permission to join the Massachusetts militia and to prepare for a war against the southern states, in order to defend "dearer rights than those which are endangered in a contest with Great Britain." Youthful thirst for experience and deep-set sectionalism led Bryant to fantasies of wreaking vengeance against the Democratic-tyrannical South. The end of the war, however, quashed his dreams of military glory and instead of enlisting Bryant moved to Great Barrington, Massachusetts, to begin the practice of law.[42]

For several more years, Bryant remained true to his roots, submitting writings to the nouveau Federalist journal the *North American Review*, reading the poems of the Connecticut Wits like Timothy Dwight and Robert Treat Paine, and socializing with the children of the Federalist jurist Theodore Sedgwick. But the declining political fortunes of the Federalist Party after 1815 foreclosed this life path. Frequently depressed, unsure about marriage, and bored in the countryside, Bryant dreamed of a more exciting life (even fantasizing about military adventures in South America).[43] Together with his friends the Sedgwicks, Bryant moved to New York City and shifted allegiance to the Democratic Party.[44] While the Sedgwicks and Bryant embraced free trade and became supporters of Andrew Jackson, they maintained the antislavery opinions of their parents. Theodore Sedgwick Jr., Bryant's close friend and intellectual mentor, spoke out against slavery as a great evil – even praising the "heroism" of southern slave rebels – although he remained leery of abolitionism throughout his life because he could not support "violent, incendiary, and revolutionary discussion."[45] Bryant, on the other hand, had been given to violent discussion since his youth and shifted naturally from denouncing Napoleon to condemning the supporters of slavery. Resisting the optimistic spirit of the so-called era of good feelings, Bryant argued that only morbid sensitivity to suffering, not a happy temperament, could motivate humanitarian action: "It is the pain which [people's sufferings] give us, that has in all ages prompted the attempts of the good and the humane

---

[41] Thomas Snell, *Repentance with Prayer... Praying for Rulers a Christian Duty* (Brookfield, Mass., 1812).

[42] William Cullen Bryant to Peter Bryant, Oct. 10, 1814, Box 1, Correspondence, Bryant-Godwin Papers, NYPL; Godwin, *Biography of William Cullen Bryant*, 129–31.

[43] William Cullen Bryant to [?], Sept. 14, 1818, Box 1, Correspondence, Bryant-Godwin Papers, NYPL.

[44] Godwin, *Biography of William Cullen Bryant*, chap. 10.

[45] Theodore Sedgwick Jr., *The Practicability of the Abolition of Slavery: A Lecture, Delivered at the Lyceum in Stockbridge, Massachusetts, February 1831* (New York, 1831), 9; "Political Portraits, No. XVIII: Theodore Sedgwick," *Democratic Review*, Feb. 1840, 129–54; "Letter," *Liberator*, Aug. 16, 1839, 130.

to improve the condition of our species."[46] His mother's and grandfather's Calvinism had deeply imprinted him with a sense of the world's sinfulness and the need to speak out against injustice.

When Bryant assumed editorship of the New York Democratic newspaper the *Evening Post* in 1829, he initially assuaged southern sympathizers within the party by criticizing abolitionism. But during the mid-1830s, when he witnessed the violent spectacle of antiabolitionist mobs rampaging through northern cities, and when he considered the suffering of black people in the United States, he embraced immediatist antislavery and opened the newspaper's pages to free discussion of slavery. Despite Bryant's rebellion against the politics of his father, the terms of his antislavery writings clearly revealed the cultural influences of his childhood. In his editorials, Bryant criticized the violence of antiabolitionist mobs in Cincinnati, New York, and Philadelphia. Echoing the sentiments of his childhood, Bryant argued that slavery "nourishes a wolfish ferocity" and "revolting brutality" among southerners, demonstrated by their mob attacks on perceived enemies. Bryant sustained these criticisms up through the Civil War, for example describing the lynching of northerners and pro-union southerners in the South during 1860 as a "reign of terror" that would "deepen into horrors which will sicken the heart."[47] Eventually, Bryant's aggressive abolitionism drove him out of the Democratic fold, and he joined first the Free-Soil Party, then the Republican Party, where his antislavery views were better received. Yet Bryant remained a true Democrat in his support for egalitarian politics and the workingman.

Anti-Jacobinism bridged Federalism to antislavery in the life experiences of abolitionists representing a diverse array of reform temperaments and tactics. In addition, anti-Jacobinism played a role in the antislavery journey of abolitionists representing diverse racial identities. Many black abolitionists from the antebellum era used anti-Jacobin discourse to attack the horrors of slavery. Some black abolitionists grew up in the Northeast, probably exposed to the same anti-Jacobin propaganda as their white counterparts. Other black abolitionists who grew up in southern slavery and later made their escape adopted anti-Jacobin rhetoric from fellow abolitionists because it proved useful to the cause.

William Cooper Nell, who wrote for the *Liberator* and was a publisher of the abolitionist journal the *North Star*, was born in 1816 into a leading black family in Boston and educated at a black common school that met at the city's African Methodist Episcopal Church. He also attended Sunday-school classes at the anti-Jacobin minister Lyman Beecher's Boston church,

---

[46] William Cullen Bryant, "On the Happy Temperament," *North American Review and Miscellaneous Journal* 19 (June 1819).

[47] William Cullen Bryant II, ed., *Power for Sanity: Selected Editorials of William Cullen Bryant, 1829–1861* (New York, 1994), 370, 364.

where he received instruction from the Garrisonian Oliver Johnson. As an adult, Nell used anti-Jacobin terminology in his extensive abolitionist writings, describing both the Fugitive Slave Law and the *Dred Scott* decision as a "reign of terror" against African Americans and comparing northern political leaders and writers who kowtowed to slaveholders to "Robespierre."[48] Likewise, the charasmatic black abolitionist Frederick Douglass, who grew up as a slave in Maryland, frequently published anti-Jacobin imagery in his newspapers the *North Star* and *Frederick Douglass's Paper*.[49] Anti-Jacobinism's ethical core and rhetorical effectiveness made it attractive even to many abolitionists who did not grow up under its shadow. Douglass's use of anti-Jacobin imagery highlights the twists and turns in the path between anti-Jacobinism and antebellum abolitionism.

Anti-Jacobinism did not lead inexorably to antebellum abolitionism; it inspired but did not determine the movement. While most white antebellum abolitionists and antislavery reformers were strongly influenced by the anti-Jacobinism of their childhoods, not all children of early national religious and political conservatives became abolitionists. Many inherited a general dislike of slavery but felt no passionate commitment to opposing the institution.[50] Personal experiences, individual temperaments, and unpredictable contingencies led individuals from passive antislavery sentiment to abolitionist action.[51] Some children of anti-Jacobins rejected antislavery completely, even labeling abolitionists "Jacobins."[52] Abolitionists, of course, vehemently protested the charge that they were Jacobins.[53] A small minority of children of anti-Jacobins, such as Jedidiah Morse's son Samuel F. B. Morse, defied all expectations and became proslavery.[54] Further complicating the anti-Jacobin/antislavery connection, many of the black participants in the abolitionist movement likely heard adults in their childhood

---

[48] Dorothy Porter Wesley, *William Cooper Nell, Nineteenth-Century African American Abolitionist, Historian, Integrationist: Selected Writings from 1832–1874* (Baltimore, Md., 2002), 253, 291, 523, 296; Robert P. Smith, "William Cooper Nell: Crusading Black Abolitionist," *Journal of Negro History* 55 (1970).

[49] For example, "The Model Republic," *North Star*, Apr. 28, 1848; "Hon. Horace of Greeley and the People of Color," *Frederick Douglass's Paper*, Jan. 29, 1852.

[50] Christopher Leslie Brown, *Moral Capital: Foundations of British Abolitionism* (Chapel Hill, N.C., 2006). Brown emphasizes the important distinction between sentiment and action.

[51] Wyatt-Brown, *Yankee Saints*.

[52] See, for example, Lucius M. Sargent, *A New Champion of the Christian Faith. Lucius Manlius Sargent vs. William Lloyd Garrison* (Boston, 1850). See also "Abolitionism," *Floridian*, Nov. 14, 1840; Joseph Tracy, *Natural Equality: A Sermon before the Vermont Colonization Society, at Montpelier, October 17, 1833* (Windsor, Vt., 1833).

[53] *Liberator*, Mar. 8, 1834; New-Hampshire Anti-Slavery Society, *Annual Report of the New-Hampshire Anti-Slavery Society* (Concord, N.H., 1835), 20; American Anti-Slavery Society, *Platform of the American Anti-Slavery Society and Its Auxiliaries* (New York, 1853), 2.

[54] Jill Lepore, *A Is for American: Letters and Other Characters in the Newly United States* (New York, 2002), chap. 6; Larry E. Tise, *Proslavery: A History of the Defense of Slavery in America, 1701–1840* (Athens, Ga., 1987).

praise the French Revolution as a lodestar for freedom or, in other words, were raised in Jacobin, not anti-Jacobin, milieus! Many exceptions disrupt attempts to define a strict formula leading from anti-Jacobinism to abolitionism. However, having given close attention to its starting point – the abolitionists' childhood milieu – evidence for the formula's usefulness can be strengthened by shifting attention to its endpoint – their abolitionist writings. Throughout the antebellum era, diverse reformers suffused their antislavery writings and speeches with anti-Jacobin tropes and Gothic rhetorical techniques to condemn slaveholder violence.

The New Reign of Terror

Diverse abolitionists drew on the anti-Jacobin legacy to advance a broad range of reform styles; yet across the spectrum of tactics and identities, opponents to slavery used the language of anti-Jacobinism in remarkably similar ways. White patricians joined black runaways, antisectarians joined Protestant evangelicals, and political partisans joined political anarchists in voicing a common set of anti-Jacobin abolitionist tropes. Most frequently, antislavery advocates illustrated the violence of their proslavery opponents by describing physical and political measures intended to suppress abolitionists as reigns of terror. In these terms, antislavery writers protested antiabolitionist rioting, attacks on abolitionist presses, the gag rule in Congress, the 1854–8 settler war in Kansas, and the lynching of northern visitors to southern states after John Brown's 1859 attack on Harper's Ferry. Abolitionists also used anti-Jacobin imagery to describe the violence suffered by black people themselves, labeling the home invasions by slave hunters following 1850 as a "reign of terror" and resuscitating early national aspersions against slaveholders as violent Jacobins. Sometimes abolitionists harkened back to an even earlier Francophobic language, by describing slavery as a bastille – the prison symbolizing Bourbon despotism that Parisians tore down at the outset of the Revolution. Despite the seeming inconsistency of identifying slavery both as Bourbon despotism and as anti-Bourbon terrorism, abolitionists perceived the Bastille and the Reign of Terror as both defined by their common violence, and thus as equally powerful proxies for slavery.

The most vociferous abolitionist use of anti-Jacobin language occurred in reaction to the mob violence of the 1830s. The renewal of the antislavery movement during the late 1820s generated intense opposition across the free states and resulted in a period of mob attacks on antislavery gatherings. In 1835 alone, there were 147 riots – 109 from July to October – more than fifty of which were directed against abolitionists or black people.[55]

---

[55] David Grimsted, *American Mobbing, 1828–1861: Toward Civil War* (New York, 1998), 3–5.

Abolitionists swiftly denounced these riots as a "reign of terror," a wave of lawless violence that threatened to destroy civil society and reduce the nation to bloody anarchy.

William Lloyd Garrison, who was captured by a mob on October 21, 1835, and dragged through the streets by a hanging rope, filled the pages of the *Liberator* with anti-Jacobin attacks on the violence of proslavery mobs. Shortly after his ordeal, Garrison published an editorial warning that "the scenes of the French Revolution [will] be re-enacted – and men and women, and children even, put to death by human butchers, until the earth be drunk with blood, and the slain cease to find a covering for the mutilated bodies."[56] Garrison's experience as a target of mob violence effected him so deeply that in the years following he embraced a radical form of pacifism, or nonresistance, which taught that any use of force, even defensive, contravened Christian justice. His Gothic descriptions of the antiabolitionist mobs of 1835 must be read not merely as cynical purple prose but also as an expression of deeply rooted concerns about bloodshed and law, informed and framed by the language of his youth.

The description of antiabolitionist mobbing as a reign of terror extended beyond Boston, the former epicenter of anti-Jacobinism.[57] When an antiabolitionist mob in 1838 burned down Philadelphia's Pennsylvania Hall, a new auditorium built to provide space for the free discussion of slavery, Theodore Dwight Weld's the *Emancipator* described the destruction as a "reign of terror."[58] African American newspapers used the same language to describe antebellum riots. After proslavery mobs in Cincinnati repeatedly destroyed the local abolitionist printing press and attacked black citizens, *Colored American* published the resolutions of a "meeting of the colored citizens of Buffalo" that "earnestly deprecated" the recent "reign of terror and destruction."[59] James Birney's Cincinnati paper the *Philanthropist* described the mob attacks in identical terms.[60] When the Washington, D.C., abolitionist newspaper the *National Era* was mobbed in 1848, Frederick Douglass's paper the *North Star* published an article by the black evangelical abolitionist Henry Highland Garnet, decrying the "reign of terror at the Capitol." Garnet's cry drew on over a decade of anti-Jacobin attacks on proslavery riots, yet his text did not simply reproduce the rhetoric of Garrison and Weld.

---

[56] "Boston: Saturday, November 7, 1835," *Liberator*, Nov. 7, 1835.

[57] For general applications, see Massachusetts Anti-Slavery Society, *Nineteenth Annual Report, Presented to the Massachusetts Anti-Slavery Society, by Its Board of Managers, January 22, 1851* (Boston, 1851), 25; Harriet Martineau, *The Martyr Age of the United States of America, with an Appeal on Behalf of the Oberlin Institute in Aid of the Abolition of Slavery* (Newcastle upon Tyne, 1838), 15.

[58] "Disgraceful Riot and Arson in Philadelphia," *Emancipator*, May 24, 1838.

[59] "Meeting of the Colored Citizens of Buffalo," *Colored American*, Nov. 13, 1841.

[60] "From the Philanthropist. The Reign of Terror," *Emancipator*, Oct. 13, 1836. See also "Reign of Terror again in Cincinnati," *Liberator*, Sept. 24, 1841.

Garnet firmly tethered his words to their historical roots, following his attack on the "reign of terror" in Washington with a vivid retelling of the story of Madame Roland, the Girondist martyr of 1793, who, "when about to submit her neck to the axe of the sanguinary Republican Robespierre," cried out "Oh liberty! what crimes are committed in thy name!"[61] Garnet's essay attacked the proslavery mob in anti-Jacobin terms because the language contained an effective critique of how violence endangered civil society.

The presence of wealthy elites among the antiabolitionists mobs did little to disrupt the association between proslavery rioters and the rioters of the French Revolution. During the 1790s, American anti-Jacobins had redefined the French Revolution as an episode of uncontrolled violence rather than a populist uprising. William Jay, the abolitionist son of the antislavery Federalist John Jay, drew on this understanding of the French Revolution when he attacked the "gentlemen of property and standing" who led the proslavery mobs of 1835: "the Jacobins of the present day are to be found among the rich and powerful."[62] To call proslavery rioters Jacobins connoted not their social class, but their willingness to use violence to defend slavery.

Jay, born in 1789, had a childhood steeped both in anti-Jacobinism and antislavery. His father, John Jay, was a Francophobic conservative who coauthored the Federalist Papers and served as an active member of the antislavery New York Manumission Society, alongside other Federalist anti-Jacobins including Gouverneur Morris and Alexander Hamilton. William Jay also received an early infusion of anti-Jacobinism from his first teacher, Thomas Ellison, an Episcopal minister who was "particularly severe on the immoralities of the French Revolution," as Jay recalled, and "detested a democrat as he did the devil." Later, William Jay's anti-Jacobin sensibilities were refined at Yale under the direction of President Timothy Dwight.[63] Following the path outlined by his father and teachers, Jay joined several Protestant reform organizations as a young man and wrote essays against violent practices such as dueling.

In 1826, after Jay had become a judge, he led a campaign to rescue a free black man from imprisonment as a runaway slave in Washington, D.C. This consciousness-raising experience inspired him to adopt immediate abolitionist principles and participate in establishing the New York City Anti-Slavery Society and the American Anti-Slavery Society. He swiftly applied his anti-Jacobin sensibility to the new cause. In an 1833 essay that Jay

61 "The Model Republic," *North Star*, Apr. 28, 1848.

62 "Letter of Judge Jay, Bedford, 26th September, 1836," *Proceedings of the First Annual Meeting of the New-York State Anti-Slavery Society* (Utica, N.Y., 1838). See also *Liberator*, Nov. 26, 1841; "The Annihilation and Disbandonment of the Whig Party!" *Daily Ohio Statesman*, Nov. 16, 1852.

63 Bayard Tuckerman and John Jay, *William Jay, and the Constitutional Movement for the Abolition of Slavery* (New York, 1893), 2, 6.

contributed to the evangelical abolitionist journal the *Emancipator*, Jay argued that antislavery fence-sitters, who feared that immediate abolition would lead to black violence against whites, needed to read about the sufferings of blacks in "strong but true colors" that would reveal the urgency of the cause; "the public needs information respecting the abominations committed," Jay wrote. A pamphlet he published soon afterwards included a section on the "cruel character of American slavery," which inspired the old Federalist jurist Chancellor Kent to write Jay praising his "horrible" descriptions of eye-opening "atrocities."[64] Jay's ethical commitment against violent disorder eventually inspired him to become a leader of the peace reform movement, and he remained committed to nonviolent antislavery until his death in 1858.[65] This aversion to disorder also caused Jay to criticize Garrison's "Jacobinical" ultraism following 1838; but he never deviated in his antislavery commitment. Rather, Jay encouraged black and white abolitionists to martyr themselves to their proslavery persecutors, and thus expose to all Americans the violence of the slaveholders' reign of terror.[66]

Charges that the mob violence against abolitionists signified a reign of terror became increasingly poweful after rioters in Alton, Illinois, murdered the abolitionist editor Elijah P. Lovejoy in 1837. Lovejoy lost his life to a "reign of terror," pronounced the Massachusetts Anti-Slavery Society in 1838 in a report that further adapted the anti-Jacobin Gothic by describing slavery as a cannibalistic feast whose "daily food was human flesh, [and] its daily drink human blood." Calling upon another image common in anti-Jacobin discourse, the report described slavery as "Moloch" – the supposed Phoenician god of human sacrifice – and warned that "civil law" was being immolated upon "its blood-stained altars."[67] William Lloyd Garrison may have been instrumental in composing the report; he had used similar language in the *Liberator*.[68] Use of this imagery extended beyond Garrison, however. The African American newspaper the *Colored American*, which was published in New York but circulated among free blacks throughout the eastern seaboard, published a letter from Alton a couple of months prior to Lovejoy's death describing the town as under "truly a reign of terror," and another letter repeating the charge after Lovejoy's martyrdom.[69]

---

[64] Ibid., 59.

[65] For a detailed examination of the Federalist elements in Jay's abolitionist ideology, see Stephen Paul Budney, "William Jay and the Influence of Federalist Antislavery" (Ph.D., University of Mississippi, 2000).

[66] Tuckerman and Jay, *William Jay*, 116, 143.

[67] Massachusetts Anti-Slavery Society, *Sixth Annual Report of the Board of Managers of the Massachusetts Anti-Slavery Society: Presented January 24, 1838* (Boston, Mass., 1838), 34–44.

[68] *Liberator*, Dec. 12, 1837. See also "Reign of Terror," *Emancipator*, Dec. 14, 1837.

[69] "Fallen Nature Disgracing the Devil," *Colored American*, Sept. 16, 1837; "A Testimonial," *Colored American*, July 20, 1839.

Although unsigned, the first letter may have come from Lovejoy himself, who, like Theodore Dwight Weld, bore the stamp of anti-Jacobinism clearly in his full name: Elijah Parish Lovejoy. Lovejoy's father, Daniel, was a Congregationalist minister who had studied under the antislavery anti-Jacobin Elijah Parish and signaled his lasting affection and gratitude by naming his firstborn son after his teacher. Elijah Parish Lovejoy was raised in "an atmosphere of stern Puritan morality" fostered by his dark and brooding father and fervently devout mother. Deeply concerned about human depravity and the state of his own soul, Lovejoy felt drawn to the world of evangelical reform and moved to St. Louis, Missouri, in 1827, where he aspired to cultivate New England values and combat democratic infidelity. In 1832, Lovejoy was swept up in the tide of the Second Great Awakening and experienced a spiritual rebirth. He started a reform paper, the *St. Louis Observer*, in 1833, which promoted an Arminian view of Christianity but attacked local Catholics and slavery with a Puritanical zeal.

Lovejoy became increasingly committed to antislavery during the 1830s as he witnessed proslavery whites use violence against blacks and abolitionists. By 1835, he had come to see slavery as a "nightmare on the body politic" that morally corrupted slave masters and slaves, and threatened American liberty. His increasingly severe denunciations of slavery and mob rule soon inspired threats of violence against himself and his press. Those threats reached a crisis point in the late summer and fall of 1837, as mobs repeatedly attacked Lovejoy's printing press and threatened his life (he had relocated his operation across the river to Alton, Illinois, following the destruction of his press in Missouri). On the evening of November 7, 1837, the editor was fatally shot while defending his newest press from a mob bent on its destruction.[70]

After Lovejoy's death, his younger brother Owen carried on the anti-Jacobin antislavery tradition in his own abolitionist career (another brother, Joseph Lovejoy, as well as their mother, Elizabeth Lovejoy, also became abolitionists). Owen Lovejoy, who had been converted to abolitionism by Theodore Dwight Weld, was present at his brother's death and pledged on the spilled blood to carry on the fight against the "reign of terror" that consumed his brother. As a minister, conductor for the Underground Railroad, antislavery congressman, and close friend of Abraham Lincoln, Owen Lovejoy drew on the rhetorical tools of anti-Jacobinism to scourge his enemies.

Owen Lovejoy was renowned as a "fiery orator."[71] In a letter addressed to the people of Alton in 1838, he described the leaders of the mob who killed his brother as similar to "Robespierre and his compeers" Danton and Marat,

[70] Merton Lynn Dillon, *Elijah P. Lovejoy, Abolitionist Editor* (Urbana, Ill., 1961).
[71] William F. Moore and Jane Ann Moore, eds., *Owen Lovejoy: His Brother's Blood, Speeches and Writings, 1838–64* (Urbana, Ill., 2004), xxii; Frederick J. Blue, *No Taint of Compromise: Crusaders in Antislavery Politics* (Baton Rouge, La., 2005), chap. 5.

encouraging the enormities of a "blood-baited and fanatical populace." In a typical Gothic trope, Owen bemoaned that "no language can exaggerate the naked atrocity of the facts – no oratory can deepen the dark colours of the truth." But if language could not "exaggerate" the tragedy, the right vocabulary could help Lovejoy capture its intensity.

During his long antislavery career, Owen Lovejoy returned repeatedly to the language of the French Revolution. He pledged to follow his conscience even while his enemies "whet their guillotines!"[72] Not intended solely for effect, remarks like these reflected Lovejoy's belief, adopted from his anti-Jacobin antislavery forebearers, that slavery was an uncivilizing institution leading naturally to bloodshed. In his most famous speech, "The Barbarism of Slavery," delivered before the House of Representatives on April 5, 1860, Lovejoy argued that "the practice of slaveholding has a tendency to drag communities back to barbarism"; it was "the sum of all villainy," a practice that combined piracy, robbery, and even cannibalism. The southern members of the House rose to their feet and brandished weapons, shouting down Lovejoy as a "black-hearted scoundrel and nigger-stealing thief." But Lovejoy continued his assault, giving Gothic examples of the tortures used in slavery.[73]

The murder of Elijah Lovejoy frequently elicited comparisons to the Reign of Terror from abolitionists, drawing an easy parallel between the bloodshed in both instances. Yet antebellum abolitionists pushed beyond this obvious connection by calling all proslavery suppression of antislavery speech a reign of terror, regardless of whether any blood was actually spilled.[74] Often abolitionists used anti-Jacobin terminology to capture the threat of violence behind southern proslavery censorship. One early abolitionist who was nearly lynched in Virginia for voicing his opinions claimed, "I told them that 'they might take my life, and, like some of the cannibals who disgraced the French revolution, they might even drink my blood. I could not die in a better cause'."[75] Rhode Island abolitionists similarly complained in 1836 that, in the South, "We are excluded by the establishment of lynch law – by the prevalence of as murderous a spirit as reigned during the bloody supremacy of French Jacobinism."[76] William Jay complained that

---

[72] Owen Lovejoy, "Open Letter to the Citizens of Alton, Illinois, 1838"; Moore and Moore, eds., *His Brother's Blood*, 5, 12–13, 23.

[73] Owen Lovejoy, "Debate on Slavery, Conducted under Hostile Conditions in Congress, April 5, 1860"; Moore and Moore, eds., *His Brother's Blood*, 191–210.

[74] American Anti-Slavery Society, *Fourth Annual Report of the American Anti-Slavery Society: With the Speeches Delivered at the Anniversary Meeting Held in the City of New York, on the 9th of May, 1837* (New York, 1837), 49.

[75] "Daring Outrage of Virginia Slaveites," *Liberator*, Oct. 1, 1831.

[76] Rhode Island Anti-Slavery Convention, *Proceedings of the Rhode-Island Anti-Slavery Convention: Held in Providence, on the 2nd, 3rd, and 4th of February, 1836* (Providence, R.I., 1837), 74–80.

the "reign of terror in the Slave states" was "crushing in the dust freedom of speech, of the press, of suffrage, and of the pulpit."[77] According to abolitionists, southern proslavery forces were destroying civil society by silencing the opposition, and thus stood guilty of giving reign to violence.

Although these comments may be seen as inflammatory sectionalist rhetoric, there is evidence to suggest that southerners in fact consciously embraced terror as the best means to silence the abolitionist movement. James Henry Hammond, the fire-eating proslavery South Carolina politician, wrote a letter to a New York editor in 1835 demanding that abolitionists "be silenced in but one way. *Terror and Death.*"[78] Recalling Thomas Jefferson's advice to James Madison during the War of 1812 that protestors should be silenced by "hemp," Hammond's remark illustrates abolitionists' logic for equating southern proslavery forces with French Jacobins: both groups seemed willing to use violence to stifle opposition.

Even when there was no immediate threat of violence, such as when the House of Representatives passed a gag rule in 1836 to prevent open congressional debate on the subject of slavery, abolitionists accused their oppressors of violent Jacobinism. John Quincy Adams, the former president turned congressman, led the fight against what he called the "reign of terror" in the Capitol.[79] Son of the first Federalist anti-Jacobin, President John Adams, Quincy Adams had himself attacked the French Revolution from its earliest days. Not only an inheritor, John Quincy Adams was in fact an original author of the antislavery anti-Jacobin trope, who managed to live long enough to direct his critique against both the Jeffersonian Republicans who usurped his father's position as well as the Jacksonian Democrats who later usurped him.

John Quincy Adams's spirited attack on the gag rule's "reign of terror" inspired many younger abolitionists, including the political antislavery editor and former Lane rebel Henry B. Stanton. Although Stanton's own father was a Jeffersonian, Stanton looked up to Adams and used anti-Jacobin language to praise his political mentor. The South, Stanton charged, had threatened to assassinate Adams because "he dared to vindicate the right of petition." Warming to his topic, Stanton passionately argued that "slavery is indeed an inexorable Moloch," and "the American Congress in now the theatre, on which is re-enacted the tragic scenes of the French Convention" during

---

[77] William Jay, *A Letter to the Committee Chosen by the American Tract Society, to Inquire into the Proceedings of Its Executive Committee in Relation to Slavery* (Boston, Mass., 1857), 15. See also Loring Moody, *A Plain Statement Addressed to All Honest Democrats* (Boston, Mass., 1856), 18.

[78] Grimsted, *American Mobbing*, 22.

[79] John Quincy Adams, *Address of John Quincy Adams, to His Constituents of the Twelfth Congressional District at Braintree, September 17th, 1842* (Boston, Mass., 1842). See also *Emancipator*, Feb. 28, 1839. For a history of the gag rule, see William Lee Miller, *Arguing about Slavery: The Great Battle in the United States Congress* (New York, 1996).

"the reign of terror, when the streets of Paris ran with blood."[80] While no guillotines had been set up on the mall, the increasingly violent conflict over slavery in Washington during the following decades reinforced Adams's and Stanton's charges that efforts to silence abolitionists constituted a reign of terror.[81]

Although abolitionists frequently depicted themselves as martyrs to the Reign of Terror, they did recognize that slaves suffered the greatest violence from southern tyrants. The Jacobin violence of slavery itself, while sometimes an afterthought, never dropped out from antebellum abolitionist rhetoric. Newspaper articles with titles like "The Slaveholders 'Reign of Terror'" connected the violence of proslavery mobs to the violence of slaveholders' selling "the bones and sinews, the flesh and blood" of their human property. Concerns about slaveholder violence against slaves and slaveholder violence against white civil society were inseparable.[82]

Many antebellum abolitionists used anti-Jacobin language to focus attention on slaves' suffering. The Afro-Canadian newspaper the *Provincial Freeman* published a lengthy commentary in 1857 on the horrors of slavery that described events in the slave South as "so strange, so unnatural, so outrageous, so undescribable, so grotesque, (if we may use the term) in their horror and wickedness" that they bore comparison to "the reign of terror of the French Revolution."[83] William Ellery Channing, an influential Unitarian minister born in 1780 who bridged the anti-Jacobin and antebellum generations, described the operation of a plantation as a "reign of terror and force."[84] The *New York Daily Times* complained that violence against blacks in southern cities like Baltimore constituted a "reign of terror."[85] Labeling the brutality enacted upon slaves in anti-Jacobin terms tied the welfare of blacks to whites, and likely increased antislavery sympathy among northern readers.

Abolitionist descriptions of the Jacobin dimensions of slaveholding brutality extended beyond brief references; some authors crafted searing anti-Jacobin imagery to describe the violence against slaves. A letter published in the *Anti-Slavery Record* in October 1837 described the story of a slave "weltering in blood" and argued that any joys that slaves experienced

---

[80] Henry Brewster Stanton, *Random Recollections* (New York, 1886). Stanton's father was a slaveholder in addition to being a Jeffersonian, and the son's rebellion against the first childhood experience may have extended to the second.

[81] "Progress of the Reign of Terror!" *Cleveland Daily Herald*, Mar. 17, 1840.

[82] "The Slaveholders' 'Reign of Terror,'" *Philadelphia National Enquirer*, Apr. 29, 1837.

[83] "Strange and Horrible Features of United States Slavery," *Provincial Freeman*, Apr. 4, 1857.

[84] William Ellery Channing, *Emancipation* (New York, 1841), 64; William Ellery Channing, *An Address Delivered at Lenox, on the First of August 1842, the Anniversary of Emancipation in the British West Indies* (Lenox, 1842). See also William Lloyd Garrison, quoted in "The New-York City Anti-Slavery Society," *New York Daily Times*, Aug. 5, 1853.

[85] "Why Do We Meddle with Slavery?" *New York Daily Times*, May 16, 1857.

"are like the pleasure that showed itself in the prisons of Paris in the days of Robespierre."[86] An article published by Frederick Douglass entitled "Reign of Terror, or Slavery as it is in Georgia," modeled after Theodore Dwight Weld's masterpiece, employed many familiar tactics of Gothic anti-Jacobinism to excite readers. The author complained about the inability of language to capture the "scene[s] of reckoning, horror and of blood" enacted in Georgia. Following this familiar profession of inability, the author proceeded to describe the whip marks and other scars that disfigured the bodies of slaves: "some have had their jaws broken, others their teeth knocked out, while others have had their ears cropped and the sides of their cheeks gashed out. Some of the poor creatures have had their noses mashed in, and some have lost the sight of one, or both of their eyes."[87] The article finished by describing the many different implements and varieties of torture.

The most disturbing anti-Jacobin narratives of slaveholder violence described incidents of torture and lynching in graphic detail. An abolitionist address from 1843 argued that slaveholders had "established a reign of terror as Insurrectionary and as sanguinary in principle as that created by the sans culottes of the French Revolution." To prove this charge, the address described the lynching of a free black man in horrifying detail:

After the flames had surrounded their prey, and when his clothes were in a blaze all over him, his eyes burnt out of his head, and his mouth seemingly parched to a cinder, some one in the crowd, more compassionate than the rest, proposed to put an end to his misery by shooting him, when it was replied, that it would be of no use, since he was already out of his pain. "No," said the wretch, "I am not, I am suffering as much as ever, shoot me, shoot me." "No, no," said one of the friends who was standing about the sacrifice they were roasting. "[H]e shall not be shot, I would sooner slacken the fire, if that would increase his misery"; and the man who said this we understand an officer of justice.[88]

Abolitionists adopted from their anti-Jacobin predecessors not only a catalog of pejorative terms but also a style of writing that described bloodshed in highly detailed and disturbing terms. Like their models, abolitionists used violent language both to inspire their audience's revulsion against that violence and to make audiences angry perhaps to the point of using violence.

Taking another page from the anti-Jacobin writers of the early national period, antebellum abolitionists argued that the violence of slaveholding led naturally to violent attacks on the law. Mobs, riots, the gag rule, and civil war all grew naturally out of the slaveholders' domineering violence on the plantation. Any abolitionist criticism of slaveholder violence against civil

[86] "Letter to a Minister of the Gospel," *Anti-Slavery Record*, Oct. 1837.

[87] "Southern Correspondence. Reign of Terror, or Slavery as It Is in Georgia," *Frederick Douglass's Paper*, Sept. 21, 1855.

[88] American and Foreign Anti-Slavery Society, *Address to the Non-Slaveholders of the South, on the Social and Political Evils of Slavery* (New York, 1843), 13, 26.

society was rooted in fundamental understandings of slaveholder violence against slaves. The Congregationalist minister David Root preached an 1835 sermon that identified "violence" as the central principle of slavery and argued that "no Jacobin of the French Revolution ever justified a more dangerous doctrine than this. Robespierre would have blushed to own such a doctrine." In a powerful image familiar to readers of the anti-Jacobin Gothic, Root described the slave laws of the South as "written in blood."[89] The Reign of Terror served as an effective trope to attack slavery because it revealed the connection between violence against slaves and violence against white civil society. Abolitionists motivated white audiences from sentiment to action by using anti-Jacobin tropes to connect the violence committed against slaves to the violent threats against white freedom. Although Gothic descriptions of slave suffering were certain to inspire sentiment in many readers, descriptions of how violence against slaves led to violence against the law could inspire white readers to action.

The murder of Elijah Lovejoy, by demonstrating the connection between violence against slaves and violence against white civil society, brought many fence-sitting white northerners into the abolitionist camp. Those who had a deep grounding in the history of the French Revolution were especially responsive to the extrajudicial killing of the abolitionist editor. Perhaps the most important abolitionist leader to join the cause after Lovejoy's assassination was Wendell Phillips. A committed Calvinist born in 1811 Boston, the son of a Federalist anti-Jacobin politician, Phillips inherited from his religiously and politically conservative family a strong belief "that passion must be controlled at all cost." In an 1831 college essay, Phillips described the French Revolution as a terrifying model of what would happen when people let their passions loose: the Revolution became "synonymous with bloodlust." Phillips' anti-Jacobin sentiments prepared him to experience revulsion at the mobs of 1835 (he witnessed Garrison's mock lynching) and later at Lovejoy's murder.

Swayed by his abolitionist wife, Ann Terry Greene (who had been trapped by the anti-Garrison mob), Phillips announced his abolitionist commitment in 1837 at a Faneuil Hall meeting to protest Lovejoy's death. Phillips's shock at the debasement of American liberty by antiabolitionist mobs and their sympathizers led to his fervent antislavery agitation in the decades following 1837. His abolitionist rhetoric stressed slavery's destruction of social and political institutions in the United States. He attacked slavery for "spreading violence, social degradation, and political tyranny" in the United States.[90]

---

[89] David Root, *Fast Sermon on Slavery: Delivered April 2, 1835, to the Congregational Church and Society in Dover, N.H.* (Dover, N.H., 1835), 8.

[90] James Brewer Stewart, *Wendell Phillips: Liberty's Hero* (Baton Rouge, La., 1986). For John Phillips's early suspicion of the French Revolution, see John Phillips, *An Oration, Pronounced July 4th, 1794: At the Request of the Inhabitants of the Town of Boston,*

Even disunion, he argued, posed a far lesser threat to liberty than did slave-holder violence. Throughout his lengthy abolitionist career, Phillips gained renown for his violent invective against slavery's supporters. From American anti-Jacobinism, Phillips learned both his hatred of disorderly violence as well as his violent rhetoric of opposition.[91]

Despite the frequency of antislavery attacks on slaveholders' reign of terror, antebellum abolitionist literature also commonly described slavery as a bastille, the ancien régime prison that held captive the victims of Bourbon tyranny. *Frederick Douglass's Newspaper* included an article in 1853 that demanded abolitionists continue their agitation "until the American Bastille falls and the long-imprisoned inmates walk forth into the pure air of freedom."[92] The *Liberator* also published multiple attacks on the bastille of slavery and the bastille of the South.[93] This seeming contradiction made sense because both the Bastille and Robespierre were identified as agents of physical violence. Abolitionists considered charges that slaveholders were both Jacobins and keepers of the Bastille to be so consistent that both claims appeared within single texts. For example, an unsigned 1839 article attacked the gag rule as worse than the despotism of Robespierre, then immediately afterward argued that the South denied the right to petition "because [petitioning] is the great door to the slave Bastile."[94]

The author of that anonymous article may have been Alvan Stewart, one of the founders of the abolitionist Liberty Party, who used strikingly similar language to argue that ending the domestic slave trade would open "the great door to the slave Bastile."[95] Stewart mixed anti-Bourbon and anti-Jacobin imagery in other writings, one time describing the gag rule as erecting a "windy bastile, an American Congress, where liberty is brought to the table or block and beheaded fifty times in a morning."[96] The conflation of Bourbons and Jacobins reveals how entirely anti-Jacobin language disassociated the French Revolution from liberty; to Stewart, for example, the Jacobin era signified a more profound tyranny than even the monarchy it had replaced.

in Commemoration of the Anniversary of American Independence (Boston, 1794). Wendell Phillips, "The Murder of Lovejoy," Nov. 7, 1837, in *Speeches, Lectures, and Letters,* Wendell Phillips and Theodore C. Pease, 2 vols. (Boston, 1863), 7.

[91] For Wendell Phillips's youth, see the excellent Stewart, *Wendell Phillips: Liberty's Hero.*

[92] "Petition to Congress," *Frederick Douglass's Paper,* Dec. 2, 1853.

[93] "Boston. Friday, June 14, 1839," *Liberator,* June 14, 1839; "The Marriage Bill," *Liberator,* Feb. 11, 1842; *Liberator,* Dec. 8, 1843; "The Rhode Island Antislavery Society," *Liberator,* Nov. 21, 1845.

[94] *Emancipator,* Feb. 28, 1839. *Bastile* was a common variant for *Bastille* during the era.

[95] Luther Rawson Marsh, ed., *Writings and Speeches of Alvan Stewart, on Slavery* (New York, 1860; repr. 1969), 176. Other Stewart references to slavery as a bastille include Marsh, ed., *Writings and Speeches,* 149, 203, 216.

[96] Marsh, ed., *Writings and Speeches,* 195.

Born in New York in 1790, Alvan Stewart began writing in opposition to the slave trade as early as 1816. Stewart came from a traditional Protestant farming family and attended Burlington College, where public lectures during his enrollment featured favorite topics of northeastern conservatism such as human depravity and dueling. Like others of his background, Stewart was deeply inculcated in the era's anti-Jacobin sentiment. This youthful influence is evident from the travel diary that Stewart kept during an 1831 visit to Europe, which he filled with negative remarks about the violence of the French Revolution and the violence and infidelity of French culture. Echoing the authorities of his childhood, Stewart described France as "a nation of infidels," populated by wild men under the influence of Rousseau and Voltaire, who spent their days "fighting, drinking, fighting dogs, monkeys, bears, and playing billiards." Stewart viewed France and its revolutionary history from the jaundiced eye of New England conservatism.

During his visit to France, Stewart took especial care to tour the major sites of the French Revolution, including the "Place de Greve, the scene of the revolutionary guillotine," the site of the Bastille, and locations associated with Napoleon. In his journal, he wrote in particularly breathless terms about his visit to Versailles: "I saw the very bed in which the ill-fated Marie Antoinette was sleeping on the night, the mob rushed into her room and killed her faithful Swiss guards on the stairs" while "the enraged multitude [were] standing below in the Palace Yard thirsting for the blood of the Royal family." Stewart clearly had read Edmund Burke's set piece about Marie Antoinette in *Reflections on the Revolution in France*. However, the mood of political unrest that gripped Paris as the one-year anniversary of the 1830 Revolution approached soon caused Stewart to concentrate on present rather than past dangers. He began to fear that he would have the opportunity to witness a "Paris mob" in person. Rather than face that danger, Stewart cut his trip short. He left Europe physically unharmed, but the experience prepared him to recoil from the antiabolitionist rioting he witnessed when he arrived back home. Soon after his return, Stewart embraced the abolitionist cause.[97]

Stewart is most famous for his legal argument that the United States represented a "document of liberty" and thus could not permit legal slavery. Like other anti-Jacobin abolitionists, Stewart was also known for his "harshness" of language. This harshness took the form of gothic evocations of slaveholder violence. Stewart defined abolitionism as a movement

[97] Alvan Stewart Papers, Special Collections, University of Miami Libraries, Coral Gables, Florida. The radical abolitionist Henry Clarke Wright, who recalled the influence of French Revolutionary tales on his boyhood in Cooperstown, New York, also toured French Revolutionary sites later in adulthood and wrote in harrowing terms about the violence of the Jacobin era; "Letter from Henry C. Wright," *Liberator*, Oct. 17, 1845; "Letter from Henry C. Wright," *Liberator*, Oct. 24, 1845; Louis C. Jones, ed., *Growing Up in the Cooper Country; Boyhood Recollections of the New York Frontier* (Syracuse, N.Y., 1965), 160.

to eliminate the stain of southern violence from the land by going "to collect the bowie-knives and revolving, hair-triggered pistols" of the slave states. Echoing William Wilberforce and the anti-Jacobins of the early American republic, Stewart described antiabolitionist laws as "written in blood" and described the leaders of abolitionist mobs as from "the school of Dante [*sic*], Marat, and Robespierre." The slaveholders whom northern rioters defended were, like Jacobins, "savage demons" guilty of ferocious cannibalism.[98] Stewart's abolitionist discourse deployed the long-familiar argument that slavery constituted an uncivilizing process.

In 1850, a year after Stewart died, the passage of a strengthened Fugitive Slave Law unleashed a new wave of anti-Jacobin abolitionist rhetoric.[99] The law, by expanding slaveholders' power to capture runaways in the North and forcibly remove them to the South, signified both a violent threat to black people and an incursion on the civil liberties of white citizens in free states. As a consequence of the act, slave hunters expanded their violent efforts to recapture runaways, while white citizens who sought to aid the runaways were exposed to prosecution, and local governments were strong-armed into cooperating with the slave power. Both black and white abolitionists responded to these fearsome developments by decrying the situation as a "reign of terror" sweeping the nation. Harriet Jacobs, well known for her affecting memoir of escaping from slavery, described the Fugitive Slave Law as sparking a "reign of terror" among people of color in the North.[100] So did the black abolitionists William Cooper Nell and William Wells Brown, as well as the British abolitionist George Thompson.[101] Applying anti-Jacobin discourse against the Fugitive Slave Law worked successfully because it highlighted how slaveholders' use of terror against black people also led to violence against the liberties of whites; and by demonstrating the threat that slavery posed to white society, abolitionists hoped to move their audiences from antislavery sentiment to antislavery action.

Several antislavery leaders expanded their anti-Jacobin criticisms of the Fugitive Slave Law beyond hasty references. In a speech to the 1854 Massachusetts Republican convention, Senator Charles Sumner compared the Fugitive Slave Law both to the Reign of Terror and to Bourbon terrorism:

---

98 Marsh, ed., *Writings and Speeches*, 40–9, 69, 88, 97, 155, 245, 264.
99 "The Reign of Terror," *Liberator*, Oct. 24, 1851; Anti-Slavery Conference, *Report of the Proceedings of the Anti-Slavery Conference and Public Meeting, Held at Manchester, on the 1st of August, 1854: In Commemoration of West India Emancipation* (London, 1854), 33.
100 Harriet Jacobs, "Incidents in the Life of a Slave Girl," in *The Classic Slave Narratives*, ed. Henry Louis Gates (New York, 1987).
101 Wesley, *William Cooper Nell*, 253, 291; *American Slavery: Report of a Meeting of Members of the Unitarian Body, Held at the Freemasons' Tavern, June 13, 1851, to Deliberate on the Duty of English Unitarians in Reference to Slavery in the United States, Rev. Dr. Hutton in the Chair* (London, 1851), 21.

"It was a judicial tribunal which, in France, during the long reign of her monarchs lent itself to be the instrument of tyranny, as during the brief reign of terror it did not hesitate to stand forth the unpitying accessory of the unpitying guillotine."[102] Sumner's comment exposed the logic of labeling the Fugitive Slave Law a reign of terror. Another Massachusetts politician, Congressman Horace Mann, also pushed comparisons between the French Revolution and the Fugitive Slave Act beyond the generic by attacking the bill's author, Daniel Webster, as a Danton and by comparing its legal procedures to the summary proceedings overseen by Robespierre.[103]

Born in 1796, Horace Mann suffered great terror during his childhood from the dark sermons of his hyper-Calvinist minister, Nathanael Emmons, on the subjects of depravity, hellfire, French anarchy, and violence.[104] Emmons so terrified young Horace Mann that the reformer became "keenly susceptible to every form of suffering."[105] Although Mann later rejected the religion of his childhood in favor of a more positive theory of Christian ethics, a Calvinist gloom haunted Mann and drove him toward relentless pursuit of reform causes. Mann's primary cause was education reform, but when he took over John Quincy Adams's seat in Congress in 1848, Mann began to speak out against slavery. Using classic Federalist and anti-Jacobin terms, Mann depicted slavery as a "barbarous institution" that nourished "imperious and violent passions," and had created "the bowie-knife style of civilization . . . a spirit of blood which defies all laws of God and man."[106] In 1850, when Mann characterized Daniel Webster as a Danton, his language testified to a deeply inculcated core of ethical concerns.

---

[102] Charles Sumner, *Speech of Hon. Charles Sumner, at the Republican Convention, at Worcester, September 7th, 1854* (Boston, Mass., 1854), 4.

[103] Horace Mann, *Slavery: Letters and Speeches* (Boston, Mass., 1851), 331, 350.

[104] See, for example, Nathanael Emmons, *National Peace the Source of National Prosperity. A Sermon Delivered at Franklin, on the Day of Annual Thanksgiving, December 15th, Mdccxcvi* (Worcester, Mass., 1797); Nathanael Emmons, *A Discourse, Delivered May 9, 1798. Being the Day of Fasting and Prayer throughout the United States* (Newburyport, Mass., 1798); Nathanael Emmons, *A Discourse, Delivered on the National Fast, April 25, 1799* (Wrentham, Mass., 1799); Nathanael Emmons, *A Discourse, Delivered July 5, 1802, in Commemoration of American Independence* (Wrentham, Mass., 1802); Nathanael Emmons, *A Discourse, Delivered on the Day of the Annual Fast in Massachusetts, April 8, 1802* (Wrentham, Mass., 1802); Nathanael Emmons, *A Discourse, Delivered on the Day of the Annual Fast in Massachusetts, April 7, 1803* (Wrentham, Mass., 1803).

[105] Mary Tyler Peabody Mann, *Life of Horace Mann. By His Wife* (Boston, Mass., 1865), 8. Another abolitionist raised in "the strictest Calvinist faith" who was haunted by visions of hell as a child and later embraced a more rationalist faith was the abolitionist editor and Liberty Party supporter Elizur Wright Jr.; Goodheart, "Child-Rearing, Conscience, and Conversion." The radical abolitionist Parker Pillsbury was also raised in an orthodox Calvinist household and retained a "gloomy personality" throughout his life, although he later embraced radical Christian anarchism; Stacey M. Roberston, *Parker Pillsbury: Radical Abolitionist, Male Feminist* (Ithaca, N.Y., 2000), 13.

[106] Mann, *Life of Horace Mann*, 74, 95, 336; Mann, *Slavery*, 27, 50–2.

Sumner and Mann's comments reveal that even as late as the 1850s, the term *reign of terror* had not become disconnected from its French Revolutionary derivation. Antislavery leaders used the term *reign of terror* to connote a well-known history, not as a dehistoricized synonym for fear. Newspapers like Gamaliel Bailey's abolitionist *National Era* prepared antislavery readers to make the connection between France's revolutionary history and the violent aggression of America's slave power by printing anti-Jacobin histories and abolitionist perorations side by side. In 1847 and 1848, Bailey published excerpts from Lamartine's "History of the Girondins," replete with Gothic descriptions of Jacobin cannibalism; descriptions of the antiabolitionist "reign of terror" in 1835; accounts of Madame Roland's execution by guillotine; reportage on the "reign of terror" against reformers in the South; warnings about a new terror unleashed by the French Revolution of 1848; and criticisms of slaveholders' disunionist "reign of terror."[107] Likewise, Frederick Douglass's *North Star* published articles on "The Fate of the Inventor of the Guillotine" and the life of Talleyrand alongside its antislavery articles.[108] When Bailey's or Douglass's readers read descriptions of the Fugitive Slave Law as a "reign of terror," they were prepared to contextualize those remarks both historically and contemporaneously.

Anti-Jacobin critiques of proslavery violence continued throughout the 1850s and even into the Civil War. The violent conflict in Kansas Territory from 1854 to 1858, between proslavery settlers and free-state settlers battling for control over the constitution-writing process and slavery's future in the soon-to-be state, generated multiple anti-Jacobin narratives in the era's newspapers, books, songs, and pulpits.[109] Predictable sources such as Garrison's *Liberator* and Gamaliel Bailey's the *National Era* repeatedly described the violence in Kansas as a reign of terror, but so too did the Afro-Canadian newspaper the *Provincial Freeman* and the Ohio *Ripley Bee*.[110] Every source agreed that the destruction of free printing presses in the territory, the use of popular violence to win elections, and the murder of

---

107 All from *National Era*: "Lamartine's History of the Girondins," Feb. 17, 1848; "The Democrat," Mar. 4, 1847; "Trouble in Accomac County," Apr. 29, 1847; "Lines from the Workshop," Feb. 3, 1848; "Doings in Congress and Out," Dec. 28, 1848; "Schemes in Regard to Fugitives," Nov. 21, 1850.

108 "The Fate of the Inventor of the Guillotine," *North Star*, May 26, 1848; "Talleyrand and Arnold," *North Star*, Sept. 22, 1848.

109 For examples, see "Kansas Matters," *State Gazette*, May 22, 1855; Eden B. Foster, *A North-Side View of Slavery: A Sermon on the Crime against Freedom, in Kansas and Washington: Preached at Henniker, N.H., August 31, 1856* (Concord, N.H., 1856); *The Republican Campaign Songster: A Collection of Lyrics, Original and Selected, Specially Prepared for the Friends of Freedom in the Campaign of Fifty-Six* (New York, 1856).

110 "The Reign of Terror in Kansas," *Liberator*, June 27, 1856; "The True State of the Case," *National Era*, Oct. 23, 1856; "The Latest," *Provincial Freeman*, June 14, 1856; "The Reign of Terror," *Ripley Bee*, June 2, 1855; "The Latest News from Southern Kansas," *Ripley Bee*, Jan. 22, 1859. See also "The Reign of Terror," *Congregationalist*, Sept. 12, 1856.

free-state settlers signified a violent abrogation of civil society and law, which resembled the bloody events of the French Revolution. Sara Robinson, the abolitionist wife of Charles Robinson, the first governor of Kansas, published a history of the territory in 1856 for free-state settlers that included an entire chapter devoted to the "Reign of Terror" there. Robinson's language typified the gothic genre; she described proslavery settlers as "demons of darkness" and "blood-thirsty" cannibals.[111]

Comparisons between the French Revolution and Bleeding Kansas resounded when the South Carolina congressman Preston Brooks savagely beat Massachusetts Senator Charles Sumner with his gold-headed gutta-percha cane in retaliation for a speech Sumner made criticizing the violence of the territory's proslavery settlers. Charles Sumner's speech "The Crime against Kansas" famously accused proslavery "border ruffians" of "raping" Kansas, and the speech allegorized slavery as a whore. (Sumner's suggestion that Brooks's relative, proslavery Senator Andrew Pickens Butler, was patronizing the whore, provided the immediate impetus for Brooks's attack.) Less well remembered is that Sumner's speech also attacked Stephen Douglas, author of the Kansas-Nebraska Act, as a "Danton," the supposed mastermind of the September Massacres.[112]

Responses to Sumner's caning adopted his idiom. One Massachusetts minister worried the Sumner's caning proved that violence had routed civil society completely: "The right of free speech will be struck down, and the reign of terror at the capitol become permanent and complete."[113] The legal scholar Theophilus Parsons Jr., son of a leading Federalist jurist of the early national era, used the language of his youth to condemn the violence of the proslavery forces that had bloodied Sumner and Kansas. "We will not have the reign of terror," Parsons pleaded with a meeting of concerned citizens in Massachusetts following the attack on Sumner; "passion is fever," Parsons warned, and northerners had to use law in their battle against slaveholding Jacobins.[114]

Anti-Jacobinism also appeared in the congressional debate on Kansas that followed the attack. Schuyler Colfax, a Republican congressman from Indiana and later vice president under Ulysses S. Grant, authored a follow-up

---

[111] Sara T. L. Robinson, *Kansas; Its Interior and Exterior Life. Including a Full View of Its Settlement, Political History, Social Life, Climate, Soil, Productions, Scenery, Etc.* (Boston, Mass., 1856), 147–53.

[112] Charles Sumner, *The Crime against Kansas. The Apologies for the Crime. The True Remedy. Speech of Hon. Charles Sumner, in the Senate of the United States, 19th and 20th May, 1856* (Washington, D.C., 1856).

[113] Edmund Hamilton Sears, *Revolution or Reform: A Discourse Occasioned by the Present Crisis: Preached at Wayland, Mass., Sunday, June 15, 1856* (Boston, Mass., 1856), 8.

[114] *The Sumner Outrage: A Full Report of the Speeches at the Meeting of Citizens in Cambridge, June 2, 1856, in Reference to the Assault on Senator Sumner, in the Senate Chamber at Washington* (Cambridge, Mass., 1856), 17.

speech titled "The 'Laws' of Kansas," which accused the proslavery Lecompton legislature of being elected by a "reign of terror and violence," and of imitating the Jacobins during "the Reign of Terror in France" by spreading "anarchy and violence" through the territory.[115] A speech made the next month by Senator Henry Wilson (who replaced Colfax as Grant's vice president after the former became involved in the Crédit Mobilier of America scandal) went even further, quoting from a letter that described proslavery violence as a "reign of terror" and proslavery settlers as "cannibals."[116] The expansion of political violence in the United States during the late 1850s gave strength to the abolitionist logic that proslavery forces were recapitulating the reign of terror. As southern congressmen arrived armed to the Capitol building, the specter of the Montagnards – the Jacobin deputies to the French National Convention – loomed threateningly over the legislature.

In the year prior to secession, an outbreak of intense political violence against northern visitors and suspected antislavery sympathizers in the South produced new anti-Jacobin grievances that carried the discourse directly into the Civil War years. William Lloyd Garrison published an 1860 account of the violence titled *The New "Reign of Terror" in the Slaveholding States*, which was a catalog of brutalities akin to *American Slavery As It Is* and earlier Gothic accounts of the French Revolution. Garrison's text included multiple anti-Jacobin references that sustained the abolitionist arguments of the previous decades.[117] Northern newspapers throughout 1860 published repeated articles describing southern violence in the same terms.[118] Bailey's *National Era* remarked that "the reign of terror in that section is marked by atrocities equal to those which desolated France seventy years ago."[119] When the southern states seceded, the *Utica Herald* complained, "The spirit that animates the Southern rebellion is brutal. It smacks of the days of Robespierre and the Massacre of St. Bartholomew. It manifests itself in a 'reign of terror.'"[120] After the attack on Fort Sumter, the *New York Herald*

[115] Schuyler Colfax, *The 'Laws' of Kansas. Speech of the Hon. Schuyler Colfax, of Indiana, in the House of Representatives, June 21, 1856* (New York, 1856), 4, 7, 9, 12.

[116] Henry Wilson, *Kansas Affairs. Speech of Hon. Henry Wilson, of Massachusetts, Delivered in the Senate of the United States, July 9, 1856* (Washington, D.C., 1856), 4.

[117] William Lloyd Garrison, *The New "Reign of Terror" in the Slaveholding States*, The Anti-Slavery Crusade in America (New York, 1969). For earlier attacks on southern extremism as a form of Jacobinism, see "The Reign of Terror – Will a Free People any Longer Endure it?" *New York Herald*, Oct. 13, 1856. See also "A Reign of Terror in Virginia." *Milwaukee Daily Sentinel*, July 16, 1856; "State of Things at the South – Letter from a Virginian," *New York Daily Times*, Sept. 6, 1856.

[118] "The Reign of Terror in the South," *Frederick Douglass's Paper*, Nov. 11, 1859; "The Reign of Terror Approaching in the United States," *New York Herald*, Jan. 4, 1860; "The Senseless Clamor of Ultra Southern Men," *Daily Evening Bulletin*, Jan. 10, 1860; "Austria and the South," *Daily State Gazette and Republican*, Jan. 27, 1860.

[119] *National Era*, Jan. 1860.

[120] Reprinted in *Liberator*, Apr. 19, 1861.

proclaimed: "In truth, this Southern rebellion has betrayed all the elements of a Southern reign of terror. The seceded States, we have some reason to believe, have fallen under the fearful despotism of a set of Jacobins, with a mob at their heels, as stupid and remorseless as the Jacobins and their mob of the first French Revolution."[121]

Throughout the war years northern newspapers continued to publish accounts of the proslavery reign of terror that persecuted unionists in the southern and border states; that seized food and men for southern armies; and that wreaked revenge on black New Yorkers during the antidraft riots of 1863.[122] Northern critics of the war and the Republican administration turned the same language against President Lincoln and his supporters, labeling them a "Jacobin crew."[123] One British writer described Thaddeus Stevens as "the Robespierre, Danton, and Marat of America, all rolled into one."[124] Northern Democrats also complained frequently about the "reign of terror" that stifled their opposition speech.[125] Advocates for racial equality still claimed the language for their own, however. Even after the Civil War had ended, anti-Jacobin discourse circulated to describe violence against black people. Frederick Douglass Jr. reported on the white supremacist violence directed at black men in the South during 1876 by describing it as a "new reign of terror."[126] For believers in racial justice, references to the violence of the French Revolution continued to hold power even after the Civil War had written a new history in words of blood.

Anti-Jacobinism served as both a lexicon and a historical logic for antebellum abolition. Most abolitionists grew up in a milieu of anti-Jacobin rhetoric and passion, which shaped their outlook on the relationship between slavery, violence, and civil society. Even those abolitionists like Frederick Douglass and Harriet Jacobs, who had grown up in the slave South far removed from New England's conservative pulpits, adopted anti-Jacobin language in their antislavery writings. While certain terms, like *reign of terror*, recurred frequently throughout antebellum antislavery discourse, abolitionists used the

---

[121] "Our Southern Rebellion," *New York Herald*, Apr. 20, 1861.

[122] "The Return of Congressman Ely," *Crisis*, Jan. 16, 1862; "The War in Kentucky," *Philadelphia Inquirer*, Feb. 3, 1862; *Daily Gazette and Republican*, Jan. 14, 1863; "The Reign of Terror at the South," *New York Herald*, Mar. 16, 1863; "Rebel Troubles," *Milwaukee Daily Sentinel*, Mar. 27, 1863; "The New York July Rioters," *Troy Weekly Times*, Apr. 9, 1864; "Letters from New York, No. XII," *Liberator*, July 14, 1864.

[123] "McClellan and the People!" Aug. 27, 1864.

[124] Quoted in James M. McPherson, *Abraham Lincoln and the Second American Revolution* (New York, 1991), 7. See also David Herbert Donald, *Lincoln* (New York, 1995), 318, 333.

[125] See especially the *Ohio Daily Statesman* and the *Wisconsin Sentinel*. See also James M. McPherson, *Battle Cry of Freedom: The Civil War Era*, The Oxford History of the United States (New York, 1988), 6:245.

[126] "A Solid South. The New Reign of Terror – Colored Men Murdered or Driven from their Homes," *New York Times*, Sept. 24, 1876.

language of anti-Jacobinism as more than flourish. Anti-Jacobin histories of the French Revolution published in serials, pedagogical materials, and books prepared antebellum audiences to view the French Revolution as an extreme episode in the violent subversion of law. When abolitionists criticized slaveholders for waging a reign of terror against slaves and their allies, audiences understood the parallel between the mob violence and summary justice executed by the Jacobins, and the rioting and lynching committed by proslavery forces.

Abolitionists used anti-Jacobin language, as their ideological predecessors had, to win support by prompting revulsion against the violence of their enemies. William Lloyd Garrison explained the purpose of his language to his more-gently inclined friend Samuel J. May: "until the term 'slave-holder' sends as deep a feeling of horror to the hearts of those who hear it applied to any one as the terms 'robber,' 'pirate,' 'murderer' do, we must use and multiply epithets."[127] The abolitionists knew no better language to send "horror to the heart" than anti-Jacobinism. But as in the 1790s and early 1800s, the language had a bipolar impact. The most radical abolitionists of the antebellum era developed such an aversion to violence that many became nonresistants, disavowing even defensive uses of physical force. Yet anti-Jacobin language also had seductive properties, generating fantasies of violent revenge among abolitionists and paving the path toward their support for the Civil War.

I Should Be a Charlotte Corday

At its origins, the anti-Jacobin and antislavery critique contained both testimonies against violence and fantasies of committing violence. Theodore Dwight, Elijah Parish, Thomas Branagan, and other first generation anti-Jacobins justified slave rebellion as a form of righteous bloodshed that slaveholders deserved to suffer. When second generation anti-Jacobins like S. M. Worcester and Joshua Leavitt began their campaigns against slavery during the 1820s, they justified slave rebellion in similar terms. Defenses of slave rebellion were a steady undercurrent in anti-Jacobin abolitionist rhetoric in the following decades. Immediately upon returning from his tour of French Revolutionary historical sites in 1835, Alvan Stewart published his first speech against slavery, challenging southern men to carry out their threats of disunion and suffer the consequences, for "slavery would *then* take care of itself, and its masters too; – in one *little month* both would become extinct."[128] In 1840, Richard Hildreth, the anti-Jacobin author of *The Slave*

---

[127] Thomas James Mumford, George B. Emerson, and Samuel May, *Memoir of Samuel Joseph May* (Boston, Mass., 1882), 149.

[128] Marsh, ed., *Writings and Speeches*, 56.

and *Despotism in America*, defended slave rebellion as an inevitable mimetic response to the violence committed by slave masters.[129] Anti-Jacobin revulsion against the violence of the French Revolution and the violence of slavery did not preclude sympathy for slave rebellions.

Instead, anti-Jacobin sentiment contained the potential for channeling support for slave rebellion. When France again erupted in revolution during 1848, William Ellery Channing (the younger) celebrated the events as holding the promise of emancipation in the French West Indies and the American South. To make this argument, Channing used horrifying imagery of the Reign of Terror to celebrate the potential for imminent slave rebellion. In a speech before an 1848 antislavery gathering, Channing

concluded by bringing before our eyes the gigantic negro who stood upon the scaffold in the *Place de la Revolution*, in the Reign of Terror, stripped to the waist, his broad black breast flecked with gore, as he shook in the face of the people, one after another, the convulsed heads of the victims of the guillotine. "Such an apparition," he exclaimed, "haunts every land of slaves!" Such a spectre disturbs the slumbers of the planters of the French sugar islands! Such a ghostly presence drives peace far away from our own Southern States![130]

In a complicated sequence of images, Channing stimulated his audience's revulsion against the bloodshed of the Reign of Terror while stoking their desire for a similarly violent end to slavery in the New World. Paradoxically, Channing simultaneously celebrated the emancipationist elements of Jacobinism while using the radicals' negative reputation for bloodthirstiness to engage a violent fantasy of horrific retribution.

Black abolitionists also found anti-Jacobinism a useful tool for defending slave rebellion during the antebellum era. Many blacks, both slave and free, had used violence to resist slavery since the institution's origins. Nineteenth-century black abolitionists often struggled bodily against slavery from personal necessity. For example, Frederick Douglass first demonstrated his commitment to antislavery violence when he fought the "negro-breaker" Edward Covey, and when he brawled with whites on the Baltimore docks.[131] After Douglass escaped and became an abolitionist orator and editor, he embraced peaceable means to combat slavery. However, he abandoned pacifism following 1850, announcing that "the only way to make the Fugitive Slave Law a dead letter [is] to make a half dozen or more dead kidnappers." To legitimize this shift, Douglass turned in part to anti-Jacobinism. Publishing

---

[129] Hildreth, *Despotism in America*, 49.
[130] Massachusetts Anti-Slavery Society, *Seventeenth Annual Report, Presented to the Massachusetts Anti-Slavery Society, by Its Board of Managers, January 24, 1849* (Boston, Mass., 1849), 52–3.
[131] Frederick Douglass, *Narrative of the Life of Frederick Douglass* (New York, 1995).

an account of a battle between runaway slaves and slave catchers in Christiana, Pennsylvania, in 1851, Douglass's newspaper argued that the "reign of terror" against black people forced them either to flee to Canada or to "shoulder our musket for revolutionizing our own."[132] An 1855 article published by Douglass titled "The Reign of Terror" warned that slaves would free themselves "if they have to cut the throats of their masters," and it argued that moral equity demanded that southerners be made to suffer for their crimes.[133] An article he published in November 1859, following John Brown's raid on Harper's Ferry, proclaimed that the "terror must and will increase." God would use slaves as the rod of his wrath to punish southerners for the sin of slavery.[134] Anti-Jacobin imagery helped Douglass to rationalize making the strategic transition from nonviolent to violent means during the 1850s.[135]

Aggressive support for violent slave rebellion rose steadily during the 1850s. Like Douglass, Wendell Phillips abandoned his pacific commitment soon after the passage of the Fugitive Slave Law. "*Sic Semper Tyrannis*," he proclaimed, "so may it ever be with slavehunters."[136] By the end of the decade Phillips's prorebellion rhetoric gave way to the Gothic, as he argued that "he was glad that every five minutes gave birth to a black baby, for in its infant wail he recognized the voice which should yet shout the war cry of insurrection; its baby hand would one day hold the dagger which should reach the master's heart." John Theophilus Kramer, author of the antislavery text *The Slave-Auction*, demanded that "a million [slaves] rise against their masters' reign of terror!" For Kramer, anti-Jacobin allusions now defended the use of violence to defeat slavery.[137]

---

[132] Jane H. Pease and William H. Pease, "Confrontation and Abolition in the 1850's," *Journal of American History* 84 (1970): 928–9. "The Christiana Patriots," *Frederick Douglass Paper*, Nov. 13, 1851. See also James H. Cook, "Fighting with Breath, Not Blows: Frederick Douglass and Antislavery Violence," in *Antislavery Violence: Sectional, Racial, and Cultural Conflict in Antebellum America*, ed. John R. McKivigan and Stanley Harrold (Knoxville, Tenn., 1999), 128–63. See a similar use of anti-Jacobin language to justify violence in defense of fugitive slaves; *The Case of William L. Chaplin; Being an Appeal to All Respecters of Law and Justice, against the Cruel and Oppressive Treatment to Which, under the Proceedings, He Has Been Subjected, in the District of Columbia and the State of Maryland* (Boston, Mass., 1851), 44.

[133] "Southern Correspondence. Reign of Terror, or Slavery as It is in Georgia," *Frederick Douglass's Paper*, Sept. 21, 1855.

[134] "The Reign of Terror in the South," *Frederick Douglass's Paper*, Nov. 11, 1859.

[135] William Wells Brown also turned anti-Jacobin language into a framework for encouraging violent resistance to slavery; see "The Abolitionists Celebrating the First of August," *New York Times*, Aug. 4, 1858.

[136] Stewart, *Wendell Phillips: Liberty's Hero*, 157. These words foreshadow John Wilkes Booth's own cry after shooting President Lincoln.

[137] John Theophilus Kramer, *The Slave-Auction. By Dr. John Theophilus Kramer, Late of New Orleans, La.* (Boston, Mass., 1859).

Anti-Jacobinism served to carve a road from nonviolence to violent means for political abolitionists as well as moral suasionists. Lysander Spooner, an ally to Alvan Stewart in the battle to prove slavery unconstitutional, shifted from legal means to violent means by the late 1850s. Spooner authored a "Plan for the Abolition of Slavery" in 1858 in which he assumed the identity of the Jacobins whom his allies had previously attacked, and announced that sometimes "the Bastille must be torn down." Spooner's plan encouraged abolitionists to start a massive slave rebellion and use violence to punish the slaveholders. One clause of Spooner's plan argued for forming vigilance committees that would arrest and chastise abusive slaveholders with their own whips. Spooner reiterated this element of the plan later in his document: "We specially advise the flogging of individual Slave-holders. This is a case where the medical principle, that like cures like, will certainly succeed. Give the Slave-holders, then, a taste of their own whips . . . stripping them and flogging them soundly, in the presence of their own Slaves."[138] Anti-Jacobin rhetoric facilitated the abandonment of the very legalities that anti-Jacobinism's originators, such as John Adams and Edmund Burke, had so highly prized.

Many Gothic outbursts in support of violence against slaveholders recalled the tropes of anti-Jacobinism more indirectly. Parker Pillsbury declaimed that he "longed to see the time when Boston would run with blood from Beacon Hill to the foot of Broad Street." Blood had served as a central symbol of the anti-Jacobin reaction, to evoke the pollution of civil society by violence. Spilled blood stained streets, altars, fields, and even language in the outcry against the French Revolution. Yet blood had a long history of symbolizing purification within Judeo–Christian theology as well. In the book of Revelation, God's servants are said to have "washed their robes, and made them white in the blood of the Lamb" (7:14). During the 1850s, as abolitionists turned to the Gothic to articulate their violent fantasies, they began to describe blood not as a pollutant but as a purifying agent. Even the Quaker-raised abolitionist Angelina Grimké declared that abolitionists should "baptize liberty in blood, if it must be so." The slave power's defeat of nonviolent antislavery means left abolitionists searching for a language to consecrate their turn to using force.[139]

The escalation of the Kansas conflict during the mid-1850s led to many more anti-Jacobin calls to action. Gamaliel Bailey, who filled the pages of the *National Era* with anti-Jacobin indictments of slavery's violence, now suggested that free settlers arm themselves to put an end to the proslavery

---

[138] C. Bradley Thompson, ed., *Antislavery Political Writings, 1833–1860* (New York, 2003), 261–4.

[139] Quotations in John Demos, "The Antislavery Movement and the Problem of Violent Means," *New England Quarterly* 37 (1964): 522.

THE

REIGN OF TERROR

IN

KANZAS.

"They covered my body with tar, and, for want of feathers, used cotton wool."—Page 20.

By which Men have been Murdered and Scalped ; Ministers of the Gospel Tarred and Feathered; Women dragged from their Homes and Violated; Printing Offices and Private Houses Burned ; Citizens Robbed, &c., by Border Ruffians.

BOSTON:
PUBLISHED BY CHARLES W. BRIGGS.
1856.

Price 12 1-2 Cents....Publishing Office, 32 Congress St.

FIGURE 9. *The Reign of Terror in Kanzas*, by Charles W. Briggs (1856). The frontispiece for this narrative of Bleeding Kansas, written by a free-state supporter, allegorizes proslavery border ruffians to the Jacobin perpetrators of the Reign of Terror in France. *Published by permission of the Kenneth Spencer Research Library, Kansas Collection, University of Kansas.*

"reign of terror."[140] The Ohio *Ripley Bee* likewise printed a letter insisting that "revolvers and other weapons" were the only recourse against the "reign of terror" in the territory.[141] Lyman Beecher's abolitionist son Henry Ward Beecher infamously supported the call to arms by raising funds to ship Sharpe's rifles, in boxes labeled "Bibles," to free-state settlers in Kansas. The *New York Daily Times* praised these shipments as "efficient corrective" for the "Reign of Terror" waged by proslavery men.[142] The newspaper later circulated reports that the abolitionist fighter Jim Lane was trying to "inaugurate the reign of terror and of blood in the Territory."[143] In Kansas, anti-Jacobin language worked simultaneously both to convict proslavery settlers of terrorizing violence and to defend the abolitionists who retaliated.

Although anti-Jacobin threats of abolitionist violence tended to be voiced by and against men, the trope also enabled female articulations of revenge fantasies. An advertisement for Sara Robinson's history of Kansas celebrated the author for raising a "Corday's arm" against the proslavery reign of terror.[144] A generation raised on tales of the French Revolution identified Charlotte Corday as the Girondist anti-Jacobin who had murdered Marat in retaliation for the September Massacres. Sara Robinson, like Charlotte Corday, would punish Jacobin–slave master violence with retaliatory bloodshed by rallying the Free Kansas troops.

Lydia Maria Child voiced the same fantasy. Born in Medford, Massachusetts, in 1802, Child attended the orthodox Calvinist church of the stalwart anti-Jacobin warrior David Osgood, and she used Osgood's anti-Jacobin library, which included the works of Abbé Barruel and John Robison, to expand her education. During adulthood, Child abandoned the religious conservatism of her youth and embraced antisectarian nonresistance. Although a passionate advocate for immediate abolitionism, Child's writings captured her pacific spirit and often served as a gentle entry point for northerners just embracing antislavery.[145] Nonetheless, by the late 1850s she was abandoning hope that slavery could ever be abolished by nonviolent means. The Fugitive Slave Law, Senator Charles Sumner's near-fatal beating on the Senate floor, and the terrorism waged against Free-Soil Kansas families, weakened her pacifist resolve. "With all my horror of bloodshed,"

---

[140] "Kansas. Nullification," *National Era*, May 24, 1855.

[141] "The Reign of Terror," *Ripley Bee*, June 2, 1855. See also "The Reign of Terror in Kansas," *Boston Daily Atlas*, May 28, 1856; "The Reign of Terror in Kansas," *Boston Daily Atlas*, May 31, 1856.

[142] "The Rifle Question," *New York Daily Times*, Mar. 27, 1856. See also "The War in Kansas," *New York Daily Times*, June 12, 1856.

[143] "Kansas Matters," *New York Times*, Dec. 4, 1857.

[144] Crosby, Nichols, and Company, "'The book out to be sold by the Thousands.' Mrs. Gov. Robinson's work on Kansas" (Boston, Mass., 1856).

[145] Lydia Maria Francis Child, *An Appeal in Favor of That Class of Americans Called Africans*, ed. Carolyn L. Karcher (Amherst, Mass., 1996).

FIGURE 10. Lydia Maria Child (1802–80) grew up in an anti-Jacobin milieu listening to negative accounts of French Revolutionary violence. The bipolar power of that language is suggested by Child's paradoxical embrace of pacifist causes and fantasy of transforming herself into Charlotte Corday, the assassin of the French Jacobin Jean-Paul Marat. *Courtesy of the Massachusetts Historical Society.*

Lydia Maria Child confessed in 1856, "I could be better resigned to that great calamity than to endure the tyranny that has so long trampled on us." On the eve of the Civil War, Child officially forsook pacifism in exchange for dreams of retributive violence. "If the monster [slave power] had one head," Child proclaimed "assuredly I should be a Charlotte Corday."[146] Janus-headed anti-Jacobinism revealed its violent face as Child imaginatively transfigured into the avenging murderess.

The most infamous avatar of antislavery violence during the 1850s, the abolitionist guerilla John Brown, emerged from the same cultural milieu as his initially peaceable allies. Brown was born in 1800 in Torrington, Connecticut, to a Calvinist antislavery family. His father, Owen Brown, had been converted to antislavery by Samuel Hopkins and Jonathan Edwards Jr., both religious conservatives. In 1805, the Brown family relocated to Hudson, Ohio, a town settled by antislavery Calvinists (the abolitionist Elizur Wright

---

[146] Lydia Maria Francis Child and John Greenleaf Whittier, *Letters of Lydia Maria Child: With a Biographical Introduction by John G. Whittier* (Boston, Mass., 1883), 79, 115, 143. After the Civil War, Child returned to her pacifist principles and engaged in the antiviolent reforms of the post-Civil War era. She was an early member of the Boston Society for the Prevention of Cruelty against Animals and continued to support the civil rights of African-Americans and American Indians.

also grew up in Hudson). As a child, Brown attended the village's Federalist school and engaged in snowball battles against children from the Democrat school (he won). The War of 1812 was a turning point for John Brown, leading him to increased consideration of the suffering of black people. But rather than take the nonviolent route of most antislavery anti-Jacobins after 1815, Brown swore "eternal war with slavery."[147] Brown engaged in a variety of antislavery activities throughout the following decades, while he formulated a plan to make war on the slave power. The biography of the Duke of Wellington, who defeated Napoleon at the Battle of Waterloo, strongly influenced Brown's planning. As the Duke of Wellington had beaten back the French Jacobins (to American eyes), so would Brown beat back the slaveholding Jacobins.[148]

The war for Kansas provided Brown with his first actual opportunity to put his principals into action. Although he had already formulated his Harper's Ferry plan, Brown moved to Kansas in 1855 along with many of his adult sons and daughters and became a leader in the antislavery guerilla violence that contributed to the era's reputation as a reign of terror. Most infamously, Brown led a nighttime raid on a slaveholding settlement at Pottawatomie, directing his sons to murder five proslavery settlers by brutally hacking their bodies with double-edged swords. Brown's archaic choice of weaponry made clear his biblical vision of purifying the land in blood. After Pottawatomie, Brown continued the antislavery fight by engaging in battles with proslavery militias at Black Jack and Osawatomie, and by liberating slaves from nearby Missouri and killing a white man in the process.

Although Brown's body count remained relatively limited, his reputation far exceeded his deeds. Brown became identified with the very Jacobin violence that had helped to provoke his youthful antislavery. The *Milwaukee Daily Sentinel* published an account of Brown's murders under the headline "A Reign of Terror in Kansas" (the article also included testimony against proslavery violence).[149] In a later article, Frederick Douglass defended the killings at Pottawatomie by alleging that "a great deal" had happened during the "Reign of Terror" in Kansas. In other words, Douglass acknowledged the charge that Brown acted with Jacobin violence in Kansas but suggested that it was justified by the violence committed by proslavery men.[150]

The charge of Jacobinism grew louder after Brown led his deadly attack on the Harper's Ferry arsenal in Virginia during 1859, intending to spark

---

[147] Franklin Benjamin Sanborn, ed., *The Life and Letters of John Brown, Liberator of Kansas, and Martyr of Virginia* (Boston, Mass., 1891), 33, 116.

[148] David S. Reynolds, *John Brown, Abolitionist: The Man Who Killed Slavery, Sparked the Civil War, and Seeded Civil Rights* (New York, 2006), 107.

[149] "A Reign of Terror in Kansas," *Milwaukee Daily Sentinel*, June 11, 1856.

[150] "Brown's Second Trial," *Frederick Douglass's Paper*, Feb. 17, 1860.

a slave rebellion throughout the South. Southerners and northern sympathizers used anti-Jacobin language to criticize Brown's actions. The *New
York Herald* protested the "Robespierrean teachings" of John Brown and
published a mournful excerpt from a southern newspaper, agonizing that
abolitionists were celebrating Harper's Ferry "as the inauguration of a reign
of terror in the South, which shall crimson our fields."[151] Yet seemingly
critical accounts of abolitionist violence also carried the potential to express
desire for bloodshed. Frederick Douglass described the southern fears of
slave rebellion that Harper's Ferry had generated as a "Reign of Terror"
but then defended slave rebellion as righteous. Douglass used anti-Jacobin
language as a framework in which to justify violence rather than to generate revulsion.[152] The *New York Herald* accused Republican editors at the
New York Times and the *Tribune* of similarly reporting on slave rebellions
in order to generate a "reign of terror" among southerners rather than to
repudiate the bloodshed. Republican reportage, according to the *Herald*,
betrayed a "devoutly wished for consummation" of "the reign of terror" in
the South.[153] Newspaper editors in the late 1850s understood that accounts
of the terror at Harper's Ferry, even when not overtly supportive, could
seduce readers with violent imagery. Violent language had a bipolar power
that operated silently at all times.

By the end of the 1850s, most of the radical participants in the nonresistance movement retreated from their pacifist commitment and began to
promote violent means to fight the slave power.[154] Historians have struggled
to understand how these radical abolitionist pacifists became advocates of
war and destruction.[155] Ironically, the same anti-Jacobin language that had
helped foster nonresistance also carved the path from nonviolent to violent antislavery means by providing abolitionists with a language that could

151 "The Reign of Terror Approaching in the United States." Jan. 4, 1860; "The Latest Mani-
     festo of the Religious and Philosophical Instructors of the Revolutionary Republican Party,"
     New York Herald, Jan. 7, 1860; "The Harper's Ferry Outbreak," *New York Herald*,
     Nov. 5, 1859.
152 "The Reign of Terror in the South," *Frederick Douglass's Paper*, Nov. 11, 1859.
153 "The Reign of Terror – the Duty of New York," *New York Herald*, Sept. 10, 1860.
154 Dan McKanan, *Identifying the Image of God: Radical Christians and Nonviolent Power
     in the Antebellum United States* (New York, 2002); Valarie H. Ziegler, *The Advocates
     of Peace in Antebellum America* (Bloomington, Ind., 1992); Perry, *Radical Abolitionism;
     Anarchy and the Government of God in Antislavery Thought*; Peter Brock, *Pacifism in the
     United States: From the Colonial Era to the First World War* (Princeton, N.J., 1968); Merle
     Eugene Curti, *The American Peace Crusade* (Durham, N.C., 1929).
155 Stanley Harrold, *The Rise of Aggressive Abolitionism: Addresses to the Slaves* (Lexington,
     Ky., 2004); McKivigan and Harrold, eds., *Antislavery Violence*; Lawrence J. Friedman,
     Gregarious Saints: Self and Community in American Abolitionism, 1830–1870 (New York,
     1982), chap. 7; Pease and Pease, "Confrontation and Abolition in the 1850's"; Demos,
     "The Problem of Violent Means"; Pease and Pease, as well as Demos, date the shift to
     antislavery violence to the 1850s, but Friedman, McKivigan, and Harrold identify earlier
     antecedents.

voice violent desires. After 1860, abolitionists dropped any pretense of disdain for the tools of Jacobin terror. The members of a Syracuse antislavery society praised William Lloyd Garrison's pamphlet *The New Reign of Terror* and declared the need to "boldly avow the doctrine of *reprisals* – tell the South plainly that this is a game two could play at."[156] Anti-Jacobinism had become an abolitionist war cry.

Anti-Jacobinism had its origins in the 1790s as a language of attack, to defeat the transatlantic forces of democratic revolution. The effectiveness of the anti-Jacobin attack, which turned the tide against the spread of political radicalism, inspired antislavery advocates to use the same language in their humanitarian cause. But for all its protests against bloodshed, anti-Jacobinism remained, throughout the first half of the nineteenth century, an offensive language intended to defeat its targets. Anti-Jacobinism's use as a language to justify violence against slaveholding society thus did not represent a falling off, or deviation, from its ethical core, but the logical fulfillment of its historical uses.

[156] "'The New Reign of Terror,'" *Liberator*, Apr. 27, 1860.

CONCLUSION

The Problem of Violence in the Early American Republic

The year 1783 brought great cause for thankfulness to the United States, as the long and brutal war for independence officially ended in victory. But for the professionally self-lacerating Congregationalist ministers of New England, 1783 also inaugurated new concerns. At a Fast Day sermon delivered in Cambridge that spring, the Reverend Charles Turner first thanked God for granting America's success over Great Britain, then threatened imminent and grave danger if his listeners did not repent for their ill deeds. According to Turner, the new nation had a lot to atone for: pride, avarice, luxurious sensuality, profaneness, and deism, among other sins. God had blessed the nation with an unlikely triumph over a great power, but now, Turner warned, Americans needed to reform their sins or suffer swift judgment. Many conservative religious authorities, the minister explained, believed that God's punishment would come at the people's own hands, as "the domineering and abusive principles of depraved nature" destroyed republican civil society. More optimistically, Turner held out hope that education could reform the people and "exclude the vile oppressing passions from their hearts," saving the nation from being "destroyed by *sudden violence.*" However, even Turner agreed that if Americans did not reform, the people could bid farewell to the nation. Human violence would unravel all that they had sacrificed to create.[1]

Charles Turner passionately supported the republican spirit of the age. The minister's political liberalism initially led him to oppose the federal Constitution when serving in the Massachusetts Ratifying Convention of 1788 – although, under the influence of Theophilus Parsons, he ultimately voted in favor of the new government.[2] Turner's anxieties about human

[1] Charles Turner, *Due Glory to Be Given to God. A Discourse Containing Two Sermons Preached in Cambridge May 15, 1783. Being a Day Appointed by Government for Publick Fasting and Prayer* (Boston, 1783), 27, 34.
[2] Justin Winsor, *A History of the Town of Duxbury, Massachusetts, with Genealogical Registers* (Boston, 1849), 202–5.

violence in the new republic stemmed not from an elitist desire to clamp down on democratic politics, but from religious belief, and probably from personal experience. The Revolution had in fact caused unsettling patterns of violence in the United States. In addition to the bloodshed in battles between the British army and the Continental army, the war exposed the United States to the bloodshed of civil war, slave rebellion and suppression, Native American war, and even increased interpersonal violence. During the age of revolution, homicide rates began to rise precipitously in the United States. If homicides are any indication of the extent of interpersonal violence within a society, then it seems that American society became markedly more violent during the 1770s. Men like Charles Turner, who was born in 1732 during a long decline in the homicide rates, probably noticed the change. The problem of violence in American society was not just a paranoid fantasy but the lived reality of Turner and others.[3]

The homicide problem worsened throughout the 1780s as the United States suffered through a series of political and economic crises. The turning point occurred during the late 1780s and 1790s, when rates of homicide in the North began to fall, eventually reaching historic lows in the 1820s. In the slave South, on the other hand, rates of homicide continued to increase. By the 1820s, the pattern of homicide in the United States differed sharply between slave society and free society, with southern whites more murderous toward both other whites and blacks than were northerners of all races.[4] What role did the vast outpouring of antiviolent rhetoric in the North throughout the 1790s and first decades of the nineteenth century play in suppressing everyday violence there? If the problem of violence in the postrevolutionary era was real, did the attempted solutions achieve real ends?

The chaos of the French Republic during the early 1790s brought to a head the sense that there was a crisis of violence in the postrevolutionary United States. The consequent outpouring of anti-Jacobin literature that anathematized bloodshed became the core of a cultural complex that contributed to the pacification of northeastern society during the early nineteenth century. That complex, most powerfully manifested within the child-rearing and pedagogy of the late eighteenth and early nineteenth centuries, gave rise to a generation of northeasterners who not only murdered one another in far lower numbers but also pursued radical reform movements to excise violence from the society at large.[5] During the age of reform, northeasterners not only protested the violence of slavery but also authored texts, passed laws, and organized movements against war, dueling, rioting,

---

[3] Randolph Roth, *American Homicide* (Cambridge, forthcoming), chap. 4.
[4] Roth, *American Homicide*, chap 5.
[5] This argument draws on Norbert Elias, *The Civilizing Process: Sociogenetic and Psychogenetic Investigations*, trans. Edmund Jephcott, rev. ed. (Malden, 2000), 369–74.

corporal punishment, capital punishment, and anger.[6] In the new republican political culture of the early American republic, fears of human depravity exacerbated by reports of the Reign of Terror produced a profound reaction, both ideological and behavioral, against violence.

Yet the United States' presently exceptional rates of homicide should testify to the fact that the problem of American violence did not resolve peacefully in 1838 with the establishment by William Lloyd Garrison and Henry Clarke Wright of the ultrapacifist New England Non-Resistant Society.[7] By the 1850s, rates of homicide and other forms civil violence such as mobbing, brawling, and guerilla fighting were again on the rise in the United States.[8] When the Civil War began, Wright and Garrison's sons (although not Garrison himself) abandoned pacifism to support the violent destruction of slave society at the cost of 620,000 lives. Wright argued for the ethical consistency of his transition, averring that "my non-resistance, my hatred of war and slavery" had led him to say to the North, 'I BLESS YOU FOR PREFERRING WAR TO SUCH A PEACE!' Be this your slogan: 'DEATH TO SLAVERY!' While Garrison never praised the war as forthrightly as Wright did, he refrained from criticizing the violence, choosing to remain silent so as not to imperil the battle against slave society.[9] As a group, the women and men who most thoroughly internalized the antiviolent critique they had heard during their childhoods became the most passionate advocates of the war.

The bipolar power of violent language transcribes two narrative arcs in this history, one leading from the perception of violence as a problem to efforts to pacify civil society, and the other leading from the perception of violent enemies as a problem to efforts to destroy those enemies. Astoundingly, anti-Jacobin language continued to circulate in both usages throughout the bloodshed of the Civil War, when contemporary events provided no shortage of alternative tropes. Americans during the Civil War both attacked

---

[6] John F. Kasson, *Rudeness & Civility: Manners in Nineteenth-Century Urban America* (New York, 1990); Louis P. Masur, *Rites of Execution: Capital Punishment and the Transformation of American Culture, 1776–1865* (New York, 1989); Paul A. Gilje, *The Road to Mobocracy: Popular Disorder in New York City, 1763–1834* (Chapel Hill, 1987); Carol Z. Stearns and Peter N. Stearns, *Anger: The Struggle for Emotional Control in America's History* (Chicago, 1986); David Brion Davis, *From Homicide to Slavery: Studies in American Culture* (New York, 1986); Myra C. Glenn, *Campaigns against Corporal Punishment: Prisoners, Sailors, Women and Children in Antebellum America* (Albany, 1984); Lewis Perry, *Radical Abolitionism: Anarchy and the Government of God in Antislavery Thought* (Ithaca, N.Y., 1973).

[7] The United States' homicide rate during the second half of the twentieth century ranged from four to ten times the rate of any other affluent democracy; Roth, *American Homicide*, introduction.

[8] Roth, *American Homicide*, chap. 5; David Grimsted, *American Mobbing, 1828–1861: Toward Civil War* (New York, 1998).

[9] Valarie H. Ziegler, *The Advocates of Peace in Antebellum America* (Bloomington, 1992), 168.

the violence of their enemies in anti-Jacobin terms and justified their violent retaliation in the same language. A black correspondent to the *Christian Recorder* in 1863 complained that when the Confederate guerilla leader William Quantrill led a raid on Lawrence, Kansas, he had executed a "reign of terror" and shot down many of the town's "best colored citizens."[10] Unionists used the old tropes to complain of the depredations committed by southern Jacobins, but rather than turning the other cheek, these complaints fueled Unionists' determination to destroy the Confederacy. If Confederate territories were under a perfect reign of terror, the Union Army should go in and execute the executioners.[11] "We should... move everywhere with overwhelming numbers; give the Rebels no chance anywhere; sweep them from the field, regardless of military forms and proportions," argued the *Philadelphia Inquirer* in 1862, "just rigor is the truest mercy," and the only means to end the rebellion and its "Reign of Terror."[12]

The use of French Revolutionary language extended beyond the anti-slavery men who had long spoken it. Many conservative northerners used anti-Jacobinism to attack the Radical Republicans and their emancipationist aims. Dissenters such as General George McClellan, whom President Lincoln had dismissed from command of the Union Army, attacked the emancipationist Radical Republicans as a "Jacobin crew."[13] Frank Blair, the conservative Missouri Republican, likewise attacked the radicals who pushed for emancipation within the border states as "Jacobins."[14] Even John Hay, Lincoln's private secretary, referred to the Radical Republicans as "Jacobins."[15] In response to the long-standing critiques of the southern repression of free speech, the Ohio Democratic newspaper the *Crisis* repeatedly attacked the Republican administration for waging a reign of terror against opponents to the war.[16]

Civil War combatants on both sides also used French Revolutionary imagery to glorify the violent conflict. During 1861, southern secessionists in Charleston and New Orleans sang "the Southern Marseillaise" in the streets, and ex-governor Henry Wise of Virginia "glorie[d] in his reputation as the 'Danton of the Secession movement in Virginia.'" One Georgia disunionist

[10] "For the Christian Recorder," *Christian Recorder*, Nov. 7, 1863.

[11] "War News," *The Farmer's Cabinet*, Jan. 2, 1862; "The War in Kentucky," *Philadelphia Inquirer*, Feb. 3, 1862.

[12] "Overwhelming Numbers," *Philadelphia Inquirer*, Feb. 2, 1862.

[13] Republican Party, *McClellan and the People!* (1864).

[14] Frank P. Blair, *The Jacobins of Missouri and Maryland. Speech of Hon. F.P. Blair, of Missouri* (Washington, D.C., 1864).

[15] David Herbert Donald, *Lincoln* (New York, 1995), 318, 333.

[16] *Crisis* published tens of articles on this theme. See, for example, "The Manner of Prosecuting the War," *Crisis*, Jan. 29, 1862; "The Eighth of January Festival," *Crisis*, Jan. 14, 1863; "The Conscription Act," *Crisis*, Dec. 12, 1863. See similar articles in the *Milwaukee Sentinel* and the *Wisconsin Daily Patriot*.

warned his political enemies that if they did not join the "revolution," "we will brand you as traitors, and chop off your heads."[17] After publishing an anti-Jacobin historical account of the French Revolution, the *Vermont Phoenix* warned that southern sympathizers in Washington whose heads had "been spared by the guillotine" should no longer be extended any sympathy.[18] The time had finally come to set the guillotine to work on Capitol Hill.

Rumors of the return of the guillotine in fact circulated throughout the United States during the Civil War. The Ohio Copperhead Democrat Clement Vallandigham attacked the 1863 Conscription Bill in Congress, alleging that the Republicans would continue destroying civil liberties in the United States until "The guillotine! the guillotine! the guillotine! the guillotine follows next."[19] Democratic newspapers printed stories in 1863 relating that President Lincoln had imported two dozen guillotines from France to begin executing domestic traitors.[20] The Confederate mouthpiece the *Macon Daily Telegraph* took up the rumor in its pages, effusively praising Vallandigham for his brave stand against the Jacobinical administration.[21] As Union and Confederate soldiers poured out their blood on the fields of Gettysburg, Chancellorsville, Vicksburg, and Chickamauga, an old man writing his memoirs declared that the scenes of the French Revolution "now, in 1863," were as "vivid in the memory as if enacted but the last year."[22] Far from a dead metaphor, the French Revolution continued to serve throughout the early 1860s to represent a deeply resonant and often dissonant chorus of arguments about the dangers and purposes of violence. The Civil War did little to resolve those arguments, which persist, along with their anti-Jacobin referents, to trouble American society today. Violence remains as problematic as it has been at any time in American society.

Historians who are concerned about the present problem of American violence often start from the supposition that our homicide rates represent an aberration that must be explained by the past. What element of American history explains why Americans are so bloodthirsty today; is slavery, the

---

[17] James M. McPherson, *Battle Cry of Freedom: The Civil War Era*, The Oxford History of the United States (New York, 1988), 240–1.

[18] "Washington Rebellious," *Vermont Phoenix*, July 3, 1862. For the historical article, see "Robespierre," *Vermont Phoenix*, May 29, 1862.

[19] Clement Laird Vallandigham, *The Record of Hon. C. L. Vallandigham on Abolition, the Union, and the Civil War* (Columbus, Ohio, 1863), 227.

[20] "Miscellaneous News Items," *Deseret News*, Jan. 7, 1863; *New York Herald*, Jan. 23, 1863; "The Reign of Terror – Good Advice," *Weekly Patriot and Union*, Mar. 5, 1863.

[21] "From the North," *Macon Daily Telegraph*, Jan. 14, 1863; "Serenade to, and Speech of, Mr. Vallandigham in New York." *Macon Daily Telegraph*, Jan. 15, 1863.

[22] Matthew Rainbow Hale, "Can You Feel It? Democratic-Republicans' Affective Engagement with the French Revolution" (paper presented at "From Colonies into Republics in an Atlantic World: North America and the Caribbean in a Revolutionary Age," Paris, France, 2006).

frontier, immigration, the Second Amendment, rampant individualism, or some other factor to blame? The question has yielded many compelling answers, but its assumptions about America's violent exceptionalism have also obscured counter-movements against violence in American history.[23] During the nineteenth century, political and religious conservatives generated a cultural reaction against the perceived dangers of democracy, reconceptualizing the United States as dependent on nonviolent social relations for survival. This reaction generated a powerful impetus to eliminate the violence of slavery and war from American society, yet at the same time it encouraged fantasies of the violent destruction of slavery through war. Despite these contradictions, it seems possible to argue that the moral balance of the reaction was positive, especially considering that most people today agree that 620,000 lives were a fair price for the abolition of slavery in the United States. Yet at this moment, in the sixth year of a horrific war in Iraq that has been justified as a means to destroy Saddam Hussein's "Reign of Terror," I wish I had at my command an alternative language, to protest violence without being seduced by it.[24]

---

[23] Roth, *American Homicide*; Eric Monkkonen, "Homicide: Explaining America's Exceptionalism," *American Historical Review* 111 (Feb. 2006); Pieter Spierenburg, "Democracy Came Too Early: A Tentative Explanation for the Problem of American Homicide," *American Historical Review* 111 (Feb. 2006); David T. Courtwright, *Violent Land: Single Men and American Violence from the Frontier to the Inner City* (Cambridge, 1996); Richard Maxwell Brown, *No Duty to Retreat: Violence and Values in American History and Society* (New York, 1991); Terry G. Jordan and Matti Kaups, *The American Backwoods Frontier: An Ethnic and Ecological Interpretation* (Baltimore, 1989); Sheldon Hackney, "Southern Violence," in *Violence in America: Historical and Comparative Perspectives*, ed. Hugh David Graham and Ted Robert Gurr (Beverly Hills, Calif., 1969).

[24] For examples, see "Hussein Will Pay for His Reign of Terror: Our Opinion: Hold Despots to Account for Human Rights Crimes," *Miami Herald*, Nov. 13, 2006; "Editorial: A Deserved End for Saddam Hussein." *News Tribune* [Tacoma, Wash.], Dec. 30, 2006. Many other journalists and editors have described Hussein's rule as a reign of terror.

APPENDIX

Digital Database Citations

American Narratives of the French Revolution

Database	Jacobin/ Jacobinism	Robespierre/ Robertspierre	Bastille/ Bastile	French Revolution/ Revolution in France	Paris and Mob	Reign of Terror	Total
Gale Thomson: 19th-century U.S. newspapers	2,705 480	3,066	650 4678	14,203 1,403	20,330	860	41,814 6,561
Gale Thomson: Sabin Americana (1789–1865)	754 311	758 3	220 569	2,537 612	2,585	1,161	8,015 1,495
Readex: America's Historical Newspapers (1789–1865)	30,535 3,551	2,027 15	321 1300	8,187 1,084	7,912	1,469	50,451 5,950
Readex: Evans Early American Series I (1639–1800)	434 29	36 1	7 15	597 209	701	28	1,803 254
Readex: Evans Early American Series II (1801–19)	870 278	431 4	120 497	1465 304	1,700	207	4,793 1,083
Proquest: American Periodicals Series (1789–1865)	2,859 569	1,909 1	602 1,586	9,577 842	2,320	2,190	19,457 2,998
Accessible Archives	66 15	89 1	26 150	376 69	190	219	966 235
Readex: American Broadsides and Ephemera	13 1	19	19 3	44 4	7	23	125 8
American State Papers, 1789–1838	5 1	7	3 1	35 4	8	2	60 6
GRAND TOTAL							146,074

Index

Printed in the USA
CPSIA information can be obtained
at www.ICGtesting.com
LVHW041311051023
760094LV00005B/145